Where the Great River Rises

Pittsburg

Colebrook

Bloomfield

Groveton

91

Lyndonville

Lancaster

St.
Johnsbury

93

Littleton

Wells
River

Woodsville

91

Fairlee

89

Hanover

White
River
Junction

89

Windsor

Claremont

Springfield

91

Bellows
Falls

Keene

Brattleboro

91

Greenfield

Where the Great River Rises

An Atlas of the Connecticut River Watershed
in Vermont and New Hampshire

Rebecca A. Brown, editor

DARTMOUTH COLLEGE PRESS ⁓ HANOVER, NEW HAMPSHIRE

Published by University Press of New England
Hanover and London
A Project of the Connecticut River Joint Commissions

Dartmouth College Press
Published by University Press of New England,
One Court Street, Lebanon, NH 03766
www.upne.com
© 2009 by the Connecticut River Joint Commissions
Printed in China
5   4   3   2   1

Published with generous financial support from the Connecticut River Joint Commissions and the National Oceanic and Atmospheric Administration.

Frontispiece: Watershed base map courtesy of VCGI and GRANIT data sets, modified by Northern Cartographic.

Library of Congress Cataloging-in-Publication Data

Where the great river rises : an atlas of the Connecticut River Watershed in Vermont and New Hampshire / Rebecca A. Brown, editor.
    p. cm.
  Includes bibliographical references and index.
  ISBN 978-1-58465-765-1 (pbk. : alk. paper)
  1. Connecticut River Watershed—Maps. I. Brown, Rebecca A., 1959– II. Title.

G1227.C62A85 2009
912.742—dc22   2008051845

Contents

Foreword

SHARON F. FRANCIS

In his poem "New Hampshire," Robert Frost described a pair of states united by a river, and he gave verse to the complementary happenstance of two political jurisdictions sharing the same geographical feature. It is this united and delightful feature that is the subject of *Where the Great River Rises*.

Not long after the New Hampshire and Vermont legislatures each established a commission for the Connecticut River in the late 1980s, the two commissions formed the Connecticut River Joint Commissions (CRJC) as a single focal point for the river and watershed. Over subsequent years, the Commissions have worked with local landowners and communities, scientists and other scholars, and state and federal agencies in a dynamic cycle of learning and communication enriching everyone's understanding of the forces, great and small, past and present, influencing this watershed.

From the outset, the Connecticut River Joint Commissions have realized that their legislative mandate to "preserve and protect the resources of the Connecticut River Valley, guide growth and development, and cooperate with the other state in doing so," would be achieved not by CRJC alone, but only by widespread public appreciation and commitment.

Thus, it was only a matter of time before CRJC and Dartmouth College found each other. Here in Hanover, overlooking the Connecticut River is a college eminent in the United States, with departments of global stature, and with faculty and students who have long studied the natural and human history of the region. The Joint Commissions approached the College and invited a collaborative project—this Atlas—to expand understanding of the Connecticut River watershed for the benefit of residents, visitors, students, and scholars, and to bring a foundation of knowledge to the intrinsic delight that people experience in this unique place.

CRJC and Dartmouth were joined by Northern Cartographic, a firm of talented cartographers based in Burlington, Vt., to bring the idea of the Atlas alive in both print and interactive Web-based form. The sponsors set about exploring what is known about this seam in the crust of the earth, and what it means in terms of natural science and human history. As they talked with experts in various fields, they recognized that these diverse experts also should be invited to become authors of the Atlas, so that its many threads of inquiry could be told by those who understand them best.

The threads of the story weave together in diverse ways, and readers will perceive a fabric of natural and human interactions, causes and effects, an ecology of people and place that continues to be dynamic as it has throughout known time. The Connecticut River, the largest river in New England, is the centerpiece of the story. The river valley has seen the ebb and flow of Native peoples and European settlers hungry for land to farm and live upon. Its valley provides a transportation corridor for people and goods. Its farmland is distinguished for fertility, the result of centuries of bathing flood waters. The scenic quality of the river lures visitors, who soon discover and appreciate, as residents already do, the valley's rare blend of sophisticated cultural, academic, and commercial enterprises, often located in distinguished historical structures, and set in a productive rural countryside.

It was not so long ago that the river was little better than a sewer. Rather than being viewed as the core of an ecologically and socially vibrant community, it was treated as a sluiceway for all manner of waste. People literally turned their back on it; mothers forbade their children to dip even a toe. In a remarkable turnaround, led by the federal Clean Water Act of a generation ago, the river is once more a destination. Swimmers, boaters, and anglers enjoy its waters, and new investment targets its neighboring lands. Success brings its own new challenges of balancing use, conservation, growth, and preservation. Today, the quality of the river—of the watershed as a whole—depends upon a sophisticated interplay of stewardship, fostered by federal and stage agencies and carried out by communities, landowners, businesses, and organizations driven by their devotion to maintaining a delightful place.

This place is rare, worth exploring, understanding, and safeguarding. Readers of *Where the Great River Rises: An Atlas of the Connecticut River Watershed in Vermont and New Hampshire* will have a stronger foundation than ever before to understand the whole interrelated fabric of the region, to appreciate today's heritage, and to shape tomorrow's possibilities.

The next chapter of this story, gentle reader, will be up to you.

Sharon F. Francis is executive director of the Connecticut River Joint Commissions.

Preface

BARRY LAWSON

This Atlas was conceived as a source of information about the Connecticut River watershed in the two states, to provide facts and insights to help local residents plan their future in relation to the waterways, to provide a guide to visitors to the region, and to educate students (and future decisionmakers) on the value of the river, its ecosystems, and its development patterns. The Atlas is intended to speak to many audiences. Its contents and potential audiences were determined largely through surveys undertaken by the Connecticut River Joint Commissions. Its vitality and promise were generated through the enthusiasm and experience of more than three dozen writers, other contributors, and a group of dedicated advisors.

We hope readers will enjoy the Atlas and use it as a basic guide to many aspects of the watershed, from its physical structure and ecological systems, to its history and economic development, to its transportation systems and historic, tourist, and recreation sites. We hope that the illustrative nature of the Atlas will encourage readers to explore and experience the region and to contribute to the long-term sustainability of the river system and its related landscape.

The maps serve as an introduction to the various resources of the watershed and have been prepared by Northern Cartographic. More detailed, special-purpose maps may be found in a range of other places, including Northern Cartographic's own work, and through the U.S. Geological Survey, which is developing a map atlas of the entire length of the Connecticut River from its headwaters at the Canadian border to the Long Island Sound.

My personal connections to the Connecticut River started when I attended Dartmouth College (Class of '64) and enjoyed weekends on the river, picnics at the Union Village Dam, and driving up and down the river from home to school. The extent of these connections were enhanced greatly when my wife and I moved to the Northeast Kingdom of Vermont after having enjoyed for many years a vacation cottage near a source of the Ottauquechee River, one of the Connecticut's important tributaries. I have canoed the West River and the upper reaches of the Connecticut from Brunswick, Vt., to Northumberland and Guildhall, capsized in the Ottauquechee on a bone-chilling early spring day, and paddled the Moore Reservoir with Timber, my late, great, golden retriever. One of my favorite memories of river travel was skating five miles from Brattleboro toward Putney, when a relatively snow-free yet frigid winter allowed this most unusual and glorious experience.

Commuting over the last four years along I-91 has provided me with the greatest appreciation of the river from a few more perspectives: as coordinator of this Atlas project, as driver-tourist enjoying the landscape and the irregular glimpses of the river, and as a researcher studying the economic development and population changes that have occurred over the past two centuries. A very special part of I-91 for me is between mile markers 95 and 100 in Bradford, where the road traveler is treated to the view of the unfolding two-state landscape bordering the river. Some days, the clouds are low and foreboding, other days the sun shines brightly and the rolling hills to the east recede into the horizon. Like the watershed and the river itself, this one view has many moods and reveals itself in endless ways.

Barry Lawson is a consultant and researcher and served as the coordinator for this project.

A Note on Map Making

BOB GAGLIUSO

The maps and graphics contained within were derived from a number of sources. These ranged from previously developed data, both public and private, to data that was created specifically for this Atlas. Regardless of the source, the goal of all the maps and graphics was more to inform rather than analyze. Given the scale restrictions imposed by the size of the Atlas pages, it was impractical to attempt any type of map or graphic that would function analytically. In this context, it would be difficult to derive some type of measurement (area or length for examples) from any of the maps or graphics.

However, this does not imply that the information presented was not analytical in nature. Indeed, the majority of maps and graphics presented within this Atlas were derived from processes that are inherently analytical. In some instances, these represent large amounts of time and effort in extracting the necessary information. The presentation of these results was designed to provide the reader the opportunity for insight, without the burden of analyses. Each of the maps and graphics contained within the Atlas typically represent large amounts of spatial and tabular data condensed to support a single idea.

Bob Gagliuso is president of Northern Cartographic in South Burlington, Vt., specializing in the use of geographic information systems for data development, database applications programming, computerized mapping, and cartographic publication.

Acknowledgments

REBECCA A. BROWN AND BARRY LAWSON

We are indebted to many people and organizations who advanced this Atlas from concept to reality. We first wish to recognize the financial support that made the project possible. Through the efforts of U.S. Senator Judd Gregg, the National Oceanographic and Atmospheric Administration provided multiyear funding. We deeply appreciate Senator Gregg's long association with and support for the work and mission of the Connecticut River Joint Commissions. The New Hampshire Charitable Foundation and its Upper Valley region, and the Vermont Community Foundation provided significant funding to launch the Atlas. The Byrne Foundation and the Windham Foundation also gave early support. TransCanada has been an ongoing friend of the project, seeing it through some critical times. We also thank the Mascoma Savings Bank Foundation, Bill Stetson and the Grace Jones Richardson Trust, and Judith (Merck) Buecker for their support.

The commissioners of CRJC and the Atlas Advisory Committee members have supported the effort from day one. Their support of and belief in the project provided the backbone for the entire effort.

We are grateful to Dartmouth College for providing an office and technology support, as well as access to professors and academic departments, and the assistance of both the College Provost and the College President's Office, especially Sheila Culbert. Provost Barry Scherr has been unfailing in encouraging the project and ensuring Dartmouth's commitment as a dependable partner.

The core of this Atlas is the maps and the fine writing of its many authors. In addition to its map making, we thank Northern Cartographic for donating a portion of its costs. We are deeply grateful to authors, many of whom received far too little for their efforts, and some of whom declined compensation entirely.

Barry Lawson wishes to thank George Demko, professor emeritus and long-time geography instructor, who was a project enthusiast from the outset, opening doors and sharing ideas, and as good a friend to the project as could ever be found. Peter Allen and Lucinda Hall of the College's Map Room were exceedingly helpful in procuring maps and atlas resources. Bob and Beatrice Ring of Peacham, Vt., contributed a very dependable computer and printer to get the project off the ground. Barbara Harris of the CRJC staff assisted greatly with the many administrative details of the project. Keith Robinson and his staff in the U.S. Geological Survey office in Pembroke, N.H., were early and constant supporters of the Atlas, and their advice and contributions are gratefully acknowledged.

Rebecca Brown wishes to recognize the forbearance of the contributors who worked with her through the long editing process. It was a pleasure working with all of the contributors, and her only regret is that their expertise far exceeds the space available to them in this volume. Thank you for your cheerfulness, creativity, and patience. She also wishes to recognize Nat Tripp, Charlie Browne, and Steve Walasewicz, who carefully read and provided thoughtful suggestions on the entire text. Several others graciously reviewed or contributed to select chapters, and they are noted therein. Finally, she thanks her colleagues Sharon Francis, Adair Mulligan, and Barry Lawson for their innumerable contributions to the entire process of writing this Atlas.

We thank many of the authors for providing graphic images and photographs. Jon Kim was especially helpful in bringing into graphic form the concepts within the Physical Landscape chapters, as was David Conant to the Flora chapter. Many other individuals added immeasurably to the graphic quality of the Atlas. Jerry Monkman's superb photographs express his creativity as an artist as well as his love and understanding of the region. Through their photographs, Susan Morse and Jim Block allow us a certain intimacy with the watershed's mammals and birds. Eric Aldrich of The Nature Conservancy, Mary Sue Henszey, David Deen, and Dave Govatski all provided many photographs from their explorations of the watershed. Artists Eric Aho and Jeannette Fournier were generous in lending images of their work. Thanks to John Rogers for making his vintage railroad photos available, to the New England Transportation Museum, and the Upper Valley Land Trust for use of their collections. We are indebted to Frank J. Barrett Jr. for access to his treasure trove of historic images of the river valley. We thank Natalie Koch and David Glovsky for their work on innumerable details critical to the project, and Emily Bryant, for her attention to detail and good cheer throughout.

We are grateful for the patience, diligence, and support of the University Press of New England staff throughout the publishing process. Mike Burton, Ellen Wicklum, Kathy Kimball, and Rachael Cohen, as well as other staff members, saw us through the sometimes painful decisions required to produce a first-rate book.

The Atlas represents the contributions of these many experts and reflects a common thread that integrates these people one to another through their teamwork and through their subject areas. This is indeed a "pot-luck" effort, not unlike the community suppers that nourish watershed residents all seasons of the year. We all lean on each other and therein resides our greatest strength. Thanks to all.

Rebecca A. Brown is editor of the Atlas and Barry Lawson is the Atlas project coordinator.

Where the Great River Rises

Introduction

Connections with the River

River is a beautiful word, beloved by poets since time immemorial for the lyrical impetus of those magic two syllables. *Valley* is a rhythmic word, too, a favorite of songwriters for countless generations. But, to my ear, *watershed* tops all its competitors, embracing as it does the meaning of those two smaller words, flowing outwards in evocation, giving us a word that works perfectly on the poetic level and the pragmatic one as well. To use the word *watershed*, even casually in a brief conversation, is to pay tribute to one of the great elemental forces in the world, and—the true magic in this difficult age—it's a force of linkage, togetherness, interconnection.

Watershed is a word, a perspective, that operates on the smallest possible scale and the largest. If I walk 10 yards up our country dirt road, I can get a view of the Connecticut River, flowing through a narrow cut between the esker over in Vermont and the matching ridges on my New Hampshire side. In November as I write, the water's surface has the flat tone of blue-gray steel—and yet the farmer's meadow that frames it is still the gentlest, softest green imaginable. (Poet Sylvia Plath has the perfect phrase for this effect: "the river's pale circumfluent stillness.") With winter closing in, with the air so surprisingly vernal, the desire to be out on the river enjoying it while I can is all but overwhelming—but no, chores and responsibilities anchor me to home.

And yet, inches away in the pebbly groove on the road's marge, water from our most recent storm is doing just that—rushing impetuously, passionately, whole-heartedly to join that blue-gray river and lose itself in its mass. Barely a half-inch deep, borne by trickles in the meadow grass, invisible to most eyes, operating on a micro level, this dancing runoff is an integral part of the watershed in which I live. Everywhere in these hills, a similar process is going on, yet this watery autumn migration goes largely uncelebrated and unnoticed. Every molecule of water, tutored by gravity, understands which watershed it belongs to, which river it must join.

Or consider the larger level, the widest perspective humans are capable of grasping. Spread before me on my desk is a large-format photo of the Connecticut taken by satellite. The dark central line of the river is unmistakable . . . in one quick journey, my eye travels from the Canadian border to Long Island Sound . . . and yet it's the branching lines, furrows, and grooves, the east-west spider webs, the ancient herringbone pattern spread across the earth that I find most captivating. This is the Connecticut River's watershed, and perhaps it's only now that we have views like this that we realize how expansive it is, how interrelated are all the parts. Up close, the watershed trickles across my boot tops; from space, it looks like a masterfully composed work of art.

The other point to make about watersheds is that there are at least two ways of dwelling in one. The first is what we might call the oblivious or blissfully ignorant way. Picture a woman living on a hill rising from the river. She appreciates the view but couldn't really tell you where the river comes from—or goes. Finishing breakfast, she rushes outside to talk to a contractor about site work she wants done for a new garage, listens impatiently to the man's explanation of drainage concerns, the possibility of a sump pump, running a pipe to "daylight." She then drives to work, wondering, idly, why it's always so foggy when she descends from her hill and hits the main road—only to be delayed by repair work on the only bridge across the river for 12 miles. She finally gets to the office, turns on all the lights, wakes up the computers, turns on the coffeemaker, visits the bathroom, flushes. That these simple tasks using power and water depend on the river never occurs to her.

Now picture another watershed resident. She wakes up early and takes a walk to a favorite spot with a commanding a view of the river, or at least of the sinuous bank of fog masking it. Knowing that geese and ducks will be flying early this autumn day, she has brought her binoculars. Before leaving for work, she remembers to write a check to a local conservation organization that's working to protect what precious farmland remains in town. She throws her kayak onto her roof rack in case it's sunny out after work and she can spend a quiet hour on the river. When she gets caught in that same bridge-construction traffic, she takes out her camera and tries to capture the gray-white churn of water rushing past the abutments down below. Reaching the office, she flushes the toilet, too. If you asked her, she could explain at least a little about the complicated (complicated in technology, complicated in governance, complicated in economics) treatment system that takes the water and renders it harmless before it reaches the river itself. Also aware of the energy draw of the lights, the computers, the coffeemakers—along with the rest of our necessities and conveniences—she makes some effort to control their use. So she turns on the computer and the necessary (compact fluorescent) lights, and looks forward to that second cup of coffee. In her awareness of the interconnections of land and water, of individual choices and cumulative effect, the watershed has a true ally, supporter, and friend.

Thinking of her involvement brings me back again to the notion of linkage. It's fashionable to dwell upon the differences between Vermont and New Hampshire—these states that are twinned so perfectly in geography, yet that can seem so different in their inner souls. But along the nearly 300-mile corridor of the Connecticut River, these differences are muted and the similarities predominate, to the point where the watershed can seem its own self-contained, semi-autonomous state. This is emphasized by the way that our villages, towns, and cities on the New Hampshire side are mirrored by matching villages, towns, and cities on the Vermont side, all the way from Canada to the Massachusetts line. Colebrook-Canaan. Woodsville-Wells River. Orford-Fairlee. Hanover-Norwich. Lebanon-Hartford. Walpole-Bellows Falls. Keene-Brattleboro. Rivals in sports, sure; subtly different, you bet—and yet these communities bridge the river in countless ways. A high school on one side educates students from the other; young men from one town marry young women from the other; commuters cross the river to go to work and shop; increasingly, the towns' planning commissions and select boards come together to find joint solutions to challenges that face them both.

It's a tribute to the hard work that has been accomplished over the last forty years in cleaning up the river and returning it to vibrant health that the challenges remaining in the watershed—challenges in housing, in conservation, in our changing economy—do not seem insurmountable. The future is bright for this valley and its people. Those who love it passionately can draw upon both inspirations: the intimate beauty of the water rushing past us almost everywhere, and the larger perspective that comes from scanning those photos from distant space.

You don't have to be a chauvinist to understand one vital fact: The watershed we live in is one of the most beautiful on earth. Surely ours will be the generation that, at long last, will give it the care and devotion is so richly deserves—and, by doing so, link us all together in ways that even water, the magic thread of it, can't manage on its own.

W. D. Wetherell, editor of This American River: Five Centuries of Writing about the Connecticut, *is also the author of numerous books. He holds the Strauss Living Award from the American Academy of Arts and Letters. Active in local and regional efforts to protect the river, he lives in Lyme, N.H.*

I   The Physical Landscape

Introduction

A trip up the Connecticut River valley on Interstate 91—or across it on Interstate 89—may be the closest thing to time travel. The roadways cut through walls of ancient rock, all telling a story about the earth's geologic history and the valley's formation.

The valley is the product of three great mountain-building events—orogenies—over hundreds of millions of years. Through the action of plate tectonics, continents crash together and break apart, forming mountains and opening oceans. The force of collisions creates great faults many miles inland, areas of weakness in the rock that are the paths of least resistance for water. Over time, these faults become the channels of the major rivers—including the Connecticut. Driving up I-91, you generally are following the faulted boundary between an ancient island complex and a small ocean basin. Fossils of scaly trilobites, coral, and primitive shellfish that have been found in Littleton, N.H., are testament to this watery past.

The bedrock on either side of the faulted boundary has some important lithochemical differences that lead to the aphorism that Vermont grows grass while New Hampshire grows trees. The contrasts at the fundamental level of bedrock have come to symbolize what many people see as landscape and even psychosocial and political differences between Vermont and New Hampshire. Yet there are also many areas of similarity in bedrock on either side of the Connecticut. As research technology advances, geologists are engaged in lively debate and reassessment of theories of the region's origins and how the two sides of the river connect. Within the watershed, the two states may have more in common than popular culture has supposed.

This Atlas starts from the ground level. In the first chapter, Jon Kim and David Wunsch expand on the formation and chemistry of the region's bedrock and describe the watershed's physiographic regions. Wunsch and Laurence Becker then take up the story with the watershed's glacial past, many signs of which are evident today. In Chapter 3, Thomas Villars describes the watershed's major soils, themselves a product of geologic history. Subsequent parts of the Atlas, from the natural environment to patterns of human settlement and development, all start here, in the story of rock.

Traveling Interstate 91 in Vermont along the Connecticut River affords ample opportunity to observe roadside geology.

1 Physiography and Bedrock Geology

The Connecticut River and its tributaries flow through rocks that range from over 1.4 billion years old to sediments that have been deposited very recently in geologic time. The river's watershed in New Hampshire and Vermont encompasses over 6,796 square miles of mountains, valleys, and plains that resulted from a complex string of geologic events that strongly influenced not only the shape and location of these features, but also the course of the river itself. The underlying geology creates the landscape of the beautiful valley we enjoy today.

The generalized bedrock geologic map shows the different types and ages of rocks that underlie the basin (Map 1). The physical makeup, relative strength, and chemistry of the rocks play an important part in the shape of the current landscape, in where groundwater occurs, and in the mineral content of overlying soils.

I-91 generally follows the western boundary of an ancient island complex (Bronson Hill Belt) and a younger ocean basin (Connecticut Valley Belt) as it winds northward along the Vermont side of the Connecticut River from Brattleboro to Newport. For most of this journey, you will see rusty gray and black schists of the Connecticut Valley Belt in the road cuts. However, if you were to drive along I-89 from Montpelier, Vt., to Concord, N.H., you would be in the Connecticut Valley Belt from Montpelier to Lebanon, N.H.; in the Bronson Hill Belt for about 12 miles east of Lebanon; and then in a small part of the Central Maine Belt halfway to Concord. The rocks would change from gray and black schists to the Bronson Hill Belt's speckled black and white granitic rocks and then to gray and black schists. Between the Bronson Hill Belt and the Central Maine Belt is a younger granite of the New Hampshire Series, but the differences are hard to distinguish at 65 mph. An instructive guide to the interstate journey is *Roadside Geology of Vermont and New Hampshire* by Bradford Van Diver, which discusses the range of rock types and formations.

Plate Tectonics

It is hard to imagine that the hills that band the New Hampshire side of the Connecticut River Valley were once tropical volcanic islands, or that the rocks of New Hampshire were added to those to the west during three mountain-building events. The geologic events that created the landforms found in the Connecticut River watershed are explained by plate tectonic theory, which describes the movement of 20 vast plates that make up the lithosphere or earth's surface (see Figure 1). For hundreds of millions of years, these rigid plates, each nearly 100 miles thick, have moved under, over, or slid alongside each other at the rate of a few inches per year. When these plates collide, compression forces up great mountain ranges—happening today in the Himalayas. When the plates pull away from each other, the earth's surface cracks open, the crack fills with lava, and the subsequent spreading forms an ocean basin—a process continuing today in the middle of the Atlantic Ocean.

A mountain building event is called an *orogeny*. The collisional forces result in high-temperature and high-pressure conditions as one plate is thrust beneath another. The high temperatures may melt the rocks and produce igneous magmas that ultimately crystallize into granite and basalt. The high pressures produce metamorphic rocks such as slate, schist, and gneiss. The crystals and minerals of these metamorphosed rocks realign and often fold in patterns that reflect the direction of the collision. The range of igneous and metamorphic rocks in the Connecticut River watershed is evidence of these collisional and separation events that have occurred over the most recent third of earth's history, approximately 1.4 billion years.

Bedrock

The bedrock underlying the Connecticut River watershed ranges from approximately 1.4 billion to 100 million years of age. It can be divided into a number of north-northeast trending belts of metamorphosed sedimentary and igneous rocks. These rocks are separated either by ancient *faults* where one belt of rock slid past the other, or by unconformities where tremendous amounts of rock were worn away by erosion.

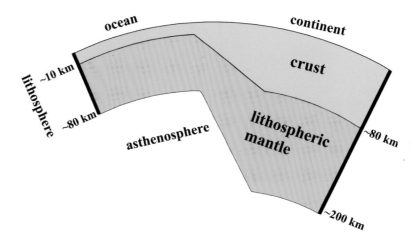

Figure 1. Structure of the Earth.

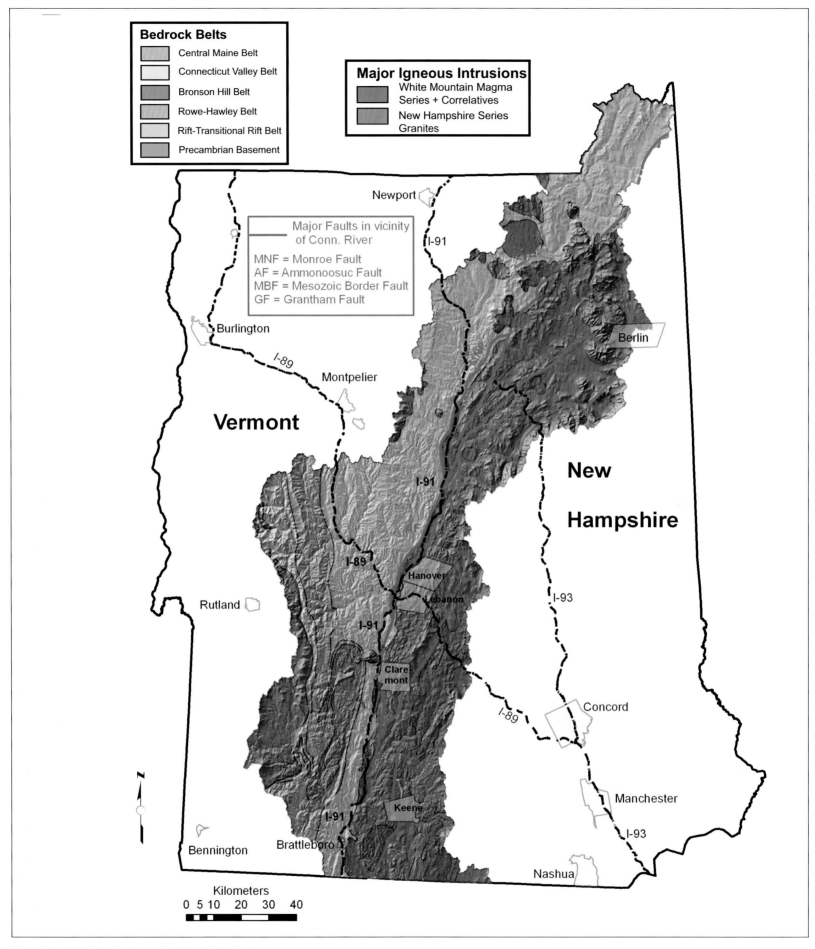

Bedrock Belts

- Central Maine Belt
- Connecticut Valley Belt
- Bronson Hill Belt
- Rowe-Hawley Belt
- Rift-Transitional Rift Belt
- Precambrian Basement

Major Igneous Intrusions

- White Mountain Magma Series + Correlatives
- New Hampshire Series Granites

Major Faults in vicinity of Conn. River

MNF = Monroe Fault
AF = Ammonoosuc Fault
MBF = Mesozoic Border Fault
GF = Grantham Fault

Newport

I-91

Burlington

I-89

Montpelier

Vermont

Berlin

New Hampshire

I-91

Rutland

I-89

I-93

Hanover

Lebanon

I-91

Clare mont

I-89

Concord

Keene

Manchester

I-91

Brattleboro

I-93

Bennington

Nashua

Kilometers
0 5 10 20 30 40

Map 1. Bedrock Belts in the Connecticut River Watershed.

6

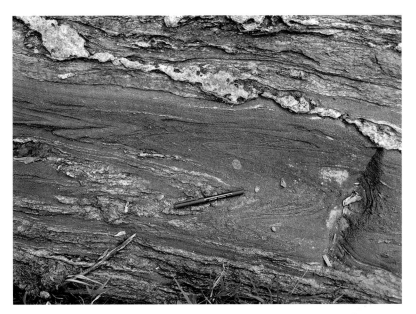

Folds in the Waits River Formation in Woodstock, Vt., are from the second mountain building event, the Acadian Orogeny, during the Devonian Period.

Garnets and hornblende in the Standing Pond Formation in the Connecticut Valley Belt in Woodstock, Vt. The garnets (red) and amphiboles (black blades) are metamorphic minerals that formed from the metamorphism of a basalt of Silurian age. One rarely sees garnets as large as these (the size of golf balls) and big *garbenschiefer* or "blades of wheat" hornblendes in metamorphic rocks.

The oldest bedrock in the watershed, dating back approximately 1.1 to 1.4 billion years (Ratcliffe, Armstrong, and Aleinikoff 1997), is found in the westernmost core of Vermont's Green Mountains (the Precambrian Basement). These rocks are remnants of an ancient continent, called Laurentia, which started to break apart approximately 590 million years ago (Late Proterozoic; e.g., van Staal et al. 1998). Rocks along the flanks of the Greens were deposited in the early stages of the continental breakup in a narrow basin that progressed from the size of the East African Rift to that of the Red Sea (Rift/Transitional Rift Belt). The Iapetus Ocean developed and rocks deposited in this ocean became much of the Rowe-Hawley Belt (see Figure 2).

Mountain Building

Just as ocean basins open by spreading or "rifting," they close through a process called *subduction*. The Bronson Hill Belt runs from the New Hampshire/Massachusetts border just south of Keene north to Berlin, at the edge of the Connecticut River watershed (see Map 1). The belt is formed above a subduction zone that was active as the ancient Iapetus Ocean closed between approximately 510 to 440 million years ago (Late Cambrian to Ordovician on Figure 3; e.g., Tucker and Robinson 1990; Karabinos et al. 1998; Ratcliffe, Armstrong, and Aleinikoff 1998; van Staal 2006). Metamorphosed igneous rocks derived from the melting of the subducting plate dominate the Bronson Hill Belt. As the plate containing Laurentia was subducted, the Iapetus Ocean progressively narrowed until the Bronson Hill Belt collided with the Laurentian continent (see Figure 3). Rocks of the Rowe-Hawley Belt were squeezed between the Laurentian Continent (Precambrian Basement–Rift/Transitional Rift Belt) and the Bronson Hill Belt, and formed a suture zone of extensively faulted rocks. The westernmost part of the Bronson Hill Belt—the Shelburne Falls Arc—formed first and may have collided with Laurentia first (Karabinos et al. 1998). This overall collision, called the Taconian Orogeny, produced a major mountain range, probably on the same scale as the Rocky Mountains. Figure 3 shows a tectonic model for the Taconian Orogeny.

After the Taconian Orogeny, the large mountain range in the collision zone began to erode, depositing sediments in small ocean basins to the west and east. This sand and mud formed sandstones and shales, respectively, whereas fossil-bearing limestones formed beneath the oceans. Rocks in the western basin became the Connecticut Valley Belt and those in the eastern basin became the Central Maine Belt. The thick sequences of interlayered shale, limestone, and sandstone were not deformed and metamorphosed until the Acadian Orogeny. It is important to realize that these rocks cover up parts of the Bronson Hill Belt shown in Map 1.

The Acadian Orogeny occurred approximately 360 to 400 million years ago during the Devonian Period (e.g., Lyons et al. 1997), when Laurentia collided with another ancient continent, Avalonia, and created a new land mass called Laurasia. This mountain-building incident was the first to deform and metamorphose the Connecticut Valley Belt and Central Maine Belt sedimentary rocks and the second to affect the metamorphic rocks of the Bronson Hill, Rowe-Hawley, Rift/Transitional Rift, and Precambrian Basement belts. Effects of the Acadian Orogeny extended as far westward as the Green Mountains. Numerous major granite intrusions of the New Hampshire Series occurred roughly at this time (see Map 1).

The next mountain-building episode occurred when Laurasia collided to the south with the ancient continent Gondwanaland, forming Pangea. This was the the Alleghenian Orogeny, occurring about 280 to 300 million years ago (e.g., Spear et al. 2003). *Terranes*, or migrating pieces of continental plates, adhered to those of North America. In the Connecticut River watershed, the Alleghenian Orogeny primarily affected easternmost Vermont and all of New Hampshire. When Pangea broke apart, it did so along new lines, leaving parts of these ter-

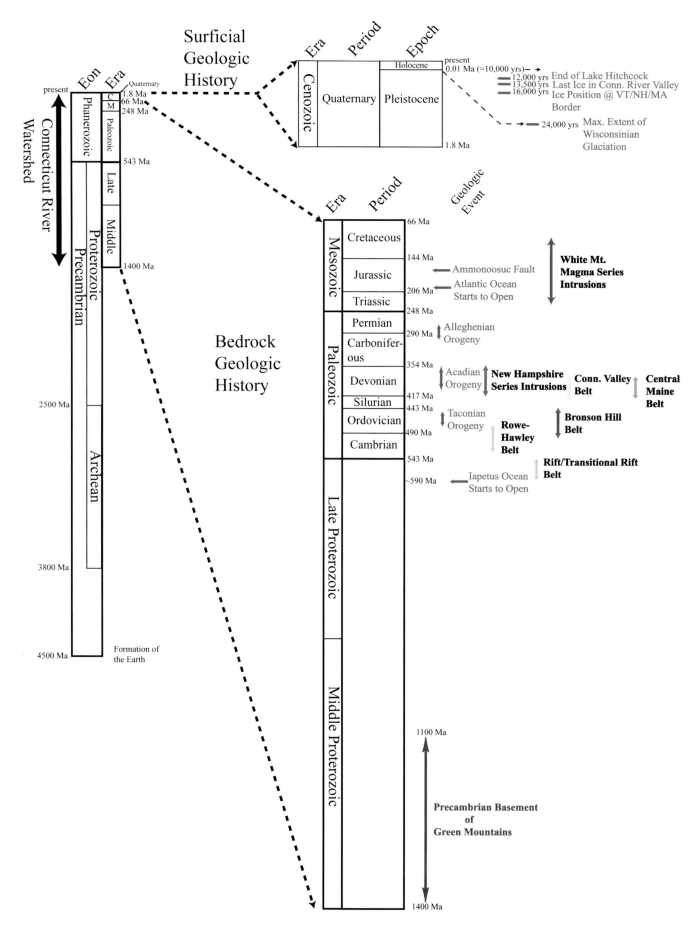

Figure 2. Geologic Time Scale for the Connecticut River Watershed.

West　　　　　　　　　　　　　　　　　　　　　East

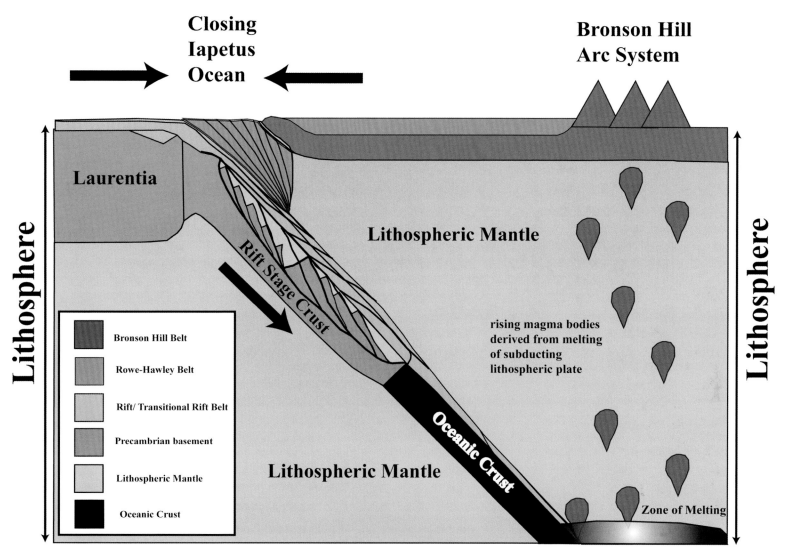

Figure 3. Tectonic Model for the Taconian Orogeny.

ranes behind in New England. As Pangea cracked and divided, valleys and basins formed, including the Connecticut River Valley. The rivers flowing through the valley emptied into the newly opening Atlantic Ocean approximately 200 million years ago.

Anorogenic (not associated with an orogeny) igneous intrusions of the White Mountain Magma Series occurred approximately between 200 and 110 million years ago (e.g., Lyons et al. 1997). In the Connecticut River watershed, these intrusions make up Gore Mountain, the Pliny Range, and Cherry Mountain in New Hampshire (160 to 200 million years ago) and Mount Ascutney in Vermont (approximately 123 million years ago; Schneiderman 1989).

The latest modification to the bedrock architecture of the Connecticut River watershed occurred during the opening of the Atlantic Ocean. As an ocean opens, the earth's crust pulls apart and steep faulting occurs where large blocks of bedrock drop down into the newly opened areas. A number of these normal faults are in the vicinity of the Connecticut River Valley. The most prominent are the Ammonoosuc and Mesozoic Border faults, which are approximately 160 million years old (see Map 1; Lyons et al. 1997).

Fault Control of the Course of Connecticut River

The overall north-northeastern trend of the rocks and structures (*faults*) of the region also has a pronounced effect on the course of the Connecticut River. The river follows this trend by flowing from north to south. From central Vermont and New Hampshire south to nearly the Massachusetts border, the course of the Connecticut River is controlled primarily by the Mesozoic Ammonoosuc Fault (see Map 1). Short segments of the Devonian Monroe Fault may exert control on the trend of certain segments of the river valley in the northern half of the watershed. From Littleton, N.H., to the Quebec border, the Connecticut River cuts across bedrock belts and faults and its course may be controlled by various fractures.

Additionally, the belts of more highly fractured schists and slates in the center of the river valley predispose the area to the erosional action of the river, which forms the river valley. In New Hampshire, the large bodies of granite resulted in prominent exposure of resistant rocks that form the core of many of the mountains found in the state, including the White Mountains. Although subsequent modification by glaciers shaped the landscape, the underlying character of the rocks

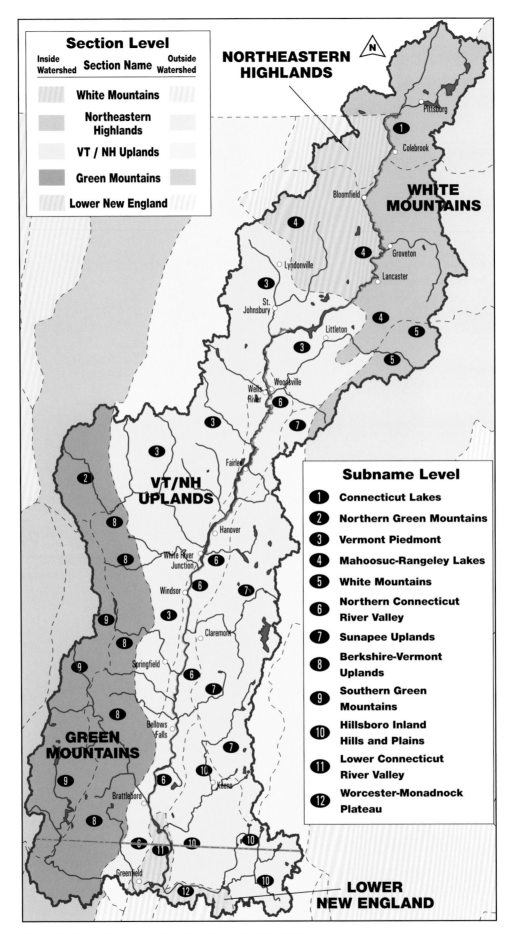

Section Level

Inside Watershed	Section Name	Outside Watershed
	White Mountains	
	Northeastern Highlands	
	VT / NH Uplands	
	Green Mountains	
	Lower New England	

NORTHEASTERN HIGHLANDS

WHITE MOUNTAINS

VT/NH UPLANDS

GREEN MOUNTAINS

LOWER NEW ENGLAND

Subname Level

1. Connecticut Lakes
2. Northern Green Mountains
3. Vermont Piedmont
4. Mahoosuc-Rangeley Lakes
5. White Mountains
6. Northern Connecticut River Valley
7. Sunapee Uplands
8. Berkshire-Vermont Uplands
9. Southern Green Mountains
10. Hillsboro Inland Hills and Plains
11. Lower Connecticut River Valley
12. Worcester-Monadnock Plateau

Map 2. Physiographic Regions of the Upper Connecticut River Valley.

has had a more pronounced effect in determining the landscape of the Connecticut River watershed (see Chapter 2, Glacial Geology).

Rock Chemistry

The complex geologic history of the Connecticut River watershed produced rocks with significantly different chemical properties. The chemistry of the minerals in these rocks affects soil development and nutrient content. Soils in turn have a pronounced effect on the distribution of plants, which influences agriculture. For example, the Connecticut Valley Belt of Vermont and northwesternmost New Hampshire has significant amounts of calcium carbonate-rich rocks, particularly metamorphosed limestones (see Map 1). These rocks usually produce soils that are rich in calcium, an important nutrient for plants, and form the fertile pasturelands that support Vermont's prominent dairy industry. Carbonate rocks are easily weathered and eroded, which results in the rolling landscapes that characterize the region. For more detail about the watershed's soils, see Chapter 3, Soils.

Physiographic Regions

Most of the topographic patterns observed throughout the watershed are directly related to the physical characteristics of the underlying bedrock. Map 2 depicts the watershed's major physiographic regions, the Green Mountains, Uplands, and White Mountains (Northeastern Highlands in Vermont; e.g., Johnson 1998; Van Diver 1987). The Green Mountain physiographic region (Precambrian basement, Rift/Transitional Rift, and part of Rowe-Hawley bedrock belts) consists of linear north-northeast trending ridges and valleys that generally parallel rock formations. Ridges generally are composed of bedrock types more resistant to erosion, whereas the reverse is true for valleys.

The highest peaks in Vermont are found in the Precambrian Basement and Rift/Transitional Rift belts. Fracture-controlled mountain streams generally flow directly downhill (roughly east or west) from the ridges to valleys where they connect at right angles with rivers that flow parallel to the north-northeast trending valley floors in a drainage pattern that is called *rectangular* (see Figure 4). River branches flowing within these valleys then connect with a main river branch that flows at right angles to the bedrock belts and form a *trellis* pattern. The largest river branches that connect with the Connecticut River are thought to follow crack (fracture) patterns in the bedrock.

The bedrock in the Uplands physiographic region (most of the Connecticut Valley, Bronson Hill, and Central Maine bedrock belts) is generally less resistant to erosion than in the adjacent Green Mountain and White Mountain regions, often forming rolling hills and short ridges. In addition, New Hampshire and White Mountain magma series granites in the Uplands region are reflected in dome-shaped hills with steep sides (Mount Ascutney, for example). The drainage pattern formed by rivers and streams in the Uplands is generally *dendritic*, which means it resembles the branches of a tree (see Figure 4).

The White Mountain physiographic region contains the highest and most rugged topography in the watershed. The northern part of the Bronson Hill, Connecticut Valley, and Central Maine belts comprise this region. A significant proportion of this region is underlain by both New Hampshire Series granites and White Mountain

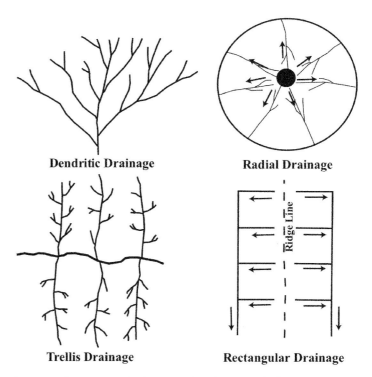

Dendritic Drainage **Radial Drainage**

Trellis Drainage **Rectangular Drainage**

Figure 4. Drainage Patterns in the Connecticut River Watershed.

magma series igneous rocks that frequently form topographic domes. Many of these domes have a drainage pattern that is *radial*, with streams flowing away from central high-elevation areas (see Figure 4). In Vermont, Mount Ascutney also has a radial drainage pattern. On the eastern edge of the watershed, Mount Washington and the Presidential Range are composed of the Littleton Formation of the Central Maine Belt.

The next chapter describes how glacial action worked within the context of the underlying geology and left the region with many of its distinctive landscape features.

Jon Kim works for the Vermont Geological Survey in Waterbury. He was first intrigued with the formation of mountains during a family camping trip to the Canadian Rockies after the ninth grade. He received his Ph.D. in geology in 1996 from SUNY at Buffalo after a stint in the oil industry.

David Wunsch is the state geologist of New Hampshire and director of the New Hampshire Geological Survey. He earned his doctorate in hydrogeology at the University of Kentucky. He has authored or co-authored more than 50 publications.

For Further Reading

Denny, C. S. 1982. *Geomorphology of New England*. U.S. Geological Survey Professional Paper 1208.

Lougee, R. J. 1939. Geology of the Connecticut River Watershed. In *Biological Survey of the Connecticut Watershed*, Survey Report No. 4. Concord, N.H.: New Hampshire Fish and Game Department.

Raymo, C., and M. E. Raymo. 1989. *Written in Stone: A Geological and Natural History of the Northeastern United States*. Chester, Conn.: Globe Pequot Press.

Van Diver, B. 1987. *Roadside Geology of Vermont and New Hampshire*. Missoula, Mont.: Mountain Press.

2 Glacial Geology

The landscape of the Connecticut River valley is influenced heavily by the underlying geology and the ongoing movement of the earth over hundreds of millions of years, as described in Chapter 1, Physiography and Bedrock Geology. However, in geologic terms, some significant features of the valley were formed only yesterday. They are the result of the action of glaciers and the passing of the last ice age.

Mountain building and erosion established the overall shape of the Connecticut River basin by the time the last great glaciers advanced over Vermont and New Hampshire. *Glaciers* are large masses of ice and compacted snow deep and heavy enough that they move, or flow, under their own weight. One of their definitive characteristics is that they are always moving. A number of major ice advances and retreats of glaciers have occurred in North America in the last 1.8 million years.

The most recent major advance was during the Pleistocene epoch. Known as the Wisconsin glaciation, it began to grow approximately 100,000 years ago in Canada. Ice up to a mile thick reached all the way to present-day New York City some 24,000 years ago. At the eastern edge of the Connecticut River basin, even the top of Mount Washington (6,288 feet above sea level) was beneath the ice. When glaciers retreat, they essentially melt backwards toward their original centers of accumulation, while still flowing forward in the direction of the retreating ice front. As the climate warmed, the ice retreated northward. Approximately 16,000 years ago, the ice front was located near the Vermont and New Hampshire borders with Massachusetts. The chronology of glacial retreat is shown in Map 3.

Current Signs of Ancient Glaciers

Abundant evidence of the movement of glaciers remains today. As glaciers move, they pull up blocks of bedrock and smooth off topographic high points while deepening existing valleys. Moving glaciers pick up boulders, cobbles, gravel, sand, silt, and clay and incorporate them into their ice mass. These materials scratch the bedrock upon which the ice is resting as the glacier flows along its path. This abrading effect is visible in the form of striations on exposed bedrock throughout the watershed.

Glacial movement has influenced the region's landscape in various other ways, including deposits of *till*, the debris left behind by the glacier. In some valleys closer to the Connecticut River, notably in the Littleton and Bethlehem, N.H., area, glacial *moraines* are found. Moraines are ridges of till deposited at a glacier's front or along its edges. The complex of moraines in the Littleton-Bethlehem area has been formed from debris piled up in successive ridges parallel to the ice front.

In most places in the basin, ice retreat occurred so rapidly that the remaining glacial till did not leave distinctive ridges. Instead, a relatively thin uniform cover of till is left over the underlying bedrock. Glacial *erratics* are large, rounded rocks and boulders that are transported by the glacial ice. A true erratic is composed of a type of rock different from the bedrock directly beneath it, indicating that the boulder had been transported from another location. These large rocks can be found in seemingly haphazard locations across the landscape, including the top of Mount Washington. They were deposited when ice first melted off the uplands, and they differ starkly from the dense till at the base of the ice, which commonly is deposited in valleys.

The ice sheet retreated in a disjointed fashion, and large fragments of ice, or *lobes*, were isolated in some valley bottoms. Lakes formed in front of some of these ice lobes, and their levels rose if the outlets through the valleys were blocked by ice and debris. Eventually, the water ran off through gaps higher in the surrounding hills and mountains. These early stages of retreat over Vermont and New Hampshire led to high-level lakes, which later filled with finer-grained sediments such as sand, silt, and clay. In Cavendish, Vt., on the Black River, pebbly sand is evidence for such a lake at an elevation of 900 feet. In Cavendish, following drainage of a high-level lake, coarser sorted material was deposited between the valley wall and retreating ice, leaving what is known as a *kame terrace*. Water rushing from the front of the glacier left *outwash deposits*. Both kames and outwash can contain stratified cobbles, gravel, and sand. Map 4 depicts an example of the geological aftermath of glacial action.

In some locations, meltwater flows in a stream under the ice of glaciers, leaving cobbles, gravel, sand, and other debris along its bed and banks. This curving, narrow ridge of debris deposited by the meltwater stream is called an *esker*. A prominent Connecticut valley esker runs from Windsor, Vt., to Lyme, N.H.

Lake Hitchcock

As the glaciers retreated, they left behind a landscape feature in present-day Connecticut that had a profound influence on the upper Connecticut River watershed. Glacial deposits created a natural dam, which expanded with the addition of tons of silt accumulating from the steady flow of glacial meltwater. Glacial Lake Hitchcock (named

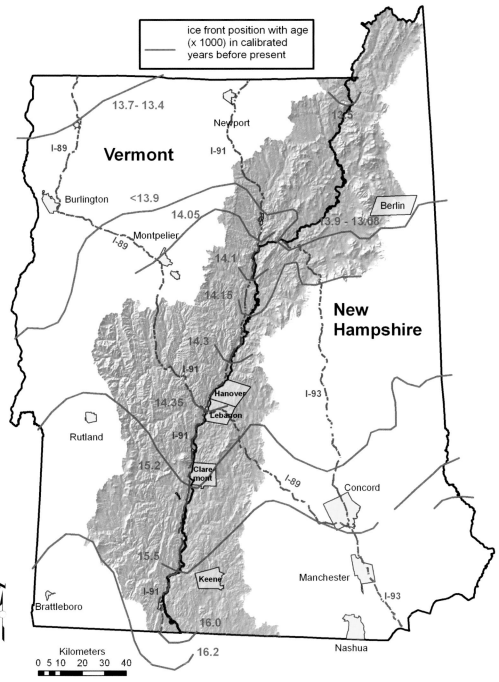

ice front position with age
(x 1000) in calibrated
years before present

13.7- 13.4

Newport

I-89

Vermont

I-91

13.5

Burlington

<13.9

14.05

Berlin

3.9 - 13.08

Montpelier

I-89

14.1

New
Hampshire

14.15

14.3

I-91

Hanover

I-93

14.35

Lebanon

I-91

Rutland

Clare-
mont

15.2

I-89

Concord

15.5

Manchester

Keene

I-91

I-93

16.0

N

Nashua

Kilometers
0 5 10 20   30   40

16.2

Map 3. Glacier Retreat Chronology for Vermont and New
Hampshire.

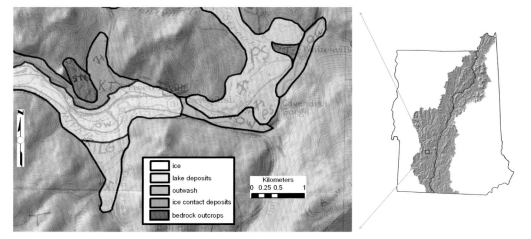

ice
lake deposits
outwash
ice contact deposits
bedrock outcrops

Kilometers
0 0.25 0.5   1

Map 4. Surficial Geology of the Cavendish, Vt., Area, and Sche-
matic Ice Position.

13

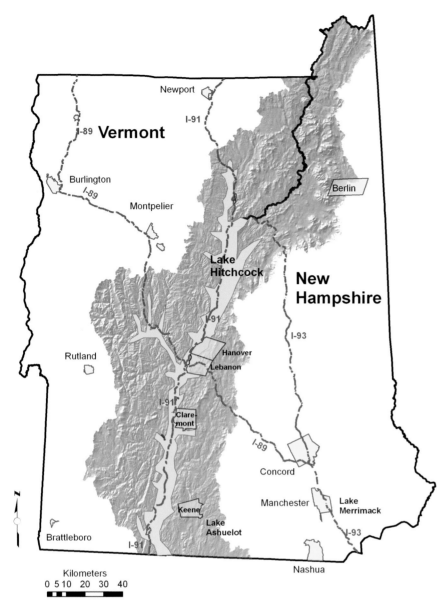

Map 5. Generalized Map of Lake Hitchcock.

for Edward Hitchcock, an Amherst College geologist who presented evidence for the lake in 1818) formed behind this dam and expanded north as ice retreat progressed. The lake existed for over 4,000 years, stretching about 250 miles from present-day Rocky Hill, Conn., to north of St. Johnsbury, Vt. It was still in place after continental ice had left the watershed entirely, but experts agree that its level fluctuated greatly during its history. North of Lake Hitchcock, smaller glacial lakes Coös and Colebrook filled the Connecticut River Valley. Lake Hitchcock is illustrated in Map 5.

Evidence of the presence and passing of Lake Hitchcock and other glacial water bodies is found in distinctive deposits of clay called *varves*. Just as tree rings show the annual growth of a tree, varves show annual activity of a glacial lake. Experts in the watershed have used them for decades to understand the timing of regional glacier retreat and the characteristics of Glacial Lake Hitchcock, although many details about its drainage remain unresolved. A stream outlet in Connecticut, called the New Britain channel, served as a spillway for the lake. This outlet was a precursor to the Connecticut River we know today.

No matter how Lake Hitchcock drained, its presence profoundly influenced the landscape of the Connecticut River Valley. A good place to see the influence is looking across the river valley from Newbury, Vt., toward Haverhill and Piermont, N.H., both of which are situated on elevated benches likely formed by glacial deposits from rivers that emptied into Lake Hitchcock. Newbury itself sits on varves that document the long existence of the lake. When the glacial ice sheet had withdrawn completely and glacial lakes had drained, streams reestablished positions on the valley floors, often in locations different from the preglacial drainage. Streams cut rapidly through fresh deposits of glacial till composed of clay, sand, and gravel, carving their way down to the new base level of the reestablished Connecticut River, and leaving a series of terraces in some valleys. Orford, N.H., sits on such a terrace above the Connecticut River. Quechee Gorge in Hartford, Vt., is a dramatic example of the valley's glacial past. At the head of the gorge, the Ottauquechee River cuts through an ancient delta of Lake Hitchcock, starting at an elevation of approximately 600 feet and cascading nearly 200 feet.

Although glacial action rounded the mountain peaks of the watershed, making steeper slopes and deeper valleys, the overall landscape form controlled by bedrock stayed largely the same. In some places, glacial movement has created rounded peaks with a *roche moutonnée* or "sheep back" shape. The northern, upstream sides are gradual slopes smoothed by the oncoming glacier, and the downstream, southern faces are steep and craggy where ice action plucked away rock. Jones Hill in Enfield, N.H., and Sargent Hill in Grantham, N.H., display the classic form, as does Cannon Mountain, which was the home of New Hampshire's famed Old Man of the Mountain.

Glacial cirques in New Hampshire's White Mountains illustrate the influence of mountain glaciers in the region's history. *Cirques* are scooped-out basins at the head of a mountain glacier valley. Two dramatic and well-known examples of cirques are Tuckerman and Huntington ravines on Mount Washington (these are just outside of the Connecticut River watershed, as their runoff flows east toward the Androscoggin River). Overall, the region's landscape today is dominated by the historical influence of continental glaciers. The retreat of continental ice left valley floors that are largely flat due to deposition of sediment from glacial meltwater. Sediments from glacier outwash and high-level lakes, including Lake Hitchcock, filled the valleys, resulting in lower relief between steeper valley sides. Open topography on the valley sides can be the result of ice contact deposits such as kame terraces.

The legacy of glacial retreat and postglacial change is a landscape with waterfalls for hydromechanical power and transportation corridors in valley floors. The forest industry is maintained by harvesting hardwood and softwood on the till-covered uplands. All are related to fertile soils overlaying glacial parent material that supports agriculture and the growth of towns and small cities. Soils are discussed in the next chapter.

Laurence Becker is the state geologist of Vermont and director of the Vermont Geological Survey. He earned his master's degree in geology from the University of Vermont, and learned his glacial geology while developing Vermont's Aquifer Protection Area mapping methodology in the early 1980s.

David Wunsch is the state geologist of New Hampshire and director of the New Hampshire Geological Survey. He earned his doctorate in hydrogeology at the University of Kentucky. He has authored or co-authored more than 50 publications.

FOR FURTHER READING

Jacobs, E. J. 1950. *The Physical Features of Vermont*. Waterbury, Vt.: Vermont State Development Department, Vermont Geological Survey.

Larsen, F. D. 1985. The last great ice sheet and the origin of Quechee Gorge, *Window of Vermont Magazine* (Summer 1985).

Lougee, R. J. 1939. Geology of the Connecticut River Watershed. In *Biological Survey of the Connecticut Watershed*, Survey Report No. 4. Concord, N.H.: New Hampshire Fish and Game Department.

Raymo, C., and M. E. Raymo. 1989. *Written in Stone: A Geological and Natural History of the Northeastern United States*. Chester, Conn.: Globe Pequot Press.

Ridge, J. C. 2003. The last deglaciation of the northeastern United States: A combined varve, paleomagnetic, and calibrated 14C chronology. In *Geoarchaeology of Landscapes in the Glaciated Northeast*, edited by David L. Cremeens and John P. Hart. New York State Museum Bulletin 497.

Stewart, D. P., and P. MacClintock. 1970. *Surficial Geologic Map of Vermont*. Waterbury, Vt.: Vermont Geological Survey, Department of Water Resources. Scale 1:250,000.

Van Diver, B. 1987. *Roadside Geology of Vermont and New Hampshire*. Missoula, Mont.: Mountain Press.

The Ottauquechee River cut the Quechee Gorge over thousands of years, starting when Glacial Lake Hitchcock began draining at the end of the last ice age.

3 Soils

For its relatively small geographic area, the upper Connecticut River region has an abundance of soil types, including some of the finest agricultural soils in the nation. Because of variations in bedrock geology, glacial history, elevation, and climate, well over 100 soil types are found in the watershed. While the soils in the uplands are all formed in glacial till, other soils have formed in alluvium on flood plains, sandy and gravelly outwash on stream terraces, lacustrine sediments from Glacial Lake Hitchcock, and organic materials in wetlands (see Map 6).

Five factors are commonly understood to interact in the formation of soils (see Figure 5). These are parent material (such as alluvium or glacial till), climate, vegetation, topography, and time. A sixth and recent factor, in terms of geologic time, is human activity. Through land clearing, cultivation, drainage, construction, and many other activities, people can have a great and lasting effect on the nature of soils in any area.

All soils have physical, chemical, and biological properties. Physical properties include the types and thickness of individual layers, called *horizons*, such as topsoil and subsoil; texture (the relative amounts of sand, silt, and clay in the soil); depth to bedrock and the seasonal high water table; and the percent slope. Horizons are shown in Figure 6. Chemical properties include pH (or acidity level), amount of organic matter, levels of plant nutrients such as potassium and calcium, and presence of other elements, including heavy metals such as lead and cadmium. Biological properties of soils include the presence and levels of bacteria and other microfauna, as well as larger organisms like earthworms and insects.

The system of soil classification developed by the United States Department of Agriculture Natural Resources Conservation Service (NRCS) is known as soil taxonomy. At the highest categorical level, it recognizes 12 different soil orders worldwide. *Entisols, histosols, inceptisols,* and *spodosols* are four of the 12 soil orders and are common in the Connecticut River watershed. At the lowest taxonomic level, there are thousands of different soils, each one classified as a *soil series.* The

Figure 5. Factors of Soil Formation.

Figure 6. A Brief Primer on the Concept of Soil Horizons.

Soil horizons, or distinctive layers of varying depths and compositions, are an important tool in defining not only the type of soil, but more importantly, how a soil will function.

Not all horizons are present in every soil type. For example, O horizons only form in areas that have an abundant source of organic materials. Soils with a history of human use, such as regular deep plowing, may lack distinct horizons altogether.

This is a profile of a Windsor soil series, found throughout the watershed.

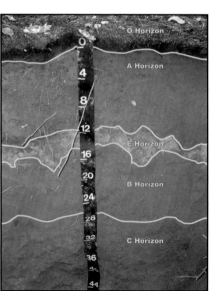

The O horizon is comprised of large amounts of organic matter in varying stages of decomposition.

A horizons vary widely in thickness and color. It is a surface horizon and is in the zone where most biological activity occurs because of higher levels of organic matter and moisture.

E horizons have been leached of their mineral and/or organic content in a process called eluviation. Eluviation leaves a pale gray layer largely composed of silicates. E horizons typically are present in acidic, sandy, and loamy soils, and are generally within a foot of the surface.

B horizons, commonly referred to as subsoil, consist of layers with concentrations of clay and other mineral compounds with iron and aluminum. In well-drained soils, they are a rusty red color due to the presence of iron oxide.

C horizons are layers too deep to be affected by typical soil-forming processes. They reflect soil parent material in the unweathered state.

Not shown in this particular soil profile is the R horizon. R horizons indicate a layer of bedrock at the base of the soil profile, and as in this example, often begin well below the depth of a typical soil pit.

One of the major contributing factors in plant-species distribution in the watershed can be linked directly to the lithology of the underlying parent material. Lithology is the study and description of rocks, especially in terms of their color, texture, and composition.

Soils are derived from these materials, and as a result, differ significantly in the types and relative amounts of essential elements. Elements such as calcium, phosphorous, and potassium determine in large part the chemical properties of a soil, which in turn determine available nutrients, and ultimately plant distributions.

This map depicts the watershed from the viewpoint of parent materials, and shows a clear delineation between those that eventually will result in soils that are calcium-rich and those that are not. Parent materials that are predominated by carbonate-rich rocks will produce calcium-rich soils.

While it might not be apparent that such differences contribute significantly to any plant-distribution patterns, they do influence what grows where and how well plants thrive. If a farmer and botanist are asked about the differences between Vermont and New Hampshire soils, they likely will describe what they see using completely different contexts. However, their descriptions will support the same conclusion: that soil chemistry plays an important role in plant distribution and composition.

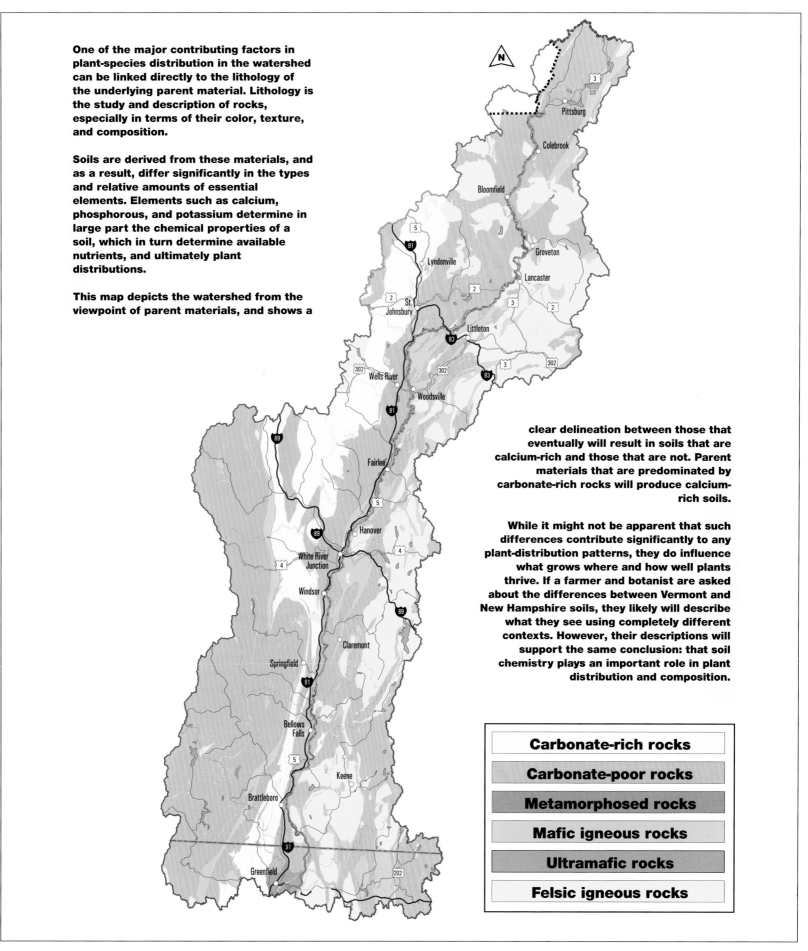

| Carbonate-rich rocks |
| Carbonate-poor rocks |
| Metamorphosed rocks |
| Mafic igneous rocks |
| Ultramafic rocks |
| Felsic igneous rocks |

Map 6. Lithology of the Upper Connecticut River Watershed.

Due to the combination of soil complexity and map scale, displaying a soils map of the entire area would not be very illuminating. However, by looking at soils data on a finer scale, the relationship between parent materials and soils series becomes obvious.

Displayed here are soils data from the Halls Brook sub-watershed of the larger Waits River watershed.

First note the soil parent material map (center). Parent material is defined loosely as rock and other substrate from which soils eventually develop. The parent material has specific chemical and physical properties that determine much of how soils behave, both physically and chemically.

This relationship can be seen in both the soil order (left) and series (right) maps. Soil orders are broad classifications of soils based on the typical physical and chemical

properties inherited from the parent material. From soil orders come soil series, a further refinement of soil properties, incorporating more of the physical and chemical properties of the soil.

Soil series is the finest delineation in the USDA classification system. Note the areas of commonality between the parent material, soil order, and soil series. Several of these have been highlighted in all three maps, but there exist many more.

On most soil survey maps, the soil series is further divided by slope classes and other physiographic features. The USDA-NRCS soil map shown (below right) may include about a dozen soil series, but there are more soil map units because the same soil can have several different slope and surface stoniness classes.

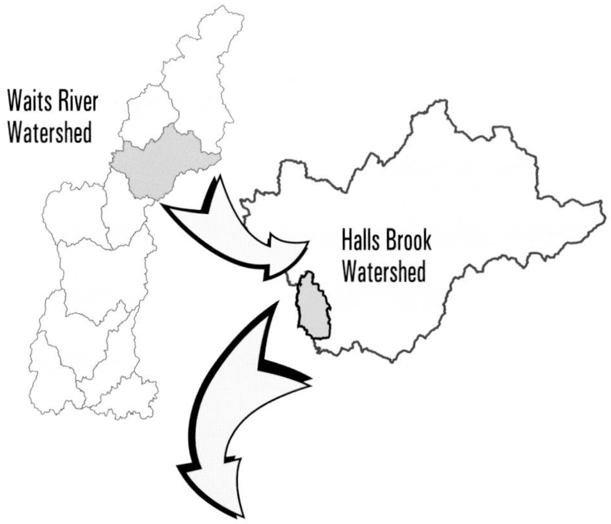

Waits River Watershed

Halls Brook Watershed

Soil parent material

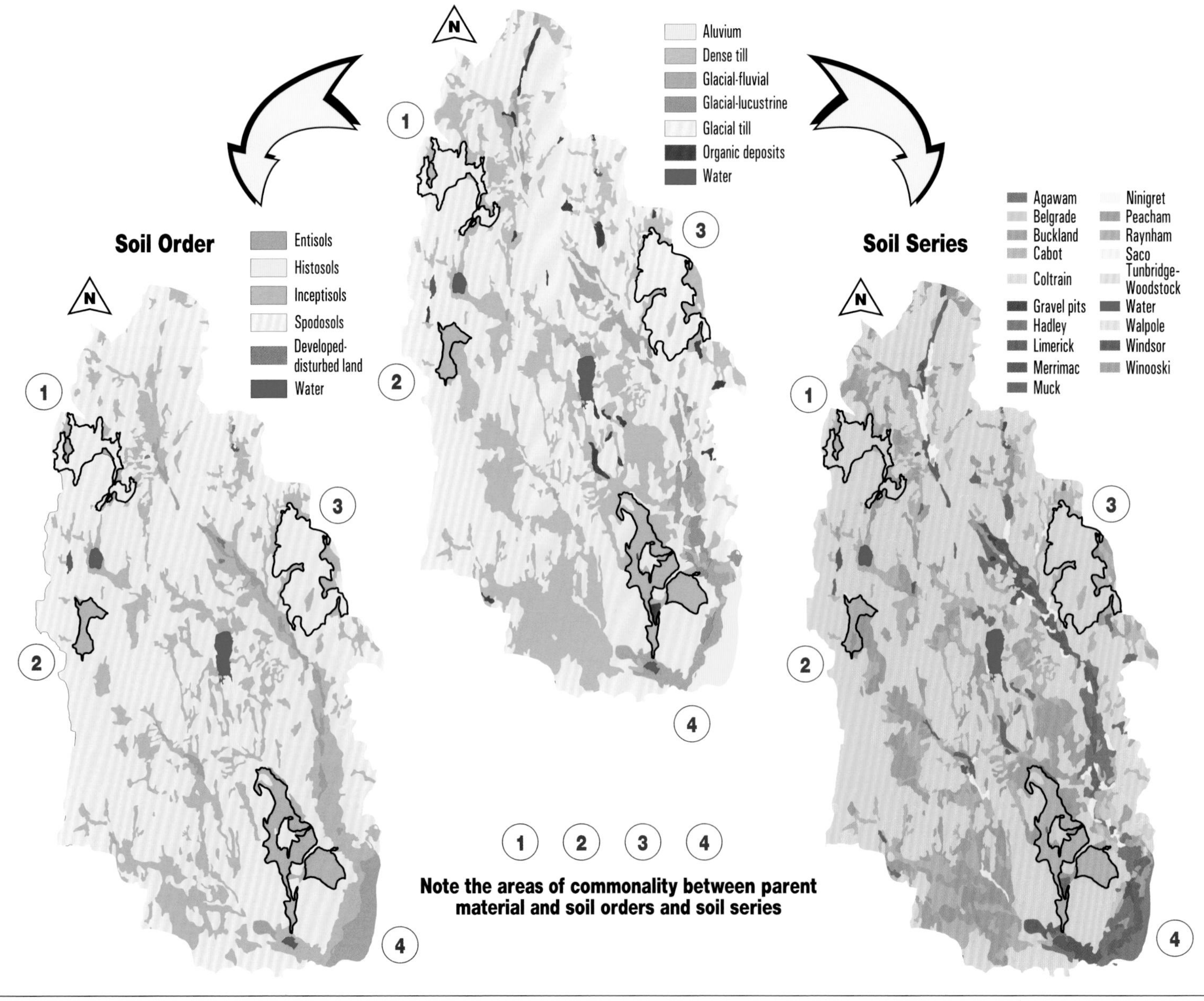

N

Aluvium
Dense till
Glacial-fluvial
Glacial-lucustrine
Glacial till
Organic deposits
Water

Soil Order

N

Entisols
Histosols
Inceptisols
Spodosols
Developed-disturbed land
Water

Soil Series

Agawam | Ninigret
Belgrade | Peacham
Buckland | Raynham
Cabot | Saco
Coltrain | Tunbridge-Woodstock
Gravel pits | Water
Hadley | Walpole
Limerick | Windsor
Merrimac | Winooski
Muck

N

Note the areas of commonality between parent material and soil orders and soil series

Map 7. Soil Parent Material: The Source of Soil Orders and Soil Series.

Tunbridge soil series, named after the town of Tunbridge, Vt., and officially designated as the Vermont State Soil, is a soil series common in the mountainous regions of the Northeast. Wherever the Tunbridge soil series is mapped, the soil characteristics and the five soil-forming factors are the same. Soil series provide a standardized frame of reference for comparing and analyzing soil characteristics at a site or among many sites. Map 7 depicts the relation between parent material and soil orders and soil series.

It is convenient to discuss the soils in the Connecticut River watershed as components of its major physiographic regions (see Table 1 and Map 2 in Chapter 1, Physiography and Bedrock Geology). The watershed is bordered by the Green Mountains to the west, the Northeastern Highlands in northern Vermont, and the White Mountains in northern New Hampshire. In the center are the Vermont/New Hampshire Uplands region, which can be subdivided into the Vermont Piedmont, the Connecticut River Valley, and the Hills and Plains region in New Hampshire.

Taxonomically speaking, the soils in the Green Mountains, the White Mountains, and the Northeastern Highlands are similar — they are almost all spodosols. These loamy, acidic, relatively infertile soils are common in the mountains of New England, but they are actually quite rare on a national scale. The soils vary primarily in depth to bedrock and drainage. The Tunbridge series, the Vermont State Soil, is well drained and only 20 to 40 inches deep to bedrock. Other spodosols, like the Marlow series, the New Hampshire State Soil, are underlain by much deeper, densely compacted glacial till.

The White Mountain and Northeastern Highland regions contain rocky, boulder-laden soils. Along with the Green Mountains, these regions comprise the most rugged and heavily forested part of the Connecticut River watershed and contain some of the most magnificent mountain landscapes in the eastern United States. Mount Washington, in the Presidential Range of the White Mountains, rises to 6,288 feet and is the highest mountain in the Northeast. Eight other mountains in the Presidential Range have elevations of more than 5,000 feet. The *cryic* soil-temperature zone is at elevations above approximately 2,500 to 3,000 feet. In this high-elevation zone, the soils are colder and even more acidic than at lower elevations and support only spruce and fir forests, or alpine vegetation above tree line. Typical soils in the cryic zone include the Glebe, Ricker, Saddleback, and Stratton series. Very poorly drained organic soils, classified as histosols, also are found in the many bogs scattered throughout the three regions, particularly in the Northeastern Highlands. Human land uses in these regions include forestry, hunting, recreation, and tourism.

The Vermont Piedmont is a hilly region that is bordered by the Green Mountains to the west and the Connecticut River Valley to the east. It is technically part of the larger Vermont/New Hampshire Uplands region, but because of the presence of thin layers of limestone in the schist and phyllite bedrock underlying the region, the soils have a higher natural fertility in comparison with soils in the New Hampshire part of this larger region. The influence of limestone is seen in higher levels of calcium and less acidic conditions in the soil. The region is home to many hill farms, due in no small part to the high soil fertility. Both the deep, moderately well-drained Buckland and poorly drained Cabot soils were formed from glacial till, and both have pH

Tunbridge Series, the Vermont State Soil.

TABLE 1. Typical Soils of the Connecticut River Watershed

PHYSIOGRAPHIC REGION	SOIL SERIES	PARENT MATERIAL	NATURAL DRAINAGE CLASS	TYPICAL LAND USES
Green Mountains, Northeastern Highlands, White Mountains, Hills and Lakes Region	Tunbridge	Acidic glacial till 20"–40" to bedrock	Well drained	Forestry, agriculture
	Lyman	Acidic glacial till 10"–20" to bedrock	Somewhat excessively drained	Forestry
	Berkshire	Acidic glacial till greater than 60" to bedrock	Well drained	Forestry, agriculture, development
	Marlow	Acidic glacial till greater than 60" to bedrock	Well drained	Forestry, agriculture, development
	Monadnock	Acidic glacial till greater than 60" to bedrock	Well drained	Forestry, agriculture, development
Green Mountains, White Mountains, above 2,500–3,000' elevation	Glebe	Highly acidic glacial till 20" to 40" to bedrock	Well drained	Limited land use — some forestry and recreation
	Stratton	Highly acidic glacial till 10" to 20" to bedrock	Well drained	Limited land use — some forestry and recreation
	Ricker	Thin organic material and glacial till 2" to 20" to bedrock	Well drained	Limited land use — some forestry and recreation
Vermont Piedmont	Buckland	Slightly acidic glacial till greater than 60" to bedrock	Moderately well drained	Agriculture, forestry, development
	Cabot	Slightly acidic glacial till greater than 60" to bedrock	Poorly drained	Wetlands, agriculture
	Vershire	Slightly acidic glacial till 20" to 40" to bedrock	Well drained	Forestry, agriculture
	Glover	Slightly acidic glacial till 10" to 20" to bedrock	Somewhat excessively drained	Forestry
Connecticut River Valley, tributaries of Vermont Piedmont	Windsor	Sandy glacial outwash	Excessively drained	Intensive land use — Agriculture, development, sand/gravel extraction
	Agawam	Loamy and sandy glacial outwash	Well drained	Intensive land use — Agriculture, development, sand/gravel extraction
	Hadley	Loamy alluvium	Well drained	Agriculture
	Winooski	Loamy alluvium	Moderately well drained	Agriculture
	Limerick	Loamy alluvium	Poorly drained	Wetlands, agriculture
	Hitchcock	Silty lacustrine material	Well drained	Development, agriculture
	Belgrade	Silty lacustrine material	Moderately well drained	Development, agriculture
	Raynham	Silty lacustrine material	Poorly drained	Wetlands, agriculture

levels near neutral. Farmland is a common land use on Buckland soils, while wetlands and some hayfields are associated with Cabot soils. The somewhat excessively drained Glover soil is less than 20 inches to bedrock and is a typical soil of hilly woodlands and ledgy pastures. In most cases, it is too steep, ledgy, and shallow to bedrock to use for farming. In the valleys, sandy and gravelly soils are on terraces and fertile alluvial soils are on floodplains. Land use is a patchwork of farms, fields, forests, and small villages.

The Connecticut River Valley, north to about Wells River, Vt., and Woodsville, N.H., is in the *mesic* soil-temperature zone, where the soils are warmer than the surrounding regions (which are in the *frigid* soil-temperature zone) and are more similar to soils in southern New England. Three main types of soils are found in this region: sandy soils such as Agawam and Windsor on terraces, silty soils like Hitchcock, Belgrade, and Raynham that formed in Glacial Lake Hitchcock sediments, and loamy soils including Hadley, Winooski, and Limerick that

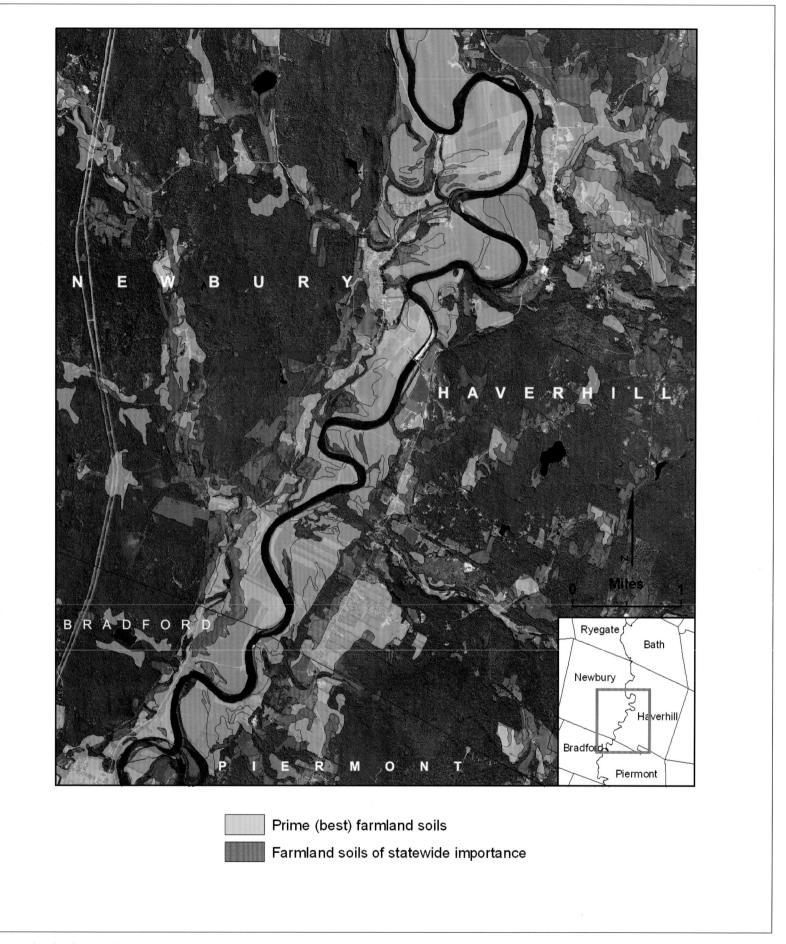

Map 8. Agricultural Soils in Newbury, Vt., and Haverhill, N.H.

Prime (best) farmland soils

Farmland soils of statewide importance

This photograph of farm fields in Haverhill, N.H. (foreground), and Newbury, Vt., shows the rich agricultural soils depicted in the soils map of the area.

formed in alluvial deposits on floodplains. All of these soils are incep-tisols or entisols. These two soil orders are common in the Northeast. Competition among various land uses is high in this region.

Some of the best farmland in northern New England is in the Connecticut River Valley. All of the soils have excellent agricultural potential. They have good moisture-holding capacity yet drain well, are nearly level and free of stones and boulders, and have good nutri-ent levels. Many of these soils have excellent development potential as well, due to their level slopes and good drainage. Coarse-textured soils like Agawam and Windsor also have good potential for sand and gravel extraction. See Map 8 and the above photo.

The Hills and Plains region includes the area in New Hampshire south of the White Mountains and east of the Connecticut River Val-ley. It is a rolling to hilly region somewhat similar to the Vermont Pied-mont but lacking in limestone bedrock. The soils are similar to those found in the lower elevations of the Green and White Mountains, but because of the more gentle topography, land use is more variable. Typ-ical soils include spodosols like Tunbridge, Marlow, Berkshire, Lyman, and Monadnock, all formed in glacial till. Land use includes farms, fields, and forests, along with many small towns and an increasing number of rural residences and vacation homes.

The main references for soils information are the NRCS county soil survey reports and soil scientists. Soil surveys are available at NRCS field offices. Most counties in the watershed have published reports; in those that don't, NRCS soil scientists working in the local offices can provide interim maps or general information about the soils in the county. Many maps and data are also available in digital and Web-based formats. The reports contain soil maps, which are based on aer-ial photographs of the land, with lines delineating and separating areas

of different soils and slope classes. Also included in the reports are descriptions of the soils and tabular data relating soil characteristics to various land uses, such as agriculture, forestry, engineering, and wild-life habitat. The reports form the basis for identifying prime farmland soils and hydric soils, which are an attribute of wetlands.

Thomas Villars is a soil resource specialist with the U.S. Department of Agri-culture Natural Resources Conservation Service in White River Junction, Vt. He has worked as a soil scientist for 30 years, in Indiana, Vermont, and New Hampshire, with short-term details to Florida and Maine. He has mapped soils on over a half-million acres of land. He lives in Norwich, Vt.

FOR FURTHER READING

Brady, N. C., and R. R. Weil. 2002. *The Nature and Properties of Soils*. Engle-wood Cliffs, N.J.: Prentice Hall.

Kohnke, H., and D. P. Franzmeier. 1995. *Soil Science Simplified*. Long Grove, Ill.: Waveland Press.

Natural Resources Conservation Service, New Hampshire. http://www. nh.nrcs.usda.gov/. New Hampshire NRCS website.

Natural Resources Conservation Service, Vermont. http://www.vt.nrcs.usda. gov/. Vermont NRCS website.

Soil Science Society of America. http://www.soils.org/smithsonian/. Smith-sonian Museum Soils Exhibit, featuring State Soils for all 50 states.

U.S. Department of Agriculture. http://soils.usda.gov/. USDA Soils website, with many links, including Official Series Descriptions.

U.S. Department of Agriculture-Natural Resources Conservation Service. 1999. *Soil Taxonomy, a Basic System of Soil Classification for Making and Interpreting Soil Surveys*. USDA-NRCS, Agricultural Handbook 436.

II Climate and Weather

Introduction

Here in New England, the rhythm of our lives moves in concert with the rhythm of the seasons, and it can be a lively tune. Midway between the North Pole and the equator, and influenced by both the continental air of the prevailing westerlies and warm, moist winds off the Atlantic, New England is a notorious battleground where storm tracks converge and variety is the norm. The upper Connecticut River Valley encompasses climate zones from USDA zone six by the Massachusetts border, where peaches can be grown safely, to zone three in the north, where July is the only month likely to be frost-free. A month's worth of precipitation may fall in a day, and the annual high and low temperatures for any given location are likely to be 120 degrees apart.

Plants and animals have adapted themselves to this dance of the seasons, and often provide us humans with important cues for our own activities. Spring spreads up the valley 100 miles every week, and ascends 100 feet in elevation each day. I enjoy watching cues such as the blossoming of the poplars and red maples while driving north and south on the interstate highways. Swelling buds mean the end of maple sugaring, just as the first long days above freezing meant the start. The Native Americans taught us that the soil has warmed enough to plant corn when the oak leaves are the size of a squirrel's ears. Spawning, blooming, hatching, planting, and growing all move ahead with the wheeling of the Sun in a complex, interdependent pattern that has evolved since the last glacier melted.

In the autumn, the pattern is reversed as "Old Man Winter" marches down the valley at about the same leisurely pace of an older man. Oaks and beech trees drop their bounty of nuts that will fatten up the deer, bears, turkeys, and smaller animals for winter. The river rises again with the arrival of autumn's rain and the drop of hardwood forest leaves. Human crops are brought in, too—corn, potatoes, big orange pumpkins. Firewood is cut and stored. Snow tires go on and skis get sharpened. We follow the season's turn just as the plants and wild animals do.

In this section's first chapter, meteorologist Steve Maleski draws on his years of forecasting to tell us why New England is such a variable place, and highlights some of particularities of the watershed's weather patterns. Extreme weather events are the stuff of New England legend, and Natalie Koch provides an overview of the watershed's most memorable weather occurrences in Chapter 5.

But what if these patterns are now suddenly shifting? What if the climate is changing? In Chapter 6, Natalie Koch outlines some of the major findings and implications of average annual temperature increases in the region. Local evidence, including temperature records, ice-out dates on lakes, and plant blooming times, show that our New England climate has warmed.

Climate modelers predict the rate of warming will increase faster still,

with temperatures rising from four to six degrees in the century to come. This would mean that the climate in Hanover, N.H., would more closely resemble that of Pennsylvania or even Virginia. If that happens, you probably can put away those skis. Our boreal forests of spruce, fir, and poplar probably would give way to the mid-Atlantic forest of oak and hickory. The maple sugar industry would continue to decline in New England, and grow in adjacent Canada. Other implications for agriculture are more serious; modelers disagree on precipitation forecasts, but any large divergence up or down from the fairly dependable 35 to 40 inches of precipitation we get each year could be catastrophic for traditional forms of agriculture. Distribution patterns of birds, reptiles, and other wildlife will shift with habitat and food supply. Some climate modelers predict greater frequency and more intense storms resulting from global climate change.

No one really knows what the effects of climate change will be. We don't know whether national and international efforts at slowing global warming—gaining traction as this Atlas is written—will have any effect. It seems likely, however, that in years to come the Connecticut River watershed will be a different place than what it is today, though to what degree is a guess. We can only hope that our valley will continue to provide the relatively well-watered and comfortable refuge that it has been in the past.

—Nat Tripp

Nat Tripp is an author, angler, and paddler who lives in Barnet, Vt. He represents Vermont on the Connecticut River Joint Commissions.

Monarch butterfly on wild aster, Sugar Hill, N.H.

4 Weather and Climate

The New England Region

New England's weather is more varied and variable than in many other places in the world. As residents are fond of stating, "If you don't like the weather, wait five minutes." This famous variability may be why New Englanders are so consumed with things meteorological. The Midwest has its reports of hog futures and corn prices; residents of Vermont and New Hampshire are insatiable in their appetite for innumerable daily weather updates served up by obliging atmospheric scientists. The region's reputation for fickle weather is well earned. This chapter summarizes the general reasons behind it, followed by a discussion of specific factors affecting weather in the Connecticut River Valley.

Three major atmospheric features dominate the wind flow at jet-stream level over North America and are responsible for New England's climate: the *polar vortex*, a cyclonic circulation center near Hudson Bay; a ridge near the Rocky Mountains; and the Azores-Bermuda high off the Atlantic coast. Changes in the amplitude of the ridge near the Rockies, and variations in the strength and orientation of the Azores-Bermuda high and the polar vortex modulate the southward flow of polar or arctic air into the lower 48 states or the northward flow of tropical air throughout eastern North America.

New England lies in a *confluent zone* — a region where various air masses often come together (see Map 9). These major air masses include continental polar air circulating around the polar vortex, milder air of Pacific origin entering North America at mid-latitudes that then becomes caught up in the peripheral circulation of the polar vortex, and warm, moist, tropical air streaming northward around the western flank of the Azores-Bermuda high.

Such zones are ones in which fronts — boundaries between different air masses — are found. When two or more air masses mix, energy is released in the form of wind and (given sufficient moisture) clouds and precipitation. The agents of mixing on this scale are waves of low pressure along the fronts. Since fronts frequently are present near New England, it's no surprise that average storm tracks across North America tend to converge on the Northeast United States and Canadian Maritimes. Some track to the west of the region, bringing showery rains or snows, depending on the season. Others track overhead or to the east. One group of lows has gained notoriety by frequently bringing to New England and the Connecticut River watershed many memorable snows and rains: Nor'easters.

These potent low-pressure systems form most often from late autumn through early spring, when surface temperature and moisture contrasts between the frigid continent and the relatively warm ocean water are at their greatest. The contrasts provide the potential energy for nascent storm systems to exploit. When the polar jet stream and any upper-level disturbances contained within it become favorably positioned over this turbulent region, the potential energy will be released and the surface system will intensify rapidly while being carried northeastward along the Atlantic Coast. In the Northern Hemisphere, air invariably circulates counterclockwise around all centers of low pressure larger than tornadic vortices. When an intensifying low moves up the Atlantic coast, New England is in the proper position to be raked by strong northeasterly winds spiraling toward the storm's center: hence their name. Some of the most storied storms of New England are nor'easters, and are discussed in the next chapter.

Precipitation Patterns in the Connecticut River Valley

The Connecticut River Valley cuts between two major mountain ranges: the Green Mountains of Vermont to the west, and New Hampshire's White Mountains to the east. Combined with the large-scale patterns of wind and air pressure described above, the mountains help create the variability in the weather of the watershed. Hikers above treeline in the higher peaks of both ranges know that conditions can change quickly and drastically, and some have experienced the oddity of being pummeled by rain or hail while watching the sun shining on a distant valley.

Large-scale storms frequently sweep across the wrinkled landscape of the Connecticut River watershed, dropping all manner of precipitation in complex yet orderly patterns. Some patterns are related to the elevation of the mountainous terrain. Annual records show a direct relationship between elevation and both total precipitation and winter snowfall. For instance, the Connecticut River Valley receives one- to two-thirds the precipitation of nearby mountain ranges. While New Hampshire's Mount Washington is drenched with a yearly average of 99 inches of liquid-equivalent precipitation (rain plus melted frozen precipitation), communities from Lancaster south to Pike see 34 to 38 inches. The reason is that during times of cross-mountain airflow, this stretch of the valley is downslope. The air passing across the spine of the Green or White mountains descends and warms. More water can exist in vapor form as the temperature increases, so during a large-scale storm, cloud bases rise and precipitation diminishes or stops in such a zone.

During nor'easters in particular, a deep precipitation shadow is evident in the portion of the valley immediately northwest of the

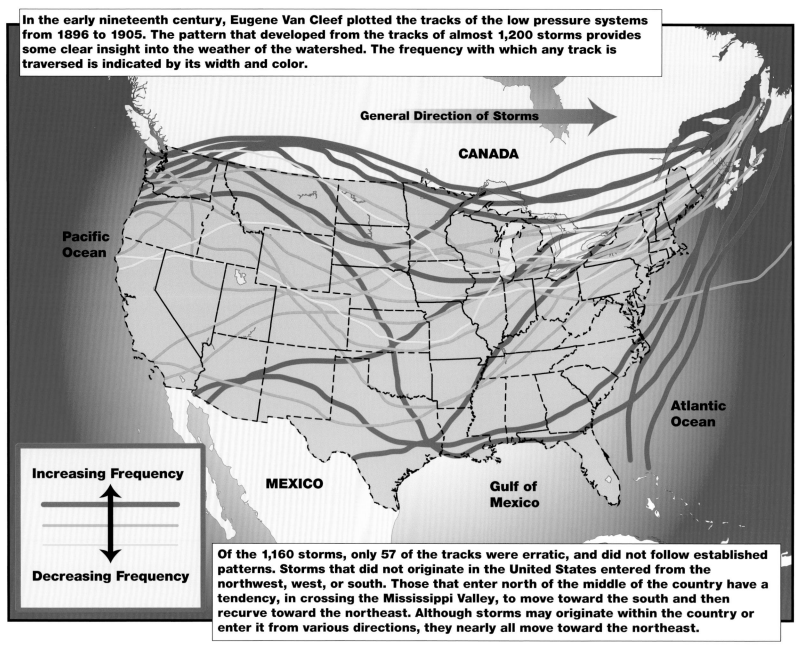

In the early nineteenth century, Eugene Van Cleef plotted the tracks of the low pressure systems from 1896 to 1905. The pattern that developed from the tracks of almost 1,200 storms provides some clear insight into the weather of the watershed. The frequency with which any track is traversed is indicated by its width and color.

General Direction of Storms

CANADA

Pacific Ocean

Atlantic Ocean

Increasing Frequency

Decreasing Frequency

MEXICO

Gulf of Mexico

Of the 1,160 storms, only 57 of the tracks were erratic, and did not follow established patterns. Storms that did not originate in the United States entered from the northwest, west, or south. Those that enter north of the middle of the country have a tendency, in crossing the Mississippi Valley, to move toward the south and then recurve toward the northeast. Although storms may originate within the country or enter it from various directions, they nearly all move toward the northeast.

Map 9. Storm Tracks Across the United States.

Presidential Range: Melted precipitation totals frequently are only 50 percent—and sometimes as little as 10 or 20 percent—of those on the windward slopes. When conditions are right, the downslope effect may be so pronounced that a strip of blue sky sometimes will appear over the valley, while moderate to heavy precipitation falls over the flanking higher terrain.

In the portion of the valley south of the Presidential Range, an easterly flow is broadly upslope, but a northwest wind is downslope. Behind a cold front, the Connecticut River Valley south of Bradford, Vt., will clear rather rapidly in such a regime. North of Bradford, however, the clearing can be much less pronounced, delayed due to the forced ascent of the air flowing out of southern Canada by both the Northeast Kingdom highlands and White Mountains.

Temperature Patterns in the Connecticut River Valley

On the whole, the valley is sunnier and drier, and usually warmer, than the surrounding high elevations. Yet like deep valleys everywhere, it is more subject to extremes of both heat and cold.

Energy is distributed through the atmosphere by three processes: conduction, convection, and radiation. *Conduction* (the transfer of energy solely by means of random motion of individual atoms or molecules coming into direct contact) is significant only when considering weather and climate on a smaller scale than in this Atlas. *Convection* (the transfer of energy through a gas or liquid by means of the free motion of large groups of atoms or molecules within it) is the more influential process at high elevations, and *radiation* (the direct propagation of energy through space via electromagnetic waves

Considerable weather data exist for St. Johnsbury, Vt., for the period 1894 to the present, collected by the Fairbanks Museum and Planetarium. Although weather patterns may vary considerably in the watershed depending on latitude, elevation, and topographical surroundings, the table provides a glimpse at the wide variety of conditions that occur here, as recorded at the museum. February 1969 certainly stands out as the preeminent month for snowfall over the 113-year period, with 60.5 inches measured. Until recently, the same winter (1968–1969) was also remembered as the year with the greatest snowfall (139.0 inches). But the winter of 2007–2008 nudged ahead with 139.2 inches of snow recorded, making it the snowiest winter yet. While January typically is the coldest month of the year, the two coldest months recorded were December 1989 and February 1934 with mean monthly temperatures of 4.58 and 6.10 degrees Fahrenheit respectively. Several different months of the year have been the wettest, with June 1973 and November 1927 each registering over 9 inches in St. Johnsbury.

The Mount Washington Observatory on the summit of New England's highest peak. Meteorological observations were made here from a weather station from 1870 to 1892. The observatory was established in 1932 as a private, nonprofit, scientific and educational institution.

Selected Monthly Meteorological Data for St. Johnsbury, Vermont (1894–2005)

GREATEST MONTHLY SNOWFALL TOTALS (IN INCHES)		COLDEST MONTHS (MEAN TEMPERATURE IN °F)		MOST PRECIPITATION (IN INCHES)	
February 1969	60.50	December 1989	4.58	June 1973	9.65
December 2007	53.70	February 1934	6.10	November 1927	9.34
December 1981	47.50	January 1970	6.40	October 2005	8.60
January 1954	47.00	January 1920	7.00	September 1999	8.59
December 1970	46.50	January 1904	7.70	September 1907	8.11
March 1956	46.00	January 1918	7.70	October 1959	8.07
January 1979	45.50	January 1912	7.80	June 1922	8.05
January 1987	45.40	January 1994	8.16	June 2006	7.92
December 1972	44.00	January 1982	8.29	May 1984	7.88
December 2003	42.90	December 1917	8.70	August 1917	7.86

Source: Data provided by the Fairbanks Museum and Planetarium.

at the speed of light) the more dominant in a valley. This is because the average wind speed is greater over higher terrain. Because winds are relatively light in a valley, both bubbles of hot and layers of cold air can develop more easily. Bubbles are parcels of air heated to a temperature higher than that of others around them. They become buoyant and begin rising through the surrounding atmosphere, much as bubbles rise through liquid water. Layers are formed because as air cools, its density increases. In the absence of wind or other mixing agents, cooling air will flow downward under the force of gravity and collect in valleys and hollows. Continued cooling of the air through radiation of its heat to space will lead to the stratification of the air by temperature. The coldest, densest air will rest at the base of the valleys and hollows, while the warmest air will be found in the free air above hills or mountaintops.

The Vermont state record maximum and minimum temperatures were both set in communities located along the Connecticut River. A blistering 105 degrees Fahrenheit was reached on August 2, 1975, at Vernon, just north of the Massachusetts border. At the other extreme, a gelid −50 degrees Fahrenheit was observed on December 30, 1933, in the hamlet of Bloomfield at the confluence of the Nulhegan and Connecticut rivers in Vermont's Northeast Kingdom. To date, this is the lowest temperature officially recorded in New England.

Although the results aren't always as dramatic, the accumulation of relatively cold, dense air along the valley floor takes place every clear, calm night. In late summer and early fall, when nights grow significantly longer but vegetation is still full, leaves transpire considerable water vapor into the atmosphere. Fog frequently forms when the air cools to its saturation point. Early on such mornings, a satellite pho-

Ice jams, like this one on the Passumpsic River in St. Johnsbury, Vt., in 1915, may result from snowmelt combined with heavy spring precipitation.

tograph will depict clearly the valley of the Connecticut River and those of some of its major tributaries as ribbons of white against the relatively dark, fog-free land surface. The last vestiges of fog may not dissipate until nearly midday if the layer of cold, saturated air is particularly deep.

On those foggy mornings, residents of the valleys will still be in sweaters while their upland neighbors don sunglasses. Just as the landscape of the Connecticut River Valley ranges from rocky peaks to gently rolling meadows, the weather is varied and variable. If you don't like it, wait — or drive — five minutes.

Steve Maleski has for many years been one of the familiar voices of the Fairbanks Museum's "Eye On The Sky" weather broadcast on Vermont Public Radio. Born and raised in Maryland, he holds a degree in philosophy from the University of Connecticut (1978) and a degree in meteorology from Lyndon State College (1981). Since 1985, he has made his home in Sutton, Vt.

FOR FURTHER READING

Ludlum, David. 1976. *The Country Journal: New England Weather Book*. Boston: Houghton Mifflin.

Zielinski, Gregory A., and Barry D. Keim. 2003. *New England Weather, New England Climate*. Hanover, N.H.: University Press of New England.

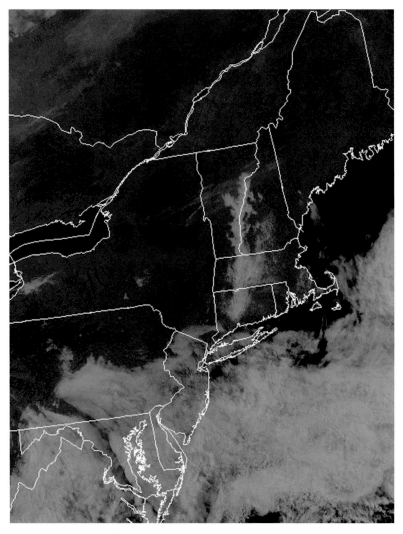

A satellite photo shows fog hanging in the Connecticut River Valley on June 15, 2007.

5 Extreme Weather Events

The truism that "all storms lead to New England" is a reality for the residents, human and otherwise, of the upper Connecticut River watershed. While resilient people expect and even welcome weather in many forms, fierce storms still have the power to disrupt life and leave lasting memories—some of them tragic. The region's forests have evolved to meet climatic and weather challenges, as many conifers are able to withstand ice and snow and hardwoods often grow back after damage from ice and wind. But severe storms may damage large swaths of forest and leave signs of devastation for years.

Rainfall, Floods, and Hurricanes

One of the most sensational events in the region is associated with excess rainfall: flooding. Intense rainfall events can have several sources, but they often are associated with hurricanes or other major storms.

The flood of March 1913 was considered a major catastrophe. Some of the most dramatic images from this flood are of the destruction that occurred to the bridges on the Connecticut River and its tributaries. Loaded freight cars were placed on railroad bridges to stabilize them, but little could be done for the covered bridges that were not built to withstand such strong and high floodwaters. The Maple Street covered bridge in Hartford, Vt., was one of those casualties, carried away by the high waters until it crashed into a downstream railroad bridge.

Severe flooding hit the valley again in 1927. That flood resulted from two storms colliding over Vermont: one from the Gulf of Mexico and one from the Great Lakes. In 45 hours, nearly 9 inches of rain fell in Vermont (Bazilchuck 1999). Somerset, Vt., received 9.65 inches of rain during the storm, while neighboring areas were estimated to have received 15 inches (Zielinski and Keim 2003). Significant damage was inflicted on private homes and public infrastructure. After the flood passed, the Vermont legislature appropriated $8 million to build and pave 200 miles of road. In the course of the following year, the state built 1,329 bridges to replace ones destroyed by the flood. The state received $2.6 million in federal aid, in addition to indirect funding that was dedicated to the Red Cross relief effort (Zielinski and Keim 2003).

Another record flood of the Connecticut River occurred just nine years later, in 1936. A snowier and colder than normal winter resulted in some 3.5 to 8 inches of water equivalent in the snowpack by early March of that year. Between March 11 and March 19, two long-duration rains soaked the region. The combination of rain and snowmelt on

The Flood of 1927 hit Vermont especially hard, as seen in these photos of Wells River. Many roads, rail lines, and bridges were damaged severely or swept away—some never to be rebuilt.

The Hurricane of '38 still looms large in the memories of many older residents of the watershed. This photo from Hartford, Vt., shows damage typical of the storm.

frozen ground sent some 8 to 25 inches of water into the ice-choked rivers, with catastrophic results throughout New England. The Connecticut was flooded along its entire length. New flow records were established from Dalton, N.H., to Hartford, Conn. At Vernon, water topped the dam by 11 feet! Many pictures of this, and other floods, have been compiled by local historical societies (see Photo 18 of the '36 Flood in Hanover, N.H., in Chapter 9, Streamflow).

With memories of the '36 flood still smarting, another epic event struck. The "Great Hurricane of 1938" was not the most severe hurricane to hit New England, but the lack of a warning meant that it caused unparalleled devastation. Originating east of the Bahamas, it traveled up the east coast and hit Connecticut, Rhode Island, and Massachusetts, killing more than 700 people before it moved north through the Connecticut River Valley. The storm traveled almost directly northward up the valley, dumping rain on its way—up to two inches per hour. Many New England rivers hit record flood levels (Zielinski and Keim 2003).

As the storm ripped across the White Mountains, extreme winds were clocked at 163 miles per hour on Mount Washington. In New Hampshire, half of the white pines were lost in the storm, as was most of the Northeast's apple crop, and three-quarters of Vermont's sugar maple trees. The timber blown down was the equivalent of 10 years' normal harvest for the state. In one of undoubtedly many similar scenarios, a husband and wife in the Green Mountains were dining in their prefabricated vacation house when the lights went out and the roof

and walls blew away. In all, 13 people died and 6,000 were left homeless in New Hampshire, and seven died in Vermont (Scotti 2003). Once the storm crossed Lake Champlain, it tracked north through Montreal and eventually expended itself in arctic Canada (Bazilchuck 1999).

Severe flooding has declined substantially with the installation of major flood-control measures on the Connecticut River and several tributaries (see Chapter 11, Water Management). Even so, major flooding still occurs. In October 2005, unusually heavy rains and a blocked culvert on a small tributary of the Cold River in southwest New Hampshire combined to create one of the watershed's most lethal flood events. When the culvert finally burst, the usually bucolic Warren Brook became a raging wall of water sweeping through a narrow valley on its way to the Cold River. After the sudden release of the culvert, the surge of floodwater down Warren Brook and the Cold River exceeded a 500-year recurrence interval. Warren Brook cut a new, deep gully, and the Cold River, formerly premier fish habitat, scoured a wide new channel, often down to bedrock. Nearly 50 homes were destroyed along the Cold River, and over the course of region-wide flooding, seven people lost their lives (Olson 2006).

Drought

Widespread drought is an infrequent visitor to the region. Because the valley lies at the confluence of several major storm tracks, the jet stream that governs formation of these large-scale storms rarely allows long periods (over nine months) of drier-than-normal weather over the entire valley. However, major droughts have occurred. Many remember the drought of 1964–1965. Precipitation was about 25 percent below the normal 40 or so inches per year average. Many test wells for monitoring groundwater levels date from this period, and New Hampshire established its first drought management plan. Another notable drought occurred in 1998–1999, and 2007 was a very dry year in some locations.

Snow Storms and Nor'easters

Annual snowfall in the Connecticut River Valley averages 55 to 65 inches. But these totals can be reached in the course of a single storm event if the conditions are right—or wrong, depending on your point of view! Many of the region's biggest snowstorms are associated with New England's signature storm: the "nor'easter" (see Chapter 4, Weather and Climate).

The Great Post-Christmas Storm of 1969 encompassed a large area from the mid-Atlantic states northward through all of New England, eastern New York State, and southern Quebec. Complex and powerful low pressure slowed to a crawl near Long Island, then tracked over Cape Cod and into the western Gulf of Maine during a three-day period. Heavy snow fell from the Green Mountains and Berkshires northwestward; moderate to heavy snow was followed by soaking rain in Maine and much of New Hampshire as the slow-moving tempest pulled mild maritime air westward from the North Atlantic. The Connecticut River Valley channeled a shallow northerly flow of subfreezing air between the Green Mountains to its west and the White Mountains and Mount Monadnock in New Hampshire to its east. Consequently, moderate to heavy freezing rain and sleet fell for more

than 24 hours from St. Johnsbury, Vt., southward to the Massachusetts border. Glaze accumulations reached nearly two inches in spots from Hanover, N.H., to Springfield, Vt. A subsequent frigid January locked the glaze on vegetation. In some cases, ice remnants were found on branches six weeks later.

Other notable storms in the region's history include the Great Snow of 1717, the blizzard of March 1888, the blizzard of February 1978, February and December storms of 1969, the "Superstorm" of March 13–14, 1993, which capped one of the snowiest winters ever, and the storm of February 1969, when St. Johnsbury received a total of 60.5 inches—the most in a century. The 1993 Superstorm has been described as one of the most intense nor'easters ever to strike the eastern United States. Record low pressures, wind speeds, low temperatures, and snowfall amounts were more than enough for this storm to gain the status of "Storm of the Century." Indeed, this storm was monumental, killing over 250 people and canceling 25 percent of air traffic across the nation for two days.

Many will long remember the Valentine's Day storm of 2007. After a nearly snowless winter, nearly three feet of snow was dumped on locations through the watershed. The two months of November and December preceding this storm were the warmest ever recorded in Vermont, and January temperatures averaged above normal as well. Interestingly, the following winter of 2007–2008 saw record snowfall totals through the region.

Ice Storms

Extreme winter weather also can take the form of ice storms. Freezing rain and sleet glazes every surface. Traffic accidents and power outages are common as roads turn to skating rinks, trees bend over or break,

The October 2005 flood on the Cold River in the Alstead, N.H., area led to several deaths and severe property and infrastructure damage. Heavy rains, the particular topography of the watershed of a tributary brook, and an overwhelmed culvert combined to create a destructive surge of water and raised streams and rivers to perilous levels.

and power lines sag under the weight of the ice or are brought down by trees. Damage may vary greatly by location, for a difference of only 1 degree Fahrenheit can determine if a given locale receives freezing or regular rain.

As destructive as ice storms are for people and their property, they are also a natural disturbance in New England forests. Conifers tend to shed the ice or bend with it, while limbs and branches of hardwoods may simply snap off. Long after the ice is gone, you may see white birches still bent to the ground. Depending on the extent of damage, trees may recover or slowly weaken and die.

The worst ice storm in recent years was in early January 1999, when widespread parts of New England went without power for days and even weeks. Destruction in the Connecticut River watershed was variable, depending on elevation and aspect (see Map 27 in Chapter 12, Habitat and Natural Communities). The storm resulted in 17 deaths in New England, and caused extensive damage to sugar maples on both sides of the river (Zielinski and Keim 2003).

Tornadoes and Wind

While the watershed's geography makes it susceptible to various forms of extreme weather, it also safeguards the region from some other events. New England has the fewest tornadoes of any geographic region east of the Rocky Mountains. For example, from 1950 to 1996, New Hampshire and Vermont experienced an average of 1.6 and 0.7 tornadoes per year respectively, compared to 125 and 51 per year in Texas and Oklahoma. Given this low overall rate of occurrence, the Vermont Storm Events Database lists a surprising number of twist-

ers. One of the earliest recorded tornadoes swept through Vermont on June 23, 1782, crossing the Connecticut near Weathersfield. The "Great New Hampshire Tornado" on September 9, 1821, was responsible for some fatalities and injuries, and took its most significant toll north of Claremont (Vermont State Climate Office; Zielinski and Keim 2003.

While tornadoes are rare, wind can really kick up its heels. The highest wind ever recorded at a land weather station in the world, 231 mph, was set at the summit of Mount Washington, at the edge of the watershed, in 1934.

While some may argue that the increase in intensity of extreme events in modern times is the result of global warming, this is a difficult claim to evaluate. However, various changes in the upper Connecticut River watershed can be predicted concretely to result from the earth's warming climate, which is the subject of the next chapter.

Natalie Koch is a 2007 graduate of Dartmouth College, where she studied geography and Russian area studies. A native of Tucson, Arizona, her love of the Connecticut River was solidified after several years of rowing for Dartmouth's women's crew team.

For Further Reading

Olson, S. A. 2006. Flood of October 8 and 9, 2005, on Cold River in Walpole, Langdon, and Alstead and on Warren Brook in Alstead, New Hampshire. U.S. Geological Survey Open-File Report 2006-1221.

Vermont State Climate Office. www.uvm.edu/~ldupigny/sc/.

Zielinski, G. A., and B. D. Keim. 2003. *New England Weather, New England Climate*. Hanover, N.H.: University Press of New England.

6 Climate Change

The issue of the earth's warming climate has exploded into popular awareness in recent years. While an incontestable scientific consensus exists as to the reality of global warming, proposed responses to it have varied widely according to political perspectives. It is important to understand the changes in the upper Connecticut River watershed that already are resulting from global warming. Since no comprehensive studies of climate change have been conducted specifically in the watershed, this section will emphasize the elements of those broader studies of New England and the Northeast.

As discussed in Chapter 4, Weather and Climate, conditions in the watershed are particularly variable. However, strong evidence has been recorded of a consistent rise in the average annual temperature. In the past 100 years, Vermont's average annual temperature has increased by 1.6°F, while New Hampshire has shown an increase of 1.8°F (Zielinski and Keim 2003). At this writing, 11 years out of a recent 12-year period (1995–2006) rank among the 12 warmest years globally since 1850, according to the Intergovernmental Panel on Climate Change. Figure 7 shows the long-term changes in temperature in the northeast portion of the United States. The rise has been 1.8 degrees over the period 1900 to 2000, with a 1.4-degree rise in average annual temperature from 1970 to 2000. A comparable analysis for winter temperatures in the northeast show a 2.8-degree rise from 1900 to 2000 and a 4.4-degree temperature rise from 1970 to 2000.

Within the watershed itself, the increase in average summer temperatures has been noted in St. Johnsbury, Vermont (see the sidebar "Window on the Weather" in Chapter 4). The Fairbanks Museum weather station reports that during the past 110 years, the mean temperature (measured as a five-year average) during the summer months of June, July, and August has increased roughly 1.5 degrees Fahrenheit (from 66 to 67.5). The effects of these increased temperatures are already quite noticeable. Descriptions of some significant trends follow.

Timing of Seasons

The four seasons are a defining characteristic of the climate of the entire Connecticut River watershed. The region's economy is bound inextricably to these seasons, particularly with a large segment of the economy heavily concentrated in outdoor activities. However, global warming has meant that the yearly timing of the seasons is changing in New England. The blooming of certain flowers and the budding of trees are indicators for the arrival of spring, and yearly data about when this occurs have been examined for trends. Analyses indicate that current first-flower (or first-bloom) dates for lilacs in the Northeast have come four days earlier since the 1960s. Over the same period, grape vines and apple trees have advanced their first-flower dates by six to eight days (Union of Concerned Scientists 2006).

Another way to understand the changing character of the seasons

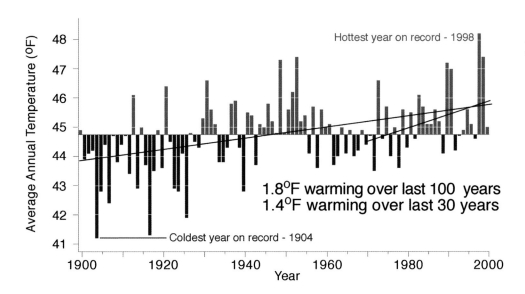

Figure 7. Average Annual Temperature for the Northeast from 1899 through 2000. This time-series is a weighted average of temperature records from 56 stations in the region.

Lilacs, like these in Charlestown, N.H., bloom an average of four days earlier than they did 40 years ago.

is through the length of the growing season, which is the number of days between the last frost of spring and the first frost of autumn — and it is particularly important for the success of agriculture. Recent years have shown an increase in the growing season's length in the Northeast. Although this may seem beneficial for farmers, those who grow cool-season crops and produce maple syrup could see production diminish significantly. If farmers were to diversify and switch to warmer-season crops, they would face intense competition from farmers with the advantages of better soil and even longer growing seasons. Farmers are also facing challenges from new pests and diseases. Data available for the Northeast from 1900 to 2001 indicate an average growing season of about 190 days in the early to mid-1900s. Since the 1990s, this average has risen to over 200 days (Lines et al. 2006).

Streamflow

The amount of water, or *streamflow*, in the Connecticut River and its tributaries is a function of climatic activity (see Chapter 9, Streamflow). The timing of the snowmelt and the breakup of ice on lakes and rivers influences this level. When this happens at the end of the winter, streamflow reaches its maximum. Conversely, streamflow is at its minimum in the mid- to late summer, when high temperatures, evaporation, and increased demand from private users, ecosystems, and agriculture exert their heaviest water demands (Union of Concerned Scientists 2006).

Winters in the Northeast have warmed by 4.4 degrees Fahrenheit since 1970, resulting in some visible changes in winter and spring streamflow and ice cover. Since 1850, the average date of spring ice-out on lakes has shifted nine days earlier in the year in the northern states of the Northeast. Consequently, the spring streamflow reaches its peak 7 to 14 days earlier than in the past. These changes are related directly to air temperature, which determines the time of ice-out and snowmelt dates (Union of Concerned Scientists 2006). This coincides with the data presented earlier about the warming of winter temperatures in general in the Northeast.

While considerable interannual variation occurs in the timing of high spring streamflow, most rivers subject to study have demonstrated statistically significant earlier timing. These observed changes are also consistent with changes in last-frost dates, lilac bloom dates, lake ice-out dates, river ice thickness, and changes in the ratio of snow to total precipitation in New England. In the fall, New England streams typically replenish, or *recharge*, with more frequent rain — a welcome respite for fish and other aquatic inhabitants that lived through low flows of the summer. Here, too, conditions are changing, as trends point to later fall recharge and low water levels earlier in the spring, meaning a lengthening of low streamflow conditions and longer periods of stress for riparian and aquatic plants and wildlife (Union of Concerned Scientists 2006; Lines et al. 2006). Fish species that rely on high flows at the right time for spawning, for instance, may have a difficult time adjusting. People also may feel the effects of a lengthened dry season. The same spring and fall rains that replenish streams also recharge drinking-water wells. More frequent and longer periods of drought may affect drinking-water supplies for the Connecticut River

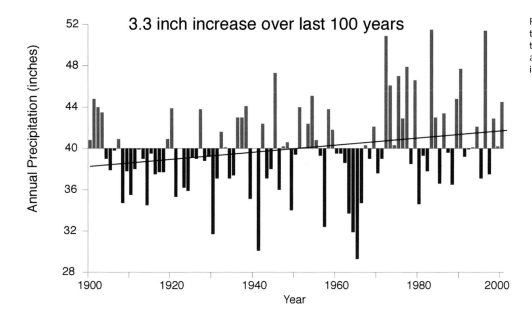

Figure 8. Average Total Annual Precipitation (in inches) of 79 Stations in the Northeast, 1900–2000. Years in red experienced more than average precipitation and years in blue experienced less. Overall, precipitation has increased 3.3 inches, with the most striking increases since the 1970s.

Valley, an historically water-rich region that relies heavily on private wells (see Chapter 8, Groundwater).

Precipitation

As the planet warms, many elements of the highly interconnected climate system are affected. While it can be highly variable, precipitation in New England is fairly consistent throughout the year. Some broader precipitation trends have been identified in recent decades—specifically a drought in the mid-1900s followed by greater precipitation thereafter. Throughout the 1960s, a severe drought in New England negatively affected agriculture, water quality and quantity, forest health, and human health, even leading to widespread forest fires and crop failures. Following the drought, precipitation increased significantly: eight of the top ten years for quantity of precipitation in New England occurred between 1970 and 2005. However, summer rainfall totals collected for St. Johnsbury, Vt., by the Fairbanks Museum and Planetarium for the past 110 years show a straight-line trend (moving average) that is practically flat for that entire period and averaging about 11 inches per summer (June–August). Figure 8 shows the increase in average annual precipitation in the Northeast since 1900.

Summers have been slightly wetter on average during the past 30 years, except for the drought years of the 1960s mentioned earlier. Annual precipitation, however, has increased 5 to 10 percent across the Northeast since 1900—until recently. Average annual precipitation now shows a slight decrease, but winter precipitation is starting to increase at a rate of up to 0.15 inch per decade. However, as winter temperatures rise, more precipitation is falling as rain and less as snow (Union of Concerned Scientists 2006). Because there is great spatial variability in precipitation, broader trends in the Northeast may not reflect accurately what is happening in the Connecticut River watershed.

Studies from 2001 indicate that southern New England precipitation increased over the last century by over 25 percent in all three states, while northern New England precipitation decreased by less than 5 percent for Vermont and New Hampshire, and by 12 percent in Maine (Zielinski and Keim 2003). As global warming continues to affect the climatic system over time, precipitation undoubtedly will be influenced increasingly. Some studies indicate that this warming will be accompanied by an increasing intensity of storms and other extreme weather events with unpredictable consequences.

Snowfall

Decreases in precipitation in the far north of New England threaten the region's economy, given the importance of skiing, snowmobiling, and other outdoor recreation activities revolving around snow. Trends relating to snowfall are thus of particular importance to the watershed. Like other precipitation, snowfall in the Northeast is highly variable. Nonetheless, strong evidence indicates a trend that snow cover extent in the Northern Hemisphere has decreased by about 10 percent since 1966 and is strongly related to increases in temperature.

The warming climate influences the amount of snow that falls each winter, but also the amount of days with snow on ground. Northeast stations indicate that there were an average of 16 fewer days with snow on ground in 2001 than in 1970 (Wake and CACP 2005). This comes as bad news for the watershed's winter recreation and tourism industry, which simply cannot make enough snow in an economical manner to compensate for these decreases. The amount of energy and water needed to do so would put great demands on the region, which would only threaten to exacerbate current problems.

Looking Ahead

As Figure 9 depicts, evidence of climate change in the northeast is noteworthy. Were trends to continue into the future, the higher temperatures identified with climate change could have significant effects on the Connecticut River Valley in a range of sectors, from the wood products industry to outdoor recreation, from farming to tourism. The anecdotal evidence of climate change recounted by residents and

Figure 9. Evidence for Climate Change in the Northeast.

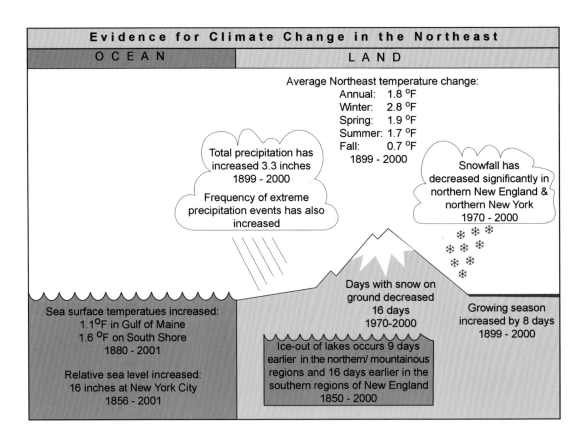

Evidence for Climate Change in the Northeast

OCEAN | **LAND**

Average Northeast temperature change:
Annual: 1.8 °F
Winter: 2.8 °F
Spring: 1.9 °F
Summer: 1.7 °F
Fall: 0.7 °F
1899 - 2000

Total precipitation has increased 3.3 inches 1899 - 2000

Frequency of extreme precipitation events has also increased

Snowfall has decreased significantly in northern New England & northern New York 1970 - 2000

Days with snow on ground decreased 16 days 1970-2000

Growing season increased by 8 days 1899 - 2000

Sea surface temperatues increased:
1.1°F in Gulf of Maine
1.6 °F on South Shore
1880 - 2001

Relative sea level increased:
16 inches at New York City
1856 - 2001

Ice-out of lakes occurs 9 days earlier in the northern/ mountainous regions and 16 days earlier in the southern regions of New England 1850 - 2000

long-time visitors—unaccustomed pests in the garden, new birds at the feeder, less snow in the winter, and more ticks, to name a few—are finding confirmation in new research. Many implications are predicted through scientific modeling, but unforeseen effects are likely. The growing body of data and analysis should allow continued evaluation and understanding of the trends, necessary as the region faces changes of a magnitude that will affect a wide range of individual, business, and public choices.

Natalie Koch, Dartmouth '07, joined the Atlas project after her graduation, writing two chapters, and researching and collecting images.

For Further Reading

Intergovernmental Panel on Climate Change. 2007. *Climate Change 2007: The Physical Science Basis.* IPCC Secretariat, World Meteorological Organization, Geneva, Switzerland, February 5, 2007.

Lines, G., C. P. Wake, et al. 2006. *Cross Border Indicators of Climate Change over the Past Century.* Gulf of Maine Council on the Marine Environment.

Union of Concerned Scientists. 2006a. *Climate Change in the U.S. Northeast: A Report of the Northeast Climate Impacts Assessment.* Cambridge, Mass.: UCS Publications.

———. 2006b. *The Changing Northeast Climate: Our Choices, Our Legacy.* Cambridge, Mass.: UCS Publications.

Wake, C. P., and Cool Air—Clean Planet. 2005. *Indicators of Climate Change in the Northeast 2005.* Durham, N.H.: The Climate Change Research Center, University of New Hampshire.

Zielinski, G. A., and B. D. Keim. 2003. *New England Weather, New England Climate.* Hanover, N.H.: University Press of New England.

III   The River and Watershed

Introduction

"The Connecticut is not a majestic river. It is, rather, a friendly stream, which invites intimacy and elicits affection," Walter Hard wrote in 1947. "To be sure, it has its periods of mad haste, but somehow it gives the impression that it is merely in a hurry to get to the next area where it may wander through peaceful meadows."

Ellsworth Grant conveyed a similar sense in 1967, beginning his homage to the Connecticut by quoting the clergyman-educator Henry van Dyke: "'A river is the most human and companionable of all inanimate things. It has a life, a character, a voice of its own.'" Grant found the qualities described by van Dyke in the Connecticut, despite admitting that the river is neither long nor ancient by world historical standards. Both he and Hard conveyed the beauty, serenity, and power of this river that have captured people's imaginations for centuries, from the Native tribes who named it in their various tongues, to late eighteenth-century scholars who set out to explore their new nation, to artists and writers today.

The Connecticut River watershed is the largest river system wholly within New England, save for its northernmost drainage from Canada. At 410 miles from source to sea, the Connecticut is also New England's longest river. Its source, Fourth Connecticut Lake, conjures up a somewhat grander vision than the reality. The "lake" is but a small pond, so close to the New Hampshire–Canadian border that one may walk the path to it with one foot literally in the Granite State and the other in the land of maple leaves. At this humble beginning, the "river" is really nothing more than a mountain brook.

As it flows south, the Connecticut slowly gains volume and speed, and empties into three successively larger waterbodies—descriptively if not imaginatively called the Third, Second, and First Connecticut lakes—though still confusing as they have been numbered from south to north, rather than as the river flows. Then the river feeds Lake Francis before freely flowing for about 10 miles to Beecher Falls, where it becomes the boundary between Vermont and New Hampshire.

Feeding the river in its upper reaches are storied tributaries, each with its own history and character: Halls Stream, Indian Stream, Nash Stream—names that conjure up the early days of the Republic and the lore of the great log drives and tough river men. Farther downriver, the Nulhegan comes in, flowing from one of Vermont's wilder regions. And on the river goes, gathering volume, flowing through dams great and small that harness its power, gathering the flows from other tributaries that themselves swell from the brooks, streams, and smaller rivers that fan out through the watershed.

This section presents the river and its watershed as a system. It begins with an explanation of hydrologic units. The maps "Hydrologic Units Defined" and "Taking Ownership of Your Watershed" show the interconnections between the Connecticut River watershed as a whole and its component watersheds. They are followed by maps of the major subwatersheds. We then turn in Chapter 8 to that basic and vital natural resource, groundwater, the sources and uses of which are described by Sarah Flanagan. Richard Moore draws on both historic and current data to illustrate the river's flow characteristics. In Chapter 10, "Water Quality," Adair D. Mulligan traces the remarkable turnaround of the river from the 1950s, when it was called "one of the best landscaped sewers in America," to today, as it supports a thriving coldwater fishery and enthusiastic human swimmers as well. The river as a source of power, and the challenges and implications of managing it for human needs, are presented by Cleve Kapala and Rebecca A. Brown in the last chapter in this part, "Water Management."

FOR FURTHER READING

Grant, Ellsworth S. 1967. The Mainstream of New England. *American Heritage* (April 1967). Reprinted in W. D. Wetherell, ed. *This American River: Five Centuries of Writing about the Connecticut*. Hanover, N.H.: University Press of New England, 2002.

Hard, Walter. 1947. *The Connecticut*. New York: Rinehart & Company.

Above Dodge Falls on the Connecticut River, Monroe, N.H.

ADAIR D. MULLIGAN

MAPS BY BOB GAGLIUSO

7 Subwatersheds and Major Tributaries

Watersheds and Hydrologic Units

A watershed is any unit of land in which all the water drains to the same point. A tiny pond has its own watershed, nested within successively larger watersheds up to the size of the Mississippi River watershed, which includes much of the central United States. Rain and snow falling on the 78-acre watershed of Fourth Connecticut Lake eventually drains into that small pond. This watershed is nested, with thousands more, in the 4.5-million-acre watershed of the mighty Connecticut River (see Map 10).

Watershed boundaries are determined by topography, and therefore cross town, state, and sometimes even national lines. Your watershed address can include dozens of sub-addresses. For example, someone living near Reservoir Pond in Lyme, N.H., could say that their home is in the Reservoir Pond watershed, but also in the Mascoma River watershed, and also within the Connecticut River watershed, since rain and snow falling on their property runs off into this pond, which drains into an unnamed stream that runs into the Mascoma River, which in turn sends its water to the Connecticut. This imaginary person's neighbor a short way down the road may have a similar street address but a different watershed address — Grant Brook watershed within the Connecticut River watershed. Rainfall on this person's property eventually travels to the Connecticut, but gets there by flowing through Grant Brook, not the Mascoma River or Reservoir Pond.

To provide a common language in which watersheds can be studied, managed, and discussed, the U.S. Geological Survey and the U.S.D.A. Natural Resources Conservation Service have created a standardized system, called the National Watershed Boundary Dataset (WBD), that assigns watersheds numeric codes. The system divides and sub-divides the country into successively smaller hydrologic units that are classified into levels, as shown in Table 2. Each hydrologic unit is identified by a unique hydrologic unit code (HUC) consisting of 2 to 12 digits based on the level of classification in the hydrologic unit system. The longer the code number, the smaller the stream.

The first level of classification divides the nation into 21 major geographic regions. Our region is the Northeastern United States, HUC 01. Within this, the large Connecticut River watershed carries the identifying HUC 0108. Within it is the subbasin watershed of the White River, 01080105. This sub-basin is subdivided into 10-digit subwatersheds, and finally into the smallest 12-digit divisions, as shown on Map 11, "Hydrologic Units Defined."

A standardized system that leaves familiar, locally used place names behind may be convenient for data managers but also has its shortcomings. On the Connecticut River, the larger sub-basins often cross state and county lines and may have "official" names that don't match those familiar to local residents. For example, the HUC system used by the federal government refers to HUC 1080104 as the "Upper Connecticut-Mascoma Watershed," a slice of the Connecticut River's drainage basin that covers tributaries on both sides of the mainstem, including the Mascoma River, but not the uppermost Connecticut. Worse, the government's official name for HUC 01080103 is "the Waits River Watershed," an area that includes the watersheds of the Wells and Ammonoosuc Rivers but not the Waits River. We have attempted to address this confusion in this Atlas where possible.

In the maps presented in this Atlas, we typically display six to eight digit hydrologic units, and in some cases show smaller geographic units, such as the Deerfield and Millers River watersheds that straddle the border of New Hampshire and Vermont with Massachusetts. This treatment is truer to the topography and tributaries than the more conventional but less accurate way of viewing nature, through the lens of political boundaries. Map 12, "Taking Ownership of Your Watershed," depicts many of these local watershed names. Major sub-watersheds are shown in Maps 13 to 22. The elevational drop of the river from its source at the Fourth Connecticut Lake to the Massachusetts border is depicted in Figure 10.

Adair D. Mulligan is conservation director for the Connecticut River Joint Commissions.

Bob Gagliuso owns and operates Northern Cartographic.

TABLE 2. The Hierarchical Structure of the WBD

LEVEL	NAME	DIGITS	AVERAGE SIZE (SQUARE MILES)
1	Region	2	178,000
2	Subregion	4	17,000
3	Basin	6	11,000
4	Subbasin	8	1,000
5	Watershed	10	60–400
6	Subwatershed	12	10–60

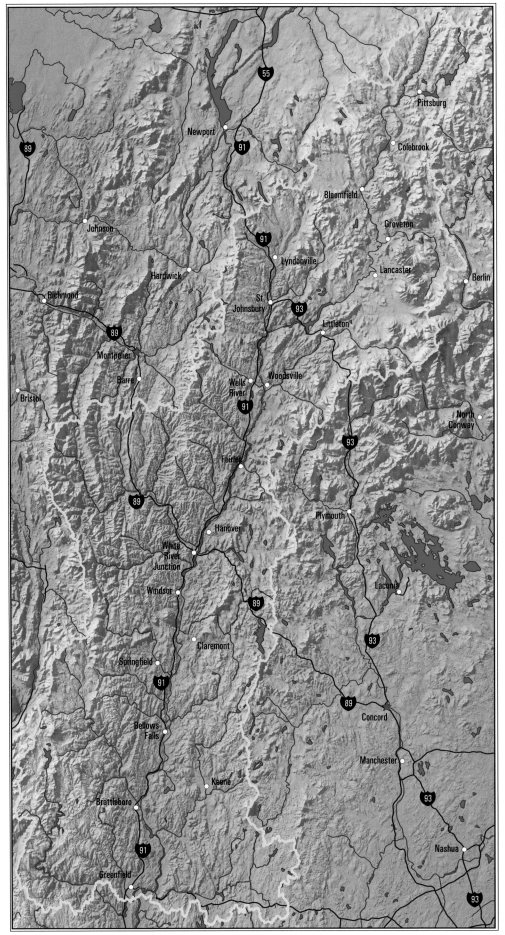

Map 10. The Upper Connecticut River Watershed.

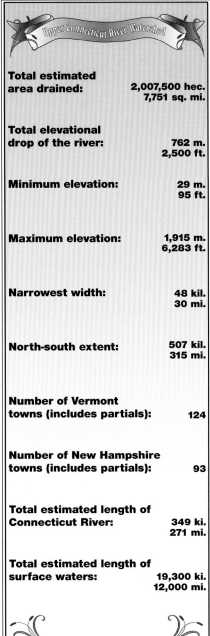

Upper Connecticut River Watershed

Total estimated area drained:	2,007,500 hec. 7,751 sq. mi.
Total elevational drop of the river:	762 m. 2,500 ft.
Minimum elevation:	29 m. 95 ft.
Maximum elevation:	1,915 m. 6,283 ft.
Narrowest width:	48 kil. 30 mi.
North-south extent:	507 kil. 315 mi.
Number of Vermont towns (includes partials):	124
Number of New Hampshire towns (includes partials):	93
Total estimated length of Connecticut River:	349 ki. 271 mi.
Total estimated length of surface waters:	19,300 ki. 12,000 mi.

The Upper Connecticut River Watershed in the Northeast

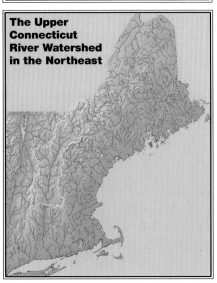

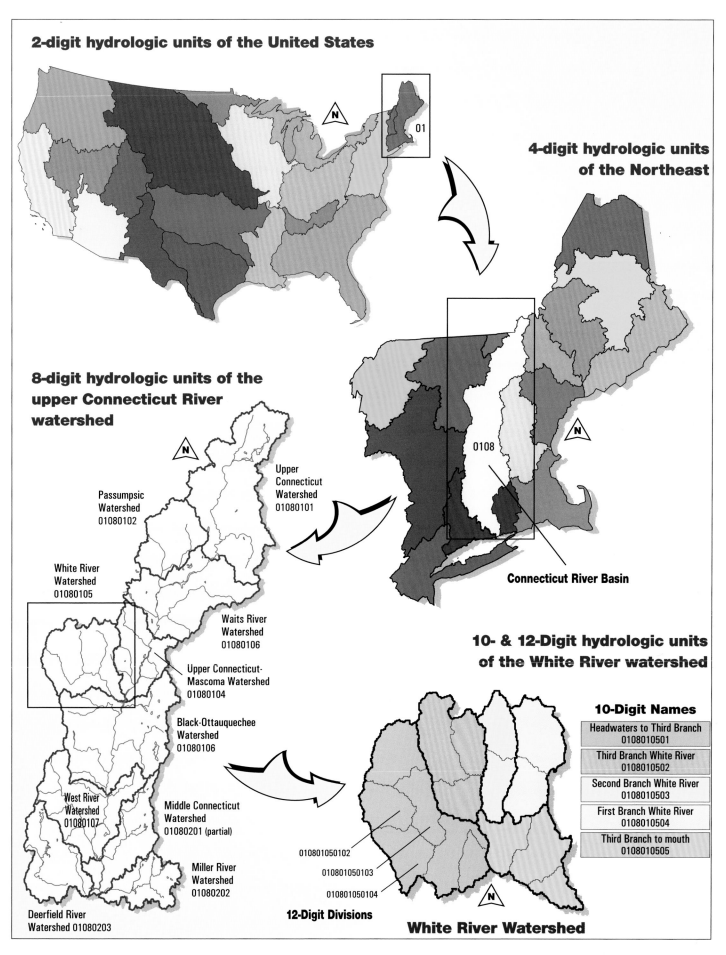

2-digit hydrologic units of the United States

01

4-digit hydrologic units of the Northeast

0108

Connecticut River Basin

8-digit hydrologic units of the upper Connecticut River watershed

Upper Connecticut Watershed 01080101

Passumpsic Watershed 01080102

White River Watershed 01080105

Waits River Watershed 01080106

Upper Connecticut-Mascoma Watershed 01080104

Black-Ottauquechee Watershed 01080106

West River Watershed 01080107

Middle Connecticut Watershed 01080201 (partial)

Miller River Watershed 01080202

Deerfield River Watershed 01080203

10- & 12-Digit hydrologic units of the White River watershed

10-Digit Names
Headwaters to Third Branch 0108010501
Third Branch White River 0108010502
Second Branch White River 0108010503
First Branch White River 0108010504
Third Branch to mouth 0108010505

010801050102

010801050103

010801050104

12-Digit Divisions

White River Watershed

Map 11. Hydrological Units Defined.

One of the goals of this Atlas is to foster a sense of place and "ownership" regarding the Connecticut River watershed and its many component watersheds. Many people identify with their local rivers, and this map shows how these rivers are the focal points of their own watersheds. The interconnectedness of the watershed as a whole system begins to take visual shape.

This map identifies local watersheds using the 10-digit hydrological unit code (see the explanation of HUC codes in Map 11). Before delving into the rest of the Atlas, spend some time with this map, identifying your own local watershed and seeing how it relates geographically to those around it.

The interconnectedness of the watershed extends to we who live here. Actions we take on a local level "trickle up" through the system just as our small local brooks "trickle down" to the Connecticut, and on to the sea. Actions such as keeping lawn fertilizer from washing into a neighborhood stream or installing culverts that allow passage of fish and other aquatic wildlife collectively add up to a healthier overall system. Don't wait for issues to be addressed on a watershed-wide basis—your individual and community-based actions make a difference!

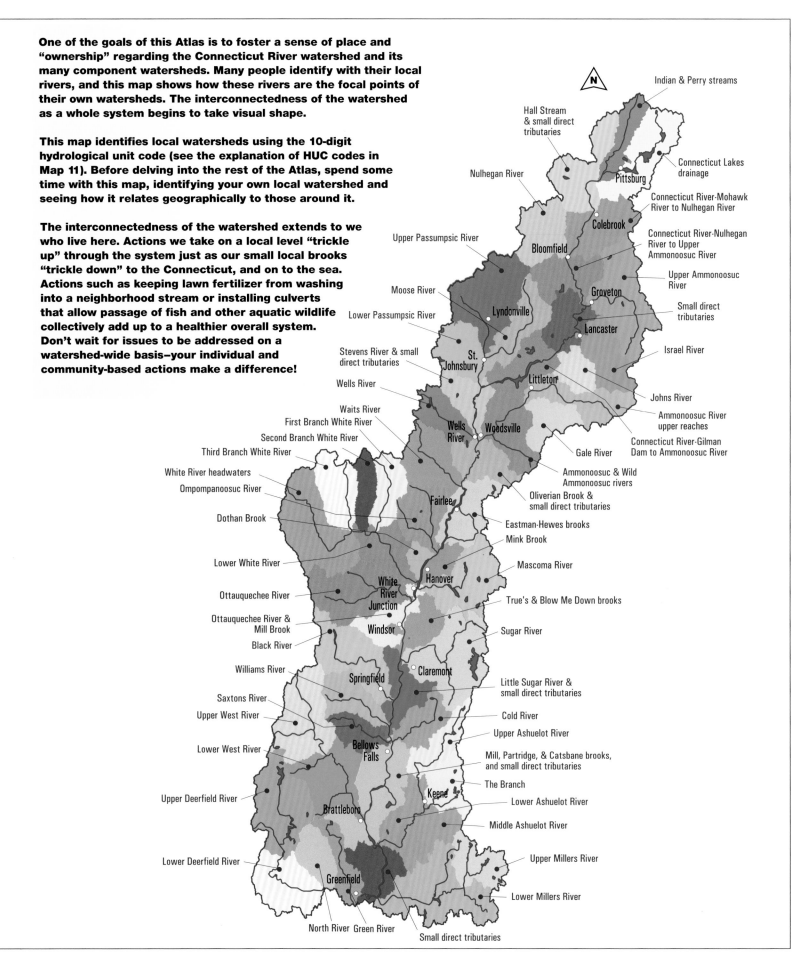

Map 12. Taking Ownership of Your Local Watershed.

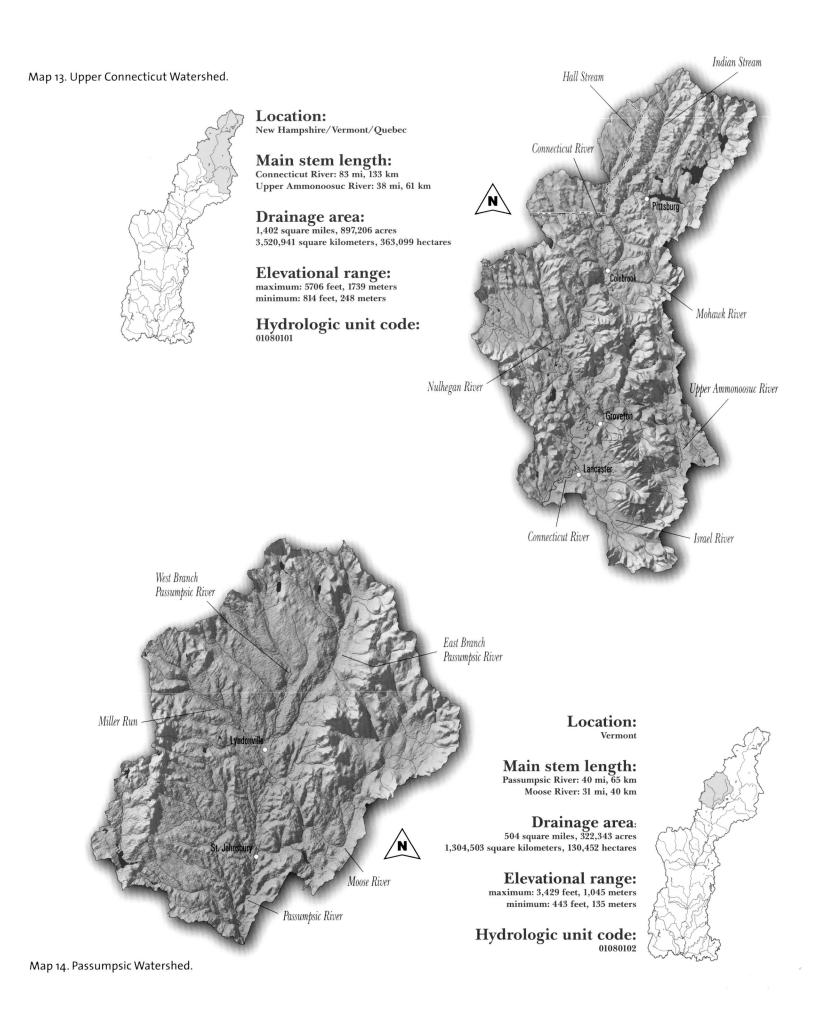

Map 13. Upper Connecticut Watershed.

Location:
New Hampshire/Vermont/Quebec

Main stem length:
Connecticut River: 83 mi, 133 km
Upper Ammonoosuc River: 38 mi, 61 km

Drainage area:
1,402 square miles, 897,206 acres
3,520,941 square kilometers, 363,099 hectares

Elevational range:
maximum: 5706 feet, 1739 meters
minimum: 814 feet, 248 meters

Hydrologic unit code:
01080101

Indian Stream

Hall Stream

Connecticut River

Pittsburg

Colebrook

Mohawk River

Nulhegan River

Groveton

Lancaster

Connecticut River

Upper Ammonoosuc River

Israel River

West Branch Passumpsic River

East Branch Passumpsic River

Miller Run

Lyndonville

St. Johnsbury

Moose River

Passumpsic River

Map 14. Passumpsic Watershed.

Location:
Vermont

Main stem length:
Passumpsic River: 40 mi, 65 km
Moose River: 31 mi, 40 km

Drainage area:
504 square miles, 322,343 acres
1,304,503 square kilometers, 130,452 hectares

Elevational range:
maximum: 3,429 feet, 1,045 meters
minimum: 443 feet, 135 meters

Hydrologic unit code:
01080102

Map 15. Wells–Ammonoosuc Watershed.

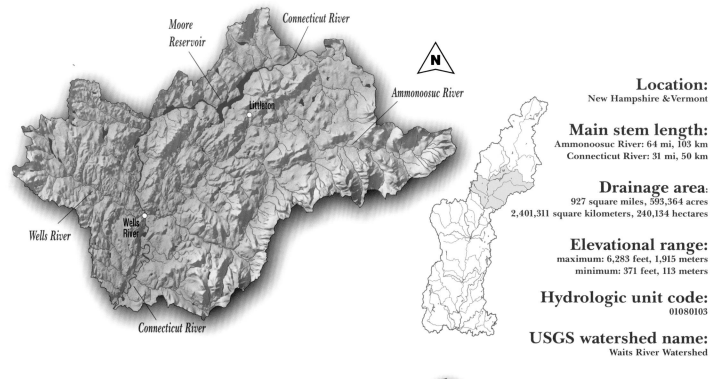

Location:
New Hampshire & Vermont

Main stem length:
Ammonoosuc River: 64 mi, 103 km
Connecticut River: 31 mi, 50 km

Drainage area:
927 square miles, 593,364 acres
2,401,311 square kilometers, 240,134 hectares

Elevational range:
maximum: 6,283 feet, 1,915 meters
minimum: 371 feet, 113 meters

Hydrologic unit code:
01080103

USGS watershed name:
Waits River Watershed

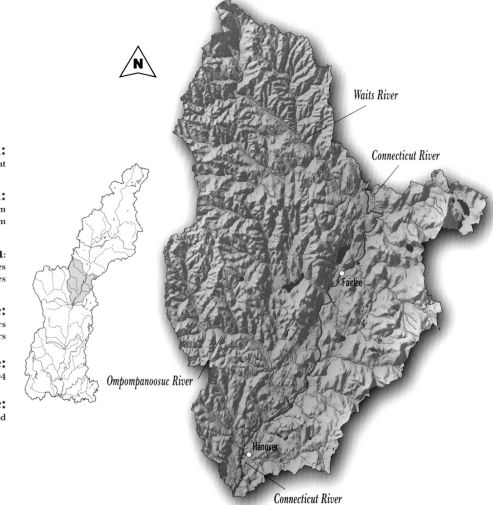

Location:
New Hampshire & Vermont

Main stem length:
Ompompanoosuc River: 41 mi, 66 km
Waits River: 19 mi, 30 km

Drainage area:
518 square miles, 330,718 acres
1,338,396 square kilometers, 133,842 hectares

Elevational range:
maximum: 3,357 feet, 1,023 meters
minimum: 318 feet, 97 meters

Hydrologic unit code:
01080104

USGS watershed name:
Upper Connecticut-Mascoma Watershed

Map 16. Waits–Ompompanoosuc–Eastman–Mink Watershed.

Map 17. White River Watershed.

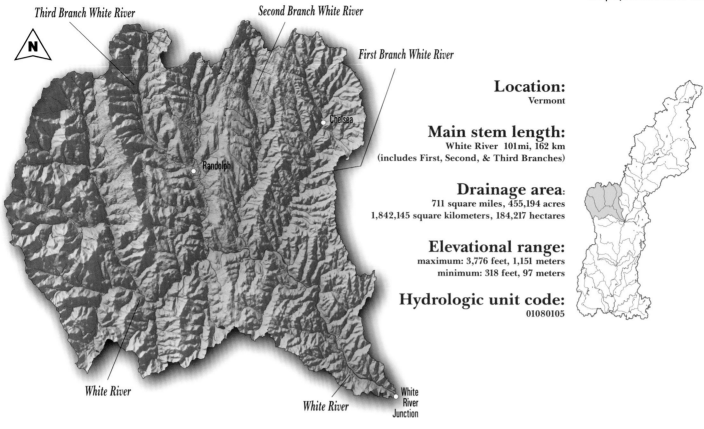

Third Branch White River

Second Branch White River

First Branch White River

Chelsea

Randolph

Location:
Vermont

Main stem length:
White River 101 mi, 162 km
(includes First, Second, & Third Branches)

Drainage area:
711 square miles, 455,194 acres
1,842,145 square kilometers, 184,217 hectares

Elevational range:
maximum: 3,776 feet, 1,151 meters
minimum: 318 feet, 97 meters

Hydrologic unit code:
01080105

White River

White River

White River Junction

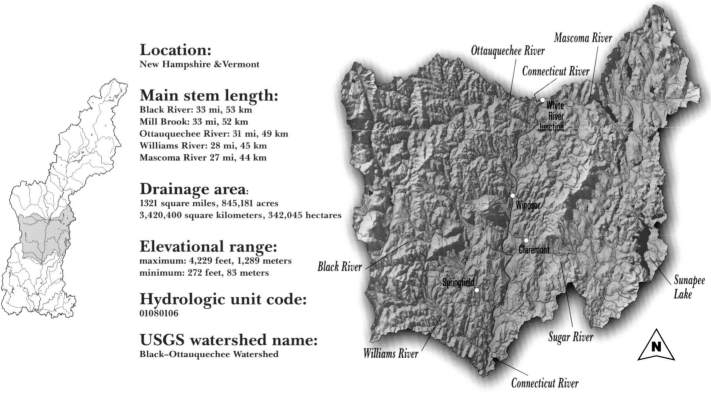

Location:
New Hampshire & Vermont

Main stem length:
Black River: 33 mi, 53 km
Mill Brook: 33 mi, 52 km
Ottauquechee River: 31 mi, 49 km
Williams River: 28 mi, 45 km
Mascoma River 27 mi, 44 km

Drainage area:
1321 square miles, 845,181 acres
3,420,400 square kilometers, 342,045 hectares

Elevational range:
maximum: 4,229 feet, 1,289 meters
minimum: 272 feet, 83 meters

Hydrologic unit code:
01080106

USGS watershed name:
Black–Ottauquechee Watershed

Mascoma River

Ottauquechee River

Connecticut River

White River Junction

Windsor

Claremont

Black River

Springfield

Sunapee Lake

Sugar River

Williams River

Connecticut River

Map 18. Ottauquechee–Black–Williams/Mascoma–Sugar Watershed.

Map 19. West–Saxtons/Cold–Partridge Watershed.

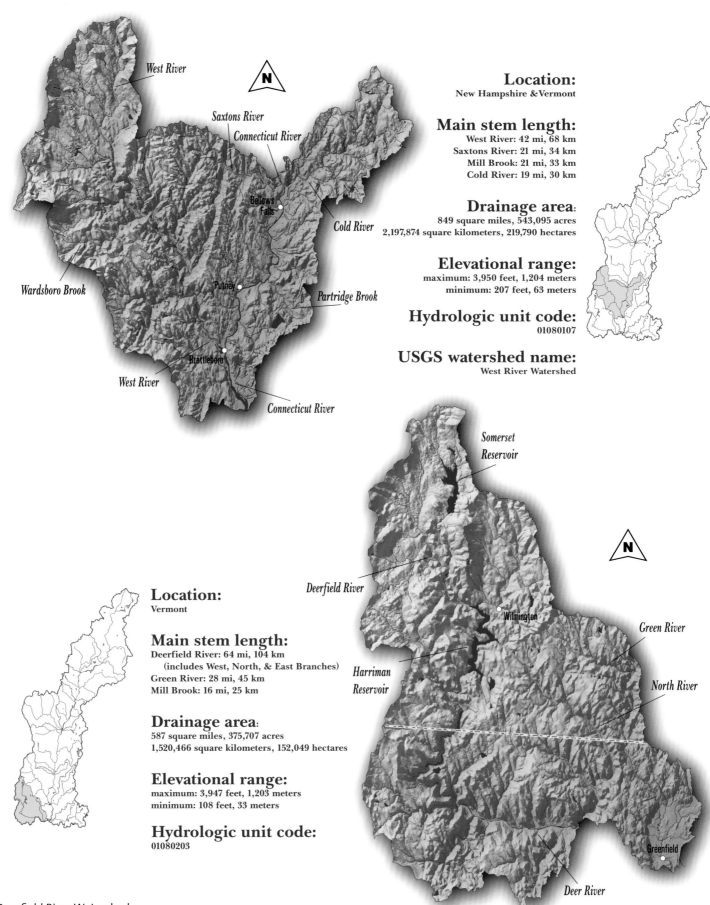

West River

Saxtons River

Connecticut River

Bellows
Falls

Cold River

Wardsboro Brook

Putney

Partridge Brook

West River

Brattleboro

Connecticut River

Location:
New Hampshire & Vermont

Main stem length:
West River: 42 mi, 68 km
Saxtons River: 21 mi, 34 km
Mill Brook: 21 mi, 33 km
Cold River: 19 mi, 30 km

Drainage area:
849 square miles, 543,095 acres
2,197,874 square kilometers, 219,790 hectares

Elevational range:
maximum: 3,950 feet, 1,204 meters
minimum: 207 feet, 63 meters

Hydrologic unit code:
01080107

USGS watershed name:
West River Watershed

*Somerset
Reservoir*

Deerfield River

Wilmington

Green River

*Harriman
Reservoir*

North River

Location:
Vermont

Main stem length:
Deerfield River: 64 mi, 104 km
   (includes West, North, & East Branches)
Green River: 28 mi, 45 km
Mill Brook: 16 mi, 25 km

Drainage area:
587 square miles, 375,707 acres
1,520,466 square kilometers, 152,049 hectares

Elevational range:
maximum: 3,947 feet, 1,203 meters
minimum: 108 feet, 33 meters

Hydrologic unit code:
01080203

Greenfield

Deer River

Map 20. Deerfield River Watershed.

Map 21. Ashuelot River Watershed.

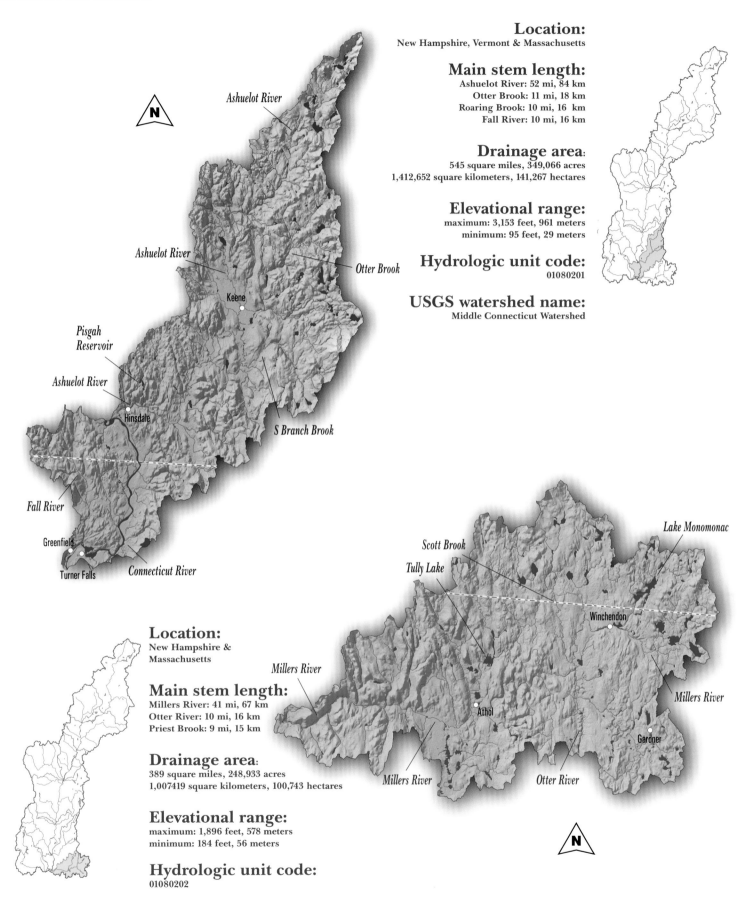

Location:
New Hampshire, Vermont & Massachusetts

Main stem length:
Ashuelot River: 52 mi, 84 km
Otter Brook: 11 mi, 18 km
Roaring Brook: 10 mi, 16 km
Fall River: 10 mi, 16 km

Drainage area:
545 square miles, 349,066 acres
1,412,652 square kilometers, 141,267 hectares

Elevational range:
maximum: 3,153 feet, 961 meters
minimum: 95 feet, 29 meters

Hydrologic unit code:
01080201

USGS watershed name:
Middle Connecticut Watershed

Ashuelot River

Ashuelot River

Otter Brook

Keene

Pisgah
Reservoir

Ashuelot River

Hinsdale

S Branch Brook

Fall River

Greenfield

Turner Falls

Connecticut River

Scott Brook

Tully Lake

Lake Monomonac

Millers River

Millers River

Winchendon

Athol

Millers River

Gardner

Millers River

Otter River

Location:
New Hampshire &
Massachusetts

Main stem length:
Millers River: 41 mi, 67 km
Otter River: 10 mi, 16 km
Priest Brook: 9 mi, 15 km

Drainage area:
389 square miles, 248,933 acres
1,007419 square kilometers, 100,743 hectares

Elevational range:
maximum: 1,896 feet, 578 meters
minimum: 184 feet, 56 meters

Hydrologic unit code:
01080202

Map 22. Millers River Watershed.

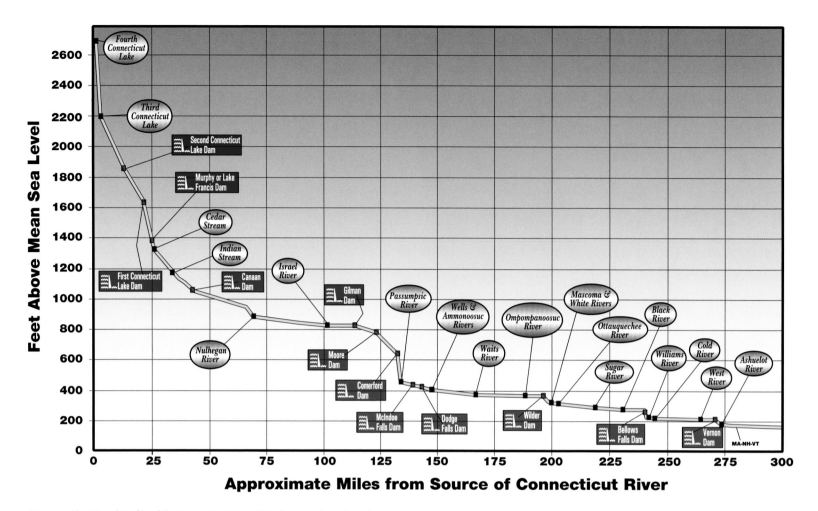

Figure 10. Elevational Profile of the Connecticut River. This diagram shows how the river drops in elevation as it falls from its source (far left) toward the sea. Dams have altered the surface elevation. Ovals show where major tributaries enter the mainstream.

8 Groundwater

Water is a natural resource that most people use in abundance but rarely think about, since using it usually means simply turning the tap. The Connecticut River Valley is rich in water resources, as evidenced by the easily seen and numerous surface-water bodies like ponds, lakes, and streams. But beneath the surface is groundwater, which, while usually hidden, is fundamental to life in the valley.

Groundwater is a crucial source of drinking water in the Connecticut River watershed. As of 2005, about 43 percent of the approximately 340,000 people living in the watershed in New Hampshire and Vermont use private wells that tap into groundwater as their primary source of drinking water, and another 36 percent of residents rely on groundwater drawn by public suppliers, according to Marilee Horn, a water use specialist with the U.S. Geological Survey. The remaining 20 percent of the population receives drinking water from public surface-water supplies such as reservoirs. These residents rely on groundwater indirectly, as groundwater also helps feed surface-water bodies.

People who live in or near larger towns typically get their water from municipal suppliers that withdraw groundwater or surface water or a combination of both. Small surface-water reservoirs have been built to store and supply municipal drinking water throughout the watershed. Other towns may use groundwater or a combination of ground and surface water as sources of drinking water.

People and businesses located in more rural or remote areas use their own private wells to supply water. Towns, or districts within them, may be supplied by wells, as are some distinct developments such as condominium complexes and schools. In some cases, water-bottling companies and farms that use irrigation systems also draw from wells. The more than 500 public-supply wells in use in the watershed serve populations ranging in size from 25 to 12,500 (Horn 2005).

Aquifers

In the Connecticut River watershed, groundwater is found beneath the land surface in two main types of aquifers: unconsolidated surficial sediments that were deposited by glaciers, and fractures in bedrock (see Figure 11).

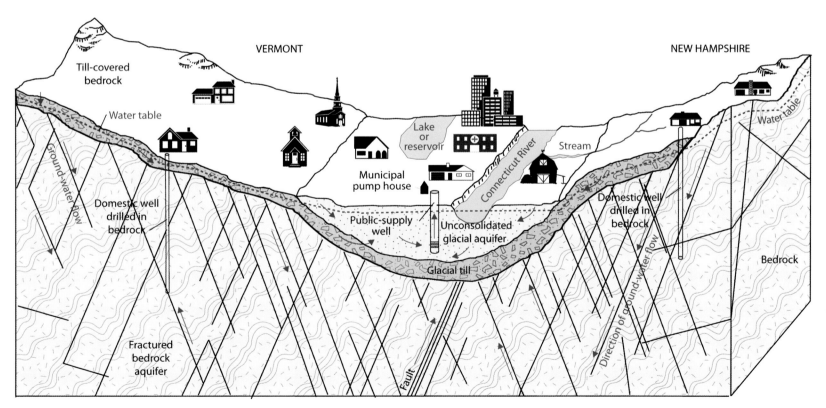

Figure 11. Generalized Geohydrologic Section of the Connecticut River Watershed. Not to scale.

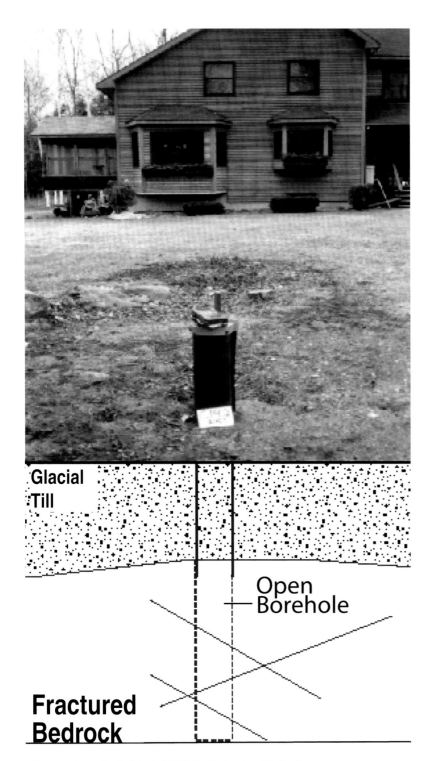

Glacial Till

Open Borehole

Fractured Bedrock

Figure 12. Example of a Private Well Drilled in Fractured Bedrock.

Sediments that were deposited from melting glaciers in river valleys and flood plains (sometimes referred to as "stratified drift") cover less than 7 percent of the land area, yet are capable of transmitting large quantities of groundwater to wells and are the most productive groundwater resource in the watershed (see Hodges and Butterfield 1967–1968; Medalie and Moore 1995). Types of glacial sediments that form productive aquifers include eskers, kame terraces, deltas, and outwash deposits (see Chapter 2, Glacial Geology). Wells that tap this groundwater resource are generally less than 100 feet deep and are most likely used for public supply, since their yields can exceed 300 to 1,000 gallons per minute (gal/min). Just one well drilled in this highly productive aquifer system can supply enough water for hundreds of homes and businesses.

The other major type of aquifer, fractured bedrock, can be tapped from anywhere within the watershed and is more likely to be used for homes and individual businesses (see Figure 12). In a bedrock aquifer, groundwater is stored in open fractures in the rock. These fractures usually are abundant enough to yield water to a single-family home (yields of 10 gal/min or less), and in some areas with large amounts of fractures (such as near fault zones), are capable of yielding enough water to supply industrial and municipal wells (yields upwards of 100 gal/min). Bedrock wells typically are drilled hundreds of feet into the ground. If few fractures are intersected during drilling, the well may be drilled more than 500 feet deep to provide enough water storage in the open borehole.

Glacial till — sediment deposited by glaciers across New England — covers the bedrock surface in most areas of the watershed. Glacial till is a minor aquifer and can be a source of water to dug wells, but these wells can go dry during droughts. Yields of wells in till typically range from 1 to 5 gallons per minute.

Groundwater Quality

Just as important as the availability of groundwater is its quality. Groundwater quality is affected partly by natural processes and partly by human activity. Natural weathering of rocks and minerals contributes most of the dissolved substances found in groundwater. These include many common substances, such as iron, manganese, magnesium, calcium, potassium, sodium, chloride, fluoride, and silica (Moore 2004). The concentrations of these substances in groundwater depend greatly on the mineral composition and geochemical properties of the aquifer and the on residence time of water in the aquifer. For example, high concentrations of dissolved iron and manganese can occur in groundwater if the water is acidic and has low levels of dissolved oxygen.

Some naturally occurring elements in groundwater are considered unsafe to human health, such as arsenic and uranium. Arsenic, an element found in many earth minerals, has been associated with some bedrock aquifers in New England. Most bedrock in New England contains some uranium, a radioactive element that leads to the eventual formation of radon gas. Certain types of bedrock, particularly those that contain igneous plutons and high-grade metamorphic rocks, usually have high concentrations of uranium, which can lead to high concentrations of radon gas dissolved in groundwater. The U.S. Surgeon

General has recognized exposure to radon gas as being second only to cigarette smoking as a cause of lung cancer. Regulating radon is complicated. It is an inert gas widely detected in groundwater, but is hazardous if accumulated in indoor air and inhaled.

Groundwater also is susceptible to human-caused contamination from applications of fertilizers and pesticides, road salt, malfunctioning septic tanks, and accidental spills and leaks of chemicals near the land surface. The unconsolidated glacial aquifers can be more vulnerable to contamination than bedrock aquifers because glacial aquifers are generally shallower than bedrock aquifers and are composed of coarse-grained sediments that allow contaminants to move downward rapidly with little opportunity for chemical degradation or filtration. Contamination of bedrock aquifers is not uncommon, however.

The U.S. Environmental Protection Agency has established enforceable drinking-water standards that apply to public water systems serving more than 25 people or 15 service connections. These primary standards protect public health by limiting the levels of contaminants in drinking water. Therefore, public water systems are monitored routinely by the utilities that own them to ensure their safety for drinking water. Groundwater used for private supply or from public wells serving fewer than 25 people typically is not regulated by the EPA or by state health agencies, so these well owners are responsible for testing to determine if their water is safe enough to drink. New Hampshire, Vermont, and the EPA encourage all private well owners to test their water periodically for contaminants.

Numerous resources are available for communities and private homeowners who wish to learn more about their water supplies and groundwater. Both states offer information on the Web, Vermont through its Water Supply Division, and New Hampshire through the Water Supply and Engineering Bureau and the Water Well Board. The New England Interstate Water Pollution Control Commission is another good resource. From all of these you can find other links of interest.

Sarah Flanagan is a hydrologist with the U.S. Geological Survey NH/VT Water Science Center in Pembroke, N.H. She has been working with the U.S. Geological Survey since 1984. A 1982 graduate of the University of New Hampshire, she started her career working on mapping the stratified-drift aquifers in New Hampshire and has worked extensively with the National Water Quality Assessment Program on a variety of groundwater quality studies.

For Further Reading

New Hampshire
N.H. Water Supply and Engineering Bureau: www.des.state.nh.us/wseb
N.H. Water Well Board: www.des.state.nh.us/WWB/index.asp
Fact sheets published by the N.H. Water Well Board to help homeowners understand and safeguard their private wells: www.des.state.nh.us/WWB/index.asp?theLink=facts

Vermont
Vermont Geological Survey: www.anr.state.vt.us/dec/geo/vgs.htm
Vermont Water Supply Division: www.vermontdrinkingwater.org

Vermont Drinking Water Quality: www.vermontdrinkingwater.org/wquality.htm

New England Regional Organizations
New England Interstate Water Pollution Control Commission (NEIWPCC): www.neiwpcc.org/. NEIWPCC studies water quality issues in New England.
U.S. Environmental Protection Agency Radon Guide for Homeowners: www.epa.gov/radon/zonemap.html

The Woodsville water supply facility on the Wild Ammonoosuc River, built in 1929. Like other communities that draw river water, Woodsville has a surface-water treatment facility.

9 Streamflow

The flow of brooks, streams, and rivers in northern New England can rise and fall dramatically and with short notice. Devastating floods, such as the one that occurred in southwestern New Hampshire in October 2005 in which seven people died, underscore the power of water and the immense damage that can result from such events. Property destruction and the loss of life itself are grim reminders of the ravages that can result from heavy rains and floods.

In more tranquil times, the natural streamflow of these same streams and rivers can provide a gorgeous backdrop to the wonders of nature and the serenity that accompanies and reflects the natural flow of life itself. All basin residents and businesses are affected by these flow regimes. This chapter provides a primer on streamflow within the Connecticut River basin, and a better understanding that comes from years of data collection and analysis as well as water management.

Streamflow, the quantity of water that flows by a given location over time, typically is expressed in cubic feet per second (cfs). A cubic foot of water is equivalent to the volume of water that could be contained in a box one foot on each side. A flow of one cubic foot per second is equivalent to that same volume of water passing a specific point in a stream within one second, about 7.5 gallons per second. *Annual flow* is an estimate of the average flow during a given year. *Mean annual flow* is the average of the yearly flows over the course of many years. Knowing the mean annual flow allows us to compare flows from various reaches on one river, and to compare rivers in the region.

Collection of Streamflow Data

The U.S. Geological Survey (USGS) provides present and historic streamflow information for sites throughout the Connecticut River watershed. It began collecting flow data on the Connecticut in Orford, N.H., in 1900, and in 1904 installed its first streamflow gage on the river in Sunderland, Mass. This first device was a staff gage — essentially a ruler reaching down into the water — fixed to a highway bridge over the river. In 1917, USGS added a graphic recorder at the bridge, a new measuring device that used a pen moved by a float or counterweight and a clock that advanced the graphic paper, on which the pen traced the changing water levels (Cooke, Socolow, and Zanca 2004). Since then, the technology has continued to advance, allowing for real-time reporting via the Web, and numerous gages have been added to the network, while some have been removed. Map 23 shows the distribution of gages in the upper Connecticut River basin.

Streamflow data are used for a variety of purposes. These include:

The river is barely a trickle at the outlet from Fourth Connecticut Lake.

- Designing, constructing, and operating reservoirs. Historical streamflow data are used to design dams, spillways, reservoir flooding area, hydropower plants, and diversion structures. Current streamflow data downstream of reservoirs are used to schedule releases for water diversions, to achieve required minimum flows, or to stay within nondamaging levels during periods of high water.
- Issuing flood warnings to protect lives and reduce property damage. Historical streamflow data are essential to the National Weather Service's ability to calibrate rainfall-runoff models that are used as the basis for flood warnings. Effective streamflow forecasting depends on historic streamflow data (for model calibration) and on current streamflow data (as the starting point for forecast-model runs).
- Designing highways and bridges. Historical peak streamflow data are used to develop generalized flow frequency curves for the design of bridges and culverts. Changes in flow patterns associated with urbanization and increased impervious areas can also be monitored.
- Mapping floodplains, based on measured and estimated high streamflows, is used to identify undesirable construction sites. Floodplain mapping is a cost-effective tool for reducing future flood damages.
- Monitoring environmental conditions to protect aquatic habitats and to maintain water quality. Pollutant discharge permits require sufficient flow to provide adequate dilution. Accurate measurements of streamflow are essential to monitor how flow and concentrations of pollutants vary over time.
- Recreational uses. Current streamflow data, which are available to the public on the Internet, are used to see if streamflow conditions are right or safe for fishing, boating, kayaking, and canoeing.

Flow volume increases as the river leaves Second Connecticut Lake in Pittsburg, N.H.

Mean Annual Flows

Starting at the Connecticut River headwaters in far northern New Hampshire, a wide range of mean annual flows have been measured in the watershed. The river originates at the Fourth Connecticut Lake just south of the Canadian border. On its way to Third Connecticut Lake, it meanders along with an estimated mean annual flow of about 1 cfs and its depth usually is measured in inches — easy enough to walk across. When the river reaches Second Connecticut Lake, its mean annual flow is about 100 cfs. There, the Connecticut River probably is difficult to wade. By the time the Connecticut River reaches Colebrook, N.H., its volume is ten times that at Second Connecticut Lake. The estimated mean annual flow just upstream of the confluence with the Mohawk River is about 1,000 cfs. By the time the Connecticut River reaches Brattleboro, Vt., its flow has increased another ten times what it was at Colebrook. There at the Massachusetts border, the estimated mean annual flow of the Connecticut River, just upstream of the confluence with the West River, is about 10,000 cfs.*

* These estimates are based on the measured streamflows at the gaged locations, extrapolated to the ungaged locations (http://nh.water.usgs.gov/projects/sparrow/; Moore et al. 2004).

Streamflow Patterns

Seasonal patterns are observed in the flow records at the USGS gages along the Connecticut River. Low streamflows generally are observed during the months of July and August and the first part of September. The seasonal pattern shows that the largest flows generally occur during the spring freshet as the winter snow melts. A secondary high also occurs in late fall. Although the flow magnitude increases downstream, the same seasonal pattern is observed all along the Connecticut River.

Charts tracking flow levels, called hydrographs, show that the daily flows in any given year can differ drastically from the daily flows averaged over the period of record, as illustrated in Figure 13.

Streamflow Runoff

Precipitation and its distribution among locations and over time directly affects runoff from the land and flow in receiving streams. The term "runoff" refers to that portion of the precipitation that actually flows out of a watershed through the stream network. Average runoff varies spatially across the watershed for several reasons. Precipitation itself varies significantly throughout the region, ranging from a high of about 60 inches or more per year at Mount Washington in New Hampshire and at Glastenbury and Stratton Mountains in Vermont, to a low of less than 34 inches per year along the Connecticut River near Moore Reservoir, which falls in the "rain shadow" of the Green and White mountain ranges (see Chapter 4, Weather and Climate).

Like precipitation data, runoff data are expressed as inches per year. Typically in New England, runoff is equal to the inches of precipitation minus the inches of evaporation per year. This assumes that the water that is absorbed by the ground either evaporates or reaches the local stream network (rather than flowing to a deep aquifer system that can transport the water to some other watershed). The careful examination of streamflow data and watershed characteristics has permitted the USGS to depict the effective runoff (Randall 1996). This is portrayed in Map 25. The area of low precipitation near Moore Reservoir, for

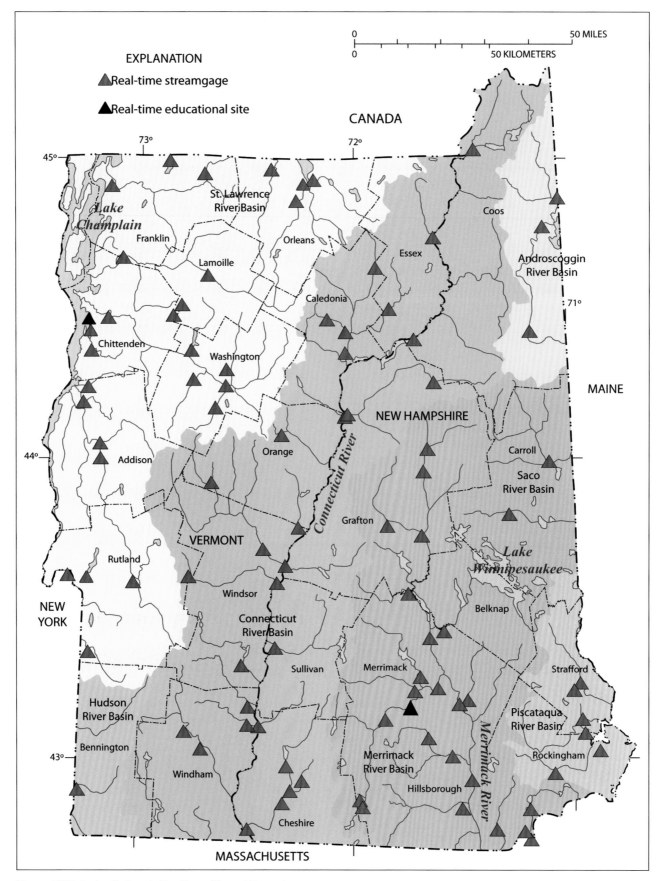

EXPLANATION

▲ Real-time streamgage

▲ Real-time educational site

CANADA

0   50 MILES
0   50 KILOMETERS

45°

73°   72°

Lake
Champlain

St. Lawrence
River Basin

Coos

Androscoggin
River Basin

Franklin

Orleans

Essex

MAINE

Lamoille

71°

Caledonia

Chittenden

Washington

NEW HAMPSHIRE

Carroll

44°

Addison

Orange

Connecticut River

Saco
River Basin

Grafton

Lake
Winnipesaukee

VERMONT

Rutland

Belknap

NEW
YORK

Windsor

Connecticut
River Basin

Merrimack River

Sullivan

Merrimack

Strafford

Hudson
River Basin

Piscataqua
River Basin

Bennington

Rockingham

43°

Windham

Merrimack
River Basin

Hillsborough

Cheshire

MASSACHUSETTS

Map 23. USGS Gaging Stations in New Hampshire and Vermont.

54

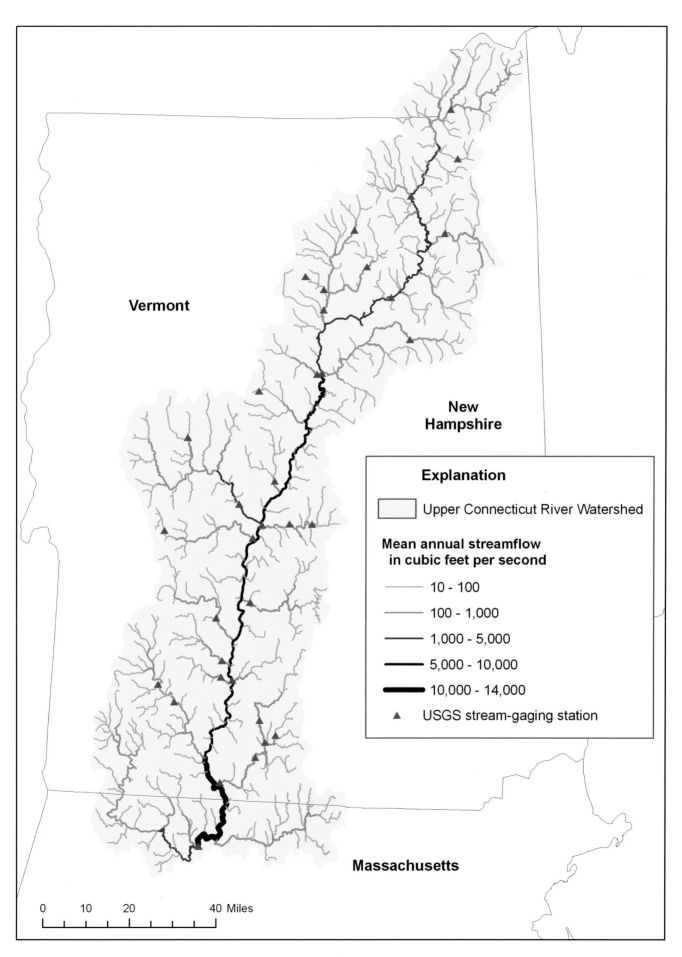

Map 24. Mean Annual Flow in the Upper Connecticut River Watershed.

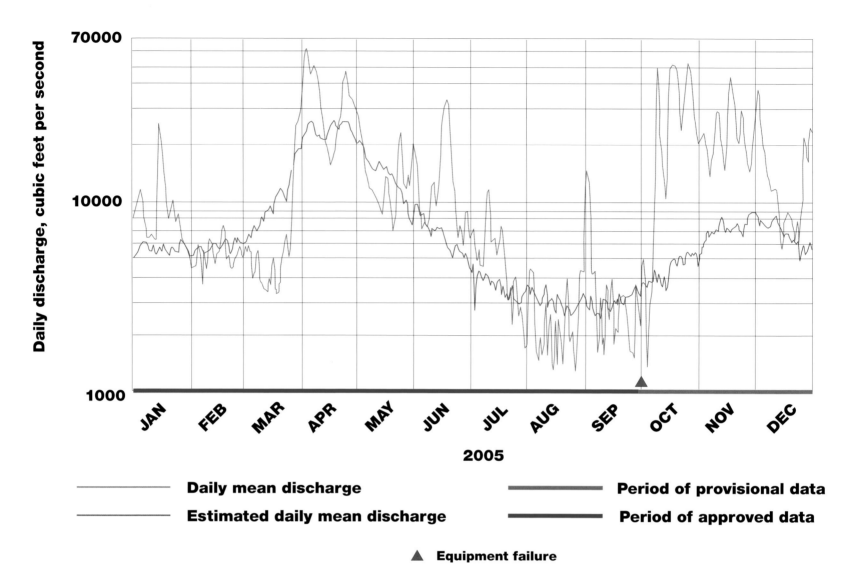

Figure 13. Connecticut River Streamflow at Walpole, N.H., 2005.

example, has low runoff, less than 18 inches per year. This is due to the low precipitation within the rain shadow and loss from evaporation.

Floods and Storm Events

Streamflow varies in response to individual storm events. An extreme example of this occurred on October 8 and 9, 2005, when 4 to 12 inches of rain fell within parts of the upper Connecticut River watershed, causing severe flooding in the Cold River, the Ashuelot River, and other rivers within the Connecticut River Basin. USGS hydrologists estimated the peak flow of the Cold River at Drewsville, N.H., downstream of Alstead, at 21,800 cfs on October 9. Historically, normal river flows at Drewsville during October are about 100 cfs (see Chapter 5, Extreme Weather Events).

The peak flow of the Cold River on October 9, 2005, was more than three times higher than the previous record, which occurred in 1973. This record peak flow was influenced by the failure of an upstream culvert, resulting in a peak greatly exceeding that expected for a return interval of 500 years. Hydrologists use "return intervals" to describe the magnitude and frequency of floods and to represent the average

interval of time over which floods of similar magnitudes may occur (see Chapter 5, Extreme Weather Events).

On October 9, peak flow at the USGS gage on the Ashuelot River in Hinsdale, N.H., was measured at 11,700 cfs, exceeding the 100-year return interval. This was the largest flood observed on the Ashuelot River since the U.S. Army Corps of Engineers built the Surry Mountain and Otter Brook flood-control reservoirs in the 1940s and '50s. Before completion of these reservoirs, the largest flood on record for the Ashuelot River at Hinsdale was 16,600 cfs in 1936. From October 14 to 16, 2005, flows on the Connecticut River near Pittsburg, N.H., peaked at 5,430 cfs, the highest on record since a gage was installed in 1957.

Peak floods resulting from storm events can be made even worse by human activities. Activities associated with increased flooding include paving and otherwise increasing impervious areas, clear-cutting forests, and filling in wetlands. Maintaining certain natural features in the landscape, such as wetlands and floodplains, helps to absorb or attenuate floodwaters. Similarly, it is critical that structures such as dams, spillways, hydropower plants, diversion structures, bridges, and culverts be properly designed and maintained to handle floodwaters.

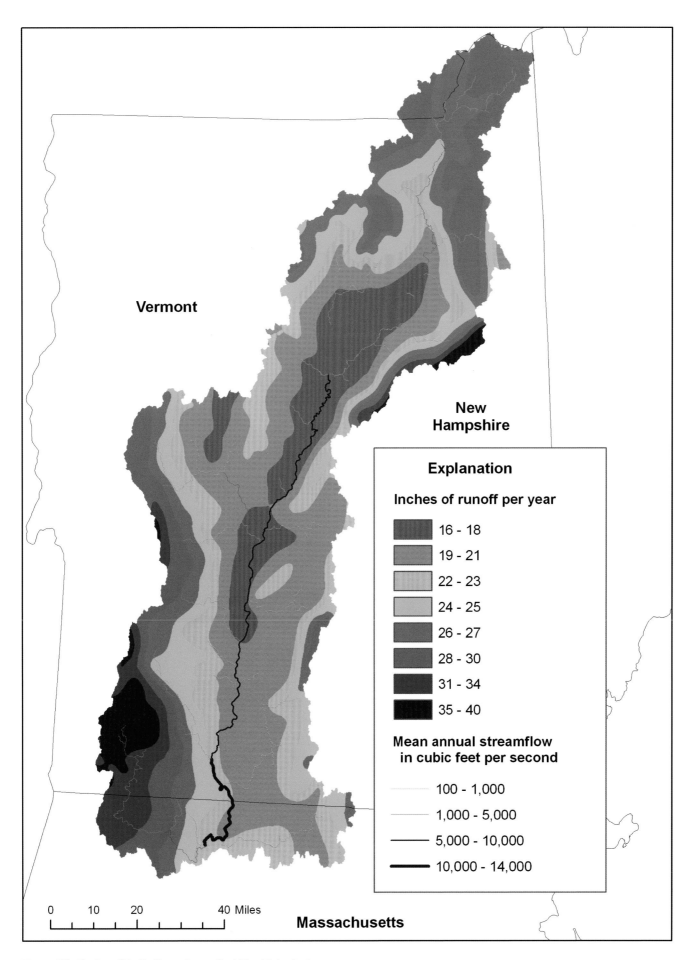

Vermont

New
Hampshire

Explanation

Inches of runoff per year

	16 - 18
	19 - 21
	22 - 23
	24 - 25
	26 - 27
	28 - 30
	31 - 34
	35 - 40

**Mean annual streamflow
in cubic feet per second**

	100 - 1,000
	1,000 - 5,000
	5,000 - 10,000
	10,000 - 14,000

0   10   20   40 Miles

Massachusetts

Map 25. Effective Runoff in the Upper Connecticut River Watershed.

The Flood of 1936 was especially hard on the Connecticut River. This photo was taken in Hanover, N.H., on March 19, 1936, looking over the Ledyard Bridge toward Norwich, Vt. It was the end of a cold winter with the ground deeply frozen and snow-covered. Then the first three weeks of March brought unseasonably high temperatures and four separate rain storms. The region's still ice-covered waterways and frozen ground couldn't absorb all the rain and snowmelt, and the Connecticut swelled to 12.6 feet above flood stage north of White River Junction, the highest flood recorded to that time. The Ledyard Bridge, completed only the previous fall, was buffeted by surging floodwaters and swirling chunks of ice. The estimated peak flow under the bridge was more than 120,000 cubic feet per second. Hanover dumped loads of gravel on the road deck to weigh down the structure, helping the bridge withstand the flow that threatened to lift its structure and severely damage it or carry it away. The bridge stood for another 60 years.

Low Flows and Competing Demands for Water

The Connecticut River is host to a number of hydroelectric facilities. There is typically a daily fluctuation in summer streamflow associated with power generation and competing demands for water. Peaks in the streamflow occur when the most electricity is being produced during the afternoon hours. The lows are associated with the holding back of water at the reservoirs so that it can be used at other times to generate electricity.

In the past, hydroelectric facilities were allowed to hold back more water than they are today. Reduced flow did not provide adequate flow for the health of the aquatic life in the river below the dams or for the dilution of effluent discharges. Beginning in the early 1970s, federal law required minimum streamflow levels to improve the quality of the river.

Richard Moore holds a B.S. degree in hydrology and a M.S. in geology from the University of New Hampshire. He has worked in New Hampshire for the U.S. Geological Survey since 1983.

For Further Reading

Current and historical streamflow conditions may be found on the Web through USGS in New Hampshire (http://nh.water.usgs.gov) with links to maps with gaging stations. Information on how the USGS collects streamflow data can be found at the same site.

Cooke, M. G., Roy S. Socolow, and J. L. Zanca. 2004. A century of service—100 years of streamflow-data collection on the Connecticut River, Montague City, Massachusetts. USGA Fact Sheet FS-2004-3049. Montague City, Mass.

10   Water Quality

Circa 1950

Not so many years ago, mothers kept their children away from the river that is today the healthy centerpiece of an astonishingly beautiful valley. It was a wise choice. The river carried untreated sewage from the homes of nearly 90,000 people and untreated wastewater from scores of industries. Inks and dyes from textile mills, caustic chemicals from metal-working shops, solids from domestic sewage, and the sulfurous effluent from paper processing created a noxious soup that led one distressed observer in the 1950s to describe the Connecticut River as "New England's best landscaped sewer."

At the same time, people routinely dumped household trash on streambanks and off bridges. Technological advances of the twentieth century brought new kinds of pollutants — automotive fluids, airborne mercury, acid rain, PCBs (polychlorinated biphenyls), and pesticides such as DDT.

The industrialized tributaries suffered the most. Many of them, like the Mascoma River in Lebanon, N.H., and the White River in Hartford, Vt., were "suitable for transportation of sewage and industrial wastes without nuisance, and for water power and navigation," according to a 1951 government report. Vermont's Passumpsic River was deemed too polluted even for power production due to discharges from sawmills, paper mills, and other industry. It, along with Sackett's Brook in Putney and Whetstone Brook in Brattleboro, were considered the most fouled rivers in the entire four-state watershed. The Black River from Springfield, Vt., to the Connecticut was labeled simply "unsatisfactory waters, nuisance exists."

The state and federal agencies that evaluated the Connecticut River basin's water quality in 1951 described five levels of water pollution: Classes A through E. Today, the states use only A and B of the original five, although they have further described subclasses of A and B, and added "waste management zones" to accommodate the mixing areas for wastewater discharges. Within Class B, Vermont also designates three Water Management Types in order to more explicitly recognize their attainable uses and the existing level of water quality protection. Table 3 describes the 1951 classes.

Circa 2006

Today, the watershed's rivers no longer run red one day and blue the next, and riverfront real estate that once was shunned as a health hazard has become expensive and desirable. What happened? The U.S. Congress passed the Clean Water Act in 1972, providing funds, energy,

TABLE 3. River Miles of Connecticut River by Class, 1951

| | RIVER MILES | |
| | CONNECTICUT | |
CLASS DESCRIPTION	RIVER	TRIBUTARIES
Class A No damages. Protected from pollution and used as public water supplies.	0	9
Class B No damages. Waters transport only "natural pollution" or have recovered from sewage and industrial waste pollution. Unsuitable for public water supply without treatment; suitable for all other uses.	44	499
Class C Damaged. Unsuitable for use as a public water supply even with treatment; for recreational uses except boating; for use in some industrial processes without treatment; and for irrigation of crops consumed without cooking. Water not always of satisfactory aesthetic quality.	219	257
Class D Damaged. Unsuitable for most legitimate water uses. Suitable only for the transportation of sewage and industrial wastes without nuisance and for power development and limited industrial uses. Aesthetic quality poor.	6	101
Class E Damaged. Unsuitable for all water uses except power development. Nuisance conditions prevail during critical periods.	0	28

Many miles of tributaries are now considered Class A. While much information is available about the quality of tributaries today, complete figures are not available for comparison with 1951 numbers. Vermont's waste management zone is not technically considered Class C, but a designated mixing area below wastewater discharges within which water is not expected to meet Class B standards.

Commerce and industry used rivers and streams as power sources, and as sluiceways for waste, such as at this c. 1880 tannery on Grant Brook in Lyme, N.H., shown in a postcard.

In contrast to a half-century ago, the Connecticut today is a safe and enjoyable place for family recreation. This photo also illustrates, on the far bank, a floodplain forest stripped of its understory and groundcover. An intact riparian forest community would better filter runoff and help prevent bank erosion.

and the force of federal law to bring this and the rest of the nation's rivers back toward a goal of "fishable, swimmable" waters. Some Connecticut River tributaries had not met this description for 200 years.

The states have adopted their own water-quality standards to measure the health of their waters, and are required to report on the status of these waters to the Environmental Protection Agency every two years. New Hampshire's 2006 description of Class B waters shows the strides made since 1951:

> Class B waters are managed to achieve and maintain a high level of quality compatible with certain beneficial values and uses. Values are high quality habitat for aquatic biota, fish and wildlife and a water quality that consistently exhibits good aesthetic value; uses are public water supply with filtration and disinfection, irrigation and other agricultural uses, swimming, and recreation, including fishing.

Massive investment by industry and also by communities using federal aid led to construction of scores of wastewater treatment systems that collect polluted water and treat it before releasing it back into rivers and streams. Investments by homeowners in modern septic systems, and by farmers in manure storage facilities, livestock fencing, and other best management practices for controlling runoff and erosion also have helped improve water quality.

While the river has recovered substantially with treatment of "point" sources of pollution—those that come from a specific point such as a discharge pipe—it still carries nutrients, sediment, trash, and other "nonpoint" or diffuse sources of pollution, and faces new challenges from increasing riverside development. The Connecticut River occupies the bed of a glacial lake, and erosion of these lakebed sediments, as well as of the soft alluvial soils later laid down by the river, is a perennial source of turbidity and sedimentation. Fertilizers carried by runoff from farm fields and residential yards enter the river whenever they are over-applied and not captured by riverside vegetation. Wastewater discharges also contain nutrients and even pharmaceuticals that are not removed during the treatment process. Research is underway to determine how much nitrogen the upper Connecticut River basin sends to Long Island Sound, where this pollutant causes dangerously low oxygen levels.

In most places, and at most times, the river today is clean enough for swimming, but there is concern about harmful bacteria in some of the most popular canoeing waters in the North Country and in the Upper Valley. Bacteria counts are likely to be higher in the river after a heavy storm. Bacteria can reach rivers through poorly functioning septic systems or drainage from areas where animals are concentrated, whether they are moose or cows, especially where they have direct access to the water. Bacteria can also reach rivers through runoff from city streets where dog walkers do not pick up after their pets, and especially through combined sewer overflows (CSOs), where runoff from heavy storms can overwhelm a wastewater treatment plant and send untreated sewage into the river. While the few cities and towns with linked stormwater and wastewater collection systems are making the time-consuming and expensive investment to separate them, CSOs remain a threat to the Passumpsic, Mascoma, and Connecticut rivers. Straight-pipe septic discharges are largely a thing of the past, but a few remain.

Farm animals can be a source of bacteria and other pollutants entering the river. Above, a Vermont farm c. 1949. Today, some cattle still have direct access to the river (below). Federal funding is available to farms for riparian buffer planting and restoration and for alternative water sources and fencing for cattle.

Mercury's reputation as an environmental poison is growing worse in the Connecticut River Valley. Mercury from atmospheric pollution threatens not only aquatic life, but also wildlife far from the water, such as the Bicknell's thrush, a rare bird of high-elevation northern New England and adjacent Canadian forests. Mercury poisons the central nervous system, leading to changes in behavior, reproduction, and body chemistry. Both New Hampshire and Vermont have issued fish consumption advisories for the Connecticut and other rivers, based on mercury levels.

The Environmental Protection Agency and the four states cooperated in 2000 on a study of fish tissue toxins in Connecticut River fish (EPA 2006). The study found that total mercury concentrations were significantly higher upstream than downstream, and particularly in Reach 7, from Moore Dam to Canaan Dam. In this part of the river system, mercury poses a risk to recreational and subsistence fishers and to fish-eating wildlife.

Much of this mercury originates in the emissions of coal-burning Midwestern power plants and arrives on prevailing winds, but it also comes from urbanized eastern seaboard emissions and local sources such as burning of hazardous waste. Once in the river, the mercury bioaccumulates in the food chain. Older fish tend to have higher levels of mercury than younger fish, and long-lived fish-eating birds such as loons are especially vulnerable.

Recent studies have linked water-level manipulations in reservoirs with mercury in fish, and identified the Fifteen Mile Falls region of the Connecticut River and similarly managed parts of the upper Androscoggin and Kennebec River watersheds as mercury hot spots (Evers 2005, 2007). On Moore, Comerford, and McIndoe Falls reservoirs, the states have issued stricter consumption guidelines.

A technician with the Environmental Protection Agency samples water quality on the Connecticut River at Sumner Falls.

Water quality monitoring for "specific conductance," a test that indicates various kinds of pollution, such as road salt runoff, shows a clear increase from upstream to downstream. Acidity is a different story, with a number of readings in the river's first 100 miles showing pH levels too low to meet state standards. In higher-elevation parts of its basin, where the river is smaller, it has less ability to bounce back from the damaging effects of the acid rain that regularly falls in its watershed.

Whether these waters are once again adequately "fishable" is a murkier question. Water quality monitoring results are generally encouraging for fish and the aquatic life upon which they depend, especially for dissolved oxygen, but most studies focus on only four aspects of the underwater world: oxygen, temperature, specific conductance, and pH. Mercury and other metals, automotive oils, PCBs, and pesticides can lurk in the sediments or in the bodies of fish and their food, and never appear in a bucket of river water. An extensive study of Connecticut River sediments by the Environmental Protection Agency in 2000 found contaminants from parking lot and road runoff at locations as far north as Pittsburg village, and traces of copper from abandoned mines high in the Waits and Ompompanoosuc watersheds of Vermont (see Chapter 23, The Industrial Era). At some sites, the contaminants were in levels high enough to threaten aquatic life. Some river sediments still contain the chemical ghosts of industrial sites later drowned by the construction of hydro dams, and harbor pesticides such as DDT, banned many years ago.

Yet, fish in the watershed have benefited from improvements such as ladders or other types of fish passage at many dams, which have allowed both native and sea-run fish such as American shad to move more freely once again within the basin. Improved gages measure water temperature. New dam licenses requiring minimum flows and ramping rates help protect aquatic habitat. Protecting water quantity is a step toward protecting water quality.

Since passage of the Clean Water Act, great efforts on behalf of water quality are being made by a growing number of citizens bearing meters and monitors, basins and beakers. Volunteers from schools, river advocacy groups, and conservation commissions have stepped forward to test the health of many Connecticut River tributaries, from the Israel River in northern New Hampshire to the West River in southern Vermont. These same citizens pitch in for river clean-ups, removing years of evidence of river abuse. Their energy and effort are a powerful catalyst for clean water for the future.

Adair D. Mulligan is conservation director for the Connecticut River Joint Commissions. She holds a master's degree in environmental biology from Smith College. She lives in Lyme Center, N.H.

FOR FURTHER READING

Evers, David C. 2005. *Mercury Connections: The Extent and Effects of Mercury Pollution in Northeastern North America*. Gorham, Maine: Biodiversity Research Institute.

Evers, David C., et al. 2007. Biological mercury hotspots in the northeastern United States and southeastern Canada." *Bioscience* 57, no. 1 (January).

The Ely Copper Mine was one of many industrial uses in the watershed that fed pollutants into rivers and streams. This c. 1896 photo shows the town and industrial buildings some years after the mine closed. The mine, and others like it, are the focus of clean-up initiatives today.

Fish ladders and other forms of passage allow both migrating and resident fish to move more freely within the watershed.

During the annual clean up by the Black River Action Team in Springfield, Vt., and other area towns, volunteers remove from the river and haul away all sorts of debris.

11 Water Management

As long as people have lived near the Connecticut River they have sought to capture its flow for human benefits. Native Americans set weirs at Bellows Falls to trap fish and diverted trickles of water to irrigate their crops. Early settlers built waterwheel-driven mills to saw lumber and grind grain. Lumbermen used the river as a highway for logs. Starting in the early twentieth century, the river was used for powering the turbines at hydroelectric dams. Later in the century, publicly funded dams were built on the larger tributaries in an effort to control flooding. Today, the river and its tributaries are seen as part of an interconnected system with multiple human interests and uses as well as critical natural functions.

Managing for Power

More than 1,000 dams have been built in the upper Connecticut River watershed, ranging from small earthen structures built to create farm ponds to the 12 mainstem dams that impound over half of the river's length. Most significant are the hydropower facilities now owned and operated by TransCanada Hydro Northeast, a private company based in Calgary, Alberta. Chapter 32, Energy, examines the history of power generation on the upper Connecticut River.

Under terms of four operating licenses issued by the Federal Energy Regulatory Commission (FERC), TransCanada owns and operates six hydroelectric generating facilities and two separate storage reservoirs on the Connecticut River. The six generating facilities are controlled remotely from company facilities in Wilder, Vt., and the Connecticut Lakes storage dams from Pittsburg, N.H. TransCanada's facilities, with their storage reservoirs and larger generating plants, are an integrated system for managing river flow for generating power. Through a water management agreement, TransCanada also operates Murphy Dam, a flood storage dam at Lake Francis in Pittsburg that is owned by the state of New Hampshire.

Hydro facilities capture the river's power in two ways: the "store-and-release" design, where dams hold back or "store" the flow until it is needed at times of high or "peak" power demand; or "run-of-river," where natural flow is used with no water storage. The TransCanada dams are all store-and-release stations, but each falls into one of three categories of management based on water storage capacity and how the company uses that storage for power generation. Seasonal cycle dams (First and Second Connecticut Lake reservoirs, Moore and Comerford stations) have large reservoirs that store water for use over the course of a year. Wilder Station, where the impoundment has less stor-

East Inlet, in the Connecticut River headwaters region, seems wild and remote. It was formed by a dam built to control flow for log drives.

The impoundment behind Moore Dam in Littleton, N.H., is effectively the Granite State's fourth-largest lake. A stone wall is a reminder of Pattenville, a village abandoned when the hydro dam flooded the area in the 1950s.

From huge concrete hydroelectric dams to farm pond dams, dams play a major part in the hydrology of the watershed. This map offers just a sampling of dams throughout the watershed, since showing the approximately 1,000 in existence would overwhelm the map. Major dams are operated by the U.S. Army Corps of Engineers for flood control, and by TransCanada and several other businesses for hydroelectric power.

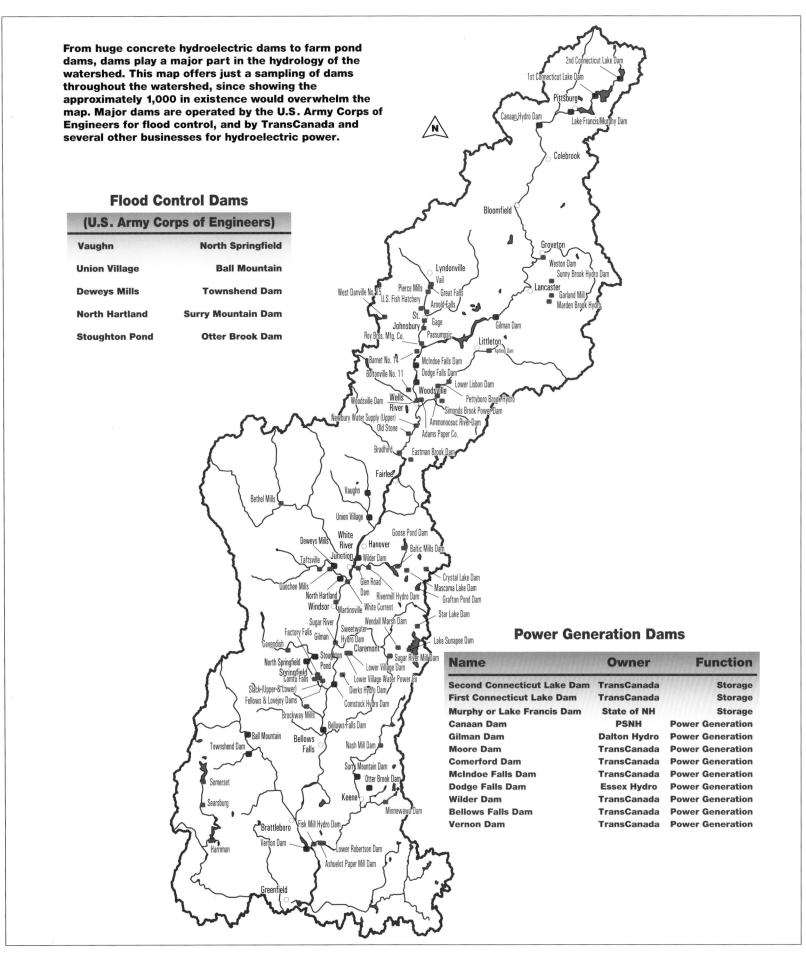

Flood Control Dams
(U.S. Army Corps of Engineers)

Vaughn	North Springfield
Union Village	Ball Mountain
Deweys Mills	Townshend Dam
North Hartland	Surry Mountain Dam
Stoughton Pond	Otter Brook Dam

Power Generation Dams

Name	Owner	Function
Second Connecticut Lake Dam	TransCanada	Storage
First Connecticut Lake Dam	TransCanada	Storage
Murphy or Lake Francis Dam	State of NH	Storage
Canaan Dam	PSNH	Power Generation
Gilman Dam	Dalton Hydro	Power Generation
Moore Dam	TransCanada	Power Generation
Comerford Dam	TransCanada	Power Generation
McIndoe Falls Dam	TransCanada	Power Generation
Dodge Falls Dam	Essex Hydro	Power Generation
Wilder Dam	TransCanada	Power Generation
Bellows Falls Dam	TransCanada	Power Generation
Vernon Dam	TransCanada	Power Generation

Map 26. Dams in the Watershed.

Where the ferocious Fifteen Mile Falls once cut a path, the river now powers New England's largest hydroelectric project. The project starts with Moore Dam, pictured here, and extends to McIndoe Falls downriver. In the background, the north and southbound bridges of Interstate 93 link Littleton, N.H., and Waterford, Vt.

age capacity, operates on a weekly cycle. Daily cycle dams (McIndoe Falls, Bellows Falls, and Vernon stations) have the smallest storage and move water on a daily basis. While natural conditions such as heavy rains, snowmelt, or drought influence management of the dams, FERC license compliance is the fundamental component of TransCanada's water management strategy.

Dam Operations

During ordinary operations, reservoir storage planning balances power, generating goals and other requirements of the operating licenses. Managers consider current weather conditions and historic patterns of precipitation and dam operations in determining the available water in storage on a weekly and seasonal basis. Minimum flow volumes needed for nonpower uses, such as fishery habitat and spawning, are also considered in determining how much water is available for power generation.

Late in the year or in the winter, managers start the drawdown of Moore Reservoir in preparation for the spring freshet. Using snow moisture content and historic records of average precipitation, they calculate how much water may be expected to flow from snowmelt in the upper watershed, and thus how much water to release and how much storage space to keep open in the reservoir. Similar calculations are made for storage reservoirs at the Connecticut Lakes and at Comerford Station. As runoff proceeds through the spring, managers manipulate storage levels through the system to balance power generation and storage needs.

Flood Management

After severe and widespread flooding in 1927, 1936, 1938, and the 1950s, Congress directed the U.S. Army Corps of Engineers to address the problem. The Army Corps constructed seven flood control dams from 1941 and 1961 with the combined capacity to control runoff from 14

SHARON F. FRANCIS

In seeking a renewal of its 40-year operating license from the Federal Energy Regulatory Commission (FERC) for Fifteen Mile Falls, New England Power Company invited key stakeholders to work with it to try to reach agreement on terms for the license application. These stakeholders included the federal and state governments, watershed groups including CRJC, regional planning commissions, and conservation, fisheries, and recreation interests.

The power company's invitation was not without risk. It asked parties with strong and differing objectives to enter into negotiations that would balance their competing interests and find a set of terms on which all could agree. There were times during the two years of study and lengthy negotiation when it was doubtful that agreement could be reached. Ultimately, however, settlement was made, and an agreement was signed on September 2, 1997.

Highlights of the settlement agreement are:

- Placement of permanent conservation easements on approximately 11,000 acres of power-company lands adjacent to Fifteen Mile Falls as well as lands surrounding the First and Second Connecticut lakes.
- Establishment of an Upper Connecticut River Mitigation and Enhancement Fund of between $10.5 million and $16.5 million, depending upon the power company's revenues, to underwrite river restoration projects, provide fish passage, remove tributary dams, improve water quality and habitat, restore and protect wetlands and stream bank buffers, and offset tax losses in communities where lands would be protected by easements.
- Establishment of minimum allowable flows and other operating conditions to protect aquatic habitat, fish passage, and enhance recreational opportunities.

The significant conservation benefits of permanent protection of 7,000 acres of land, and of a multimillion-dollar fund that could be used for other conservation improvements, gained the support of the two governors, federal and state agencies, and conservation organization leaders. Because of the settlement agreement, none of the parties contested the application for a renewed operating license to the Federal Energy Regulatory Commission. Incorporating the settlement terms, FERC issued the license in 2002. The FERC licenses for TransCanada's three other hydropower dams expire in 2018.

Sharon F. Francis is executive director of the Connecticut River Joint Commissions.

Floodplain forests along the Connecticut and its tributaries play a natural and crucial role in absorbing, storing, and dispersing high water.

percent of the upper Connecticut River watershed (Lambert 1998). Areas within these sites are open for public recreation (see Chapter 36, Recreation).

The Army Corps Reservoir Regulation Team, located in Concord, Mass., uses radio and satellite communications to monitor river conditions that influence management of flood-control dams throughout New England. At the dam sites, park rangers regulate the amount of water through the dam by raising or lowering gates.

Managing for flood conditions is also part of TransCanada's water management practices. The power company also works with the Army Corps to coordinate flows during flood conditions, and supplies owners of downstream hydroelectric stations with daily discharge data so that the smaller operators may implement effective flow management for their facilities.

Natural Flood Storage

The persistence of major flooding is a reminder that despite people's efforts to contain it through built infrastructure like dams or retaining walls, a great river like the Connecticut—as well as its tributaries—

The natural floodplain along the Ammonoosuc River in Lisbon, N.H., provides space for ice to pile up during spring ice-out.

cannot truly be controlled. Nor'easters, hurricanes, and the combination of heavy spring rains with rapid snowmelt and ice jams have all caused the river to overflow its banks in the past, and will continue to do so in the future (see chapter 5, Extreme Weather Events). For this reason, there is growing interest in preserving what is referred to as natural valley flood storage by protecting floodplains from development.

Floodplains are natural sponges that help absorb overflow from the river. However, because these ordinarily flat, broad areas offer riverfront views and often have access to major roads, some regard them as prime development areas. Most communities in the watershed still allow building within 100-year floodplains. The Army Corps of Engineers has recognized the long-term utility of permanently protecting floodplains with conservation agreements with private landowners. The Corps has identified two major natural valley flood storage areas on the upper Connecticut: between Stewartstown and Lancaster, N.H./ Canaan and Lunenburg, Vt.; and between Haverhill and Piermont, N.H./Newbury and Bradford, Vt. Leaving these floodplains undeveloped will help prevent increased flooding throughout the immediate area and downstream. Many floodplains are also prime agricultural lands or are inhabited by unique natural communities, meaning that conserving them may serve multiple interests, including maintaining local agriculture, providing public recreational areas and scenic views, and preserving habitat (see Chapter 12, Habitat and Natural Communities, and Chapter 15, Flora).

Different Flow, Different River

As a result of active water management, the Connecticut, like most of New England's major rivers, is a very different river than the one navigated by Native Americans and white settlers. Placid stretches of impounded flatwater now cover many formerly muscular rapids and steep waterfalls. Where one could have walked from New Hampshire to Vermont through the river channel and barely have gotten wet feet during summer droughts, the river now carries more consistent flow through the year.

At the same time, flow management for flood control and power generation may alter unique natural communities that border the river, such as high terrace floodplain forests. Recent research suggests that since the Connecticut and other tributaries have been dammed,

Throughout the watershed, some old and inactive dams, like this one on Pearl Lake Brook, a tributary of the Ammonoosuc River in Lisbon, N.H., are slated for removal. Some have fallen into disrepair and are considered unsafe. Others, while still active, have outlived their designed life expectancy and are deteriorating, posing liabilities to their owners. Old dams also disrupt natural streamflow, posing obstacles to fish and other aquatic species, and contribute to erosion. Both New Hampshire and Vermont have programs aimed at identifying and removing dams that no longer serve the public interest.

floods have occurred less frequently, are of shorter duration, and affect less of the natural floodplain than before the dams were built. Riparian plant and animal communities and individual species evolved in the historic natural regime of flood disturbance. Floodplain communities are decreasing in size and extent along the river—in part due to the encroachment of agricultural and residential development. Research suggests that these natural communities, which represent some of the most botanically diverse habitats in the watershed, may be weakened further by changes in hydrology resulting from alterations to the river's natural flow (Nislow et al. 2002).

Flow Alteration, Erosion, and New River Science

A river is a dynamic system, always changing and evolving in response to current conditions. Historical evidence suggests that nineteenth-century timber companies changed the system dynamics when they straightened the river to keep timber from piling up in the meanders during the log drives. It is also likely that railroad builders and farmers straightened some sections of the river to suit their purposes. At the same time, people were clearing land along the river for agriculture, cutting timber on forested slopes, and building dams on the tributaries—all of which affected runoff, flow, and the overall river system.

Erosion in some areas and sediment deposition in others is part of the natural behavior of a river system, but can be accelerated by human action. Recent assessments by the Connecticut River Joint Commissions using fluvial geomorphology, the study of river dynamics, show that those historical changes affect the flow of the river today, accelerating erosion in some areas and creating new erosion problems

in others (Field 2004 and 2006). Erosion eats away riverbanks, sometimes reaching public roads, sometimes carrying away edges of farm fields. Sediment loosened by erosion can harm water quality, affecting fish and other aquatic life, and can create new sand and gravel bars, which in turn divert flow and cause more erosion. Research by CRJC indicates that restoring sediment storage capacity in tributaries can decrease sediment entering the mainstem and reduce the erosion problems it causes there.

With this knowledge, CRJC and public agencies are working with communities and private landowners to address the causes of erosion as well as to find solutions. Bioengineering—using large tree trunks with root wads rather than traditional rock riprap—often can help stabilize banks and encourage growth of new vegetation on the bank, known as riparian buffers, and provide fish habitat. The new river science is advancing understanding of flood dynamics, as well as erosion and sedimentation, with long-term, cost-effective solutions, and a river returned to a more stable condition, as the hoped-for outcomes.

In conclusion, while people have successfully captured the river's flow for everything from power generation to white-water kayaking, it can safely be said that this great natural resource cannot be controlled fully. The river will continue to exert itself as it has for millennia, sometimes as a roiling flood, sometimes as a tranquil current.

Cleve Kapala is a New Hampshire member of the Connecticut River Joint Commissions. He is director of government affairs for TransCanada. He lives in Hopkinton, N.H.

Rebecca A. Brown is communications director for the Connecticut River Joint Commissions. She lives in Sugar Hill, N.H.

Good Culverts / Bad Culverts

ERIC ALDRICH

As you drive or ride or walk down roads in the Connecticut River watershed, you cross culverts—lots of them. They are the big pipes, concrete boxes, and other structures made to let streams flow under roads. In addition to being part of our road infrastructure, culverts are important links in the network of streams, brooks, and rivers in the watershed. How culverts do their job has a big effect on the health of a stream.

Consider water spilling three feet from a culvert before hitting the stream below. Could a brook trout get up that waterfall to reach cooler, deeper pools or spawning habitat upstream? What about darters, or turtles, or crayfish? Can they make it up the waterfall? Not likely.

The three-foot waterfall is a sign of a poorly designed culvert. Culverts can be bad for fish and wildlife in many other ways. They can be too small or too shallow. They can cause water to halt to a trickle. Culvert bottoms made of metal or concrete can block some species that need a natural streambed. Some culverts cause scouring and erosion. Others clog and become dams. All of these present barriers to the movement and health of wildlife that live in or use streams for travel, breeding, or feeding.

Good culverts are essentially invisible to fish and wildlife (Nedeau 2005). They don't require Herculean efforts to get through. They allow a natural flow and don't choke the stream. For instance, an open arch (as opposed to a pipe) lets a stream run its course over a natural streambed. Open-bottomed box culverts work the same way.

Realizing that well-designed culverts can reconnect miles of stream habitat, some communities are replacing and upgrading them. In watersheds of the West River in Vermont and the Ashuelot River in New Hampshire, The Nature Conservancy has launched detailed studies of culverts, dams, and other road-stream crossings. TNC has also ranked each crossing in terms of habitat quality and stream mileage. It has found that replacing one bad culvert may reconnect 99 miles of high-quality up- and downstream habitat.

TNC is sharing its findings with local and state highway departments. As agencies plan to replace aging culverts, often for added flood control, TNC hopes that better culverts will become part of those plans. Simple fixes to the built infrastructure may make remarkable improvements to the natural infrastructure.

Eric Aldrich served as communications director for the New Hampshire chapter of The Nature Conservancy.

Sources

Nedeau, Ethan, and Massachusetts Riverways Program. 2005. *Massachusetts Stream Crossings Handbook*. Boston: Mass. Department of Fish and Game.

Bechtel, Douglas. 2007. *River Continuity Assessment of the Ashuelot River Basin*. Concord, N.H.: The Nature Conservancy.

A volunteer for The Nature Conservancy measures a culvert in the Ashuelot River watershed as part of an inventory of culverts and other stream crossings.

For Further Reading

Field, John. 2006. *Fluvial Geomorphology Assessment of the Northern Connecticut River Tributaries*. Charlestown, N.H.: Connecticut River Joint Commissions.

———. 2004. *Fluvial Geomorphology Assessment of the Northern Connecticut River, Vermont and New Hampshire*. Charlestown, N.H.: Connecticut River Joint Commissions.

Lambert, Kathy Fallon. 1998. *Instream Flow Uses, Values and Policies in the Upper Connecticut River Watershed*. Charlestown, N.H.: Connecticut River Joint Commissions.

Nislow, Keith. H., Francis. J. Magilligan, Heidi Fassnacht, Doug Bechtel, and Ana Ruesinka. Effects of impoundment on the flood regime of natural floodplain communities in the Upper Connecticut River. *Journal of the American Water Resources Association* (December).

IV The Natural Environment

Introduction

Seen from far above, the Connecticut River uniting Vermont and New Hampshire runs like a sinuous ribbon, stretching from its humble beginnings in a small pond in northern New Hampshire to its broad, flat course through wide valley floors as it crosses into Massachusetts. From the air, the larger tributaries sparkle in the sun: the Ammonoosuc, the Ottauquechee, the White, the Black. It all looks like a seamless system, mostly unbroken by major human interruptions.

Coming closer, the details of the land become clear, and the imprint of human impact is everywhere: the change in forest cover where loggers worked last winter, the neat rows of crops, the roads, the houses, the industrial parks. But it's that first, overall impression of interconnectedness of the valley's natural parts that sets the scene for this chapter on ecosystems. The watershed is a natural system, composed of innumerable subsystems, in which humans are the mammals with the greatest footprint. The human story will be told in due time. But first, this Atlas focuses on the natural and wild inhabitants of the region, the plants, mammals, reptiles and amphibians, fish, and birds, and the ecosystems in which they live.

The river itself provides some of the story. In its seasons, ebbing and flowing according to rainfall and snowmelt and the vast power of its ice flows, over time it has created the conditions for distinct natural communities.

Many of us are familiar with wild plant and animal species found in and around the river, and up through the hills and mountains that edge the valley. Some enjoy finding the watershed's unusual plants, such as the remarkable showy lady slipper. Birders know where to look for the jewels of spring, the orioles and tanagers and other neotropical migrants, as well as the harbingers of fall: the big flocks of ducks and geese. Hunters understand the habitats and habits of grouse, woodcock, and deer, and anglers know the aquatic environments that favor pike, brook trout, or smallmouth bass. Many of us look forward to the first warm March or April day when we hear spring peepers—outrageously noisy, given their diminutive size.

In the first chapter, Ned Swanberg asks us to look beyond individual species to the interconnected space in which they live, to topography, aspects of heat and light, moisture and water availability, food sources, and relationships among the plant and animal species found in natural communities. David Conant urges us to look closely, to discern the small but telling details that help tell the story of where and how different plant species thrive. Through Charles Cogbill's eyes we can imagine flora on a grander scale, from the return of tree species after the retreat of the glaciers, to the change in forests since European settlement. Brett Engstrom describes the richness of the region's wetlands, some created literally before our eyes by beavers, others the result of glacial movement 10,000 years ago.

Charlie Browne recounts the rich diversity of bird species that migrate

Deer don't just live "in the woods." They need a variety of resources, including water, cover, and a food source, all of which are present for this white-tailed buck in northern Vermont.

through and live in the watershed, while David Deen informs us that some of our river's best known fish species arrived here by very unconventional means. Jim Andrews draws on his years of observation as well as historical accounts to depict the status of the region's reptiles and amphibians, and Ted Levin goes back into history to illuminate stories of the region's mammals.

Taken together, these essays remind of us that we share this valley with remarkable inhabitants, both plant and animal, which have been shaped by millennia to what we witness today.

12   Habitats and Natural Communities

Considering "Habitat"

The Connecticut River watershed encompasses extremely diverse places, from the haunts of spruce grouse in the Nulhegan Basin to riverside seeps along the White River. How can we describe and understand this array? How can we understand the changes that humans have made in this mosaic over several thousand years?

We may begin to understand the interconnectedness of these very different places by considering *habitat*. Habitat reflects the needs of a type of living thing, such as brook trout or white-tailed deer. Habitat also may be considered as a distinct kind of natural place, such as a bog, or a pitch pine forest on a rocky summit. These two meanings of the term "habitat" can be tangled, but together they will help expand our understanding of ecological relationships.

Consider the habitat needs of a herd of white-tailed deer. The herd requires a mosaic of resources including water, food, air, cover, and space. They need meadow plants and leaves for summer forage, and twigs and low branches to survive the winter. In our region, they also need a special type of winter cover called a deeryard. In a deeryard, dense conifers shield the ground from heavy snow, making it easier for deer to find food and escape predators. To improve habitat quality for deer, land managers try to increase whatever resource is in shortest supply. Typically, when managing a timber harvesting operation, for example, a forester will try to protect deeryards.

Natural Communities

The second approach to habitat refers to what biologists call *natural communities*. A natural community is a distinct association of living things that occurs in a place and is shaped by natural physical and biological processes. Examples of such communities include alder swamps, spruce-fir stands, and alpine tundra. Natural communities are defined by the ecological connections among organisms and include the soil, solar aspect, moisture, and periodic disturbances that alter the site (Sperduto and Nichols 2004).

Natural communities can help us understand what would grow in a spot without human intervention. For instance, what naturally had been a "rich sugar maple/ash/oak/hickory forested floodplain" natural community along the Connecticut River in Hinsdale might now be a cornfield. Biologists believe that if corn growing ceased, the soils and other natural conditions at the site would favor it growing back to the natural assemblage of trees and understory plants once found there, along with the insects, birds, mammals, and other wildlife species it once sheltered.

Natural communities are assigned specific names based on where they occur (e.g., floodplains) and the indicator organisms found there (e.g., silver maple). They are defined primarily by their dominant plants. Natural community classifications convey a picture of the interrelationships of the plants and animals that live there with each other and their environment. New Hampshire and Vermont have two different taxonomies of natural communities, but the systems share most characteristics. The sidebar on page 80 depicts how a particular land area may be viewed through the lenses of habitat and natural communities.

The resource definition of habitat is used most commonly when wildlife managers, for instance, try to increase the populations of game animals like woodcock, or develop recovery plans for rare animals such as bald eagles. The natural community meaning of habitat is used more frequently to focus on plants in their living context, including soils, pollinators, herbivores, predators, seed dispersers, and so on.

Five Critical Resources

Following is a shared framework of five resources to compare and contrast the two understandings of habitat. Where one of these things is in short supply or missing, it limits the population size, productivity, or range of a species. This framework may be applied to any region, but examples within it are drawn from the Connecticut River Valley.

Air may be easy for people to take for granted, but in an aquatic environment it is critical. In a pond, the amount of dissolved oxygen in the water can easily become too low to sustain stoneflies or brook trout. In dramatic situations, sewage entering the water can stimulate the growth of bacteria populations until they use up all of the available oxygen. In these circumstances, the trout may leave the area or die.

Along the Connecticut River and its tributaries, landowners are increasingly aware of how important it is to keep trees growing along the bank. Shade helps keep water cooler, allowing it to retain a higher level of oxygen. Higher dissolved oxygen means that a wider range of fish may survive in that reach.

Some natural communities are shaped by oxygen availability. Floodplain forests are natural communities found on low terraces along the Connecticut River and its tributaries. These forests are flooded periodically during the growing season. When floodwaters cover the soil for an extended period, most plant roots and soil-dwelling animals cannot survive. However, silver maple and ostrich fern have special adaptations to endure low oxygen in the root zone. They become prominent

- Northern hardwood forest, Lord's Hill Natural Area, Groton State Forest, Groton, Vt. (this is a widespread type of "matrix" forest with many variants)
- Hemlock–spruce–northern hardwood forest (this is another type of matrix forest more common to the area around Mount Cube and north)
- Rich fen, Eshqua Bog, Hartland, Vt.
- Black spruce bog, Philbrick-Cricenti Bog, New London, N.H.
- Red Maple–Black gum swamp, J. Maynard Miller Memorial Town Forest, Vernon, Vt.
- Sugar maple–silver maple–white ash floodplain forest, Bedell Bridge State Park, Haverhill, N.H.
- Temperate lichen talus barren, Mount Wantastiquet, Hindsdale, N.H.
- Cattail marsh, Herrick's Cove, Rockingham, Vt.

The J. Maynard Miller Town Forest in Vernon, Vt., contains fine examples of red maple–black gum swamps. Black gum (*Nyssa sylvatica*) may be found in various stages of growth and decline, with some trees dating back centuries.

components of the natural community called the silver maple–ostrich fern riverine floodplain forest.

Water is a physiological requirement for life. Water works within both plants and animals in transporting food, waste, and gases. It is necessary for photosynthesis, making it the foundation of life on this planet.

Since rooted plants cannot move quickly, the minimum level of soil moisture is one factor that determines which plants survive. Even with roughly 40 inches of precipitation per year in our region, certain types of soils are typically dry. During a period of drought, some types of plants will die out. Natural communities that form along a windswept and dry ridge will thus be very different from communities found at the foot of a slope where there is more abundant and constant moisture. Gravel and sand bars along the White and Connecticut rivers often experience drought conditions by late summer, and big bluestem (*Andropogon gerardii*), a deep-rooted, drought-resistant prairie grass, thrives in these locations as part of the cobble-sand river channel community.

Energy is critical to growth, healing, and reproduction. For animals, energy comes as ingested food. In the hungry winter season, some animals sleep (such as bats and bears) or migrate (such as bank swallows and bluebirds), while others, like white-tailed deer, survive by foraging on woody shrubs and saplings.

Plants need energy as well, in the form of sunlight. The amount of sunlight at a site influences the types of plants that will thrive. Plants also require nutrients, including nitrogen, phosphorus, potassium, calcium, and magnesium, which are found in soil and can come from underlying bedrock. The diversity and character of natural communities is very much shaped by bedrock, soils, and the nutrients they make available for plants. The quality of sunlight through the day also affects natural communities, as shown in Map 27. See also Map 6, Lithology, in Chapter 3, Soils.

Wetlands communities around the John's River in Jefferson, N.H., include spruce–fir–tamarack swamp, alder swamp, and peaty shallow emergent marsh.

The quantity and quality of sunlight is influenced by orientation (aspect) and steepness (slope). Solar radiation is an important determinant in the development of natural communities. Natural communities develop through an elegant and continuous interplay between energy (the Sun) and resource (the Earth). The maps presented here demonstrate the influence of slope and aspect on solar radiation. The analytical process uses elevation changes to determine both slope and aspect at any given point. These values are then utilized to calculate what is known as a *Slope-Aspect Index*. Shading the results, by taking into account the direction of the Sun and its height in the sky (time of day), gives insight into the biological processes driven by the most basic of resources: sunlight.

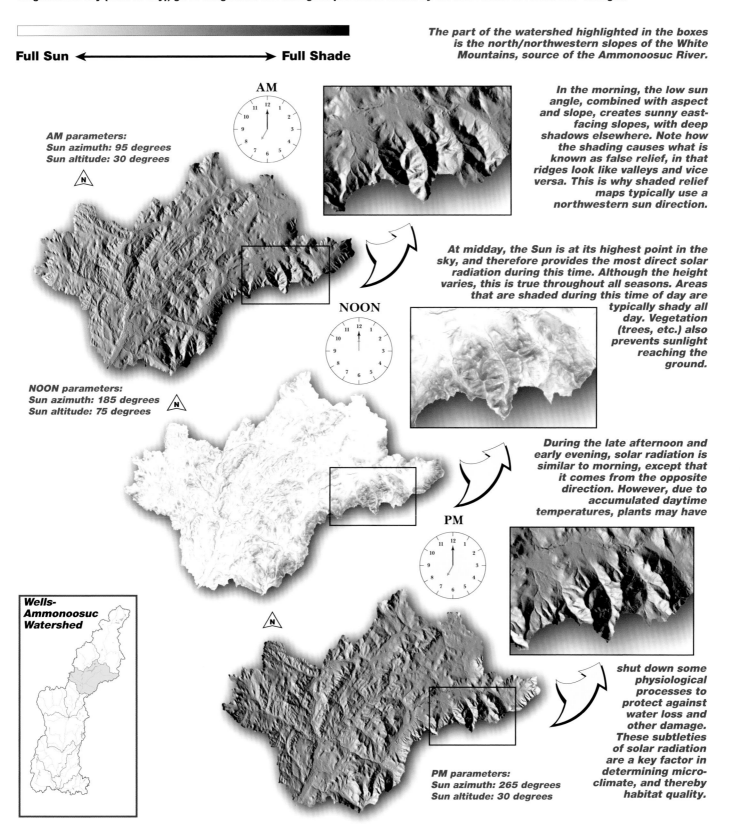

Full Sun ←——————————→ Full Shade

The part of the watershed highlighted in the boxes is the north/northwestern slopes of the White Mountains, source of the Ammonoosuc River.

AM

AM parameters:
Sun azimuth: 95 degrees
Sun altitude: 30 degrees

In the morning, the low sun angle, combined with aspect and slope, creates sunny east-facing slopes, with deep shadows elsewhere. Note how the shading causes what is known as false relief, in that ridges look like valleys and vice versa. This is why shaded relief maps typically use a northwestern sun direction.

At midday, the Sun is at its highest point in the sky, and therefore provides the most direct solar radiation during this time. Although the height varies, this is true throughout all seasons. Areas that are shaded during this time of day are typically shady all day. Vegetation (trees, etc.) also prevents sunlight reaching the ground.

NOON

NOON parameters:
Sun azimuth: 185 degrees
Sun altitude: 75 degrees

During the late afternoon and early evening, solar radiation is similar to morning, except that it comes from the opposite direction. However, due to accumulated daytime temperatures, plants may have

PM

Wells-
Ammonoosuc
Watershed

PM parameters:
Sun azimuth: 265 degrees
Sun altitude: 30 degrees

shut down some physiological processes to protect against water loss and other damage. These subtleties of solar radiation are a key factor in determining micro-climate, and thereby habitat quality.

Map 27. Natural Community Development and Solar Radiation: A Relationship of Aspect and Slope.

Black bears need large amounts of space with varied habitat.

Silver maples and ostrich ferns are dominant species in the floodplain community at Bedell Bridge State Park in Haverhill, N.H.

Cover refers to natural structures (like rock piles or thickets) offering animals places to hide from predators, or shelter from extreme weather. Many animals need special nesting cover for their young. The reproductive stage may be the most precarious for any population. Because of reproductive habitat requirements, foresters often will mark and protect dead standing hardwood trees to provide cavities for nesting birds and other wildlife.

Cover also influences the creation of natural communities. Where cover is scant, such as along a windswept ridge, or a frequently flooded stream terrace, only particular plants will survive. The character and frequency of disturbance is a dramatic and critical factor in the formation of natural communities such as the silver maple–sensitive fern riverine floodplain forest.

Space is often overlooked as a habitat component. The concept includes the idea of minimum territorial space, and even more significantly, optimum ecological space in which critical habitat resources are connected. The importance of space is illustrated by black bears. In southern Vermont, a female black bear ranges over an area of roughly 8,600 acres, or an area the size of the forest on Mount Ascutney. This area cannot accommodate a second female, a male, or the female's grown cubs. Mount Ascutney by itself, therefore, is insufficient in size to maintain a population of black bears. The bears sighted in the nearby valley often are wandering in search of better habitat elsewhere. While the bear population is rebounding in the Connecticut River Valley, bear habitat, or space for bears, is not as extensive as it once was. It is fragmented by roads, farms, and housing developments with the distracting and disastrous temptation offered by bird feeders and household garbage.

Other species are faring well, as their habitat is in greater supply. The upper Connecticut River watershed is considerably more forested now than it was 150 years ago during the height of timber harvesting and agricultural expansion. With this evolution, species including fisher, beaver, and turkeys have been reintroduced or re-entered the region on their own. Moose, once a rarity, are a common site in the northern watershed, and the white-tailed deer population has grown dramatically. Other species have not recovered, such as mountain lions and timber wolves, predators that require large amounts of space unfragmented by human habitation and infrastructure.

The spatial risks for natural communities are related to size and isolation. When natural communities become too small and isolated, they may lose member species and never recruit replacements. Small-sized pockets of natural communities are also more vulnerable to being destroyed by a single event such as a fire, or by the intrusion of invasive species.

The Nature Conservancy has identified a reach between Hanover and Claremont as the Connecticut River Rapids Macrosite. This area has high concentrations of ecologically significant natural communities. Living there are species considered rare, threatened, or endangered species at state, federal, and global levels. If one of these species disappears from the macrosite, it is unlikely to return, for its "replacement population" is too distant. For this reason, of great concern is the growing presence of invasive species, including purple loosestrife, which can crowd out rare species like Jesup's milk-vetch (*Astralagus robbinsii* var. *jesupii*).

Fragmentation of the landscape diminishes biodiversity. Ultimately, the natural communities of the watershed, together with the particular species that live here, depend on the same factors. We all need energy, water, air, cover, and space. To retain the living diversity of the Connecticut River Valley, we need to work with a broad understanding of habitat. To retain the fragile and rare plants and animals, we need to understand the five resource elements of habitat and how they limit populations. To promote the full array of natural diversity in our region, we need to develop a language of natural communities that speaks to the dynamic landscape in the world around us.

Naturalist Ned Swanberg lives in Hartland, Vt., near Sumner Falls in the midst of highly modified mesic red oak–northern hardwood forest.

For Further Reading

DeGraaf, Richard M., and Mariko Yamasaki. 2001. *New England Wildlife: Habitat, Natural History, and Distribution*. (Hanover, N.H.: University Press of New England.

DeGraaf, Richard M., Mariko Yamasaki, William B. Leak, and Anna M. Lester. 2006. *Technical Guide to Forest Wildlife Habitat Management in New England*. Burlington, Vt.: University of Vermont Press.

Sperduto, Daniel, and W. Nichols. 2004. *Natural Communities of New Hampshire*. Concord, N.H.: New Hampshire Natural Heritage Bureau and The Nature Conservancy.

Thompson, E. and E. Sorenson. 2005. *Wetland, Woodland, Wildland: A Guide to the Natural Communities of Vermont*. Waterbury, Vt.: Vermont Department of Fish and Wildlife and The Nature Conservancy.

Wooster, Chuck. 2007. *The Outside Story*. Corinth, Vt.: Northern Woodlands.

Jesup's milk-vetch *(left)* is a rare plant found at the Connecticut River Macrosite, a 15-mile-long stretch in the Upper Valley that harbors a number of very rare plants and animals. Because habitat includes ledges that receive periodic ice scouring, it is affected by how and when water flows through dams. It is also threatened by invasive plants such as Japanese knotweed and purple loosestrife *(above)*.

West Mountain wildlife management area

When land managers consider any given property, large or small, one of the first questions asked is "What is there?" This simple question has a large number of management implications, not the least of which is how to define the resource being managed.

The context in which a manager views the landscape often defines how the landscape is managed. Foresters, wildlife biologists, botanists, and soil scientists, to name a few, were all professions that viewed the landscape from very different perspectives. Often the goals of management favored one use over another, for example timber production over water quality.

In the last decade, there has been a positive movement in management toward the combining of previously separate disciplines. As part of the trend, managers have been defining the landscape in broader ecological terms than previously considered.

Natural community mapping provides one such tool in viewing the ecosystem as an entity, rather than as individual parts. In considering natural communities,

Legend

Natural community types

| Northern hardwood forests |
| Red spruce-hardwood forests |
| Lowland spruce-fir forests |

| Montane forests |
| Riparian / alluvial |
| Open peatland |
| Shrub and herbaceous wetlands |
| Coniferous swamp forests |

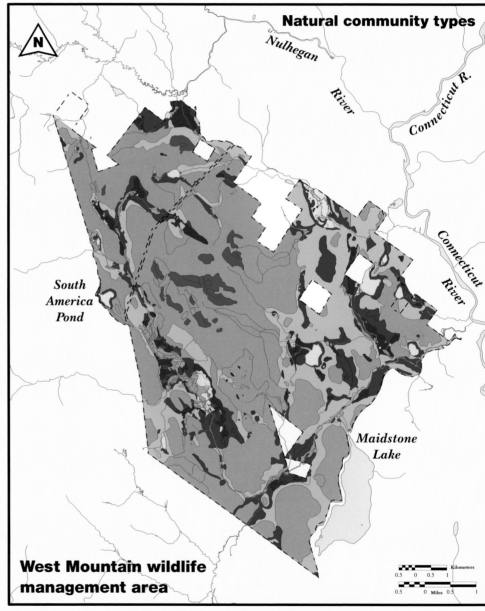

Natural community types

Nulhegan River

Connecticut R.

Connecticut River

South America Pond

Maidstone Lake

West Mountain wildlife management area

Comparative categories of classification

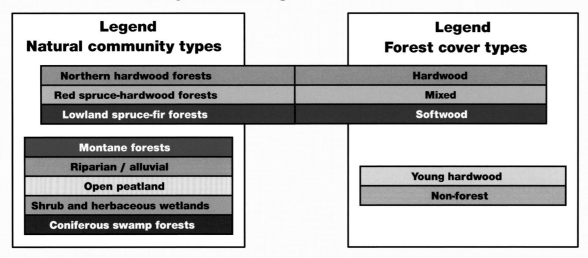

**Legend
Natural community types**

| Northern hardwood forests |
| Red spruce-hardwood forests |
| Lowland spruce-fir forests |

| Montane forests |
| Riparian / alluvial |
| Open peatland |
| Shrub and herbaceous wetlands |
| Coniferous swamp forests |

**Legend
Forest cover types**

| Hardwood |
| Mixed |
| Softwood |

| Young hardwood |
| Non-forest |

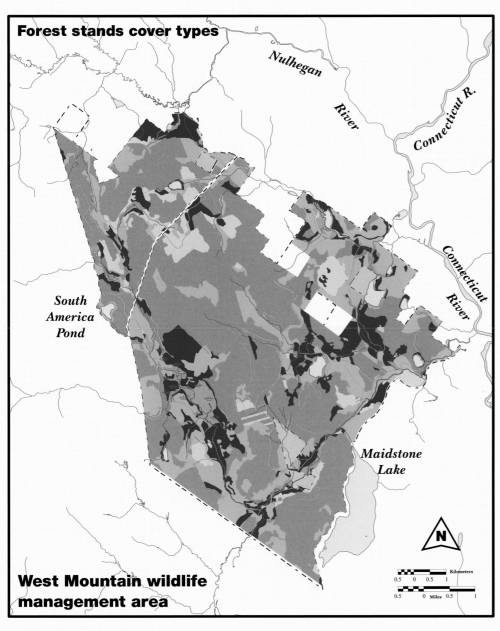

Forest stands cover types

Nulhegan River

Connecticut R.

South America Pond

Connecticut River

Maidstone Lake

West Mountain wildlife management area

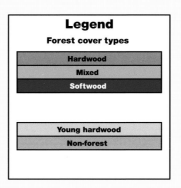

0.5 0 0.5   1   Kilometers

0.5   0 Miles 0.5   1

managers include a range of ecosystem functions and characteristics.

One of the first examples of natural community mapping in the watershed was undertaken by the State of Vermont and the U.S. Fish & Wildlife Service when they purchased and conserved a large block of previously commercial timberland in the Northeast Kingdom. The maps displayed here are of the West Mountain wildlife management area, and show the subtle, but important, differences in forest stand mapping and natural-community based mapping. Note through the legend how more specific detail is provided with natural communities. This distinction allows managers to consider the individual natural communities, rather than over-looking them within categories more conducive to resource extraction than ecosystem management.

Legend

Forest cover types

| Hardwood |
| Mixed |
| Softwood |

| Young hardwood |
| Non-forest |

SOURCES: Base maps: VCGI and Northern Cartographic datasets. Natural community data and forest stands data: Vermont Department of Parks and Recreation, derived from Champion Lands Management Plan.

13 Forests

Trees, like this magnificent oak in Vernon, Vt., are a foundation of the watershed's ecosystem.

The Nature of Forests

For millennia, forests have dominated the landscape of the upper Connecticut River Valley. Broadleaf, deciduous trees (beech, birch, maple) mixed with scattered conifers (hemlock, pine, spruce) grow over the rolling hills stretching away from the river. A moist, seasonal climate and relatively young glacial soils are conducive to the growth, reproduction, and maintenance of these temperate tree species. In the absence of catastrophic disturbances, these forests naturally maintain an unbroken coverage and continuously replace themselves.

Trees are a foundation of the ecosystem. They produce vast amounts of food energy via photosynthesis, which is the beginning of most terrestrial and water-based food chains. Forests also control microclimates, water flow, and the recycling of nutrients within terrestrial ecosystems.

The role of forests goes beyond what is immediately visible. Roots are a substantial part of any tree and dominate much of the below-ground environment. Even after they die, trees continue to play an essential role in the ecosystem, from sheltering invertebrates in fallen logs, to providing nutrients and organic matter for fungus and microbes as the wood decays.

Forests are one of the most visible and influential components of the watershed's landscape. Because of this, the condition of the forest becomes a prominent indicator of the overall integrity and health of the Connecticut River Valley.

History

Studies of tree pollen deposited in lake sediments give us a picture of species and their relative abundance after the retreat of the last glaciers (Davis et al. 1980). Spruce, fir, poplar, birch, and pine were the first species to reestablish. They later were joined by oak and maple approximately 10,500 years ago, hemlock (9,000 years ago), and beech (7,500 years ago). Only 2,000 years ago, American chestnut (*Castanea dentata*) advanced into southern Vermont, and from isolated populations along the foggy coast, red spruce (*Picea rubens*) expanded inland to cover mountain slopes.

Each species moved at a different rate following a different route as successive generations "migrated" into the formerly glaciated landscape. The trees entered New England from the south and, generally following the lower elevations, took several thousand more years to become fully established at the northern and higher elevations. The early forests of boreal conifers gradually transformed to pine–oak and then hemlock–northern hardwood (beech–birch–maple) forests. Even after current species became established, changes continued to occur in the New England forests. About 5,000 years ago, the hemlock virtually disappeared throughout its range, including the Connecticut River Valley, most likely as the result of an insect predator. Interestingly, hemlock took several thousand years to recover and today has returned to its previous abundance, although insect predation is again threatening in the form of the invasive wooly adelgid (*Adelges tsugae*).

Forest Geography

Today, northern New England supports a mosaic of plant communities that are direct descendants of forests established after the last glacial age. This ancient pattern is seen in the current range and abundance of tree species across the watershed. For example, oaks are distributed widely on the southern uplands, but their range narrows farther northwards until they are just found on dry south-facing hills near the river or are mere threads along the banks of the Connecticut River and its larger tributaries.

To the north, yellow birch (*Betula alleghaniensis*) and other hardwoods increasingly become mixed with fir and spruce. In the Nulhegan Basin of northeastern Vermont and the upper elevations of Coös County, N.H., are widespread conifer-dominated forests. Similarly, at higher elevations in the White and Green mountains the cool, cloudy forests are dominated by mountain conifers, especially balsam fir (*Abies balsamea*).

To the south, one finds such so-called "southern" hardwoods as oak, and pitch pine (*Pinus rigida*) forests. What some scientists call the "New England tension zone" marks the quite dramatic transition from northern to southern hardwoods. This line crosses all of southern New England, looping northward up the Connecticut River to roughly Charlestown, N.H. Isolated islands of southern species extend even farther north along the river corridor in Vermont, with red oak (*Quercus rubra*) reaching as far as Maidstone, Vt.; white oak (*Quercus alba*) to Ryegate, Vt.; bitternut hickory (*Carya cordiformis*) and pitch pine to Newbury, Vt.; shagbark hickory (*Carya ovata*) to Norwich, Vt.; and black oak (*Quercus velutina*) to Windsor, Vt. These species, together with white pine (*Pinus strobus*), generally tolerate fire and vigorously sprout after wildfire. Southern New England and parts of the Connecticut River Valley, with a warmer climate, drier soils, and larger Native American populations, had a distinct history of wildfire that favored this suite of southern trees (Day 1953). Chapter 15, Flora, discusses other tree species that reach their range limits in the watershed.

Forest Communities

The watershed's conifers and broadleaved deciduous tree species assemble into many natural communities (see the previous chapter for a discussion of natural communities in the watershed). The most widespread type is hemlock–white pine–northern hardwoods, dominated by communities of its namesake temperate conifers, plus beech, yellow birch, and sugar maple (Braun 1950).

The mosaic of forest communities is not random. If one knows the

Sturdy red spruce, which expanded into the northern watershed only about 2,000 years ago, was a prime species for nineteenth-century timber harvesting.

geographic setting, particularly the elevation, topography, and soil conditions, the composition of a particular forest can be predicted accurately.

Some other widespread natural forest communities and their dominant tree species are (Thompson and Sorenson 2000):

- balsam fir, mountain birch (*Betula lenta*) and red spruce forests: found on the slopes of the higher hills and mountains;
- spruce forests: rocky ledges, in wet depressions, or lakeshores;
- beech (*Fagus grandifolia*), yellow birch, red spruce forests: glacial till soils at moderate elevation;
- beech and yellow birch: infertile schist and granitic soils, especially in New Hampshire;
- sugar maple (*Acer saccharum*) with butternut (*Juglans cinerea*), basswood (*Tilia americana*), and white ash (*Fraxinus americana*) forest: nutrient-rich soils or lime-rich rocks, especially in Vermont;

Tamaracks, which turn golden in the fall, contrast with black spruce and other Northern Forest conifers in Jefferson, N.H., on the watershed's eastern edge, framed by the White Mountains.

- black spruce (*Picea mariana*), northern white cedar (*Thuja occidentalis*), and black ash (*Fraxinus nigra*) forests: poorly drained lowlands, swamps, and bogs;
- hemlock (*Tsuga canadensis*) forest: poor thin soils and in cool ravines, especially in the southern uplands;
- silver maple (*Acer saccharinum*), cottonwood (*Populus deltoides*), elm (*Ulmus americana*), sycamore (*Platanus occidentalis*) forests: lower river terraces of the floodplain;
- pitch and white pines: sandy floodplains;
- red oak forests: south-facing slope of hills and river banks;
- white birch (*Betula papyrifera*), white pine, cherry (*Prunus serotina*), and aspen (*Betula populifolia*, locally known as "popple"): severely disturbed forests.

Human Legacies

Comparison of the current forest composition with forests at the time of European settlement shows that the relative abundance of the species has shifted dramatically (see "Witness Trees," p. 85). Beech is 15 percent of what it was 200 years ago and hemlock is 40 percent of what it used to be. Meanwhile, maple and birch have doubled their proportion of the forest. Species that occur in second-growth forests (fir, poplar, and cherries) have increased by five- to tenfold. White pine has increased 50 percent. Maps 28 and 29 show the forest conditions in the watershed by county, circa 1800 and circa 1997.

Snapshots of forest conditions 200 years apart tell only part of the story. In between, the valley experienced dramatic loss and then regrowth of forests. By the end of the nineteenth century, virtually the entire watershed was altered as farmers cleared the forests and loggers cut the woodlands. Land that had been 98 percent forested became on average only 55 percent forest by 1880 (Harper 1918).

The actual amount of forest clearing varied greatly by county. In southern areas, the clearing peaked by 1850, while in the north it was at least 30 years later. Windsor and Orange counties were cleared to only 30 percent forest, but Coös County retained 87 percent of its forest. In general, mountainous and northern areas were less suitable for agriculture and were often just cut for timber. The southern half of the Connecticut River Valley was left with only 33 percent forest, although in recent years it has grown back and is now 80 percent forest.

Today, forested land shows evidence of at least five distinctly different past uses. Specifically, a forest may never have been cut, or may have been industrial or commercial timberland, a farm woodlot, a pasture, or tilled land. Map 30 illustrates the proportion of current forests with these particular human histories. Many examples of these legacies may be seen on the ground. White pine thrive on the former cleared fields in the valleys, sugarbushes grow in old farm woodlots, and northern hardwood forests cover the mountain slopes where the red spruce has been removed permanently by logging.

Future Forests

While natural conditions of soil, topography, and climate are still primary influences, current changes in forest patterns increasingly are caused by humans. In the last 100 years, the Connecticut River Valley has been changing once again as former agricultural land gradually returns to forest. At the same time, growth and development has converted many forests to residential or commercial land use.

Many of the original tree species remain dominant in the region,

Light-tolerant white birch is one of the first tree species to grow back after a harvest, ice storm, or other disturbance. It is the state tree of New Hampshire.

Beech and yellow birch populate a rocky New Hampshire hillside formerly pastured for sheep.

Northern hardwoods cast autumn colors. In the future, these could give way to more southern species like oak and hickory.

but the status of several has changed. The decline in chestnut, elm, butternut, beech, and potentially hemlock all are due largely to insects or diseases imported by humans. As the climate changes, species composition is expected to shift, with a decline in species like sugar maple, which is valuable as saw timber, for fall foliage, and for maple syrup, and an increase in more southern species like hickory and oak. Natural disturbances such as hurricanes, ice storms, snow breakage, insect outbreaks, and thunderstorms will continue, possibly with greater frequency or intensity as a result of climate change. In the future, much of the watershed will support forests, but substantially altered from the presettlement conditions. Especially in the former farmlands of the valley, future forests will be young, relatively homogeneous, dominated by fewer species, simple in structure, and infested by alien species. Forests still will dominate the valley, but with a different character from today.

Charles V. Cogbill is a freelance ecologist living in Plainfield, Vt. He was educated at Dartmouth College, Cornell University, and the University of Toronto and currently is associated with several academic institutions. He is engaged actively in research on historical ecology of the Northeast and in field studies on the vegetation of eastern North America.

FOR FURTHER READING

Davis, M. B., R. W. Spear, and L. C. K. Shane. 1980. Holocene climate of New England. *Quaternary Research* 14: 240–50.

Harper, R. M. 1918. Changes in the forest area of New England in three centuries. *Journal of Forestry* 16: 442–52.

Wessels, T. 1999. *Reading the Forested Landscape.* Woodstock, Vt.: Countryman Press.

Whitney, G. G. 1994. *From Coastal Wilderness to Fruited Plain.* New York: Cambridge University Press.

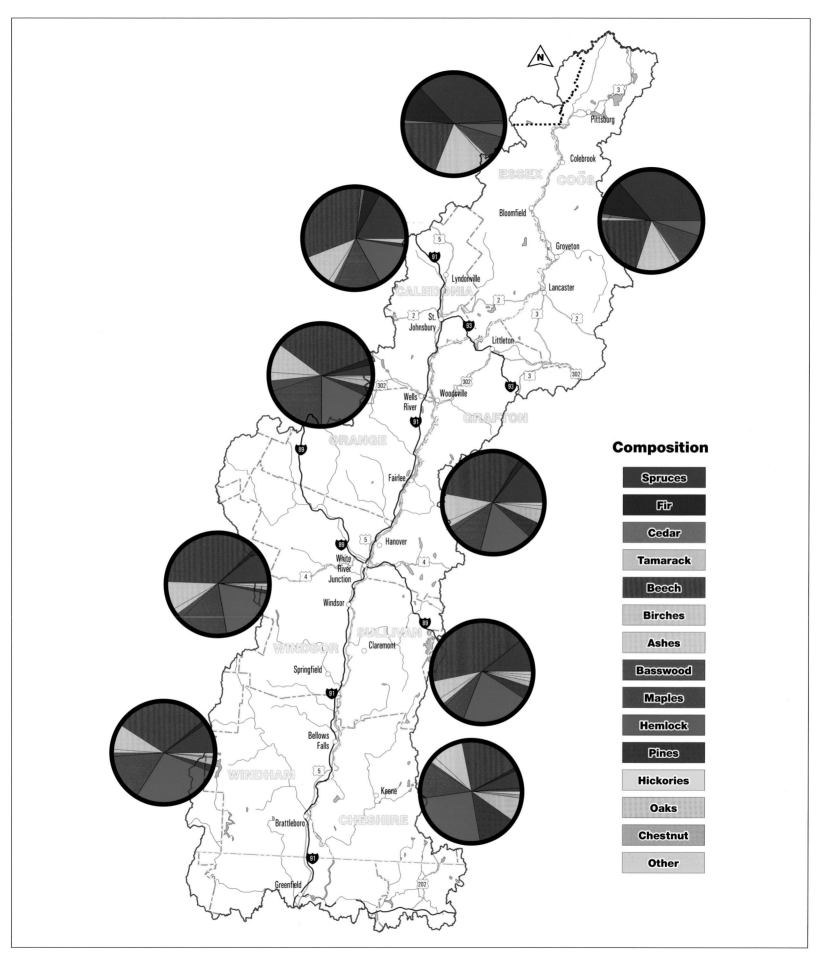

Map 28. Forest Composition in the Upper Connecticut River Watershed, Circa 1800.

Composition

- Spruces
- Fir
- Cedar
- Tamarack
- Beech
- Birches
- Ashes
- Basswood
- Maples
- Hemlock
- Pines
- Hickories
- Oaks
- Chestnut
- Other

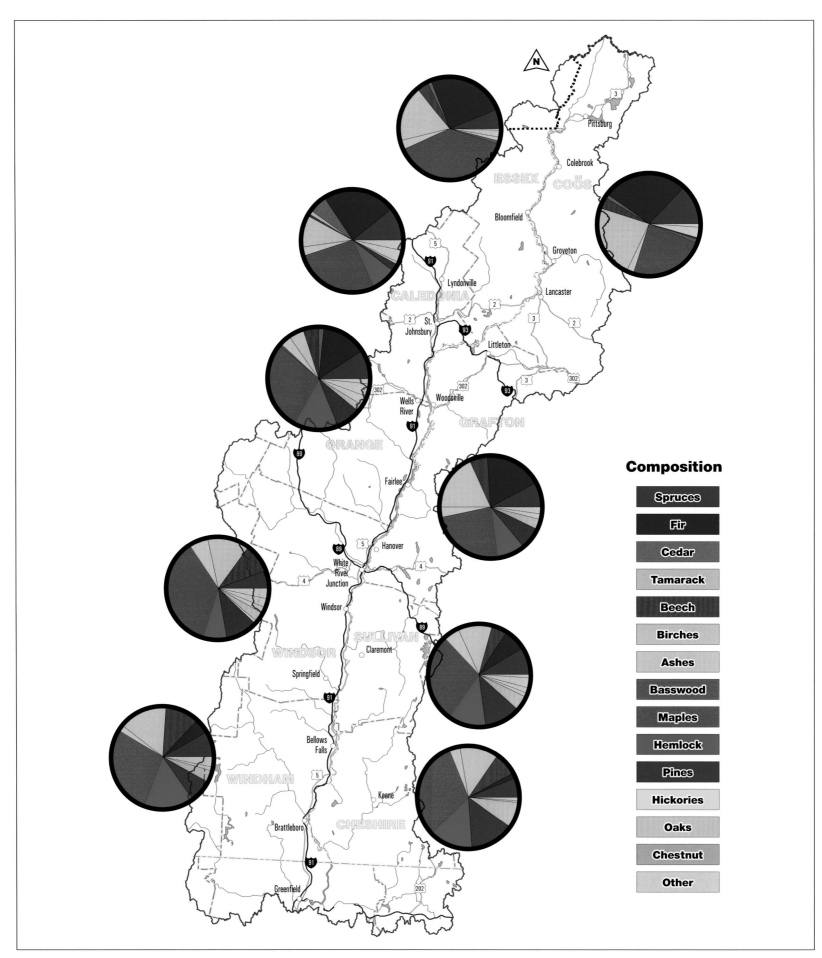

Map 29. Forest Composition in the Upper Connecticut River Watershed, Circa 1997.

Composition

Spruces
Fir
Cedar
Tamarack
Beech
Birches
Ashes
Basswood
Maples
Hemlock
Pines
Hickories
Oaks
Chestnut
Other

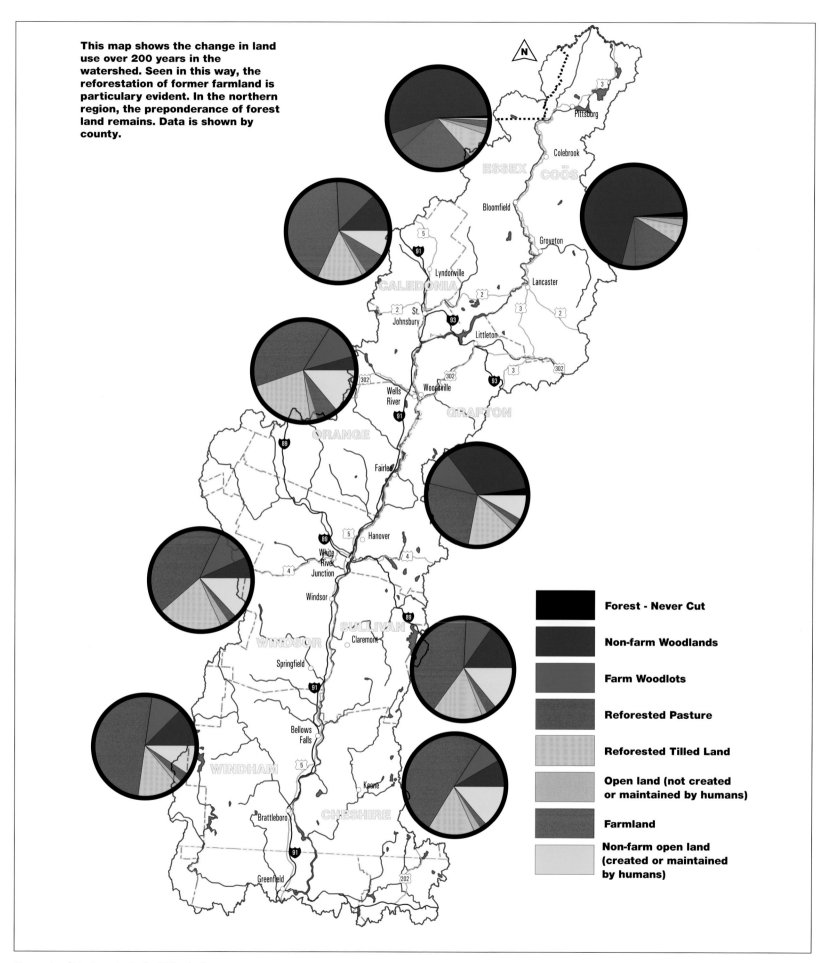

This map shows the change in land use over 200 years in the watershed. Seen in this way, the reforestation of former farmland is particulary evident. In the northern region, the preponderance of forest land remains. Data is shown by county.

Forest - Never Cut

Non-farm Woodlands

Farm Woodlots

Reforested Pasture

Reforested Tilled Land

Open land (not created or maintained by humans)

Farmland

Non-farm open land (created or maintained by humans)

Map 30. Land Use Legacies in the Watershed.

14 Wetlands

Wetlands are just what their name implies: places where soils are permanently saturated or are wet for significant periods. These conditions lead to distinct "hydric" soils and groups of plants and animals often not found in uplands or in open water. While wetlands occupy a small portion of the landscape, their importance for biodiversity and watershed health is enormous. In addition to providing habitat for a variety of animal and plant species, wetlands also serve critical functions as water filters. They trap sediments, excessive nutrients, and toxins, and act as great sponges that help prevent flooding. River and lakeshore wetlands also help prevent soil erosion.

The understanding of the critical function of wetlands is a fairly recent phenomenon. For years, these soggy, mosquito-infested places were seen as impediments to more obvious economically valuable uses like commercial or residential development and agriculture, and they often were drained and filled. Now, their importance has been recognized in state and federal laws established to protect them or at least minimize damage when land is developed.

Wetland Ecology

Wetlands often lie between uplands and aquatic environments such as lakes and streams. Wetlands may occur in basins or general low points of land; in drainages or at or near the bottom of slopes; and also on slopes themselves where there is groundwater discharge. As part of the great hydrological cycle, wetlands are fed by rain, surface-water runoff, and groundwater, and drained by evapotranspiration, streams, and seepage below ground.

A critical variable of wetland ecology is the duration of water in the soil. For example, a bog has permanently saturated soil, while the soil of a floodplain forest is saturated only periodically. Different water saturation periods lead to the formation of different types of soils. Two of the most common wetland soil types are *muck* and *gley*. Muck soils are found in many permanently saturated wetlands. They are formed by the decay of organic debris such as leaves and twigs in a largely anaerobic, or oxygen-free, environment, and are typically black in color. A layer of muck soil may be a few inches or many feet deep.

In contrast, gley soils are composed of mineral particles (clay, silt, sand), with little or no organic matter. They often are characterized by striking grey or blue-grey coloring. Like muck, gley soils result from a lack of oxygen in the soil. Gley layers frequently are found below muck soil surface layers. (See Chapter 3, Soils.)

Wetland Classifications

Because of different hydrology, soils, and local climate, many different types of wetlands are found in the Connecticut River watershed. Marshes and swamps are among the most common wetlands in the region. Bogs and floodplains are less common types.

There are different systems for classifying specific types of wetlands. The U.S. Fish and Wildlife Service developed one of the first national classification systems, now the basis for National Wetlands Inventory (NWI) maps. Map 31 depicts the three major wetland systems in the watershed according to the NWI. Map 32 depicts the relationship between the wetlands inventory and wetland types. Many town planning boards and other government agencies rely on NWI maps. Map 33 shows a sample wetlands inventory for Lyme, N.H.

A newer way of categorizing wetlands is by natural community classification. As described in Chapter 12, natural communities are characterized by particular species of plants, consistent physical structure, and key physical features, such as water availability or elevation. For instance, we may refer generally to a wetland area, or "community" along the Connecticut River as a floodplain forest, and identify it specifically as a "silver maple–wood nettle–ostrich fern floodplain forest," named for its dominant plant species. Using the Vermont natural community classification names, some of the most common wetlands in the watershed are shallow emergent marsh, alder swamp, and spruce–fir–tamarack swamp.

Marshes and Swamps

Shallow emergent marshes and alder swamps are natural communities commonly associated with old beaver ponds. These communities often form when beavers abandon their ponds, leaving their dams to deteriorate and water to escape. As the water level drops, mud is exposed along the pond bottom, and a variety of grasses, especially bluejoint (*Calamagrostis canadensis*), sedges, and herbs such as spotted Joe-pye weed (*Eupatorium maculatum*), begin to colonize. A familiar type of shallow emergent marsh is the cattail marsh. The common cattail (*Typha latifolia*) is emblematic of these marshes, but increasingly, the invasive purple loosestrife (*Lythrum salicaria*) is crowding them out. Typical birds include red-winged blackbirds, swamp sparrows, and American bitterns.

In the process called succession, the grasses and sedges of the emergent marsh give way to woody shrubs, such as speckled alder (*Alnus incana* subsp. *rugosa*), as soils build up from decomposing plant matter

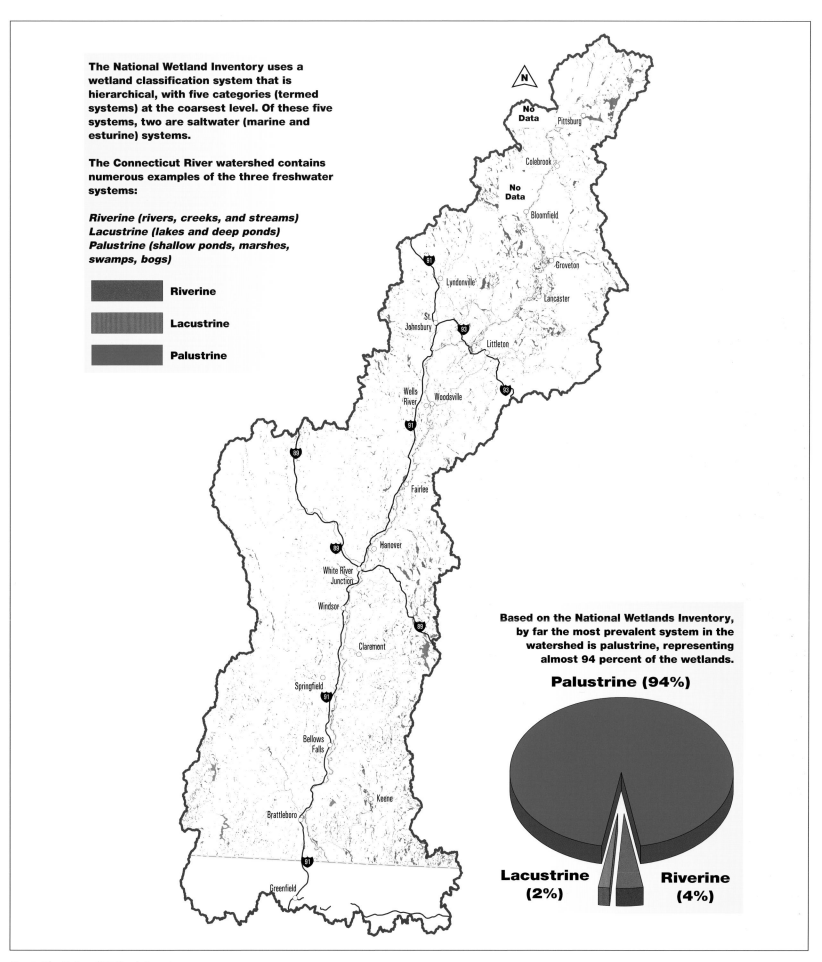

The National Wetland Inventory uses a wetland classification system that is hierarchical, with five categories (termed systems) at the coarsest level. Of these five systems, two are saltwater (marine and esturine) systems.

The Connecticut River watershed contains numerous examples of the three freshwater systems:

Riverine (rivers, creeks, and streams)
Lacustrine (lakes and deep ponds)
Palustrine (shallow ponds, marshes, swamps, bogs)

█ **Riverine**

▒ **Lacustrine**

█ **Palustrine**

Based on the National Wetlands Inventory, by far the most prevalent system in the watershed is palustrine, representing almost 94 percent of the wetlands.

Palustrine (94%)

Lacustrine (2%)

Riverine (4%)

Map 31. The National Wetlands Inventory.

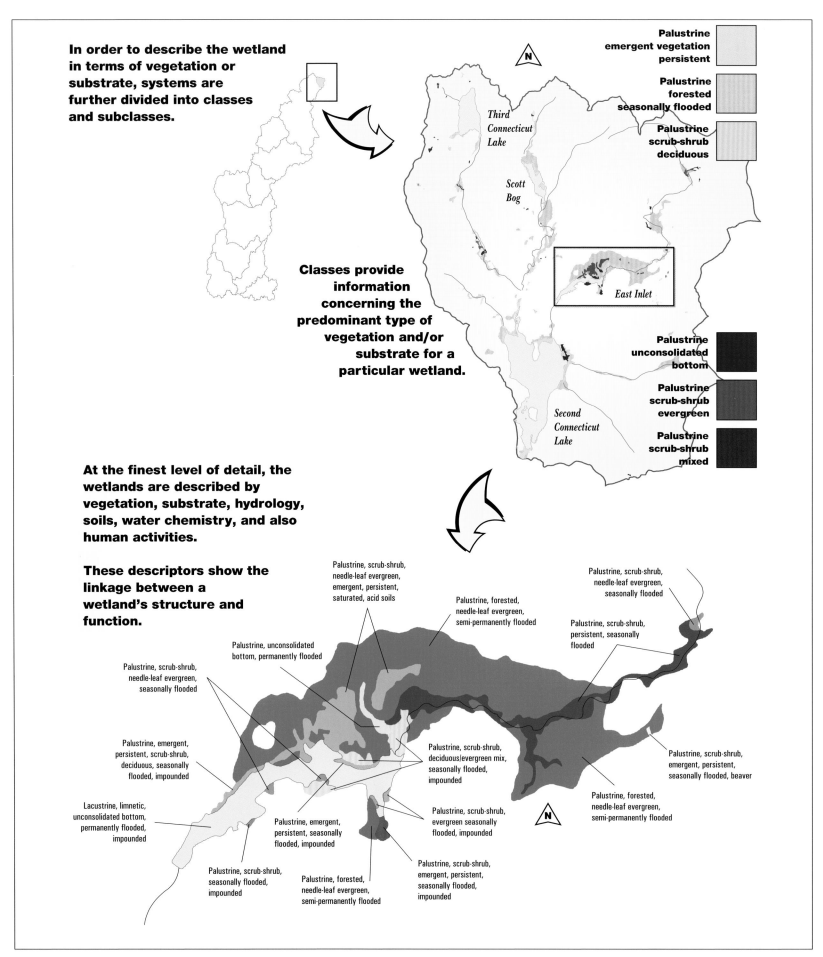

In order to describe the wetland in terms of vegetation or substrate, systems are further divided into classes and subclasses.

Palustrine emergent vegetation persistent

Palustrine forested seasonally flooded

Palustrine scrub-shrub deciduous

Third Connecticut Lake

Scott Bog

East Inlet

Palustrine unconsolidated bottom

Palustrine scrub-shrub evergreen

Palustrine scrub-shrub mixed

Second Connecticut Lake

Classes provide information concerning the predominant type of vegetation and/or substrate for a particular wetland.

At the finest level of detail, the wetlands are described by vegetation, substrate, hydrology, soils, water chemistry, and also human activities.

These descriptors show the linkage between a wetland's structure and function.

Palustrine, scrub-shrub, needle-leaf evergreen, emergent, persistent, saturated, acid soils

Palustrine, forested, needle-leaf evergreen, semi-permanently flooded

Palustrine, scrub-shrub, needle-leaf evergreen, seasonally flooded

Palustrine, scrub-shrub, persistent, seasonally flooded

Palustrine, unconsolidated bottom, permanently flooded

Palustrine, scrub-shrub, needle-leaf evergreen, seasonally flooded

Palustrine, emergent, persistent, scrub-shrub, deciduous, seasonally flooded, impounded

Palustrine, scrub-shrub, deciduous/evergreen mix, seasonally flooded, impounded

Palustrine, scrub-shrub, emergent, persistent, seasonally flooded, beaver

Lacustrine, limnetic, unconsolidated bottom, permanently flooded, impounded

Palustrine, emergent, persistent, seasonally flooded, impounded

Palustrine, scrub-shrub, evergreen seasonally flooded, impounded

Palustrine, forested, needle-leaf evergreen, semi-permanently flooded

Palustrine, scrub-shrub, seasonally flooded, impounded

Palustrine, forested, needle-leaf evergreen, semi-permanently flooded

Palustrine, scrub-shrub, emergent, persistent, seasonally flooded, impounded

Map 32. The National Wetlands Inventory: Wetland Types.

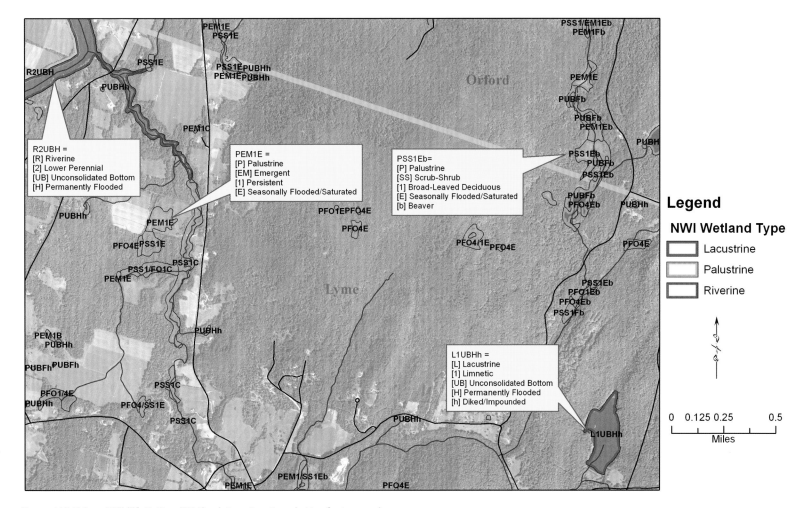

Map 33. U.S. Fish and Wildlife National Wetlands Inventory Sample Map for Lyme and Orford, N.H.

and other conditions slowly change. The 6- to 12-foot-tall woody shrub structure of an alder swamp provides habitat for additional species of birds such as alder flycatchers and other animals including numerous insects and other invertebrate species. A spruce–fir–tamarack swamp, which occurs on deep muck soil, is dominated by its named conifers, and typically has a well-developed layer of 2- to 3-foot-tall cinnamon ferns (*Osmunda cinnamomea*) and hummocky ground carpeted with bog mosses (*Sphagnum* spp.)

Another distinctive wetland that contains peat and muck soils is the red maple–black gum swamp. While unusual in the watershed, this type of swamp is found in some isolated basins perched atop rocky ridges in the southernmost part of the region. With maturity, black gum trees (*Nyssa sylvatica*) grow bark with blocky, flat-topped ridges unlike any other hardwood tree in the region. Black gums may grow very old, and ancient trees are one of the distinctive features of this rare type of wetland. One black gum in Vernon, Vt., has been aged at 435 years, and black gum in nearby swamps of southeastern New Hampshire have been documented at 562 years! These venerable New Hampshire black gum are the oldest documented trees in New England, and possibly the oldest broadleaf deciduous trees in North America. A good place to visit a red maple–black gum swamp is the J. Maynard Miller Town Forest in Vernon.

Bogs and Fens

Bogs and fens are less common wetlands occurring in the Connecticut River Valley. Bogs usually are isolated from significant surface and groundwater flow, and are most frequent in regions of acidic soils and bedrock. This isolation creates acid, nutrient-poor peat soils that support a very distinct flora, including an abundance of bog mosses (*Sphagnum* spp.) and insectivorous flowering plants, such as pitcher plant (*Sarracenia purpurea*) and sundew (*Drosera rotundifolia*). A preponderance of low heath shrubs, as well as stunted and lollipop-shaped black spruce (*Picea mariana*), are also common to bogs. Several rare dragonfly and butterfly species, such as the bog copper butterfly, are associated with bogs as well as that great symbol of the north, the moose. A floating mat of mosses—which moves or "quakes" when walked upon—also may surround the open water frequently found in the center of bogs.

The Mollie Beattie Bog within the Nulhegan Division of the Silvio O. Conte National Fish and Wildlife Refuge in Brunswick, Vt., the New London Conservation Commission's Philbrick-Cricenti Bog in New London, N.H., and the Pondicherry National Wildlife Refuge in Jefferson and Whitefield, N.H., are excellent places to explore bog natural communities in the watershed.

In contrast to bogs, fens are open peatlands that are influenced

Shallow emergent marshes and alder swamps are natural communities commonly associated with old beaver ponds. The grassy mound in the foreground of this Lisbon, N.H., marsh is a beaver house abandoned for several years. The earlier wetlands was spruce–fir–tamarack, and may revert back to that condition as the pond fills in and a succession of vegetation grows. These old conifer swamps attract cavity-nesting birds to the dead snags. More than one wetland type may be found together as a wetlands complex.

Cherry Pond at the Pondicherry National Wildlife Refuge in Whitefield and Jefferson, N.H., is bordered by spruce–fir–tamarack swamp. In the foreground is rhodora (*Rhododendron canadense*), a common species of peaty bogs and swamps.

primarily by groundwater, making the soil less acidic. Dominant vegetation includes sedges and herbaceous species. Fens, especially the most nutrient-rich types known as "rich fens," occur in regions where the bedrock contains lime. The Connecticut River Valley, particularly Vermont's White River watershed, has some of the best rich fens in the northeastern United States. Eshqua Bog in Hartland, owned jointly by the New England Wildflower Society and The Nature Conservancy, is an excellent example of a rich fen. Visitors to Eshqua Bog during the first half of July may be treated to blossoming showy lady's slipper (*Cypripedium reginae*), an uncommon orchid most frequently found in fens.

Floodplain Forests

A floodplain forest is a wetland with soils created by the cyclical deposition of sands and silts during floods. The layered soils of a floodplain, known as alluvial soils, are recycled completely when over many years, a river's channel shifts position, thereby eroding banks and depositing sediment downstream. The nonorganic soils of these wetlands can be deceptively dry for most of the year. But during floods, these soils can be inundated with water.

The classic floodplain natural community is the silver maple–ostrich fern riverine floodplain forest. With a potential height of over 100 feet and girth of over 30 inches, cottonwood (*Populus deltoides*) is also a characteristic canopy species of this community. This floodplain community is found along the main stem of the Connecticut River on stretches where the river gradient is low and its channel tends to meander. Because of the associated highly fertile, stone-free soils, most of this unique wetland forest type was converted to agricultural fields during European settlement. More recently, the construction of dams and the resulting reservoirs flooded out large areas of riparian forest. Good places to see remaining floodplain forests are the White River Wildlife Management Area in Sharon, Vt., the Cheshire County Farm in Westmoreland, N.H., and along the Connecticut River at Maidstone Bends. Additional characteristics of floodplain forests are found in Chapter 15, Flora.

Some of the largest wetlands in the region occur in the upper reaches of the watershed, especially the Nulhegan Basin in Essex County, Vt., and the Connecticut Lakes Headwaters Natural Area in Pittsburg, N.H. In these areas, wetlands form large complexes of several natural communities grading into one another, as well as occurring in isolated units scattered across the landscape.

Vernal Pools

Vernal pools are wetlands communities characterized by drying out. These small, isolated depressions are wet only seasonally, usually in the spring and fall, when rain and snowmelt fill them. They typically dry out in the summer. Because of this wet/dry cycle, fish can't survive in vernal pools. Without fish predation, a host of invertebrates, reptiles, and amphibians breed and feed in them. Of course, other predators are drawn to vernal pools, including otters, herons, and raccoons. The animals that live there, not the plants, define vernal pools biologically (Sperduto and Nichols 2004). Characteristic inhabitants include spring

The showy lady slipper is a beautiful and uncommon orchid most frequently found in the watershed's rich fens.

Silver maples like these along the Connecticut River in Newbury, Vt., are adapted to living through periods of inundation, or flood.

The Yellow Branch of the Nulhegan River in Lewis, Vt., part of the Silvio O. Conte National Fish and Wildlife Refuge, flows through a mosaic of wetland natural communities typical of northern New England. Among them are spruce–fir–tamarack swamp, black spruce swamp, alder swamp, and peaty shallow emergent marsh.

A woodland vernal pool in Sugar Hill, N.H. *(above)*, attracts spotted salamanders, wood frogs, and spring peepers for courtship and breeding in the absence of predatory fish. By August *(above right)*, the pool has dried up.

peepers, the diminutive frogs whose piercing calls herald the beginning of spring in the Connecticut River Valley. Because of the uniqueness of vernal pools and their importance to wildlife, some towns are now identifying and mapping their vernal pools so they might be left undisturbed when land is developed.

There are many other types of fascinating wetland natural communities that are beyond the scope of this brief chapter, including dynamic wetland river cobble shore, the small forest seep, northern white cedar swamp, and even small peat lands unique to the alpine areas of the White Mountains. Whether large or small, there are wetlands in every town that contribute to biodiversity and flood control, and many can be visited. Each one is unique and adds tremendously to the overall biodiversity of an area.

Brett Engstrom is a field naturalist living in Marshfield, Vt. For the past 17 years, he has inventoried natural communities and rare, threatened, and endangered plants throughout northern New England and adjacent New York. He holds a B.A. in biology from Earlham College and a M.S. in the field naturalist program at the University of Vermont.

FOR FURTHER READING

Johnson, Charles W. 1985. *Bogs of the Northeast*. Hanover, N.H.: University Press of New England.

Sperduto, Daniel D., and William F. Nichols. 2004. *Natural Communities of New Hampshire*. Concord, N.H.: New Hampshire Natural Heritage Bureau and The Nature Conservancy.

Thompson, Elizabeth H., and Eric R. Sorenson. 2005. *Wetland, Woodland, Wildland: A Guide to the Natural Communities of Vermont*. Waterbury, Vt.: Vermont Department of Fish and Wildlife and The Nature Conservancy of Vermont.

Tiner, R. W. 1998. *In Search of Swampland: A Wetland Sourcebook and Field Guide*. New Brunswick, N.J.: Rutgers University Press.

15 Flora

St. John's wort (*Hypericum perforatum*, the yellow flower) and invasive purple loosestrife (*Lythrum salicaria*) at Dodge Falls, in Monroe, N.H.

The flora of New England includes species with geographic distributions ranging in size from most of eastern North America to less than one acre. The flora of the Connecticut River valley reflects this mix, with some species found broadly and others with very limited ranges. The river itself is a dynamic system, actively contributing to the mix of species and natural communities as it creates and changes habitats over the course of seasons and millennia.

The flora changes remarkably as one proceeds upriver, with some southern plants reaching the northern limit of their ranges, while other northern species reach their southern limit, as discussed in Chapter 13, Forests. In the river-bottom forests of southern New Hampshire and Vermont along the Connecticut River and its tributaries, one finds the stately sycamore tree (*Platanus occidentalis*). Never far from water, this large tree with mottled white and brown bark occurs as far north as Windsor County, Vt., and Sullivan County, N.H. Other species that reach the northern limit of their range in the Upper Valley region include the black birch (*Betula lenta*), Eastern red cedar (*Juniperus virginiana*), and the bladdernut (*Staphylea trifolia*). Range limits of several species are shown in Map 34.

Farther north, in the vicinity of St. Johnsbury, Vt., near the confluence with the Passumpsic River, hackberry (*Celtis occidentalis*) and ironwood (also called American hornbeam or musclewood, *Carpinus caroliniana*), reach the northern limits of their ranges in the Connecticut River Valley. These two species extend farther to the north in Orleans and Franklin counties of Vermont.

Red oak (*Quercus rubra*) generally is scarce north of the Connecticut River Valley towns of Waterford, Vt., and Monroe, N.H. However, it does occur at upper elevations in eastern Coös County, N.H., and at lower elevation sites in Guildhall and Maidstone, Vt. Proceeding northward, one encounters plants such as the satin willow (*Salix pellita*), a northern species that reaches the southern limit of its range in Essex County, Vt., and Coös County, N.H.

There are also east to west changes in flora, apparently associated with differences in the geology of the two sides of the river (see Map 6 in Chapter 3, Soils). East of the river, the soils are derived from granitic bedrock and are more acidic. West of the river, soils derived from metamorphic rocks have a higher pH and calcium content. A few species, such as the bog aster (*Aster nemoralis*), are restricted almost entirely to the region east of the river, although one station occurs on the west side in Essex County. Similarly, the great St. John's-wort (*Hypericum pyramidatum*), a riparian plant of the Midwest, reaches the eastern limit of its range along the Connecticut River.

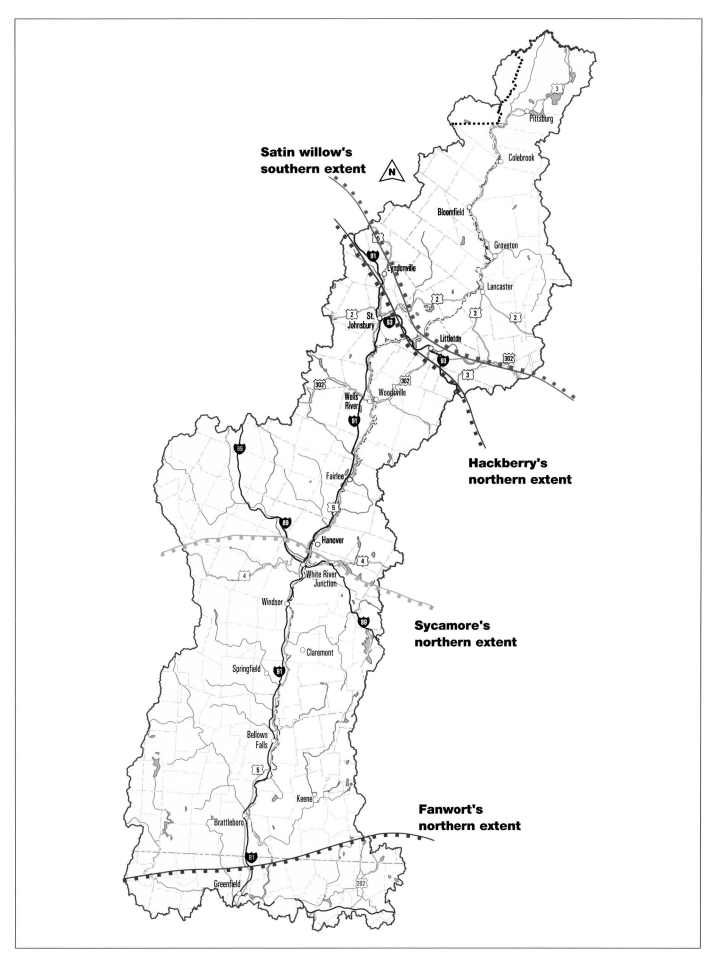

Map 34. Northern and Southern Extents of Selected Species in the Watershed.

Floodplain Forest

The most extensive riparian community in the Connecticut River Valley is the floodplain forest, which at one time covered most low-lying areas (see Chapter 14, Wetlands).

Trees of the riparian floodplain forest community thrive despite being inundated by floods for weeks each spring. Dominant species include silver maple (*Acer saccharinum*) and boxelder (*Acer negundo*). Frequently found are sycamore, white ash, black ash, American elm, and slippery elm. Growing in the deep deposits of fine sandy loam, these species all possess the remarkable ability to withstand and recover from the ravages of severe ice scouring—the wounds from which can be seen on the trunks of many trees along the riverbank. The roots of these riverbank trees, and those of a select group of shrubs including the red osier dogwood and speckled alder, serve to hold fine soil in place against the erosive force of periodic flooding.

Away from the riverbank in the shadier understory, the forest floor is covered with herbaceous vegetation dominated by vast thickets of ostrich fern (*Matteuccia struthiopteris*) interspersed with Joe-pye weed, meadow rue, and Canada lily, and shorter plants including Jack-in-the-pulpit and red baneberry, as well as a great variety of other small herbs.

Oxbow Ponds

The changing course of the river has also created new plant communities. Some are found in oxbow ponds, formed when the river cut new, straighter paths through sharp bends and eventually left the bends as isolated ponds. Figure 14 shows the formation of oxbow ponds. The first submerged aquatic plant communities in these oxbow ponds are the same plants that form so-called weed beds in the main stem of the river.

Common species in oxbow ponds include ribbon-leaf pondweed, perfoliate pondweed, variable pondweed, common water-weed, free-flowered water-weed and floating bur-reed. Because they are isolated from the free-flowing main stem of the river, water in oxbow ponds moves only during spring flooding. The rest of the year it is stagnant. These conditions favor a succession of plant communities that wouldn't survive the ravages of fast-running water. Submerged aquatics found in oxbow ponds include floating pondweed, northern snail-seed pondweed, common bladderwort, green water-milfoil, water-shield, and hornwort.

As oxbow ponds fill with sediment and organic matter, their flora succeeds to emergent aquatics that like quiet water: common arrowhead, pickerelweed, and water parsnip, sedges, and grasses such as rice cutgrass and rattlesnake manna grass. These emergent aquatics produce flowers on stems that stand above the surface of the water for pollination by insects or through the wind. Fast-flowing water would knock over their flower stalks, making it hard for insects and the wind to reach them.

As sediment continues to accumulate, oxbow ponds are invaded by

Joe-pye weed (*Eupatorium fistulosum*) on the banks of the West River in Jamaica, Vt.

Common pondweeds characteristic of free-flowing northern Connecticut River. Stems and leaves of these plants are flexible and oriented with the direction of current. Below rock, *Potamogeton perfoliatus*; above rock, *Potamogeton epihydrus*.

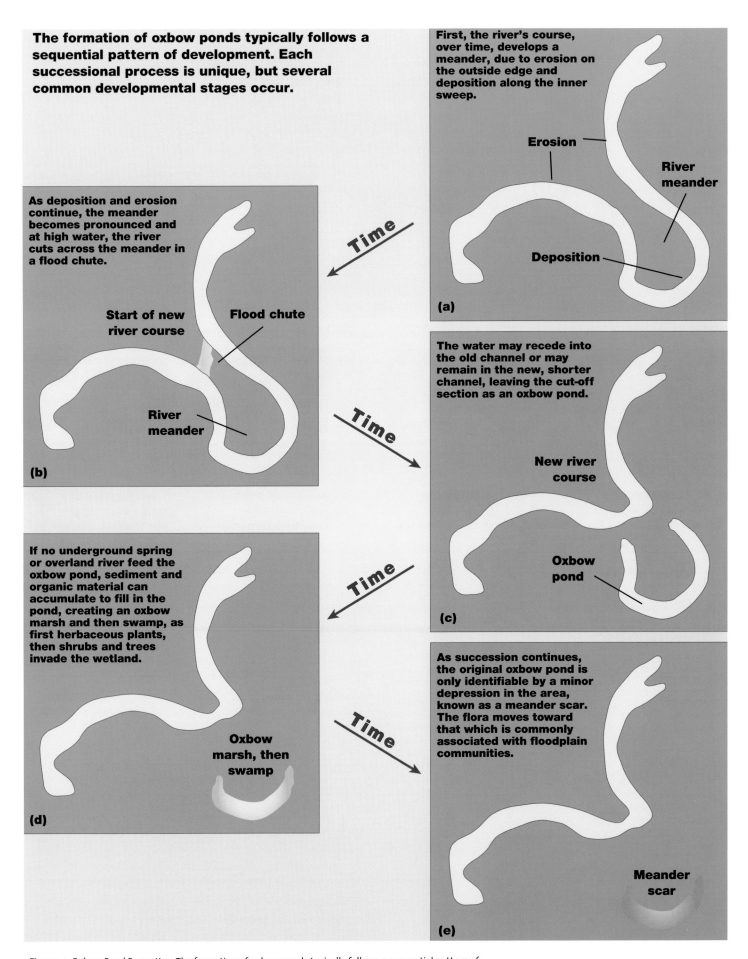

The formation of oxbow ponds typically follows a sequential pattern of development. Each successional process is unique, but several common developmental stages occur.

First, the river's course, over time, develops a meander, due to erosion on the outside edge and deposition along the inner sweep.

Erosion

River meander

Deposition

(a)

Time

As deposition and erosion continue, the meander becomes pronounced and at high water, the river cuts across the meander in a flood chute.

Start of new river course

Flood chute

River meander

(b)

Time

The water may recede into the old channel or may remain in the new, shorter channel, leaving the cut-off section as an oxbow pond.

New river course

Oxbow pond

(c)

Time

If no underground spring or overland river feed the oxbow pond, sediment and organic material can accumulate to fill in the pond, creating an oxbow marsh and then swamp, as first herbaceous plants, then shrubs and trees invade the wetland.

Oxbow marsh, then swamp

(d)

Time

As succession continues, the original oxbow pond is only identifiable by a minor depression in the area, known as a meander scar. The flora moves toward that which is commonly associated with floodplain communities.

Meander scar

(e)

Figure 14. Oxbow Pond Formation. The formation of oxbow ponds typically follows a sequential pattern of development. Each successional process is unique, but several common developmental stages occur.

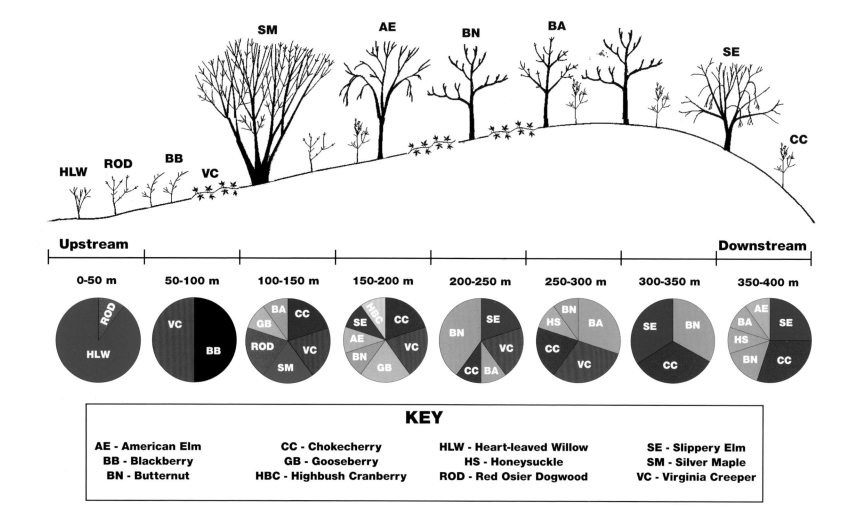

Figure 15. Vegetation Distribution and Succession on Islands in the Connecticut River. North-south transect of large island in Stratford, N.H., showing relative frequencies of woody plant species. The transect begins at the upstream end (left) and continues 420 meters down the middle of the island to the downstream end (right). Pie charts show frequencies of woody plants encountered in each 50-meter interval along the transect line. Silhouettes depict common woody plant species.

The first 50 meters of the upstream end of the island is the highest-energy region and is dominated by heart-leaved willow. The next 50 meters encompass a region where there is active deposition of ice, driftwood, and other debris during spring floods. This disturbed region is dominated by early successional species such as blackberry and Virginia creeper. On this island, the forest begins about 100 meters below the upstream end and is dominated by species such as silver maple that are most tolerant of the heavy scouring that ice and debris inflict. Farther downstream, trees such as American elm, butternut, black ash, and slippery elm form a mixed forest with slippery elm becoming increasingly abundant toward the downstream end.

a suite of shrubs, especially species of willow, which in turn eventually give way to the dominant trees of the floodplain forest. The creation of impoundments by dams has created vast shallow setbacks, areas that mimic oxbows but are still part of the main river. Setbacks are not a natural component of the riparian community, but are regions where dams have created new habitats where species that probably were associated originally only with oxbows have now become abundant.

Islands

Dozens of larger and many smaller islands occur along the course of the Connecticut River. Some of these, formed when the river changed course and cut off an oxbow, are inhabited by the same riparian forest described above. Other islands, however, have a different origin and harbor quite different plant communities.

Some islands and gravel bars are formed by the deposition of sediment in the bed of the river. Gravel bars frequently are submerged by water, but harbor a few hardy plants, including spreading dogbane, types of sedges, field horsetail, and several small willows. As these plants increase in number, they add surface texture, called "roughness," to the gravel bar. The plants resist the flow of water, slowing down the

A dense stand of invasive Japanese knotweed (*Polygonum cuspidatum*) grows on the right bank of the Ammonoosuc River in Bath, N.H. The bank on the far side of the channel is susceptible to erosion given the absence of a wide vegetative buffer.

flow so finer sediments are deposited. As soil accumulates, a wider variety of herbs, shrubs, and tree seedlings appear. As the plant communities on these islands develop, roughness increases and sediment deposition continues. Thus, it is the presence of plants that results in the accumulation of soil and in the vertical growth of the island.

Plant communities of the upstream ends of the islands differ markedly from those of the downstream ends. The upstream end of an island is where high-energy water hits first. This end of the island often remains as a low gravel bar inhabited by only the hardiest species. The downstream end is where more sediment accumulates, often as a high sand deposit followed by a lower sand bar, each with a different set of species. Figure 15 depicts the frequencies of woody plant species along a longitudinal transect of an island in Stratford, N.H.

Nonnative Species

Frequent disturbance from such factors as floods, ice, and debris is a common characteristic of all riparian plant communities. *Weeds*, which are nonnative plants mostly from Europe and Asia, depend on disturbance to persist in our region. These immigrant plants generally cannot compete effectively for space in native plant communities,

unless constant disturbance creates niches for them. It is not surprising, therefore, that riparian communities subject to ice scouring and flooding include a large number of nonnative species. Many of these are the common roadside weeds such as ox-eye daisy, wild madder, gill-over-the-ground, self-heal, common milkweed, moneywort, and many others. A few are becoming invasive.

Invasive species are introduced plants that have made the transition from growing as weeds to competing for space in our *undisturbed* native plant communities. Invasives have several advantages over native species that can make them more abundant. They may be susceptible to fewer diseases, may be eaten by fewer animals, and often have rapid growth rates enabling them to absorb a greater share of scarce nutrients. Some invasives carpet the ground with leaves and dense stems, discouraging the germination of seeds of native plants. This same mass of vegetation can insulate the surface of the ground so it thaws more slowly in the spring, affecting the emergence of insects and other animals from winter dormancy. Thus, the impact of invasive plants is not limited to other plants, but can be felt up the food chain.

In the Connecticut River Valley, some of the invasive species are aquatic, some are terrestrial, and some occupy the zone in between.

Nature Conservancy workers remove Japanese knotweed (*Polygonum cuspidatum*) from the banks of the Connecticut River.

Purple loosestrife invades the watershed along roads, rivers, and through wetlands.

Eurasian milfoil (*Myriophyllum spicatum*) occurs in the waters of the southern Connecticut River, and has been found as far north as Fairlee, Vt., as of 2007. Fanwort (*Cabomba aquatica*), an invasive aquatic plant from the southeastern United States, is well-established in the Connecticut River as far north as Northampton, Mass. Both of these aquatic invasive species have the potential to clog waterways and, as excess vegetation decays, reduce dissolved oxygen limiting the number of fish species able to survive.

Several terrestrial invasive species are also becoming serious problems. Japanese knotweed (*Polygonum cuspidatum*), honeysuckle (*Lonicera japonica*), and purple loosestrife (*Lythrum salicaria*) form large stands on the banks of the river and on islands. The first two now occur throughout the Connecticut River Valley, and purple loosestrife is steadily making its way north.

The River and Beyond

Trees and other forms of plant life constitute the biological foundation of the watershed. Healthy forests recycle up to 40 percent of rainfall back to the atmosphere by evapotranspiration, and the abundance and diversity of animal life is related directly to the abundance and diversity of plant life.

Huge efforts have been made in the last 40 to 50 years to improve water quality in the Connecticut and its tributaries. People now recognize that the river is just one part of a larger and more complex watershed, and are learning to manage the environmental quality of the whole, rather than just the water quality of the river. Methods to deal with invasive plant species, and strategies for preserving and protecting floodplains and other riparian habitat, are examples of ways some organizations, towns, states, and local landowners are facing this challenge.

David S. Conant is a professor of biology at Lyndon State College in Lyndonville, Vt. He lives in Barnet, Vt.

For Further Reading

Crow, G. E., and C. B. Hellquist. 2000. *Aquatic and Wetland Plants of Northeastern North America, a Revised and Enlarged Edition of Norman C. Fassett's A Manual of Aquatic Plants. Volumes 1 & 2.* Madison: University of Wisconsin Press.

Gleason, H. A., and A. Cronquist. 1991. *Manual of Vascular Plants of Northeastern United States and Adjacent Canada.* New York: New York Botanical Garden.

Magee, D. W., and H. E. Ahles. 1999. *Flora of the Northeast: A Manual of the Vascular Flora of New England and Adjacent New York.* Amherst: University of Massachusetts Press.

CHARLIE BROWNE
PHOTOS BY JIM BLOCK

16 Birds

Bird Biology and Ecology

A ghostly still great blue heron hunts the calm shallows on a cool foggy morning. A belted kingfisher rattles raucously as it rises to rest on a riverside limb. The unearthly flute of a Bicknell's thrush trails away on a timberline breeze. Tree swallows, glinting deep blue and green, sweep across still water, gorging on the spring hatch of midges. Bobolinks chatter from dry tufts above floodplain hay meadows, then flutter into the deep grass toward their hidden nests. And a bald eagle, unbelievably large, flaps and glides with magisterial dignity along the broad river's wooded shore.

In these fleeting moments with the birds, we are reassured that life's diversity is resilient, worthy in and of itself, and beautiful beyond imagining. Birds, so gracefully released from the two dimensions of the landscape, are inseparable from our conceptions of that landscape. At the ecological level, they are messengers of environmental health; at a more intimate scale, the frenetic presence of a black-capped chickadee on a subzero morning is a sure sign of a system that works!

Birds of the Connecticut River Valley, as in every natural system, find food, nesting territories, and sheltering rest sites in the landscape. Some forage for seeds; others gorge on emerging insects; some chisel beetle grubs from mealy wood; still others prey on small mammals and other birds. Birds process and deposit seeds, redistributing plants in their natural communities; they excavate deadwood, the first crumbling steps in decomposition and recycling; they consume clouds of insects, reducing forest and crop losses and easing the seasonal annoyance of flies and mosquitoes.

Birds are vertebrates of feverish metabolism. Their energy consumption is by our standards colossal, and their inner furnaces burn above 100 degrees Fahrenheit. As warm-blooded animals, birds need a steady supply of energy, but as airborne travelers, they can carry no excess baggage. Even the meager fat deposits of a long-distance migrant are efficient, borne in dense packets near the balancing keel of the sternum. Similarly, their reproductive cycle of egg laying and external incubation keep mother birds lightweight and mobile.

Migration

In our climate, birds face long seasons of sub-freezing weather, when two essentials — liquid water and invertebrate food — become scarce or unavailable. Seasonal migration is their adaptive response, its timing and distances shaped by the cycles of the postglacial climate.

The ancient north-south trend of the Connecticut River Valley has long offered a migratory flyway to the inland breeders of the boreal forests and the eastern Arctic tundra. The long-distance neotropical migrants, such as warblers and flycatchers, are cued by dwindling autumn light, which triggers the hormones that drive their migratory urges. Many fly at night, stopping to feed and rest during the warmth of the day. More opportunistic migrants, including many blackbirds, sparrows, waterfowl, and raptors, move south with a vaguer sense of purpose, their destinations the moving targets of frost-free, bare ground winter in the southern states and beyond. Though the valley does not host spectacular hawk migrations, good autumn viewing locations include Mount Prospect in Lancaster, N.H., Gile Mountain in Norwich, Vt., and Mount Cube in Orford, N.H. Map 35 shows how the Connecticut River Valley fits into the large Atlantic Flyway.

The return of spring draws birds to northern breeding grounds for a prolific but compressed summer season where long hours of daylight offer warmth and a season of prodigious biological productivity. Up the valley in April and May they come, averaging 100 miles northward and 1,000 feet upslope each week. The northward migration of neotropical migrants is exquisitely synchronized with the leaf-out of our northern hardwoods and the emergence of leaf-feeding insect larvae. Research shows that in the spring, migrants use riverside forests as staging areas from which they then branch out into favored habitat.

In some winters, birds of the far north, including common redpolls and snow buntings from the tundra, and pine siskins and pine grosbeaks from the forests of Ontario and Quebec, wander down in search of abundant cone and seed crops. Similarly, when rodent populations in the far north crash, their hungry predators, snowy owls, rough-legged hawks, northern shrikes, and great gray, boreal, and northern hawk owls "irrupt" into northern New England and even further south, down along the Connecticut River Valley and its wooded upland slopes, in search of voles and mice.

Habitat

The watershed embraces a wealth of bird habitats, each a complex community of physiographic features, plants, animals, and human disturbance. Near the river's source are the boreal forests of the Nulhegan and Victory basins in Vermont, and the Connecticut headwaters in New Hampshire, where gray jays, spruce grouse, black-backed woodpeckers, boreal chickadees, white-winged crossbills, saw-whet owls, and a score of warbler species inhabit the swampy stands of black

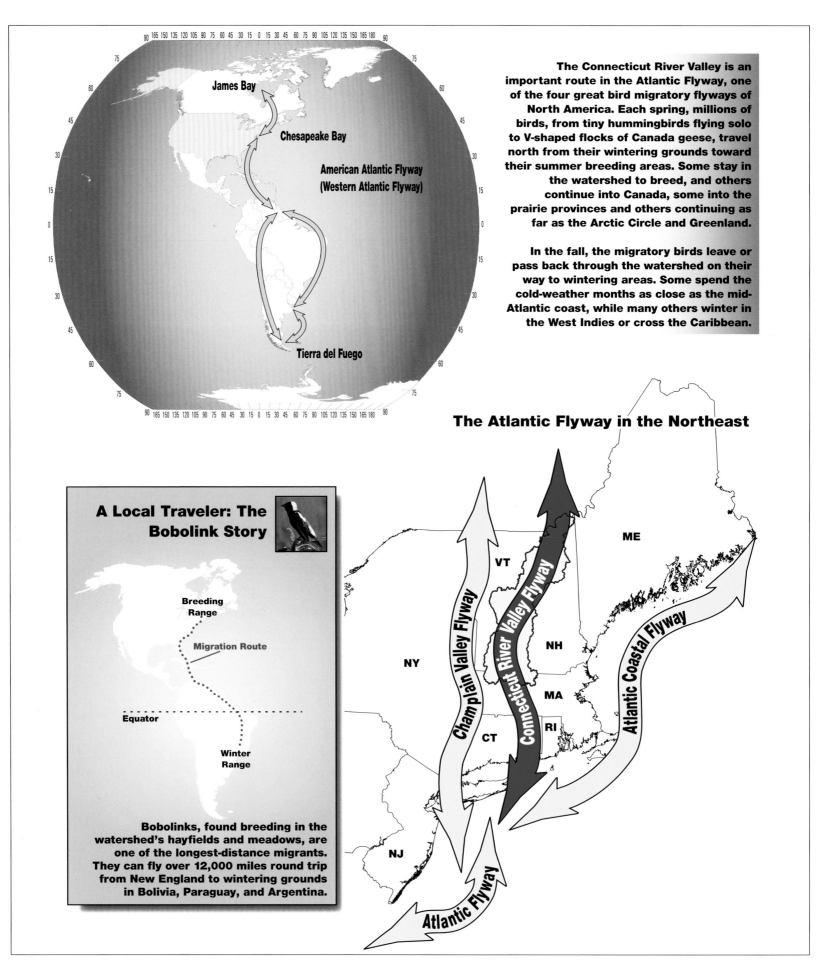

The Connecticut River Valley is an important route in the Atlantic Flyway, one of the four great bird migratory flyways of North America. Each spring, millions of birds, from tiny hummingbirds flying solo to V-shaped flocks of Canada geese, travel north from their wintering grounds toward their summer breeding areas. Some stay in the watershed to breed, and others continue into Canada, some into the prairie provinces and others continuing as far as the Arctic Circle and Greenland.

In the fall, the migratory birds leave or pass back through the watershed on their way to wintering areas. Some spend the cold-weather months as close as the mid-Atlantic coast, while many others winter in the West Indies or cross the Caribbean.

James Bay

Chesapeake Bay

American Atlantic Flyway
(Western Atlantic Flyway)

Tierra del Fuego

The Atlantic Flyway in the Northeast

ME

VT

Champlain Valley Flyway

Connecticut River Valley Flyway

Atlantic Coastal Flyway

NY

NH

MA

RI

CT

NJ

Atlantic Flyway

A Local Traveler: The Bobolink Story

Breeding Range

Migration Route

Equator

Winter Range

Bobolinks, found breeding in the watershed's hayfields and meadows, are one of the longest-distance migrants. They can fly over 12,000 miles round trip from New England to wintering grounds in Bolivia, Paraguay, and Argentina.

Map 35. The Atlantic Flyway in the Americas and the Connecticut River Watershed.

The bobolink (*Dolichonyx oryzivorus*) enlivens summer hay meadows with its tinkling call. Its numbers are declining in the Northeast due to habitat loss, as grasslands and former agricultural fields grow up to young forest or are converted to house lots. It is a long-distant migrant, traveling over 12,000 miles round-trip from its wintering grounds in South America.

spruce and larch, balsam fir, and speckled alder. Vireos, flycatchers, and wrens often are found in forests regrowing after logging.

Southward, the upland forests of maple, beech, and birch lure yellow-bellied sapsuckers, ruffed grouse, red-tailed hawks, purple finches, hermit thrushes, and a hundred other breeding species, while fertile floodplain farms host eastern bluebirds, savannah sparrows, bobolinks, and barn swallows. Lowland forests in the valley, with their mix of conifers and hardwoods, welcome barred owls and broad-winged hawks, and the incessant voices of red-eyed vireos. It is along the margins of these common habitats, the edges between farm and forest, shrubby roadside and wooded riverbank, that we encounter some of our most beloved birds: the song sparrows whose arrival assures us of spring's return, the gaudy Baltimore orioles, and foraging winter flocks of chickadees and nuthatches.

Up in the high mountain boundaries of the watershed, where the summer season is most compressed, one can find blackpoll warblers, golden-crowned kinglets, northern ravens, and Bicknell's thrush. Peregrine falcons tend their gravel-scrape nests on the steepest ledges above glacial talus slopes, I-91 highway cuts, and rock quarries. After precipitous declines because of the pesticide DDT, these fierce and flashy falcons are being restored to their historic numbers thanks to the work of dedicated scientists, volunteer nest monitors, and the protection of the federal Endangered Species Act.

The glacial forces that shaped the valley dammed clear upland lakes along many of the tributaries. On lakes Maidstone and Tarleton, Christine and Groton, the wail of the common loon—another restoration success story—echoes through predawn mists. Elsewhere on the Connecticut and its larger tributaries, dams transformed riffles, rapids, and riverine habitats to lazy lake shore. In floodplain meadows and marshes, such as designated Important Bird Area Herrick's Cove, on the Connecticut River in Rockingham, Vt., one may find American bitterns, marsh wrens, secretive Virginia rails, and a great diversity of migrating shorebirds and waterfowl. Another excellent place to find such wetland habitat and bird species is Pondicherry Division of the Silvio O. Conte National Fish and Wildlife Refuge in Whitefield and Jefferson, N.H., also designated an Important Bird Area by the National Audubon Society.

Population Trends

More than 220 species of birds live in, visit, or pass through the upper Connecticut River Valley each year, but the mix of species has changed over the past 250 years. Changing land use and habitat loss have had the most dramatic impact. Early European settlers found vast forest resources here, but driven by the imperatives of an agrarian economy, converted much of the landscape to working farmland. Grassland sparrows and blackbirds, as well as open-country predators such as American kestrels and northern harriers, thrived while species of the deep woodlands retreated to the remaining forest patches.

In the twentieth century, abandoned farms grew back into productive forest habitats. Today, those forests are falling to vacation homes and woodland getaways, commercial strip development, the proliferating network of secondary roads, trails for mechanized recreation and shoreline access, and new development on ridgelines and mountain tops. Those birds best adapted to urban and suburban life and human disturbance, such as house sparrows, European starlings, rock pigeons, and American crows, are doing well, while those needing large tracts of undisturbed habitat, such as scarlet tanagers, are declining.

The enchanting song of the hermit thrush (*Catharus guttatus*) echoes in deep woods throughout the watershed. The Vermont State Bird, the hermit thrush is the only member of its genus to spend its winters in North America.

A powerful flier, the peregrine falcon (*Falco peregrinus*) nests on high ledges in several locations in the watershed, including the Palisades in Fairlee, Vt., and Holt's Ledge in Lyme, N.H. A conservation success story, it has recovered from extirpation in the 1960s in the Northeast sufficiently to be removed from the federal Endangered Species Act in 1999.

The diminutive golden-crowned kinglet (*Regulus satrapa*) may be seen flitting about the boughs of spruce, fir, and other conifers in search of insects and other food.

For reasons that may include the moderation of the valley's climate, the shade trees, ornamental shrubs, and lawns that come with suburbanization, and the popularity of feeding birds, the past several decades have brought a changing bird population mix in the region. Northern cardinals, northern mockingbirds, tufted titmice, red-bellied woodpeckers, and turkey vultures are "southern" birds that have become familiar sights. At the same time, common raven populations have expanded southward through the watershed. For reasons more directly attributable to maturing forests, the valley is seeing an increase in populations of Cooper's hawks, common mergansers, pileated woodpeckers, and, most explosively, wild turkeys. New Hampshire reintroduced 25 turkeys from New York and Vermont to the river valley in 1975. A healthy river and more protected shoreline promise a growing bald eagle population, which is recovering from the ravages of the pesticide DDT.

Some species are declining. Of particular concern is the Bicknell's thrush, federally endangered and breeding high in the White Mountains. Mercury deposition from Midwest power plants is a likely contributor to its falling population. Birds that require grasslands, such as bobolinks and meadowlarks, are losing habitat to development or reforestation. Similarly, species like chestnut-side warblers that are found in early successional forest habitat, characterized by the shrubs, bushes, grasses, and saplings, that grow back after a timber harvest, blowdown, or other disturbance, are also in decline as forests mature or land is converted to development.

Research

Considerable research is being conducted on the status of bird species in the Connecticut River Valley. The Vermont Ecostudies Center and New Hampshire Audubon are among the organizations involved in field research projects. Christmas Bird Counts and backyard bird surveys take place in both states. Annual status reports are made on bald eagles, ospreys, and peregrine falcons in each state. Research is being done in the Important Bird Areas in the watershed, and ongoing work is aimed at identifying other such areas. The state wildlife agencies and academic institutions often conduct research on game bird species (such as turkeys and woodcock) and nongame species like the Bicknell's thrush.

Resources

Many resources are available for learning more about the birds of the upper Connecticut River Valley. For bird enthusiasts, the Connecticut River Birding Trail maps feature public locations for bird and nature study in New Hampshire and Vermont. The American Birding Association's publication, *A Birder's Guide to New Hampshire*, offers maps, driving loops, and site information for the entire state. Similarly, *Birdwatching in Vermont* offers guidance on how and where to find birds in the Green Mountain State. The *Vermont Breeding Bird Atlas* provides maps of confirmed locations for breeding bird species in Vermont, with map overlays of habitat and topography. The *Atlas of Breeding Birds in New Hampshire* provides similar data for the Granite State. For

The Cooper's hawk (*Accipiter cooperii*) breeds in forests throughout the watershed. It is a stealthy hunter of other birds. Unlike many species, it is tolerant of forest fragmentation and human disturbance, so its numbers may be increasing.

109

The American bittern (*Botaurus lentiginosus*) nests almost exclusively in large cattail marshes. Its numbers are declining as wetland habitat dwindles. Sometimes it may be observed standing stock still, head aloft, with its long striped neck meant to blend in with cattail stalks and marsh grasses.

current sightings, see New Hampshire Audubon at www.nhaudubon .org and Vermont eBird at http://ebird.org/vt.

A lifelong birder, Charlie Browne is executive director of the Fairbanks Museum & Planetarium in St. Johnsbury, Vt. He lives in Peacham, Vt.

FOR FURTHER READING

Delorey, A. 1996. *A Birder's Guide to New Hampshire*. Colorado Springs: American Birding Association.

Foss, Carol R., ed. 1994. *Atlas of Breeding Birds in New Hampshire*. Dover, N.H.: Arcadia Publishing for New Hampshire Audubon.

Laughlin, S. and D. Kibbe. 1985. *The Atlas of Breeding Birds of Vermont*. Hanover, N.H.: University Press of New England for Vermont Institute of Natural Science.

Murin, T. and B. Pfeiffer. 2002. *Birdwatching in Vermont*. Hanover, N.H.: University Press of New England.

Shepard, W., et al. *Connecticut River Birding Trail*. 3 maps. White River Junction, Vt. www.birdtrail.org.

17 Fish

After the Glaciers

Little is known about fish in the Connecticut River before the Ice Age, but scientists theorize that species that were present were pushed southward as the glaciers advanced. Then, when the glaciers melted and Lake Hitchcock drained some 12,000 years ago, fish migrated back into the river from southern and coastal regions. The returning species, including brook trout (*Salvelinus fontinalis*), darters, sculpin, Atlantic salmon (*Salmo salar*), and pickerel, either swam their way into this reopened habitat or were transported by birds as eggs or small fish. John Ridge of the Department of Geology at Tufts University describes fossil evidence of their path that may be seen today in the varved lake bottom deposits of Glacial Lake Hitchcock, where researchers have found swimming and resting trails of what they believe were freshwater sculpin (*Cottidae* sp.).

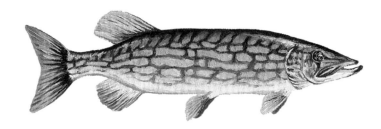

Chain pickerel are found in warm, shallow, still waters with lots of aquatic vegetation.

Human Introductions

Some of our favorite and most familiar fish species in the Connecticut are not native to the river system but were brought here by people. These include smallmouth and largemouth bass, rainbow and brown trout, walleye, and pike. Humans introduced these species as game fish to the watershed, most after the railroads and steamboats allowed for fast shipment of fish or eggs from the Great Lakes, the Mississippi River watershed (especially smallmouth bass, *Micropterus dolomieu*, from the Ohio River), and Europe (especially brown trout, *Salmo trutta*) in the mid- to late 1800s. In 1873, fish breeder Livingston Stone of Charlestown, N.H., developed the aquarium car for rail transport of fish, speeding cross-continental introduction of fish species.

The most recent arrival is the western rainbow trout (*Oncorhynchus mykiss*). Since 1938, it has been the species of choice for hatcheries because of its ability to adjust to a wide variety of habitat conditions. Rainbow trout are now found in all but three of the lower 48 states. Most people mistakenly look on these fish as native, given that they are so plentiful throughout the watershed.

A species originally found in only four ponds in New Hampshire, Vermont, and Maine is the Sunapee trout (*Salvelinus aureolus oquassa*). Hybridizing with introduced lake trout (*Salvelinus namaycush*), native to the very northern watershed, has diminished this species.

Lake trout thrive in cold (50 degree) water near the bottom of big lakes.

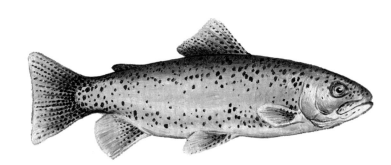

Oxygen and Temperature

Anglers refer to cold-, cool-, and warm-water species of fish. Cold-water species include trout and salmon, and some people consider

A common but introduced species, the adaptable rainbow trout thrives best in cold water, but can withstand temperatures up to 77 degrees if the water is well aerated.

Smallmouth bass like cooler summer temperatures than largemouth bass, and move into deeper, cooler water in the warm-weather months.

Largemouth bass prefer warm, shallow, mud-bottomed and weedy lakes, ponds, rivers, and streams.

Walleye need clean water and prefers a firm bottom, such as gravel or bedrock.

pickerel a cold-water species. Cool-water species include smallmouth bass and for some anglers, walleye. Warm-water species include largemouth bass (*Micropterus salmoides*), northern pike (*Esox lucius*), and rock bass (*Ambloplites rupestris*).

Although these anglers' categories are not scientific, they are descriptive, because habitat and water quality determine where species of fish live. Regardless of their size or habitat niche, all fish in the Connecticut River require clean, well-oxygenated water to survive. But different species require different levels of dissolved oxygen, with trout demanding the most oxygen-rich conditions. The temperature of water determines the level of dissolved oxygen, with levels falling as the water warms.

From its source near the Canadian border to where it crosses into Massachusetts, the river is subject to natural warming of approximately 20 degrees Fahrenheit given changes in both latitude and altitude. It drops from 2,670 feet above sea level at Fourth Connecticut Lake to 240 feet at Brattleboro, Vt. Trout thrive in the cold, far-northern waters. Moving downriver, the species mix changes to cool- and warm-water species: walleye (*Sander vitreus vitreus*), bass, and perch.

The creation of reservoirs and the effects of land use changes have altered the river extensively. These changes have created substantial warm-water habitat where only cool- and cold-water habitat existed previously. Since the early twentieth century, nine hydroelectric dams along with three water-storage dams have been built on the main river north of the Massachusetts border. Each reservoir adds heat to the river because of the wide expanse of slow-moving, unshaded water.

While the water above the dams is warm, flow just downriver of the hydro facilities actually is cooler, because the turbines draw water from mid-levels of the reservoirs. Thus, trout often are found in the colder, well-aerated water below the dams. Cold-water favoring trout may also be found in southern reaches where major tributaries join the main river or where there is moving and roiled water. Examples include the mouth of the Cold River below the dam in Bellows Falls, and Sumner Falls, the last free-flowing reach of river from Wilder, Vt., to Holyoke, Mass. Both are places where trout may be found in what otherwise is a bass fishery.

Migration

Each year, some fish make their way from the Atlantic Ocean up the Connecticut River as part of their life cycle. Others migrate from the Connecticut into its tributaries. *Anadromous* fish return to freshwater from saltwater to spawn the next generation. In the upper Connecticut River, these species include Atlantic salmon, American shad, blueback herring, sea lamprey, and striped bass. *Catadromous* fish return to saltwater from fresh to spawn the next generation. In the Connecticut, the American eel is our only catadromous species. *Potamodromous* fish spend all of their lives in freshwater. They may migrate from rivers to streams to spawn the next generation. Trout, bass, pickerel, and walleye species are potamodromous. Map 36 shows ranges for four anadromous species.

Historical references place the strong swimming Atlantic salmon as far north as Beecher's Falls, near the Canadian border. Today, reintroduced young salmon have been as far up the Connecticut River

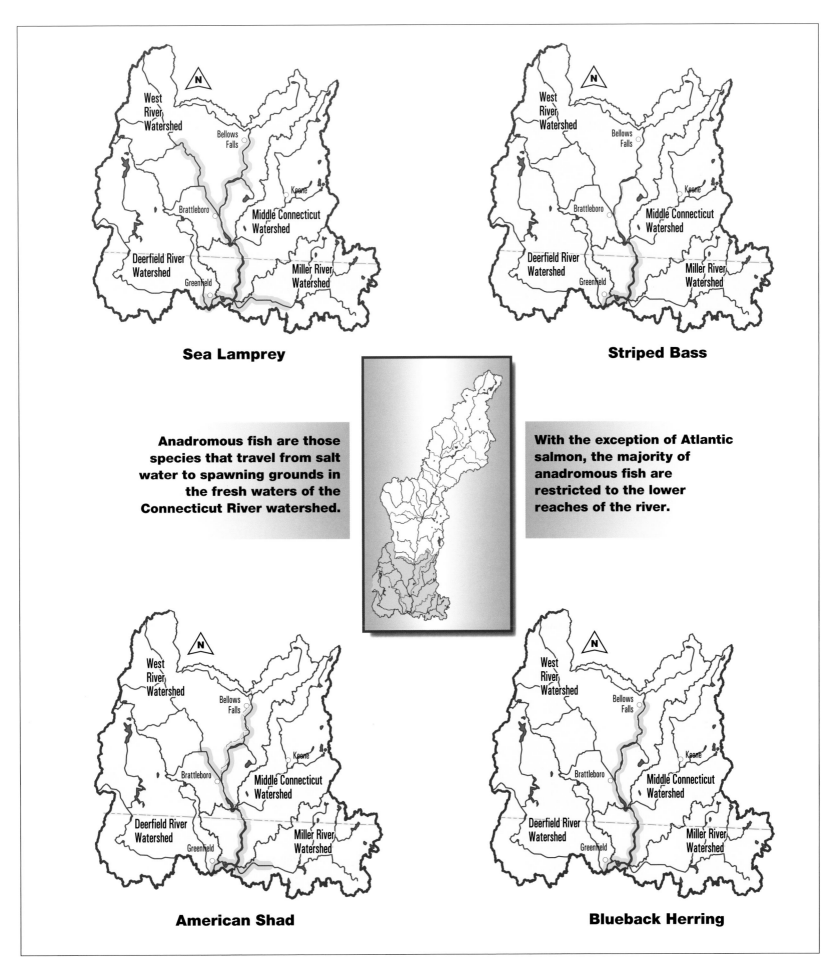

Sea Lamprey

Striped Bass

Anadromous fish are those species that travel from salt water to spawning grounds in the fresh waters of the Connecticut River watershed.

With the exception of Atlantic salmon, the majority of anadromous fish are restricted to the lower reaches of the river.

American Shad

Blueback Herring

Map 36. Anadromous Fish Species in the Upper Connecticut River Watershed.

Even in the southern reaches of the watershed, turbulent conditions create habitat for cool- and cold-water species, such as on stretches of the White River.

system as the Ammonoosuc River. American shad can't make it past Bellows Falls, approximately 35 miles north of the Massachusetts border, so angling for shad stops there. There is no open season for sea-run salmon anywhere in the watershed.

Finding Fish

Because the northern reaches of the river are cooler, the region is a reliable trout fishery even in the heat of summer. The northern stretch is considered a prime cold-water fishery. Cool-water species are found in the mid-reaches of the river. Smallmouth bass and pike can be found throughout the river from McIndoe Falls Dam downstream, including in the lower reaches of the tributaries. Smallmouth bass (*Micropterus dolomieu*) and trout may be found in the same pools in the larger tributaries. It is not at all unusual to catch three or four species in a day of fishing on the lower White River, where anglers may find everything from bass to brook trout.

The dams are useful as guides of where to look for different species of fish along the river. In the reservoirs behind the Vernon, Bellows Falls, and Wilder dams are found the warm- and cool-water species including smallmouth bass and pike.

The lowest reach of the main river welcomes the warm-water largemouth bass, particularly in the reservoirs behind the hydroelectric dams. Trout also may be found in the lower main river at the confluence with smaller tributaries that send cool, oxygenated water into the mainstem.

The Return of the Salmon

The Connecticut River stock of Atlantic salmon became extinct in the early 1800s due to dam construction, overfishing, and pollution. Restoration efforts, which started as early as the 1860s, were formalized when Congress authorized the Connecticut River Basin Salmon Compact in 1983. The compact is a four-state initiative to restore the fish through habitat protection and restoration, research, and stocking. Every spring, volunteers help stock salmon fry in the river and some tributaries. The Connecticut River stock of Atlantic salmon currently is not considered an endangered species, unlike the remnant stocks in some Maine rivers. The maps on pages 000 and 000 show the number of salmon returning to the watershed and the placement of dams that do or do not impede fish migration.

In the Connecticut River system, most adult salmon migrate from the ocean to the river in the spring. A smaller number migrate upriver in early fall. They stop eating when they enter freshwater, living off their body fat and tissues for up to a year. The adult salmon seek cold-water areas to spend the summer, moving to smaller, swift-running, gravelly tributaries to spawn in October and November. Unlike their Pacific cousins, Atlantic salmon do not always die after spawning, and can return to the ocean.

Salmon deposit their eggs in gravel nests, called redds. Eggs hatch in March and April. After three to four weeks under the gravel, the fry emerge to seek food and establish feeding territories. The young salmon, called parr, spend one to three years in their natal stream. When they are about 6 inches long, the salmon, now called smolts, undergo physical changes (so they can live in saltwater), become silvery in color, and migrate to the ocean. They travel thousands of miles to their North Atlantic feeding grounds, where they remain for up to three years before returning to their natal stream in the Connecticut River basin to reproduce.

More information about salmon and other fish habitat restoration efforts, including daily fish counts, is available from the U.S. Fish and Wildlife Service Connecticut River Coordinators Office, on the Web at www.fws.gov/r5crc.

Source

Gephard, Stephan, and James McMenemy. 2004. An overview of the program to restore Atlantic salmon and other diadromous fishes to the Connecticut River with notes on the current status of these species in the river. Springfield, Vt.: American Fisheries Society.

Atlantic salmon.

Because brook trout are so sensitive to changes in water quality, biologists consider them an indicator species of overall river health. Eastern brook trout—the watershed's native trout (though technically a char), so-named by Pilgrims—were ubiquitous at the time of European settlement and well into the nineteenth century. Visitors to northern New Hampshire told of catching literally hundreds of the brightly speckled "square tails" on any given day. But industrialization was cruel to these fish of free-running waters. Dams for mills and later for power slowed the rivers, land was cleared, and water temperatures rose. Loggers used the rivers for transporting timber, and factory waste and farm runoff poured into waterways. Brook trout populations dropped throughout the watershed and disappeared completely from some areas.

More recently, restoration efforts for wild brook trout are underway, led by the multi-party Eastern Brook Trout Joint Venture. In the Connecticut River watershed, one such effort is at Nash Stream, once a prime trout fishery in northern New Hampshire. Trout Unlimited, the N.H. Fish and Game Department, and several other state and federal partners are working to restore in-stream and floodplain habitat, much of which was damaged from a major dam failure in 1969.

A native species of the watershed, brook trout require well-oxygenated cold water, 68 degrees or cooler.

SOURCE

Trout Unlimited. 2005. *The New England Brook Trout: Protecting a Fish, Restoring a Region*. Arlington, Va.: Trout Unlimited.

Fish and the Watershed Economy

Few economic statistics about the impact of fishing relate specifically to the Connecticut River, but statewide totals give a picture of the importance of fishing—and healthy fisheries—to the economy. When added together, freshwater fishing expenditures for Vermont and New Hampshire in 2001 amounted to $257 million. National studies suggest that 41 percent of that is spent on the fishing trip (food, lodging, transportation, entertainment), 50 percent on fishing gear (rods, waders, nets, hats, etc.) and 9 percent is spent on other items such as licenses, magazines, donations, and memberships.

David L. Deen is the river steward for Vermont and New Hampshire for the Connecticut River Watershed Council. He has served on Connecticut River Joint Commissions, and is a long-time member of the Vermont legislature. He operates Strictly Trout, a guide service, and lives in Westminster, Vt.

FOR FURTHER READING

Langdon, Richard W., Mark T. Ferguson, and Kenneth M. Cox. 2006. *Fishes of Vermont*. Waterbury, Vt.: Vermont Fish & Wildlife Department.

Little, Richard D. 1986. *Dinosaurs, Dunes and Drifting Continents: The Geohistory of the Connecticut Valley*. Greenfield, Mass.: Valley Geo Publications.

McClane, A. J. 1974. *McClane's New Standard Fishing Encyclopedia*. New York: Henry Holt & Co.

Scarola, John F. 1987. *Freshwater Fish of New Hampshire*. Concord, N.H.: New Hampshire Fish and Game Department.

Generations ago, Atlantic salmon were abundant in many New England rivers, having migrated upstream from the Atlantic Ocean to spawn. The construction of a dam on the Connecticut River at Turner's Falls, Massachusetts, in the 1790s ended the historic runs of salmon into the upper watershed. Today, the entire Connecticut River watershed is at the center of an effort to reintroduce the salmon. Every spring, volunteers release salmon fry into tributary rivers and streams. Many schools in the upper watershed devote classroom and field time to the salmon, including raising salmon in the classroom. The White River National Fish Hatchery in Bethel, Vermont, raises broodstock salmon and incubates millions of eggs.

Numbers of returning adult salmon remain well below what is required to reestablish a sustainable fishery, and significantly less than the levels set for allowing their harvest. The challenges facing efforts to reintroduce the Atlantic salmon are enormous. All four Connecticut River states are experiencing changes in land use that affect water quality and salmon habitat, and many dams still block the tributaries salmon rely upon for successful spawning. In addition, much is still unknown about the lives of salmon in the ocean, where other environmental factors are affecting them.

At the same time, other anadromous fish species in the watershed are doing well. American shad, sea lamprey, and blueback herring migrate as far as the dam at Bellows Falls. Unlike salmon, these species were never extirpated from the river. Also unlike salmon, these species do not rely on full access to the smaller tributaries for successful spawning. As the upper watershed opened up through the construction of fish passage at the dams, they have returned to their historic ranges. They have reestablished in all waters accessible to them, including the lower reaches of the tributaries. The restoration of these species, although below historic levels, are a significant side benefit of the effort to restore the salmon.

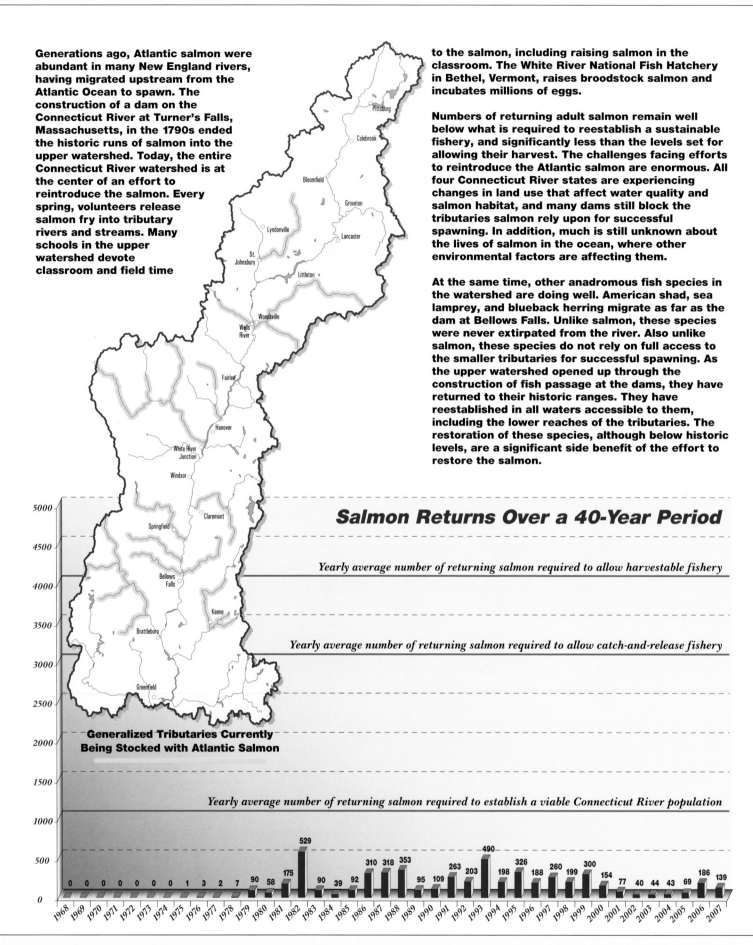

Salmon Returns Over a 40-Year Period

Yearly average number of returning salmon required to allow harvestable fishery

Yearly average number of returning salmon required to allow catch-and-release fishery

Yearly average number of returning salmon required to establish a viable Connecticut River population

Generalized Tributaries Currently Being Stocked with Atlantic Salmon

Year	Returns
1968	0
1969	0
1970	0
1971	0
1972	0
1973	0
1974	0
1975	1
1976	3
1977	2
1978	7
1979	90
1980	58
1981	175
1982	529
1983	90
1984	39
1985	92
1986	310
1987	318
1988	353
1989	95
1990	109
1991	263
1992	203
1993	490
1994	198
1995	326
1996	188
1997	260
1998	199
1999	300
2000	154
2001	77
2002	40
2003	44
2004	43
2005	69
2006	186
2007	139

Atlantic Salmon Restoration in the Connecticut River Watershed. Base map: VCGI and GRANIT data sets, modified by Northern Cartographic. Salmon returns graph: from *Vermont Trout Streams* © Northern Cartographic, derived from U.S. Fish and Wildlife salmon return data for the Connecticut River.

Management of anadromous and native fish includes ensuring that fish populations can move freely to and from spawning grounds and feeding areas. In the past, this need for fish passage was not considered when dams were designed and constructed across rivers. Blockage of migratory fish movement by dams has been an issue throughout the United States, with many fish populations in severe decline as a result.

In 1986 Congress tackled the issue head on, and gave federal and state fish and wildlife agencies "equal" consideration with power production sponsors when issuing renewal licenses for existing dams or when new dams are proposed.

When dam owners apply for a renewed license, the Federal Energy Regulatory Commission (FERC) can require the construction of "fish ladders" or other features that can allow fish to migrate in both directions. FERC can also require minimum flow releases to ensure both quantity and quality of water for fish in the reservoir and below the dam.

We are fortunate in the Connecticut River watershed that many of the dams now provide fish passage. However, as shown on the map to the left, there are still some notable exceptions.

While fish ladders are helpful, they do not eliminate all mortality of fish populations passing dam structures. Many young fish on their way to the ocean get caught in turbines and do not survive. Thus hatcheries raise and release enormous numbers of young migrants, hoping a reasonable number will survive the journey to the sea and the perils of growing there before their return.

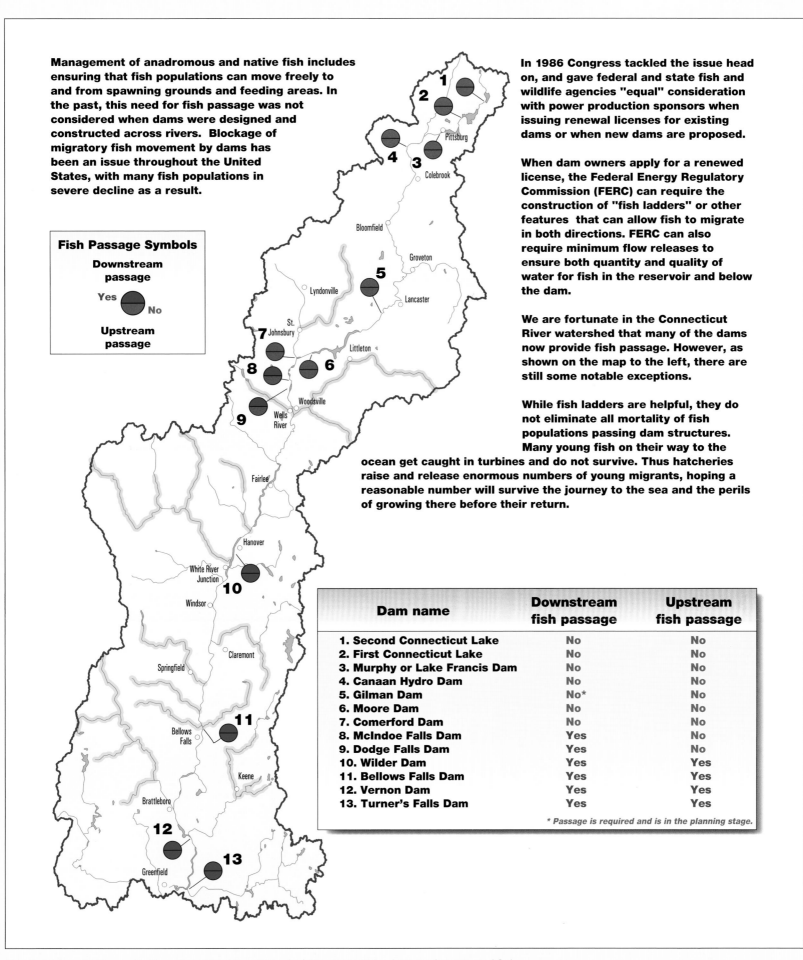

Fish Passage Symbols

Downstream passage

Yes / No

Upstream passage

Dam name	Downstream fish passage	Upstream fish passage
1. Second Connecticut Lake	No	No
2. First Connecticut Lake	No	No
3. Murphy or Lake Francis Dam	No	No
4. Canaan Hydro Dam	No	No
5. Gilman Dam	No*	No
6. Moore Dam	No	No
7. Comerford Dam	No	No
8. McIndoe Falls Dam	Yes	No
9. Dodge Falls Dam	Yes	No
10. Wilder Dam	Yes	Yes
11. Bellows Falls Dam	Yes	Yes
12. Vernon Dam	Yes	Yes
13. Turner's Falls Dam	Yes	Yes

Passage is required and is in the planning stage.

Atlantic Salmon and Dams in the Upper Connecticut River Watershed. Base map: VCGI and GRANIT data sets, modified by Northern Cartographic. Dam names and locations: VCGI and N.H. Department of Environmental Protection data-sets. Passage information from Connecticut River Joint Commissions staff.

18   Reptiles and Amphibians

Most people would be surprised at the diversity and beauty of the many reptiles and amphibians found in the Connecticut River watershed. The watershed hosts 21 known amphibian species (salamanders and frogs) and 14 known reptile species (snakes and turtles).

Salamander species range from the tiny and secretive four-toed salamander (*Hemidactylium scutatum*) to the hefty (12-inch-or-larger), totally aquatic mudpuppy (*Necturus maculosus*). Turtles range from the very large and prehistoric-looking snapping turtles (*Chelydra serpentina*) that only leave the water to lay their eggs, to the largely terrestrial, more friendly-looking wood turtle (*Glyptemys insculpta*), which winters in streams but feeds primarily on land. Frogs range in size from the tiny spring peepers (*Pseudacris crucifer*) that loudly and persistently announce the spring season to the giant, bellowing American bullfrogs (*Lithobates catesbeianus*) that may dine on prey as large as chipmunks. The ubiquitous common gartersnake (*Thamnophis sirtalis*) is the most likely of the snake species to be seen, but many more-secretive but beautifully colored species, such as the ringneck snake (*Diadophis punctatus*), also reside in the watershed (Andrews 2002).

Southern Species
Some of the most unusual reptiles and amphibians are southern species for whom the upper Connecticut River watershed is the northern extreme of their ranges. These species are able to survive farther north than usual, partially as a result of the relatively moderate temperatures in and along the floodplain of the Connecticut River. These species include the eastern racer, spotted turtle, marbled salamander, Fowler's toad, and possibly the timber rattlesnake (Taylor 1993).

The North American racer (*Coluber constrictor*) is a large, fast, and wary snake that reaches a known length of 6 feet in this watershed. In the Connecticut River Valley, it has been found as far north as Cheshire County, N.H., and Windham County, Vt. The racer lives in early successional open lands, such as in pastures and under power lines. Racers may travel as much as two miles from their dens to feed.

The spotted turtle (*Clemmys guttata*) is currently known only in Windham County, Vt., and southern Grafton County, N.H. It is a small (6-inch-long) black turtle with yellow spots on its shell. It requires a mosaic of wetlands and undeveloped adjacent uplands for its survival. Spending the winter in permanent water, such as marshes or ponds, it travels over land to vernal pools to feed on amphibian eggs in the spring. Like other turtles, it lays its eggs in open areas on land. Its occurrences are depicted in Map 37.

The marbled salamander (*Ambystoma opacum*) is a chunky black salamander with pewter bars across its back. It is unusual in that it migrates to breeding pools to lay its eggs in the late summer and fall instead of the early spring, as do other members of the genus *Amby-*

The sonorous American bullfrog.

Spring peepers are diminutive, but their combined voices fill early summer evenings when they congregate in ponds and vernal pools for breeding. Later in the summer, their solitary voices may be heard surprisingly far from water.

American racers, which can grow to 6 feet, get their name from the illusion of speed they create when they glide away. They are also excellent tree climbers.

stoma. Its eggs hatch that fall; by the following spring, its larvae can feed on newly hatched spotted salamander larvae and wood frog tadpoles. The marbled salamander currently is known only from Cheshire County in the New Hampshire portion of the watershed. It has been reported from only one other county in the state.

The discovery of a Fowler's toad (*Bufo fowleri*) in White River Junction, Vt., in the 1980s made biologists aware that two species of toad breed in the watershed. Previously, the widespread and abundant American toad (*Bufo americanus*) was the only documented species. The American toad has a long, musical, vibrato call during its mating season, while the rare Fowler's toad is most easily identified by its entirely unmusical bleating call. Fowler's can also be identified by its largely unmarked belly, and by the absence of large warts on its legs or within the dark patches on its back. The American toad has black markings on its belly and large warts on its legs and within the patches on its back. Currently, Fowler's toad is found only in a very limited area of Windham County, Vt., but other scattered reports (still undocumented) exist within the watershed.

Although the timber rattlesnake (*Crotalus horridus*) was known historically from both sides of the Connecticut River, it has not been documented within the watershed in recent years. At this latitude, this species dens communally in sunny and exposed rockslides but forages in woodlands up to a few miles away. The *Vermonter* magazine reported in 1901 that "on some farms it is so abundant that it is difficult to keep a hired man" (Titcomb 1901). Most documented reports of rattlesnakes from the watershed ended in the 1950s. Habitat loss, bounties, and persecution eliminated most of these snakes. Here is a 1883 quote from the *Brattleboro Reformer* referring to a New Hampshire population:

Spotted turtles live in marshes, ponds, and streams with aquatic vegetation. The temperature at which eggs are incubated determines gender of the hatchlings, with warmer temperatures producing females.

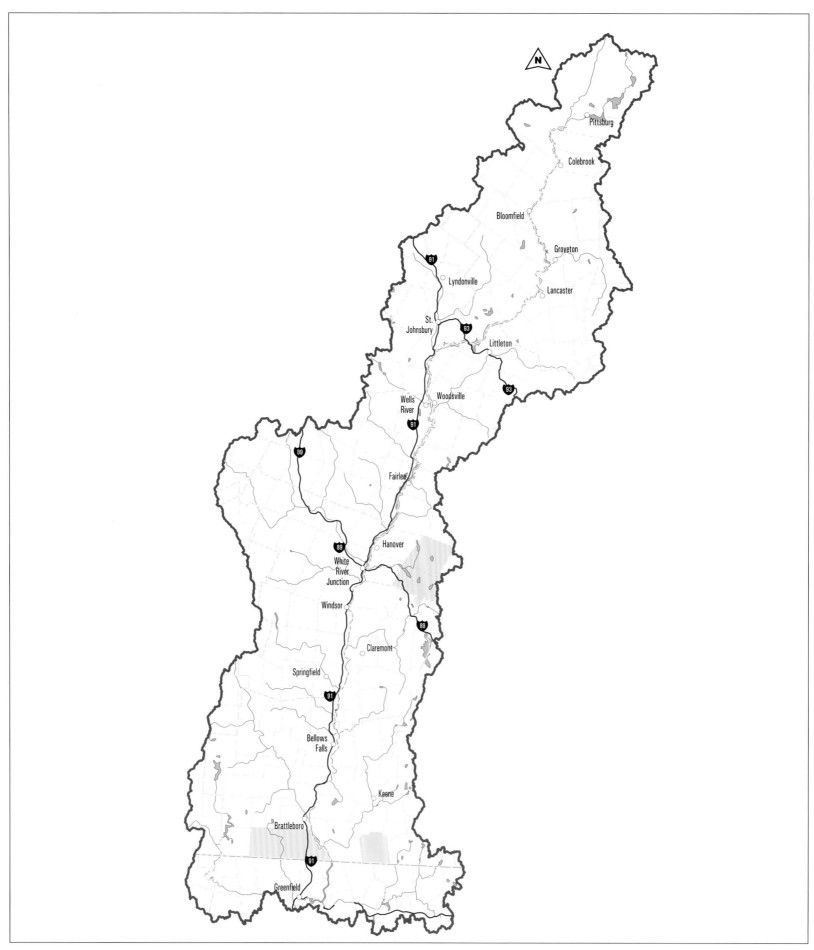

Map 37. Spotted Turtle Occurrences.

Mr. Thomas has undoubtedly had the most experience in capturing them, he having caught and sold as many as 100 within the past two years. One day he brought in eight alive, securing them by a slip-noose made of strong cord and attached to a four-foot stick; these he mostly sold to local cigar-makers for from $3.50 or $4.50 and as high as $10, who generally put them in fruit or candy-jars filled with alcohol and sent them to New York, but for what purpose he was not apprised. (Childs 1883)

One Northern Species

One species in the watershed is at the southern extreme of its range. The mink frog (*Lithobates septentrionalis*) is a Canadian species that breeds in the northeastern corner of Vermont and across the northern tip of New Hampshire. The climate of this area is colder and the vegetation includes a higher percentage of boreal tree species such as spruce and fir than elsewhere in the watershed. Like the mammal it is named after, the mink frog can produce an unpleasant odor. Consequently, it is sometimes referred to as the scratch-and-sniff frog. Luckily, the rotten onion odor it produces does not last long. Other than by smell, this species can be distinguished by the oval spots oriented along the axis of its legs. Otherwise, it easily could be confused with the very common green frog (*Lithobates clamitans*). Bands on the green frog's legs cross at right angles to the axis.

Conservation Needs

Whether the reptile and amphibian species currently in the watershed survive into the coming decades depends on how well we conserve their habitat. Most herptile species need to move among habitat types over the course of their lives. For instance, spotted salamanders (*Ambystoma maculatum*) travel from over-wintering sites in upland deciduous woods to woodland pools and ponds to lay their eggs. On rainy nights, green frogs leave their ponds and travel and feed on land. American racers travel a couple miles from their ridge-top dens to lowland feeding sites. Female painted turtles (*Chrysemys picta*) leave their ponds and travel over land to find egg-laying sites every June. All of these species and most others use a variety of habitat types over the course of their lives. Consequently, they also need to be able to move safely among those habitats. Unfortunately, increased development and fragmentation of habitat is threatening many of these species. For instance, mortality from increased road traffic has become significant. Many species will need the assistance of an informed and caring public if they are to persist.

In Vermont, according to the U.S. Environmental Protection Agency, roughly 10 square miles of habitat are developed every year and New Hampshire is growing even faster. We cannot sustain this loss of habitat without losing populations of herptiles. As individuals, towns, and states, we need to be conserving and managing land in a way that allows these species to survive.

Learning More

Much is yet to be learned about the current distribution of these species within the watershed. Additional breeding populations of species

American toads live most of the year on land, but like many amphibians, flock to vernal pools and ponds for breeding. The musical trill of the male is a familiar sound of early summer.

The surprisingly large (eight inches and longer) spotted salamander is one of the first amphibians to emerge in spring. They spend most of the year in forest leaf litter or under other cover. They are drawn out on the first rainy nights in early spring, sometimes when snow is still on the ground and ice still occupies vernal pools and other breeding ponds.

such as the box turtle may yet be discovered. You can help by reporting your Vermont sightings to the Vermont Reptile and Amphibian Atlas, on-line at www.middlebury.edu/herpatlas or by calling 802-443-5648. To report New Hampshire sightings, contact RAARP (Reptile and Amphibian Reporting Program) at 603-271-3016 or e-mailing wilddiv@wildlife.state.nh.us. Additional information on the New Hampshire RAARP program is available at on the Web.

Jim Andrews is a research herpetologist at Middlebury College in Middlebury, Vt.

FOR FURTHER READING

Andrews, James S. 2001. *The Atlas of the Reptiles and Amphibians of Vermont.* Middlebury, Vt.: Middlebury College Press. Digital 2005 edition available at http://community.middlebury.edu/~herpatlas/.

Childs, F. 1883. Sees snakes. *Brattleboro Reformer,* August 24.

New Hampshire Wildlife Action Plan. 2005. Concord, N.H.: N.H. Fish and Game Department.

Taylor, James. 1993. *The Amphibians and Reptiles of New Hampshire.* Concord, N.H.: N.H. Fish and Game Deparment.

Titcomb, J. 1901. Twentieth century history of Vermont: Animal life of Vermont. *The Vermonter: A State Magazine,* June.

19 Mammals

The Connecticut River watershed hosts many mammal species whose abundance and variety have changed over time. Glaciers, fur trade, hunting, and human land use all have affected the diversity of wild mammals in the valley.

Approximately 12,000 years ago, glaciers that had locked the upper Connecticut River valley in ice melted. Land not flooded by ancient meltwater lakes was colonized by Arctic and boreal plants, which in turn attracted Arctic and boreal mammals. American mastodons (*Mammut americanum*) browsed black spruce, hemlock, and larch, while wooly mammoths (*Mammuthus primigenius*) and caribou (*Rangifer tarandus*) grazed an assortment of tundra plants. Nine thousand years ago, mastodon and mammoth vanished from eastern North America, victims of postglacial warming and a subsequent shift in plant communities, as well as the depredations of a newly arrived predator: man. By 1900, caribou, which had become a casual visitor to New Hampshire and Vermont, were seen for the last time in either state as a herd of 17 milled about the First Connecticut Lake, near the headwaters of the Connecticut River.

Decline of Native Species

During the seventeenth and eighteenth centuries, as European explorers and settlers began displacing Native Americans, commercial trapping and hunting began exacting a heavy toll on large and moderate-sized mammals. The Connecticut River was the highway south. Hides of deer, moose, beaver, catamount, bobcat, lynx, wolf, black bear, otter, fisher, and pine marten were shipped downstream to a trading post in Springfield, Mass. By the time of the Revolutionary War, however, the importance of the fur trade had dwindled and the upper Connecticut River Valley had become a region largely of farm and pasture, the great woods having fallen before the long-handled ax and the crosscut saw. Habitat destruction, bounties, and wholesale slaughter took a toll on native wildlife. By the late nineteenth century, moose were found only in northern Coös County, N.H. By 1853, the wolverine (*Gulo gulo*) was extinct in Vermont; 20 years later, the state imported white-tailed deer from New York to bolster its diminished herd.

On Thanksgiving Day, 1881, the last known catamount, or mountain lion (*Puma concolor*), in Vermont was shot in Barnard. New Hampshire's last wolves were gone by 1895 and Vermont's by 1902. Beaver had been trapped out of the Connecticut River watershed before the turn of the twentieth century. In 1918, two wolverine cubs were taken from Coös County, the last wolverines recorded east of Minnesota.

In 1929, Vermont closed the season on fisher (*Martes pennanti*); New Hampshire followed suit in 1934, then a year later, closed the season on the American (pine) marten (*Martes americana*), which were already gone from the entire Connecticut River watershed.

New Colonists

In the late seventeenth century, when pioneers first paddled the upper Connecticut River, red fox (*Vulpes vulpes*) were absent. This was the land of the gray fox (*Urocyon cinereoargenteus*), the small, tree-climbing canid of eastern broadleaf forest. Red fox arrived with the colonists, a nonnative mammal brought to the New World by British fox hunters. It prospered during the era of land clearing and is common today wherever there is a mix of forests and fields.

Two species of mammals colonized the region in the twentieth century: the opossum (*Didelphis virginiana*) and the coyote (*Canis latrans*). The opossum spread steadily northward from the Middle Atlantic states since the sixteenth century—perhaps because of a natural warming trend more recently augmented by global warming—and was first recorded in Warner, N.H., in 1915 and in Dorset, Vt., in 1921. Now the opossum is found well north in the watershed.

Coyotes were first recorded in New Hampshire in 1944, according to the state Fish and Game Department, and in Vermont in 1948. Their population moved in from the Midwest, through Canada and into the northern reaches of Vermont and New Hampshire, and now has spread throughout the watershed. Tissue analyses of eastern coyotes in New England have shown a great deal of wolf blood related to the gray wolf (*Canis lupus*) of Quebec. This interbreeding has led to the eastern coyote being significantly larger than its western counterpart. While the large tracts of habitat in the northern watershed of both states may be suitable for wolves, sightings of wolves have not been verified in either state for over a century.

Coyotes aren't picky eaters. They're known to eat mammals from mice to deer; birds from sparrows to wild turkeys; plus bird eggs, reptiles, amphibians, insects, domestic and wild carrion, garbage, shoe leather, green corn, nuts, and fruit. They're particularly fond of cantaloupes and apples.

In the decades after the Civil War, as people left New England to settle the Midwest, trees began to regenerate across abandoned pastures and farms. Eventually, forest mammals reclaimed lost ground. By the dawn of the twenty-first century, the population of white-tailed deer (*Odocoileus virginianus*) was at an all-time high. Populations

The adaptable coyote uses a wide range of field and forest habitats.

of both moose (*Alces alces*) and black bear (*Ursus americanus*) have grown exponentially. Both have become familiar sights along waterways, roads, orchards, and other open spaces; periodically, bear and moose cross suburban yards, often in daylight.

Reintroductions

As abandoned farmland gave way to regenerating forests, state wildlife agencies brought several species of extirpated mammals back to the upper Connecticut River valley. Between 1957 and 1969, Vermont released 124 Maine-trapped fishers. By 1971, descendants of these animals, augmented by New Hampshire's native stock that had spread out of the White Mountains, recolonized the watershed. Fishers feast on squirrels, mice, snowshoe hare, ground-nesting birds, apples, nuts, and the occasional porcupine and raccoon. Less frequently, fishers prey on bobcat kits, fawns, and adult foxes.

Both New Hampshire and Vermont reintroduced American martens. In 1975, New Hampshire released 25 animals from Maine, and

animals were released in Vermont's Green Mountain National Forest between 1989 and 1991. These efforts appeared unsuccessful at first, but now this lithe, arboreal member of the weasel family once again is gaining a foothold in the northern watershed, where it prefers higher elevation forests.

Canada lynx (*Lynx canadensis*), a boreal wildcat of the most remote corners of northern New England, disappeared as a breeding population from the White Mountains by the late 1970s. A verified lynx track found in the White Mountains in 2006 caused considerable excitement, and in 2007 their presence was confirmed in Vermont's Northeast Kingdom. Bobcat (*Lynx rufus*), a southern relative of the lynx, has a different history. Before settlement, wolves and catamounts stole prey from bobcats and lynx. In the absence of the big predators, the watershed's bobcat population peaked in the 1930s and 1940s. Since the arrival of the carcass-stealing coyote, bobcat populations have declined. These shy mammals are seldom seen.

The Connecticut River separates the Green Mountains and the White Mountains, draining their east and west slopes respectively.

The forest-dwelling American marten is listed as endangered in Vermont and threatened in New Hampshire. It has been reintroduced in both states. This one was found on Mount Pierce, on the watershed's eastern edge in New Hampshire.

The bobcat is an elusive but not uncommon watershed resident that requires dense forest understories and a healthy population of its major prey, the snowshoe hare. This one was spotted in Lyme, N.H.

Because much of the land in both mountain ranges has been protected by the federal government as national forests, sections of the river valley are vital corridors that permit the genes of adjacent populations of wide-ranging mammals—bobcat, black bear, moose, fisher, otter, and now American marten—to move between areas. If the corridors were lost to residential and commercial development, movement between the refuges would end and the species would become geographically confined. Inbreeding, which becomes common in small, isolated populations of wide-ranging mammals, severely reduces genetic diversity and is thus a prescription for local extinction.

Semi-Aquatic Species

Besides beaver and otter, the upper Connecticut River watershed is home to a number of semi-aquatic mammals: mink, muskrat, water shrew, and star-nosed mole. The mink (*Mustela vison*) is a major predator on fish and frogs and rodents up to the size of young muskrats. The northern water shrew (*Sorex palustris*) feeds on small fish,

tadpoles, and aquatic insects. Although the star-nosed mole (*Condylura cristata*) feeds primarily on earthworms, it also enters the water to catch small fish and tadpoles. Muskrats (*Ondatra zibethicus*) feed mainly on cattails, arrowhead, water lilies, and pickerel weed, but also eat sluggish aquatic animals, including freshwater clams, crayfish, and snails.

Beaver (*Castor canadensis*), once extirpated from the watershed but reintroduced in the 1920s, are once again its principal habitat architects. Their ponds provide homes to all other semi-aquatic mammals, wood ducks and black ducks, American bitterns, swamp sparrows, willow flycatchers, eastern kingbirds, red-winged blackbirds, and brook trout. Small woodpeckers and other cavity-nesting species, from chickadees to saw-whet owls, are attracted by the scores of drowned, dead trees standing in the midst of beaver ponds. Moose, deer, and black bear feed in ponds, while predators from goshawks to bobcats hunt the borders.

The river otter (*Lutra canadensis*) is the watershed's specialist. Otter families travel up to 50 miles of river, stream, and lakeshores, some-

These tracks of a lynx were found during a wildlife crossing survey near the border of Jefferson and Randolph, N.H., in January 2006. The last confirmed lynx sighting in New Hampshire was in the early 1990s. The Route 2/Route 115 wildlife crossing investigation sponsored by New Hampshire Audubon identified the locations where wildlife prefer to cross highways, then identified the roadway, habitat, and landscape elements associated with those crossing areas. During the course of the study (December 2005 to May 2006), over 7,000 animal tracks were recorded along the highway.

The beaver is North America's largest rodent. It creates its own habitat by building dams.

times crossing miles over land to reach a particular pond or marsh. The passage of the federal Clean Water Act in 1972 and a widespread decline in the trapping of furbearers have combined to make the river otter a more common sight. The state of their population also reflects the overall health of the watershed; with their need for miles of intact wetland habitat, they are the canaries of our aquatic "coal mine." While the otter population seems to be holding its own, it bears watching. Fragmentation of habitat through road construction, filling of wetlands, and conversion of land to development may affect them. Like all the watershed's mammals, they live in an interdependent relationship with the land and environment.

Ted Levin is a naturalist and writer living in Thetford Center, Vt. In 2004, he was awarded the Burroughs Medal for nature writing.

River otters travel widely using riparian corridors. They prefer areas with complex vegetative structures, such as fallen and submerged trees, tall grass patches, and dense thickets of shrubs.

FOR FURTHER READING

DeGraaf, Richard M., and Mariko Yamasaki. 2001. *New England Wildlife: Habitat, Natural History, and Distribution*. Hanover, N.H.: University Press of New England.

New Hampshire Wildlife Action Plan. 2005. Concord, N.H.: N.H. Fish and Wildlife Department. www.wildlife.state.nh.us/Wildlife/wildlife_plan.htm.

Klyza, Christopher McGrory. 2001. *Wilderness Comes Home: Rewilding the Northeast*. Hanover, N.H.: University Press of New England.

Silver, Helenette. 1957. *A History of New Hampshire Game and Furbearers*. Concord, N.H.: Evans Printing Co.

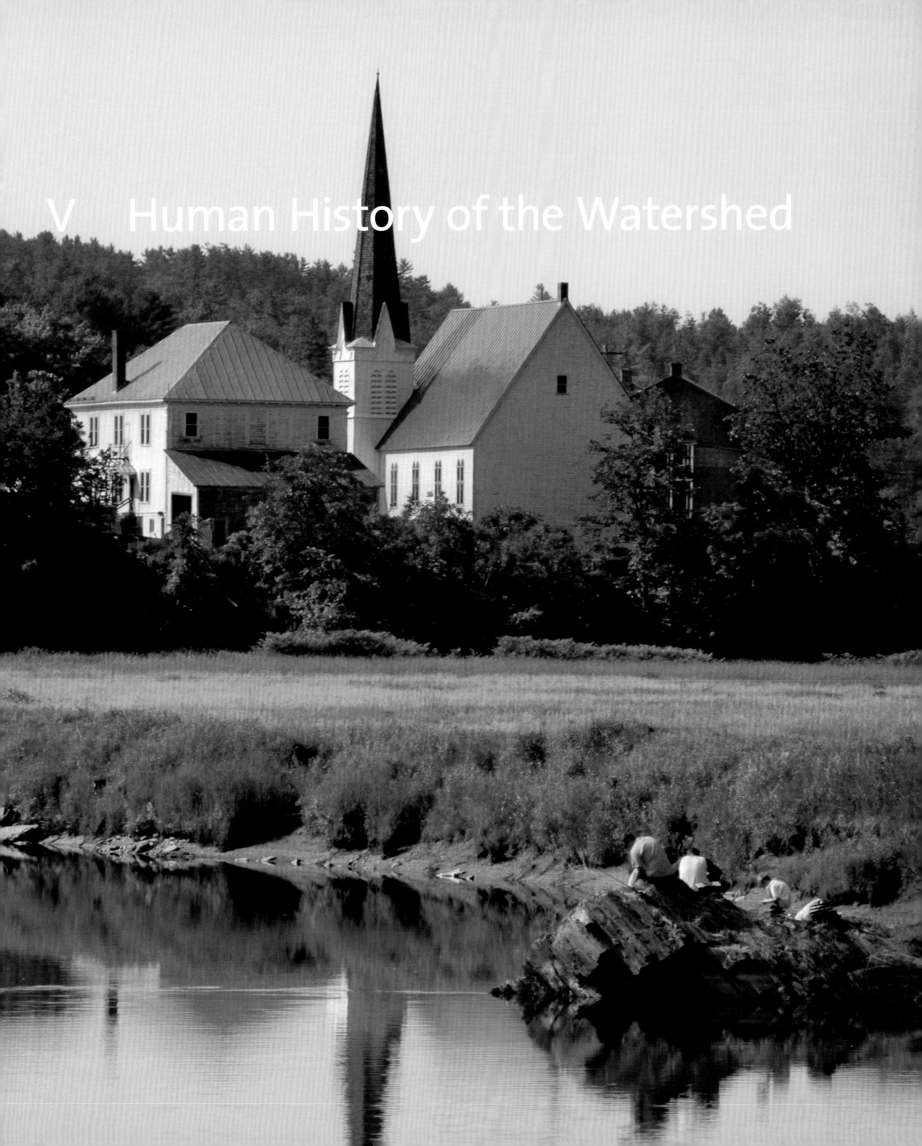

Introduction

Seen as a seamless green ribbon from far above, the Connecticut River Valley is a study in contrasts on a human scale. Its human history ranges from the earliest settlements of paleo-Indians who followed the glaciers' retreat, to seventeenth-century European fur traders, to colonial conflicts among the British, French, and shifting alliances of Indian allies and foes, to the founding days of the Republic, to the formation of an economy that evolved from pastoral to industrial.

The contrast between industrial and pastoral eras still may be seen at the opposite ends of the river valley. In the south, Brattleboro is the gateway to the Precision Valley, as the region became known in the nineteenth century for its ascendant machine tool industry. In the north, there are still forested hollows so remote that with a little imagination, one can conjure up the crackle of an Abenaki fire. On roiling stretches of the Connecticut, it's easy to imagine river drivers armed with peaveys and clad in spiked boots. Along the river valley, some farmers still work land first cleared by white settlers.

This section traces the human history of the valley. In many ways, the story is a microcosm of that of the nation itself: the forays into the wilderness by Europeans seeking to capitalize on the region's bountiful natural resources and their varied interactions, some peaceful, many bloody, with the region's Native population; the bending of the land to the new settlers' uses; and later, the ingenuity of inventors and engineers who harnessed the river's power to turn their mill stones and turbines. The river has always been a central player in the story. It was a passageway for traders and native paddlers, for explorers and for armies. As the dividing line between Vermont and New Hampshire, the river has served as a handy reference point from the states' very founding. But as Jere Daniell tells us in Chapter 21, Early Settlement, this boundary was not always so clear. Some New Hampshire river towns actually seceded for a time and joined Vermont—and a countermovement arose from a few towns in the Green Mountain State that sought to join New Hampshire. Today's conception of the river as a uniting and dividing place for the states actually has deep historical roots.

This account begins thousands of years before the American Revolution, with the native tribes who were the earliest human residents of the valley. Their story of the valley's creation and the place of Native Americans in its history, is eloquently told by Lisa Brooks, Donna Roberts Moody, and John Moody in Chapter 20, Native Space. The struggle of colonial settlers to carve out farmland from the wilderness, and to take advantage of the river valley's rich bottomlands is told in Chapter 22 by Steve Taylor, who describes the back breaking labor of forest clearing, followed decades later by the unimaginable riches for those lucky or perspicacious enough to ride the crest of the craze for Merino wool. In Chapter 24, Richard Ewald starts his account of the rise of industry in the valley with a visionary business owner whose new methods for making paper from wood pulp helped spark an economic revolution.

An early French illustration of an eighteenth-century Abenaki couple.

20 Native Space

Abenaki Adaptation in the Kwanitekw Valley

For the Alnôbak who are indigenous to the abundant intervales and forested mountains of Kwanitekw, this "long river" has always been a center of adaptation, subsistence, and exchange.* While the settlers of Vermont and New Hampshire designated this river as a boundary, within Native Space, Kwanitekw has operated as a major trade corridor, travel route, and gathering place for indigenous families.† It represents a nexus of life in Wôbanaki, the land of the dawn.

Creation of the River Valley

Kwanitekw is uniquely situated between two key emergence places, Bitabakw (Lake Champlain) and Wôbiadenak (the White Mountains). In the traditional Abenaki creation story, it is said that Odzihozo, "he who shapes himself from something," moved through the landscape, his body forming fertile bowl-shaped valleys, or *wôlhanak*, as he dragged himself around by his strong arms, pushing up the land into the mountains that formed on either side, and sending boulders crashing in his wake. Exhausted and satisfied with his work, Odzihozo came to rest on Bitabakw, beside the wôlhana of Winooskik, where you can see him sitting amongst his family still. Colonial governors recorded the offerings left by Native people when they passed by Odzihozo in their canoes, to ensure they would not be overturned by his yet-powerful wake.

In what is now known as the upper Connecticut River Valley, two regional *wôlhanak* emerged from within the abundant bowls carved by Odzihozo, forming the lower homeland of Sokwakik, the south place, the home of those who separated, and the upper homeland of Koesek, the north place, the place of pines. Here, where the spring fishing was abundant, and the game was good, families of the Alnôbak gathered. Women cultivated the medicinal and edible plants that grew in the marshes, while men learned to work with the forest, cultivating fire and cutting wood to ensure the most hospitable environment for hunting game. The Kwanitekw valley was not a wilderness, but an environment in which many beings participated, including humans, plants, and animals, and in particular, beavers. The people were dependent on the plants that grew in the marshes created by beavers, as well as on the game animals that followed the beaver in their cycle of flooding, retreat, and return. People learned from watching beavers, and told stories that helped them to remember how to live in this dynamic, changing land.

The old stories tell of Ktsi Amiskw, the Great Beaver, who held back the waters of Kwanitekw, hoarding them behind his mighty dam. It is said that Hobomok, a southern cousin to Odzihozo, punished the beaver for his greed, breaking his back in half, and releasing the water for all the people, plants, and animals who suffered from drought.‡ You can see Ktsi Amiskw still, below the great falls of Pocumtuc, or Deerfield, Mass. This story tells us about the geography and geology of the region—the formation of the great bowl left by a glacial lake, and of the mountain that forms the end of a long ridge, allowing for navigation within the landscape—but it also tells us of our history, and of how to navigate through the problematic landscape of the present. This story contains hard memories of the beaver wars that coursed through the landscape when Europeans entered Native Space in the seventeenth century, transforming the extensive trade networks of Kwanitekw, disrupting the beavers' cycle, and creating a world of imbalance. As colonial war flooded the landscape, the Alnôbak, like the beaver, entered into a new cycle of adaptation and change.

---

*Alnôbak is the traditional name that Abenaki people have used to describe ourselves. It simply means "human beings" (as opposed to all the other living beings with whom we share this land). Since colonization, however, it has evolved in usage to mean the indigenous people of this land. "Abenaki" is the term that is in most frequent use, both within and outside of Native communities, to refer to the related family bands indigenous to present-day Vermont, New Hampshire, northwestern Massachusetts, and southern Quebec, who are described by anthropologists and historians as the Western (and sometimes Central) Abenaki. Abenaki comes from the word Wôbanaki or Wabanaki, which describes all of the "people of the dawn," including the Eastern nations of the Penobscot, Passamaquoddy, Maliseet, and Mik'maq. This word refers to both the people and the place to which we belong, and literally translates to "dawnland," because we are the first to greet the light of the Sun, as it emerges off the coast on its daily round.

†When European colonists arrived on the Algonquian coast, they entered into Native Space, a network of relations and waterways containing many different groups of indigenous people as well as animal, plant, and rock beings that was sustained through the constant transformative activity of its inhabitants.

‡These stories that revolve around what anthropologists term "transformers" are common throughout the Northeast. We think of these creative beings who shaped and formed the land as relations to one another, since they play similar roles in regional stories, but are rooted firmly in particular places and communities. These "transformers" or "earthshapers" include Odzihozo in Western Abenaki country, Gluskabe in Eastern Abenaki country, Maushop in Wampanoag, Narragansett, and Mohegan/Pequot country, and Hobomok in the lower Kwanitekw valley (as well as contiguous regions). Many of these stories, like that of Ktsi Amiskw, demonstrate the connections among families within the network of relations that constitutes the expansive Native space of the Northeast. Related oral traditions take shape in multiple regions, often communicating similar information about how to be human in a shared landscape, but remaining firmly rooted in particular places and landforms. For a thorough exploration of this topic, see Marge Bruchac, "Earthshapers and Placemakers: Algonkian Indian Stories and the Landscape," in *Indigenous Archaeologies: Politics and Practice*, ed. H. Martin Wobst and Claire Smith (London: Routledge Press, 2003).

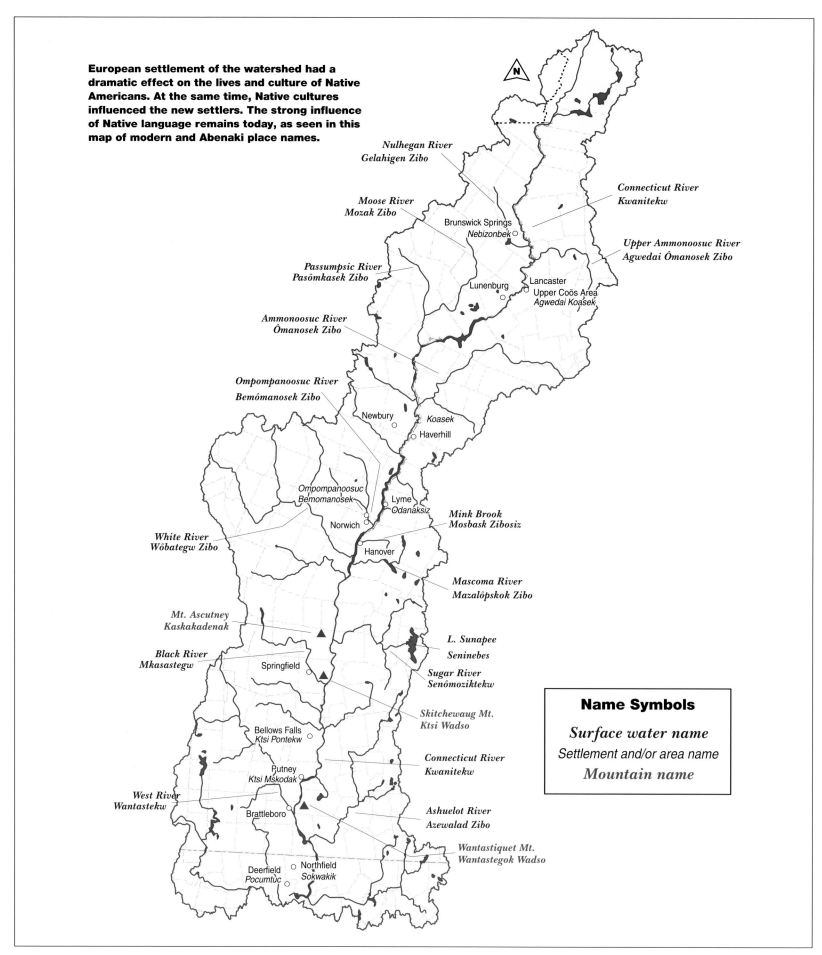

European settlement of the watershed had a dramatic effect on the lives and culture of Native Americans. At the same time, Native cultures influenced the new settlers. The strong influence of Native language remains today, as seen in this map of modern and Abenaki place names.

Nulhegan River
Gelahigen Zibo

Connecticut River
Kwanitekw

Moose River
Mozak Zibo

Brunswick Springs
Nebizonbek ○

Upper Ammonoosuc River
Agwedai Ômanosek Zibo

Passumpsic River
Pasômkasek Zibo

Lancaster
Upper Coös Area
Agwedai Koasek

Lunenburg
○

Ammonoosuc River
Ômanosek Zibo

Ompompanoosuc River
Bemômanosek Zibo

Newbury
○

Koasek

○ Haverhill

Ompompanoosuc
Bemomanosek

Lyme
Odanáksiz

Mink Brook
Mosbask Zibosiz

Norwich ○

White River
Wôbategw Zibo

Hanover
○

Mascoma River
Mazalôpskok Zibo

Mt. Ascutney
Kaskakadenak

L. Sunapee
Seninebes

Black River
Mkasastegw

Springfield
○

Sugar River
Senômoziktekw

Skitchewaug Mt.
Ktsi Wadso

Bellows Falls
Ktsi Pontekw
○

Connecticut River
Kwanitekw

Putney
Ktsi Mskodak

West River
Wantastekw

Brattleboro
○

Ashuelot River
Azewalad Zibo

Wantastiquet Mt.
Wantastegok Wadso

Deerfield
Pocumtùc
○

○ Northfield
Sokwakik

Name Symbols

Surface water name
Settlement and/or area name
Mountain name

Map 38. Native and European Names in the Watershed.

134

Seasons of Adaptation and Change

Long before the transformations wrought by the entry of Europeans, the Alnôbak had learned to accommodate change, to adapt and survive. An extensive network of trails and waterways connected Kwanitekw to the Native nations along Sobagw (Atlantic Ocean) and within the deep woodland interiors to the north and west. The people who traveled by footpath and canoe brought knowledge, material goods, as well as the stories that shaped them. Corn traveled all the way from its origin point in Mexico to Kwanitekw accompanied by the Corn Mother story, which revealed how to cultivate good relations with the plants and their keepers. Before the coming of corn, women had learned to cultivate flowering plants in the marshes, butternut trees on the riverbanks, and squash in the village fields. They quickly learned to adapt this newcomer to their river valley. From the banks of Kwanitekw, a seasonal system emerged that would sustain the Alnôbak for generations to come.

Every year, as the snow began to melt, icy cold spring waters would descend from the mountains and the river would fill. The people themselves would descend from the surrounding forested uplands, where they had their winter hunting camps. As spring waters broke through the ice, the sap in the maple trees would start to flow, and families gathered to boil the slow-moving sap into syrup. Soon after, the salmon and shad made their way upstream from the ocean to spawn in the icy rapids of Kwanitekw. The fish were so abundant below the "great falls" of Ktsipontekw (Bellows Falls) that it is said one could walk across the river on their backs. As the fish came upstream, families coalesced around the falls, to seine and smoke salmon and shad. After a long hard winter, fresh fish was a welcome sight in pots and over fires, and the maple syrup seemed a sweet gift. This sustenance enabled the women to then begin their planting on the banks. It was hard work. The people had to cultivate and harvest enough food for themselves, and also for visitors who would come to trade as the months grew warmer under the light of the sun.

The River Valley in War and Peace

Kwanitekw emerged as a center of human activity and cultural exchange. Families gathered at Sokwakik and Koasek to trade goods and exchange news, to renew longstanding relationships, and to forge new ones through marriage. Here, culture was renewed and remade, dances and songs created, stories recalled. Here, conflicts were ameliorated and families made.

When Europeans entered from the sea to the southern stretch of the valley, the Alnôbak attempted to incorporate them into this network of relations and trade. Long councils were held on the banks of Kwanitekw, with French and English, Kanienkehaga (Mohawk), and Abenaki, under the same tent. Agreements emerged, in the wake of war, for sharing the space of the valley. However, the English desire for land seemed to mirror the Great Beaver's desire for water. As the forts and settlements pushed upriver, Abenaki raiding parties traveled south. Contrary to popular belief, the "frontier" did not thrust continually west and north. Rather, for 150 years, there was a dynamic force of recede, retreat, and return, for both Abenaki and English, in

ABENAKI PLACE NAMES IN THE CONNECTICUT RIVER VALLEY

There are still a few Native place names surviving in the Connecticut River watershed, including Kwanitekw, the Connecticut River's original Abenaki name. Not until the 1950s did scholars realize that the entire upper Connecticut River watershed had been the homeland of one people, the Abenaki, for thousands of years. For over two centuries, newcomers have tried to sort out Abenaki place names, often adding more confusion than clarity to the process.

Today we have a small but reliable set of sources to sort out these place names' meanings and spellings, based on Abenaki speakers from over four centuries. These insights are a rare gift and give the reader a long look back at the most enduring geography of the upper Connecticut River Valley.

The accompanying table provides the reader with the contemporary place name, the correct Abenaki names (where possible), and the translation. Several names—noted with an asterisk on the table— represent our best translation, pending further research.

There are literally thousands of other Abenaki place names that are indigenous to the upper Connecticut River Valley. Most Abenaki place names lean toward being practical and directly observable rather than the romanticized, nineteenth-century versions found throughout American literature. We have found that the translations cited in John Huden's and Esther Swift's Vermont and New England place name works repeat some of these common misconceptions, whereas the works by Joseph Laurent, Henry Masta, Jesse Bruchac, and Gordon Day are much more grounded in the Abenaki language.

SOURCES

Bruchac, Jesse. 1995. "Abenaki Place Names in Vermont," manuscript in possession of the authors.

Day, Gordon. 1994/1995. *Western Abenaki Dictionary*. 2 vols. Hull, Quebec: Canadian Museum of Civilization, Mercury Series, nos. 128 and 129.

———. 1975. *The Mots Loup of Father Mathevet*. Ontario: Canadian Museum of Civilization, Mercury Series, no. 8.

Huden, John C. 1962. *Indian Place Names of New England*. New York: Heye Foundation.

———. 1957. *Indian Place Names of Vermont*. Montpelier, Vt.: Vermont Historical Society. Monograph Number 1.

Masta, Henry Lorne. 1932. *Abenaki Indian Legends, Grammar, and Place Names*. Victoriaville, Quebec: La Voix des Bois-Francs.

Laurent, Joseph. 1884. *Abenaki and English Dialogues*. Quebec City, Quebec: Leger Brosseau.

Shea, Peter. 1985. "A New and Accurate Map of Philip's Grant." *Vermont History* 53, no. 1: 36–42.

Swift, Esther Munroe. 1977. *Vermont Place Names—Footprints of History*. Brattleboro, Vt.: Stephen Greene Press.

Translations of Selected Abenaki Names in the Connecticut River Watershed

CONTEMPORARY NAME	ABENAKI NAME	TRANSLATION
Pocumtuc, Deerfield, Mass., & Deerfield River in Mass. & Vt.*	Pokw'mtekw	Very narrow river
Connecticut River	Kwanitekw	Long River
Northfield, Mass./Squakheag	Sokwakik	Land of the People who separated
South Vernon, Vt.	Koasek	Pine Tree Place
Meadows south of Brattleboro	Odanak	Village
Whetstone Brook, Brattleboro, Vt.	Kitadowôgani Zibosiz	Whetstone Brook
West River	Wantastekw	Lost River
Wantastiquet Mountain	Wantastegok Wadso	Lost Place Mountain
Ashuelot River	Azewalad Zibo†	One carries (rather than canoes) someone across or up the River
Great Meadows, Putney, Vt.	Ktsi Mskodak	Great Meadows
Mount Monadnock	Menonadenak	Smooth Mountain
Bellows Falls	Ktsi Pontekw	Great Falls
Black River	Mkasawitekw	Black River
Skitchewaug Mountain	Ktsi Wadso	Big Mountain (Also Abenaki Man's Name)
Sugar River	Senômoziktekw	Sugar Maple River
Lake Sunapee	Seninebes	Rock Lake
Mount Ascutney	Kaskakadenak	Wide Mountain
Mascoma River	Mazalôpskok Zibo	Clap place River (Also Sokwaki Man's Name)
White River	Wôbatekw	Clear River
Mink Brook, Hanover, N.H.	Mosbasak Zibosiz	Mink Brook
Ompompanoosuc River	Bemômanosek Zibo	Fishing place River
Pompanossuc, Norwich, Vt.	Bemômanosek	Fishing place
Ordanakis, Lyme, N.H.	Odanaksiz	Little village
Kikon, Bradford, Vt.	Kikônek	Place of the Field
Mount Moosilauke	Mozalhlakik Wadso	Cow Moose Land Mountain
Newbury, Vt., & Haverhill, N.H.	Koasek	Pine Tree Place
Upper Coös, Lunenburg, Vt., Lancaster, N.H.	Agwedai Koasek	Upstream/Upper Pine Tree
Musquash Meadows, Newbury, Vt.	Moskwasak Mskodak	Muskrat Meadows
Lake Tarleton, Piermont, N.H.	Nitamibakw	First Lake
Passumpsic River	Pasômkasek Zibo	Sandy bottom River
Moose River	Mozak Zibo	Moose River
Ammonoosuc River	Ômanosek Zibo	Fishing River
Upper Ammonoosuc River	Agwedai Ômanosek Zibo	Upstream/Upper Fishing River
Brunswick Springs	Nebizônbek	Medicine Springs
Nulhegan River	Gelahigen Zibo†	Deadfall Trap River
Clyde River	Mskwamatekw	Red Fish/Salmon River
Island Pond	Menahanibakw	Island Lake
Lake Memphremagog	Mamhlibakok	Wide or Expansive Lake
Barton River, Orleans & Newport, Vt.	Kikômkwak Zibo	Carp River
Mt. Metalak, Millsfield, N.H., Metallak Island	Môlôdakw	Cedar Man (Name of Abenaki Man)
Molls Rock, Errol, N.H.	Mali Senek	Molly's Rock (Named for an Abenaki Woman)
Lake Umbagog	Wôbakok	Clear Lake Place
Saco River	Zawakwtekw Msoakwtekw	Dead Trees River
Lake Winnipesaukee	Wiwinebeskik	Lake Region Place
Pemigewasett River	Bemijijoasek	Side Current River
Merrimack River	Molôdemak Zibo	Deep Water River
Missisquoi River	Wazawatekw	Crooked River
Lamoille River	Wintekw	Bone Marrow River
Winooski River	Winoskitekw	Onion Land River
Otter Creek	Onegigwtekw	Otter River
St. Francis River	Alsigôntekw	Empty Cabin River
Green Mountains of Vt.	Askaskwigek Adenak	Green Mountains
White Mountains of N.H.	Wôbiadenak	White Mountains
Mount Washington	Gôdagwadso	Hidden Mountain
Mount Washington	Ôgawakwadso†	Shaded Mountain

*The Pocumtuc People's name for themselves is Amiskwolowôkoiak, translated as Beaver Tail Hill People.
†Best translation currently available, pending further research.

the land of Sokwakik. Finally, the great Abenaki orator Atecuando sent a message to the English:

> You have the sea for your share from the place where you reside; you can trade there. But we expressly forbid you to kill a single beaver, or to take a single stick of timber on the lands we inhabit . . . We acknowledge no other boundaries of yours than your settlements whereon you have built, and we will not, under any pretext whatsoever, that you pass beyond them. The lands we possess have been given to us by the Master of Life. We acknowledge to hold only from him. (Calloway 1997)

In the wake of colonization, many Abenaki families sought shelter from the storm in the familiar, protected, upland hunting territories in the mountains. The north country of Koasek was connected by well-traveled trails and portages to all of the rivers of Wobanaki that converged above Wôbiadenak, the White Mountains. Here, in these high, sheltered peaks, it is said that the Alnôbak took refuge during a great flood. Perhaps this was the flood let loose when Hobomok released the water from Ktsi Amiskw's dam. Perhaps this was the ice age that swept through the landscape thousands of years ago, leaving only a few places where survivors might find shelter and vegetation. This story tells us that the mountains are a place of shelter, a place to which we can return in times of trouble. And as the flood of colonial warfare transformed the networks that connected Wôbanaki, the Alnôbak sought refuge in this storied place, hidden deep by the mountains to the north.

Families Lead the Culture Forward

During the years before, after, and during the American Revolution, family groups survived in the "north country" of Koasek, living a subsistence existence and maintaining a low profile. They fought on both sides of the war, served as scouts, traded goods, and provided medicine and knowledge of the landscape to their newcomer neighbors. When the tourist trade entered the north country, families developed fancy basket styles, and included hotels and resorts in their seasonal travels, incorporating the tourist trade into the subsistence cycle. Numerous families still maintain the old subsistence ways and the tradition of basketry, as well as the deep knowledge of the land in the north country of Koasek today. At the same time, Kwanitekw is in a new cycle of rebound and return. The beavers have returned to reconstruct their marshes, and likewise, Alnôbak families who originated in the south place have returned to the fertile valley to reconstruct its history. Abenaki women have been particularly active in this endeavor.

During those years prior and subsequent to the American Revolutionary War, Indian doctors such as Molly Ockett and Sally Soisen frequented the colonial settlements in the river valley, visiting the settlers who depended on their knowledge of plants and indigenous medicine. In fact, although often erased in American history, women always have been prominent in the Native Space of Kwanitekw. They were at the center of the development of agriculture over the course of thousands of years. Their names appear on the early deeds, acknowledging their "ownership" of the villages that they planted, and representing their special power over the community space and planting grounds.

When Dartmouth College was founded in "the wood of Coos" for the education of Indian youth, oral tradition tells us that its founders had to contract with the women who gathered at Mosbasak Zibosis (Mink Brook, a tributary of Kwanitekw), where Abenaki families have continued to live and gather until the present day.*

While women like Molly Ockett and Sally Soisen are often represented in town histories as anomalies from an Indian past, "descendants" of great nations, or "the last of their kind," in truth, they were only the most public face of extensive family networks that continued to inhabit the Kwanitekw valley, and particularly, the surrounding mountains, where "hiding in plain sight" was more feasible. Families who had occupied the fertile valleys supplanted by colonial towns, like many of the beaver and other animal families, retreated into areas that would still allow for cover and subsistence. Here, today, Alnôbaiwi, the ancient Abenaki way of life, is reemerging, as its families continue to adapt creatively to changes in the physical and social environment, and continue to survive as part of this dynamic, changing land of Wôbanakik.

Lisa Brooks is an Abenaki scholar with family roots in the headwaters of the Missisquoi River and the White Mountains. She is an assistant professor of history and literature and of folklore and mythology at Harvard University.

Donna Roberts Moody is an Abenaki mother and grandmother with deep roots in the Kwanitekw river valley. She is the repatriation and site protection coordinator for the Abenaki Nation, and the director of Winter Center for Indigenous Traditions based in the Upper Valley of Vermont and New Hampshire.

John Moody is an ethnohistorian. He is the co-founder and project coordinator for Winter Center for Indigenous Traditions.

For Further Reading

Bruchac, Joseph. 1995. *Long River*. Golden, Colo.: Fulcrum Publishing.

Calloway, Colin G. 1997. *After King Philip's War: Presence and Persistence in Indian New England*. Hanover, N.H.: University Press of New England.

Haviland, William A., and Marjory W. Power. 1994. *The Original Vermonters: Native Inhabitants, Past and Present*. Hanover, N.H.: University Press of New England.

Moody, John. 1982. The Native American Legacy. In *Always in Season: Folk Art and Traditional Culture in Vermont*. Middlebury: Vermont Council on the Arts.

* It was the famous Mohegan minister, Samson Occom, who expressed great disappointment that his mentor, Eleazar Wheelock, planned to locate his Indian school in "the woods of Coos," another variation of Koasek. Occom had traveled to England and raised a tremendous amount of funds for the school, which he believed would serve his relations in the south, as its predecessor, the Moors Indian Charity School in Lebanon, Conn., had. The Mohegans had worked as scouts for the English in their wars with the Abenaki, and the last place that Occom wanted to send his young nephews and nieces was a place that was still quite clearly Abenaki space. Indeed, more Abenaki than Mohegan students would attend Dartmouth College in the decades that followed.

21 Early Settlement

The rebuilt Fort at No. 4 in Charlestown, N.H., is a living museum of the early settlement era.

Fewer than a thousand Euro-Americans lived in the Connecticut River valley above the Massachusetts border in the beginning of the 1760s. More would have liked to, but for the past several decades France and England, each with Indian allies, had engaged in a series of bloody wars that made settlement unsafe. Construction of a fortification in Charlestown (Fort at No. 4) and another downriver near Brattleboro had provided only marginal security. Most settlers who had chanced migration lived south of the forts.

Migration into the River Valley

The wars ended in 1760. The previous September, the English had captured Quebec, and a year later Montreal fell. Canada's governor then surrendered the entire province. Even though formal cession didn't take place for another three years—in the Treaty of Paris—land-hungry English families in New England's four colonies began planning to move north into the valley's fertile bottomlands. Connecticut, whose population already exceeded agricultural carrying capacity, provided the bulk of the potential migrants; residents of central Massachusetts, eastern New Hampshire, and Rhode Island also thought of settling in the river valley.

Migrating required careful planning. The first step: acquire some land. In the early 1760s, the colony of New Hampshire assumed jurisdiction over all of what now is the Granite State and Vermont. Its governor and appointed council had begun chartering a township below Fort No. 4 a decade earlier. Obtaining land in a township was neither complicated nor costly.

The process started with a group of roughly 60 men (and occasionally women) petitioning the provincial authorities, choosing someone to visit Portsmouth and select the specific territory, and making payment, which totaled roughly a month's wages for each of the 60. The group members then became "proprietors" and assumed responsibility for dividing and developing the township. Each proprietor received a "right" to about three hundred acres. In 1761 alone, the governor and council created 35 new townships either on the Connecticut River or one tier back from it. Fifteen more came in the next three years. Individual proprietors, once assigned land, could keep, sell, or lease it. The one factor complicating this simple way of distributing land to potential settlers was an English court decision in 1764 making the acreage west of the river (today's Vermont) part of New York. New York, however, found it difficult to extend its authority into the valley,

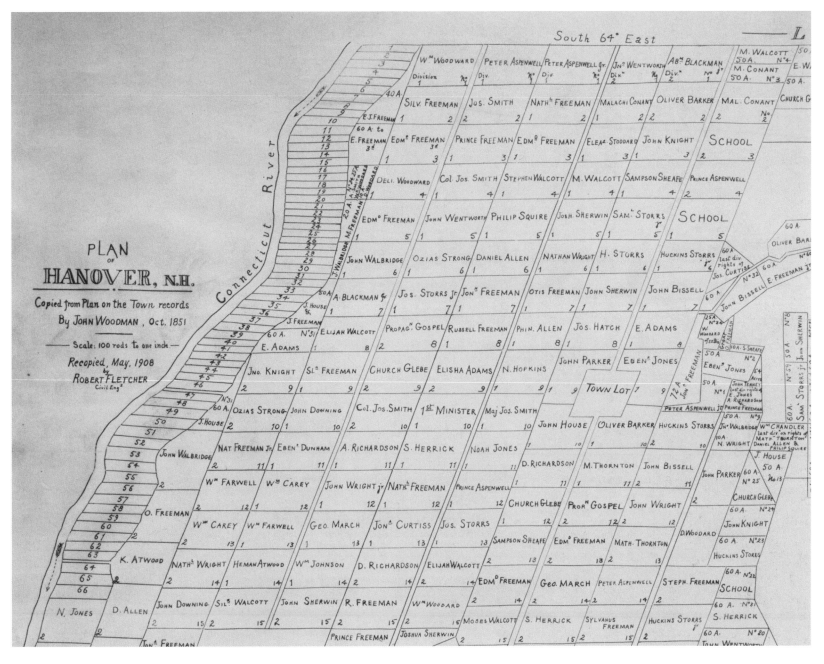

Plan of the town of Hanover, circa 1851, copied from a 1908 document.

so agreed to confirm — at a price — many of the grants made by New Hampshire.

The second step for obtaining land: those migrating had physically to move. Most were young men from downriver. North of the cross-river pairing of Lyme and Thetford, many of the migrants were former residents of New Hampshire's coastal region. Frequently the potential settler would spend summers preparing his land, then return home for the winter. Many married and brought their new brides north when the homestead was ready. The resulting valley population was very young. Half the residents, according to a 1786 New Hampshire census, were age 16 or under. Men outnumbered women, and few townspeople exceeded 50 years in age.

Creating Community

Once settled, most of the new arrivals adopted the familiar routines of agricultural life that their parents and grandparents had known. They cleared land, improved dwellings, let weather and the seasons dictate daily activities, and raised their children. Neighborhood and town defined community life. The former provided opportunities for socializing, labor for work like barn-raisings, and bartering partners for services and goods. The latter provided religious and political organization.

Incorporated towns existed throughout New England. Even though a valley town contained newcomers from all over the region, everyone knew about Congregational churches, ministers' rates (the form

THE
DRESDEN  MERCURY,
AND
Universal
THE
Intelligencer.

TUESDAY, *July* 13, 1779.   [*Number* 11.

Free as the Savage roams his native Wood,——Or finny Nations cleave the briny Flood.

DRESDEN: Printed by JUDAH-PADOCK & ALDEN SPOONER, in the South End of *Dartmouth* College.

To the People of the NEW HAMPSHIRE GRANTS, *East and West of Connecticut River.*

My Friends and Fellow-Countrymen,

To you I beg leave to address myself, who have before the world, signalized yourselves, almost four years, in that which unerringly marks the free born—a vigorous contest for your civil rights and liberties. Many and various have been the measures to accomplish so desirable an end——Various have been your prospects, and as various your feelings;—but you resolutely entered upon the necessary labor, while you were apprised of the only alternative, fatal ruin, should you fail before the completion. Time after time successively have been eclipsed by brighter ones—and now you have almost reached the closing period—your cause has gained the particular attention of the tribunal of America.——For this once, at least, add virtues to your resolution—convince the honorable Committee from Congress, who will soon be here, and will make a strict report of your true situation—that you are not so capricious that a meer brook or river can divide your sentiments——If you are united and determined to be together, you have nothing to fear. The reasons for dispute are not whether you shall all be with New-Hampshire, as before the year 1764, or whether you shall be organized into a new State; for your rights may be as permanently secured in the former, as in the latter case—this point is out of the question. The scale ponderates between New-York and New-Hampshire, so we have great reason to believe it is considered in the eye of Congress—Why then do you substitute an ideal in the place of your real interest—excuse the comparison—like the Dog in the fable, *while it was catching the shadow, lost the substance?* Be not deceived—think not that the members of Congress talk so open and free in favor of the State of Vermont—there are other and greater interests respecting the New Hampshire Grants, that influence their attention; they mean not to fabricate a new state out of ruins created by divisions caused by ambition and imprudence——connect with this idea the situation of Berkshire county in the Massachusetts; the fractured condition of some other states on the continent, and then reflect on the nature and influence of a precedent or example, and candidly say if you can, that Vermont, in its present situation, will be recognized.——Be not traduced by designing men, those whose mangled reputations depend only on the success of a party; but let every one carry his heart in his hand, be wrought upon by truth more than by characters, and support the essential union east and west of the Grants——Congress itself considers the Grants as existing on a common principle—their very latest declaration holds it forth—they resolve, " That a Committee be appointed to repair to the inhabitants of a *certain district*, known by the name of the New Hampshire Grants——" that is, both sides of Connecticut River; and if they consider you as being connected, why should you divide yourselves?—Pardon me for pressing the matter, that if you do not cement the union, and rivit the band, your neglect may prove your ruin—but if a general harmony, prudence, and zeal co operate, success will be the ernest of your future happiness.

A PATRIOT.

From the Exeter Journal of May 18.

OBSERVATIONS on the internal policy of the governments of New Hampshire and Vermont, so far as it seems to interfere with each other, or so far as unskilful politicians or designing men, or both together, have in some degree occasioned discord, by propagating among the inhabitants of each state, unjust motives of an imaginary selfish interest by enlarging and enriching the one, on the ruin of the other—— Witness the unjust and impolitic union, (which is now fully dissolved) which was formed between the state of Vermont, and a number of discontented towns on the east side of Connecticut River,—and also a late petition preferred to the General Assembly of New Hampshire, by Brigadier General Jacob Bailey, and Mr. Davenport Phelps, desiring them to assert a jurisdictional claim to the territory of the state of Vermont, the consideration thereof being laid over to the session of their Assembly in June next.

A number of designing geniuses on both sides of Connecticut River, and contiguous thereto, had best it into the heads of the inhabitants of that vicinity, that the Grants east of the River to the old Mason line, were unconnected with any government, as to their internal police, and that they were at liberty to connect with any government or political body. This delusion was with great art and industry propagated amongst the freemen of Vermont; and the magical influence of it was so great, that it charmed a majority of their House of Assembly, and young Vermont, in June 1778, stretched her wings over near one third part of the territory of New Hampshire; but a little cool reflection brought them (at their sessions in February 1779) to a sense of their mistake and danger, and excited them to withdraw it to the west side of the river again; nevertheless, it met with a small sprain, but is in a fair way to recover.

These disappointed schemers, who designed to connect the whole of the Grants west of the Mason line, into one entire state, and bring the centre of the government to Connecticut River; adopted a second scheme, viz. to use their magical influence with New-Hampshire, to lay a claim to the territory of Vermont, and accordingly circular letters were distributed though New Hampshire for that purpose.

This projection seems to be supported by the influence of part of the members of the Assembly of New Hampshire. Such part of the state as lies contiguous to Connecticut River, and whose inhabitants are desirous of bringing the seat of government into their neighbourhood, may be prevailed upon to endeavour the ruin of Vermont; to corroborate their interested view of extending jurisdiction over the premises others may be inclined to extend such a claim, as they may imagine that the acquisition of the territory of Vermont, would be a large addition of wealth and strength to New-Hampshire, and afford it great assistance in the heavy list of paying taxes. To this I beg leave to observe, that from the same parity of reasoning, the Grants east of Connecticut River to the Mason line, would have been a valuable acquisition to Vermont, (if they could have got it.) However both of these projections are as equally destitute of justice as of sound policy; and I apprehend that they are equally impracticable.

The circular letter prepared the laying in of the said claim, with a design of friendship to the inhabitants of Vermont; and I doubt not but that part of those gentlemen, who are in favor

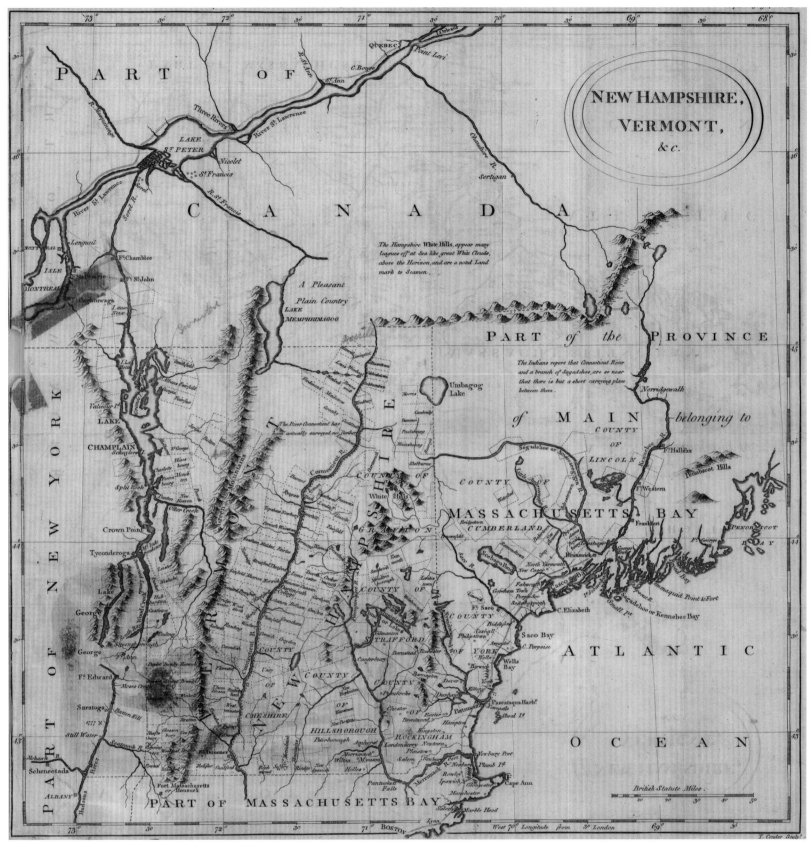

Map of the White Mountains (then called the White Hills), c. 1788.

The most unusual settlement narrative of the postrevolutionary period took place in what became the town of Pittsburg, N.H. Both Canada and United States claimed land north and west of the Connecticut River headwaters.

The disputed territory—named for Indian Stream, which flowed though it—began attracting frontiersmen early in the 1800s. Some were squatters, most held land company titles. In 1824, New Hampshire asserted jurisdiction by annexing Indian Stream to Coös County. Seven years later, the King of the Netherlands, asked to arbitrate the boundary dispute, awarded the land to Canada. Even though the United States Congress rejected the King's recommendations, the settlers took action. They declared independence by writing a constitution for what they called the Indian Stream Republic, elected their own government, and refused to obey any external authority. Two years of instability followed. Competing officials from Canada, New Hampshire, and the Republic arrested each other, and these detainees frequently were rescued back from their captors. Combat, however, was mostly verbal and nobody suffered serious injury.

In November 1835, New Hampshire sent the militia in, Canada backed off, and things calmed down. The end of the story: settlers forgot about independence, New Hampshire in 1840 incorporated Indian Stream as a town named Pittsburg, and the Webster Ashburton Treaty of 1842 set the northwest boundary with Canada where it sits today. Thus the short-lived Indian Stream Republic came to a quiet end.

Source

Doan, Daniel. 1997. *Indian Stream Republic: Settling a New England Frontier, 1785–1842.* Hanover, N.H.: University Press of New England.

of taxation), and annual meetings to select local officials. New Hampshire, moreover, facilitated quick creation of functioning town governments by authorizing proprietors to organize them before people moved. Hanover's initial town meeting, for example, took place in a Mansfield, Conn., tavern.

Revolution and Secession

One development seriously disrupted both northward migration and life in the incorporated communities already inhabited. Coastal colonists throughout America became first restless with—and then defiant toward—their transatlantic English rulers. The American Revolution had a major impact in the valley. Young men served in the military; rumors circulated that the British planned to invade from Canada; individual homesteads became small armed camps as they had during earlier wars; essential commodities became scarce; and fewer new settlers arrived. After American troops defeated the British at Saratoga in October 1777, the military threat subsided. But a different kind

of combat accelerated, one that involved words and institutions, not bullets. Many townspeople on both sides of the Connecticut River wanted to live in the same state. Those who acquired land before the 1764 boundary decision had assumed that New Hampshire reached over the Green Mountains, and even after the decision, retained the habits, friends, and beliefs stemming from their common Connecticut heritage.

In the summer of 1777, men from west of the Greens spearheaded a movement to secede from New York, wrote a constitution (while meeting in Windsor, on the west bank of the Connecticut) and declared the existence of a new state called Vermont. Settlers on both sides of the river took this as an opportunity to unite. In 1778, 14 valley towns on the east bank formally rejected New Hampshire authority and joined Vermont; 22 more joined the original 14 when a second union—the first lasted only a few months—took place in 1781 (see Map 39). Between the two east-bank secessions, a less aggressively organized campaign vied to have Vermont towns east of the Green Mountains join New Hampshire.

The logic of secessionists included the belief that revolution had erased all governmental allegiance except the loyalty individuals owed to their towns. Towns, then, could join whichever state they wanted. Practical, not theoretical, matters determined the outcome of these conflicts. The western Vermont leaders, especially Revolutionary War hero Ethan Allen and his brother Ira, worried that all those added New Hampshire towns would mean Connecticut River Valley control of the state they and their friends had created. Similar worries from the Piscataqua and Merrimack valley killed the idea of eastern Vermont joining New Hampshire. Once George Washington, speaking for the Continental Congress, told Vermont leaders that if they ever wanted to be admitted to the United States they should forget about expansion, the valley unionist movements collapsed.

Revolutionary Heritage

Two remnants of these aborted regional rebellions are with us today. One is local: shortly before the first union, parts of Hanover and Lebanon formed a "district" called Dresden to serve as the seat of government for a cross-river state to be called "New Connecticut." Dresden never became operational, but was reborn in the modern interstate Dresden School District of Norwich and Hanover. The other is national: the first union played an essential role in the creation of constitutional conventions. Valley towns east of the river justified their secession by complaining that they hadn't participated in writing New Hampshire's revolutionary constitution, nor been asked to either approve or reject it. The legislature agreed, and convened a special "Constitutional Convention" with representation from all towns to rewrite the existing document and submit it to voters for approval. Massachusetts also used a special convention to write its constitution, with the eventual result that other states followed the model created here in northern New England.

Another Treaty of Paris was signed in 1783, 20 years after the first one. In the new treaty, England recognized the independent United States of America. By that time, it was clear that the Connecticut River north of Massachusetts would remain a permanent boundary between

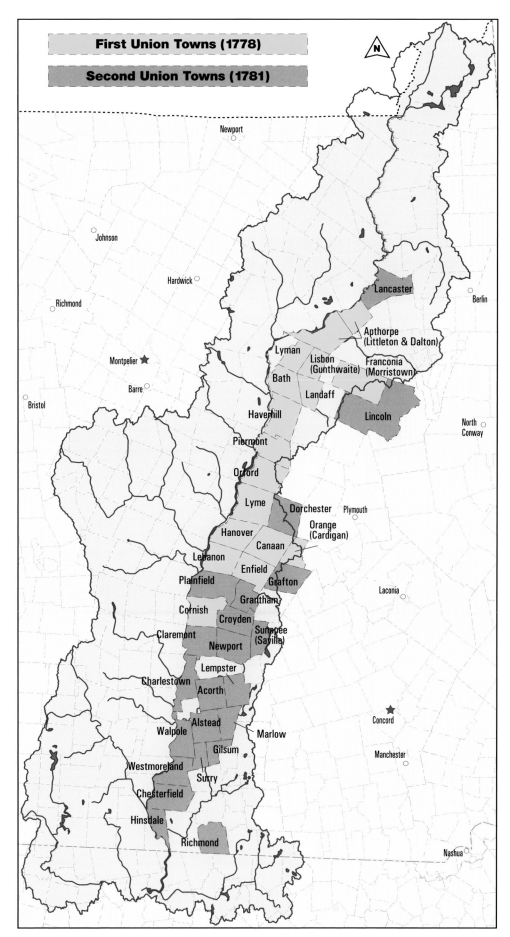

N

Newport

Johnson

Hardwick

Richmond

Berlin

Lancaster

Montpelier ★

Apthorpe
(Littleton & Dalton)

Lyman

Lisbon
(Gunthwaite)

Franconia
(Morristown)

Barre

Bath

Bristol

Landaff

Lincoln

North
Conway

Haverhill

Piermont

Orford

Lyme

Dorchester

Plymouth

Orange
(Cardigan)

Hanover

Canaan

Lebanon

Enfield

Laconia

Plainfield

Grafton

Grantham

Cornish

Croyden

Claremont

Sunepee
(Saville)

Newport

Lempster

Concord ★

Charlestown

Acorth

Alstead

Walpole

Marlow

Manchester

Gilsum

Westmoreland

Surry

Chesterfield

Hinsdale

Richmond

Nashua

Map 39. New Hampshire Towns Admitted to Vermont in 1778 and 1781.

The Constitution House in Windsor, Vt.

two different states. The valley, however, would remain a community in many senses. This Atlas testifies to the continued existence of a united valley heritage.

Jere Daniell is a retired professor of early American history at Dartmouth College. He is the author of three books on early New Hampshire history. He lives in Hanover, N.H.

FOR FURTHER READING

Bacon, Edwin M. 1911. *The Connecticut River Valley and the Valley of the Connecticut.* New York: G.P. Putnam.

Daniell, Jere R. 1981. *Colonial New Hampshire: A History.* Millwood, N.Y.: KTO Press.

———. 1970. *Experiment in Republicanism: New Hampshire Politics and the American Revolution, 1741–1794.* Cambridge, Mass.: Harvard University Press.

Williamson, Chilton. 1949. *Vermont in Quandary, 1763–1825.* Montpelier, Vt.: Vermont Historical Society.

22   Early Agriculture

Clearing the Land

The Connecticut River watershed, with its vast pine and hardwood forests, presented both great opportunity and tremendous challenges to the men and women who took up grants of land and set about to establish farms and settlements.

Standing timber was an immediately available resource for fuel, for construction of buildings, and for harvest as a cash crop. But the towering trees were also a great impediment to getting production of grain and animal forage crops underway. Opening the land for crop production was the first imperative of the settlers as they moved northward.

The strategy settlers commonly used to create tillable land was called "stubbing." They began by cutting the bark all the way around, or girdling, the tree. The tree would die and not leaf out, and sunlight would reach the forest floor the following year. Soil around the trees was then raked, hoed, or otherwise scarified so that seeds could be planted and a crop begun. Barley, oats, and wheat yielded grain and the residual straw provided roughage for livestock. Native grasses also sprang forth where the soil was bathed in sunlight, and these also could be harvested for hay to feed animals.

Removing the dead trees entailed much hard, dangerous work, and often took 15 or 20 years to accomplish. Usually the settlers built a fire around the base of each tree and burned as much of it as they could. After days or even weeks of stoking the fire, limbs and the upper trunk eventually would be consumed or fall to the ground, but the lower portion of the trunk would remain, leaving a blackened "stub." The stub could stand for years before the roots rotted enough that it could be pulled over with a chain and ox power. With these stubs removed, the landscape finally took on the familiar appearance of fields, meadows, and pastures that we know today.

Today we have little concept of the toil and danger that clearing the watershed's land for agriculture entailed. It was a process that spanned more than 200 years, and went forward amid all the work of planting and harvesting crops, building roads, erecting houses, barns, churches, and mills, and establishing public institutions such as the town meeting government.

The Cow Ascendant

A critical element in sustaining the earliest pioneer settlement was the cow, without which the opening of the forest for farming and establishment of communities would have been even more problematic. The cow provided several important products necessary for sustain-

Merino sheep loomed large in the watershed.

The Nelson farm in Ryegate, Vt., c. 1880, in a stereoscopic image.

ing human life in the remote, hostile environment of the pre-Revolutionary Connecticut River Valley countryside. A cow's milk yielded protein and fat for the human diet that could be stored in the form of cheese for later consumption. Cows produced offspring that could be raised for meat or for draft purposes. Their manure fertilized crops and their hides became leather.

Town by town, settlement crept north up the river. Land closest to the river was the first to be cleared. As more settlers came, agricultural activity spread along the banks of tributary streams and onto the hillsides. By the end of the Revolutionary War, agricultural activity was well established in the lower two-thirds of the watershed, with tens of thousands of acres of land cleared, villages with mills, stores, and public buildings developed, and networks of roads in place. The opening of the land for agriculture would continue in the northern reaches of the region well into the early part of the nineteenth century.

From Subsistence to Market

Most farming in the early years of colonial and postrevolutionary settlement was subsistence agriculture: crop production and raising livestock primarily for family sustenance. But as the productivity of farms increased, modest surpluses of grain, hay, and food animals on many farms enabled the development of a commercial, or cash crop,

dimension of agriculture. Thus came the drovers, entrepreneurs who assembled and herded cattle, hogs, sheep, and turkeys down the roads to markets as far off as Boston, Mass., and Hartford, Conn. Similarly, commerce sprang up in hay and grains, which were transported overland and by boat down the river.

By 1800, aggressive clearing of the land was continuing, primarily to create more cropland and pastures, but also to harvest timber for growing markets for lumber. Rather than burning trees to get rid of them, landowners were harvesting trees, pine and oak in particular, as another type of crop.

The Sheep Craze

With as much as 80 percent of the land area of many towns cleared for agriculture in the middle and lower reaches of the watershed by the turn of the eighteenth century, the stage was set for the only period of true agricultural prosperity the region has ever known. The engine: sheep.

Sheep commonly were raised for mutton by farmers of English ancestry, with animals yielding minimal amounts of wool. But in 1809, William Jarvis of Weathersfield, Vt., President Thomas Jefferson's envoy to the Spanish Court, arranged the importation of several thousand valuable Merino sheep from the Iberian Peninsula into

The home of Merino sheep entrepreneur William Jarvis in Weathersfield Bow, Vt.

the United States. These animals became the genetic foundation for a huge expansion of sheep numbers and dramatic increases in wool production.

In what came to be called the "Merino Craze," farmers throughout New England took to raising sheep to capture the profits from producing wool for the numerous textile mills that were springing up. By 1825, several towns in the watershed were home to 10,000 or more head of sheep, and virtually every town had a substantial sheep population. Map 40 depicts the preponderance of sheep in some watershed towns, and Figure 16 compares sheep and human populations by town.

The first imperative of this massive sheep enterprise was fencing in the flock. Thousands of miles of walls were laid on the landscape using the most common building material to be had: stones. Sheep were pastured in the warm-weather months on the uplands, and the more fertile lands near the streams were used to grow the hay necessary to feed the flocks over the long winters.

Fortunes were made with sheep, but competition from elsewhere in the world lowered the value of wool by 1840. The enduring legacies of the sheep era endure, however, as stonewalls are a signature part of the valley's landscape, as are the fine period architecture of homes built by those who enjoyed the profits of the wool trade.

As important as they were to the watershed's agricultural and cultural history, Merino sheep may be considered a fad, or a phase that

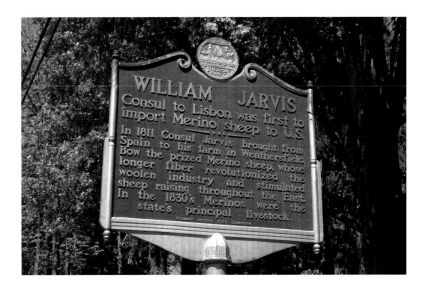

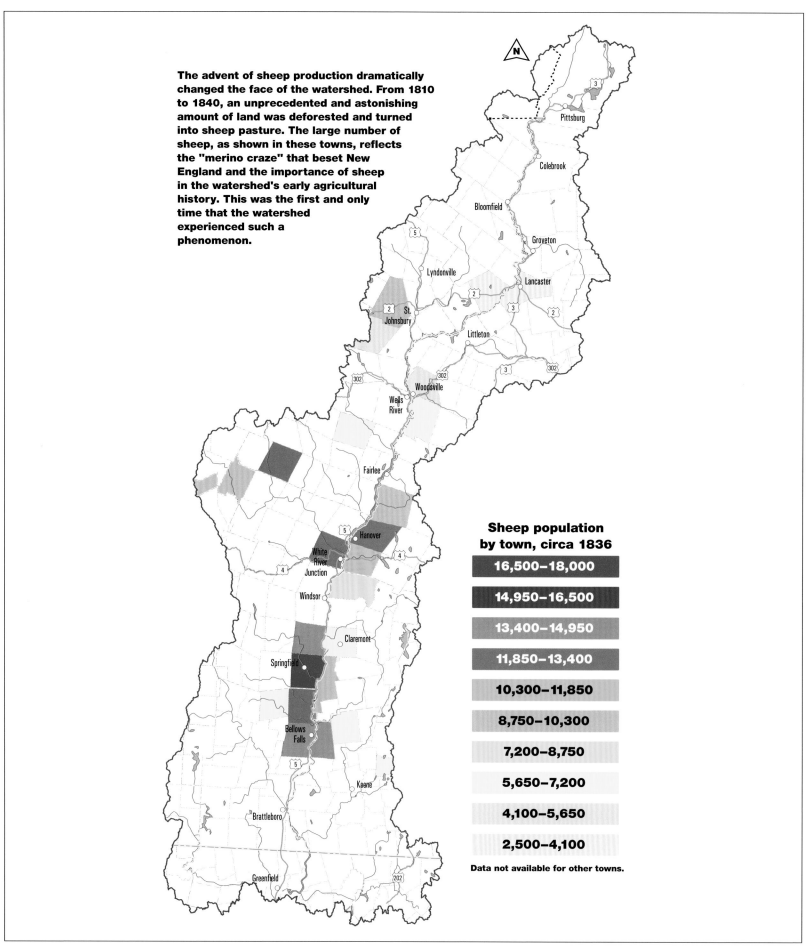

The advent of sheep production dramatically changed the face of the watershed. From 1810 to 1840, an unprecedented and astonishing amount of land was deforested and turned into sheep pasture. The large number of sheep, as shown in these towns, reflects the "merino craze" that beset New England and the importance of sheep in the watershed's early agricultural history. This was the first and only time that the watershed experienced such a phenomenon.

Sheep population by town, circa 1836

16,500–18,000

14,950–16,500

13,400–14,950

11,850–13,400

10,300–11,850

8,750–10,300

7,200–8,750

5,650–7,200

4,100–5,650

2,500–4,100

Data not available for other towns.

Map 40. The Merino Craze.

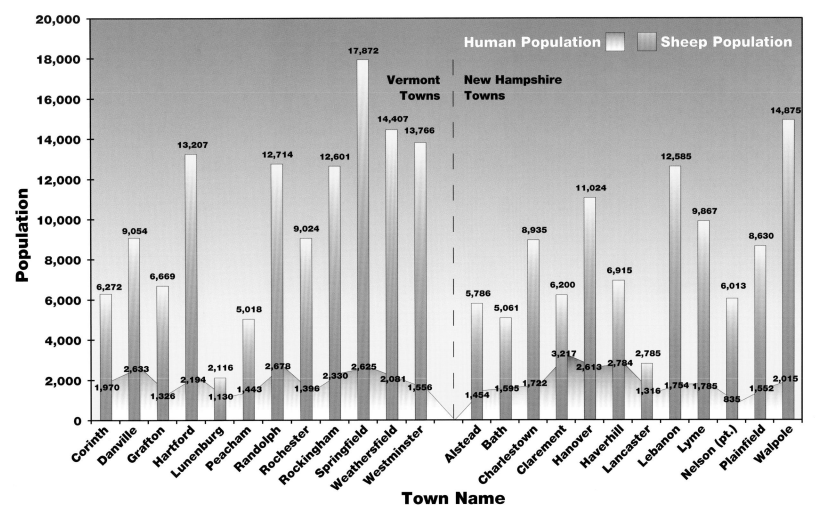

Figure 16. Human versus Sheep Population in the Connecticut River Valley, circa 1840.

A dog and stone walls help this c. 1945 Ryegate, Vt., farmer contain his sheep.

County fairs have a long history in the watershed.

came and left. Meanwhile, cows and dairy farming endured. Chapter 24, Contemporary Agriculture, traces the evolution of dairy farming in the watershed and emerging trends in farming.

Steve Taylor served as the New Hampshire Commissioner of Agriculture for 25 years, retiring in 2007. He lives and farms in Plainfield, N.H.

FOR FURTHER READING

Goodwin, Harry Samuel. 1986. *The Clock Turned Back: Reminiscences of a Nineteenth Century Childhood.* Portsmouth, N.H: Peter E. Randall.

Hudson, Robert F., ed. 1976. *The Yankee Farmer.* Topsfield, Mass.: Americana Archives.

Russell, Howard S. 1982. *A Long, Deep Furrow: Three Centuries of Farming in New England.* Hanover, N.H.: University Press of New England.

Wilson, Harold Fisher. 1936. *The Hill Country of Northern New England: Its Social and Economic History, 1790–1930.* New York: Columbia University Press.

23 The Industrial Era

On April 15, 1869, Massachusetts entrepreneur and budding industrialist William Russell scouted prospects in Bellows Falls, Vt. He was looking for a place to try a new commercial method of making paper from wood pulp. He walked along railroad tracks introduced less than 20 years before, and surveyed the leaking walls and locks of the adjacent 1802 Bellows Falls Canal. He saw the potential for vast waterpower, and considered the enormous forest reserves of northern Vermont and New Hampshire, raw material that the region's waterways, as well as the new railroads, could bring right to his door.

Geographically, Russell stood on the banks of the Connecticut River. Historically, he stood on the brink of an industrial expansion that would lift Connecticut River Valley communities out of the economic and cultural stagnation of the post–Civil War era. It would propel them into the twentieth century, in step with a nation then creating the world's first large-scale commercial and consumer economy. These industries grew directly from the valley's natural resources and landscape.

A New Economy Emerges

The scale of Russell's vision—and those of other entrepreneurs of the era—stood in marked contrast to the medieval, preindustrial technology European immigrants brought to the region in the last quarter of the 1700s. Upon arrival, settlers scattered throughout the watershed, establishing subsistence farms and locating mills anywhere an appreciable volume of water fell toward the valley floors. Their water-powered, site-specific mills sawed lumber or ground wheat and grains for people and farm animals. These mills adequately served the modest demands placed on them by an agriculture-based rural economy founded on cash, barter, and limited credit.

Other enterprises rose and fell depending on the extent and quality of natural resources available. The need to clear forests for farming coincided with a need for charcoal and potash, created by burning the downed trees. The tree-harvesting culture evolved into large-scale seasonal logging camps in the remote northern forests and river-choking log drives whose dangers are now legendary. Other resources lay beneath the ground, and small operations to utilize them sprouted at the surface. Workers molded and baked clay into bricks, quarried out granite for building materials, and coaxed lime from limestone in tiny kilns in every town in the region.

Some extraction industries were launched in the nineteenth century and grew and survived into the twentieth, including iron foundries and mines producing copper and talc. In St. Johnsbury, the Fairbanks family established an iron foundry in 1823 and invented the platform scale in 1830. Fairbanks Scales became one of the region's foremost iron-working industries as well as the world's largest producer of platform scales for a century. It also improved standards for the accurate commercial measurement of goods throughout the United States.

A vein of copper running through Vershire, Strafford, and Corinth, Vt., was the basis for the most significant mining operations in the region. These mines helped make Vermont one of the nation's largest producers of copper for a short period of time in the late nineteenth century, second only to operations around Lake Superior.

Mass Production and the Industrial Revolution

In the first half of the nineteenth century, in small workshops on both sides of the Atlantic, inspired tinkerers were coming up with new ideas about how to make things better and faster. Their creation of new objects and processes so transformed manufacturing and Western culture that the trend became known as the Industrial Revolution. An example of this revolution in production comes from Eli Whitney. In 1798, several years after inventing the cotton gin, Whitney established a factory in New Haven, Conn., to make muskets for the federal gov-

Robbins & Lawrence advertisement, c. 1850.

REBECCA A. BROWN AND BARRY LAWSON

It may be hard to imagine today, but the mining of copper, iron, and even gold was once big business in the Connecticut River watershed. Early maps show mines dotted across the landscape in both states. Today, piles of tailings and debris-filled entrances to mines may be found on rugged mountainsides, and such names as Copper Mine Brook give further clues. When iron ore was discovered in the town now called Sugar Hill in the 1790s, it was said to be the richest deposit in the nation (Aldrich 1996). A stone furnace stack built in the early nineteenth century still stands next to the Gale River in nearby Franconia. Iron from that forge helped build the surrounding towns for many years.

While never inspiring the "rush" of California, gold mining was conducted in the river valley years ago, and prospecting continues today. In Vermont, gold mines operated with minor success in the Black River and Ottauquechee River watersheds. However, as George H. Perkins, state geologist from 1898 to 1933 is said to have declared, "it is entirely useless to throw away money, time and labor seeking gold in Vermont." New Hampshire proved somewhat more lucrative. In 1878, State Geologist Charles Hitchcock was so enthusiastic about deposits found in the region, including in Lyman, Monroe, Bath, and Lisbon, that he labeled the area the Ammonoosuc Gold District. Small gold mines operated all over the district in the nineteenth century before being shut down as uneconomical. Today, recreational gold panners still seek their fortune in the Wild Ammonoosuc River, which rushes down from the White Mountains and meets the Ammonoosuc between Woodsville and Bath.

Vermont was once a major copper supplier, and two of its three most significant mines are in the Connecticut River Valley. Deposits in what became the Elizabeth Mine in South Strafford were discovered in 1793. Production varied in intensity and ownership over the next century, and the mine was revitalized during World War II as the largest operation in New England. The Elizabeth Mine closed for good in 1958, but its tailings, or waste piles, continue to be a source of acidic runoff into the west branch of the Ompomponoosuc River. Copper was processed at the Ely Mine in Vershire from 1821 to 1920. By 1880, it produced three-fifths of the nation's copper and employed 2,000 men, but declining copper prices and mismanagement put it out of business soon thereafter. Like the Elizabeth Mine, it is now a source of acid runoff into nearby streams. A third operation, Pike Hill in Corinth, produced copper in three separate mines from the mid-nineteenth century through World War I. It, too, is now a source of soil and water contamination. All three mines have been declared EPA Superfund sites. Multi-agency study efforts in recent years may lead to eventual clean up and reclamation.

The Copperfield mine, Vershire, Vt., about 1900.

SOURCES

Aldrich, Roger W. 1996. *The Iron Industry in Franconia & Sugar Hill, 1805–1860?* Sugar Hill, N.H.: self-published.

Abbott, Collamer. 1973. *Green Mountain Copper: The Story of Vermont's Red Metal*. Randolph, Vt.

Hammarstrom, J. M., J. C. Jackson, R. Barden, and R. R. Seal. 1999. *Characterization of Mine Waste at the Abandoned Elizabeth Copper Mine, Vermont* [abs.]. Geological Society of America, Abstracts with Programs (NE), vol. 31, p. A-20.

REBECCA A. BROWN

The industrial era is thought of as a time of heavy metal and clanking machinery. But the factory floor was not the only place pulsing with the sounds of a growing nation. The Northern Forest echoed with the thump of lumberjacks' axes and the zing of their crosscut saws, the jingle of horse and oxen harnesses, and later, the steam whistles and roar of chugging locomotives. Hundreds of men cut countless virgin red spruce in the winter, used draft animals to haul the logs to tributary rivers to wait for spring breakup, then floated and goaded the timber down the Connecticut River to sawmills that fed construction in Boston, Hartford, and other cities. The double-ended bateau, the sharp-hooked peavey, and spiked boots were the tools of the river drivers who shepherded millions of board feet of lumber down the Connecticut.

Logging camps bustled with hundreds of men and beasts. The bunkhouses buzzed with many languages: French, Slavic, Scandinavian, English, and Abenaki, as tough men from all over slept side by side, and at meal times heaped their plates with the traditional camp fare of sourdough biscuits, baked beans, coffee, and donuts.

Tall trees had been cut in the southern river valley of Vermont and New Hampshire as far back as the early 1700s. The British Navy favored the white pine for masts for His Majesty's ships, and the royal "broad arrow" marked the prime trees as off-limits for all other uses. A century later, timber harvesting had become a commercial enterprise. Entrepreneurs including David Sumner, for whom the falls below Hartland, Vt., are named, purchased large tracts of forestland and built sawmills along the river.

The first efforts at floating logs from the Connecticut headwaters all the way to Massachusetts came after the Civil War. The skilled river drivers, many of them from Maine, maneuvered thousands of 40-foot logs through such obstacles as the fierce Fifteen Mile Falls, using dynamite when necessary to loosen log jams. With the success of the first drives and the vast northern forestland beckoning, the timber-harvesting industry went into full swing. Dozens of dams were built on rivers and streams to hold back the flow until the drive was ready, and then loosed to flush the timber downstream. The Connecticut River log drives became the largest the country had ever seen.

The leading timber concern was the Connecticut River Lumber Company, incorporated in 1879. In its heyday, CRL Co. owned about 350,000 acres of virgin forest in the headwaters region. The company's leader was George van Dyke, born in Quebec, who started working in the woods when he was

14. Van Dyke made his reputation as the most aggressive and energetic among the era's larger-than-life timber barons. He died in 1909, when his chauffeur apparently hit the wrong pedal and sent the car plunging into the Connecticut at Turners Falls, where van Dyke had been watching his river drivers at work. By 1915, the seemingly endless supply of merchantable sawtimber was depleted, and that year saw the last of the great log drives on the Connecticut.

Timber harvesting was not over, however. The woods continued to grow, and smaller trees were used as raw material for the next big product: paper. Pulpwood in four-foot lengths fed the new paper mills, and within a few years, the north woods were owned by a new cast of companies with names like St. Regis and International Paper. Pulpwood was floated down the Connecticut until 1949, when more efficient overland transportation made river driving obsolete.

SOURCES

Gove, Bill. 2003. *Log Drives on the Connecticut River*. Littleton, N.H.: Bondcliff Books.

WGBY. 2006. *Dynamite, Whiskey and Wood: Connecticut Log Drives 1870–1915*. Video. Springfield, Mass.: WGBY.

River drivers use peaveys and wear spiked boots to work logs under the Ledyard Bridge in Hanover, N.H., in 1912. The view is toward what was the Vermont village of Lewiston, currently part of the town of Norwich.

The International Paper Company used two of the valley's great natural resources: the river and the timberlands. The paper mill, established in the early 1880s and shown here in 1927, occupied the Wilder, Vt., side of the river. The pulp mill was across the river in Lebanon. Some remains are visible today, but most were submerged following construction of the Wilder Dam.

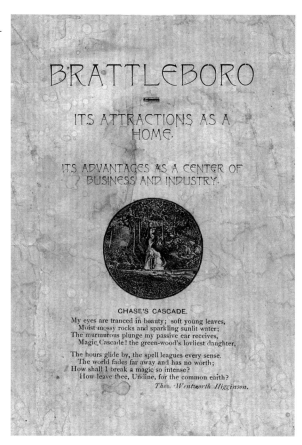

Promotional booklet issued by the Brattleboro Board of Trade, 1887.

ernment. Rather than hire craftsmen to build each gun by hand, as had been the practice, Whitney had workers manufacture interchangeable parts and assemble them into complete rifles.

The concept of mass production took root in the Connecticut River Valley over the succeeding decades, and was applied many different ways. The most notable achievement was in 1846, at the Robbins and Lawrence Armory and Machine Shop in Windsor, Vt. The shop's first big job was to manufacture rifles for the federal government—and do it a lot faster than Whitney had a half-century before. Later, the business invented machines that shaped and milled metals, which themselves were assembled into metal-processing equipment, making possible a quantum leap in production capacity and quality. After seeing Robbins and Lawrence machinery at the Crystal Palace Industrial Exhibition in London in 1851, a British parliamentary commission came to Windsor to study the details of the "American system," and ordered machines to be shipped to British arsenals. The Windsor mill now houses the American Precision Museum.

So-called precision manufacturing brought economic success and international renown to Windsor and Springfield, Vt., just as it did to Springfield, Mass., and Windsor, Conn. Soon, accurately fitted metal parts made possible the mass production of items like sewing machines, typewriters, farm equipment, bicycles, and (outside the river valley) automobiles. The arrival of the railroads in the mid-nineteenth century provided for the efficient transport of raw materials and finished products.

The Brattleboro Board of Trade promoted the Estey Organ Company in its 1887 promotional booklet.

It was into this industrial environment that William Russell stepped in 1869, when he helped shift the paper industry's reliance on scarce rags to plentiful wood pulp. Before he died 30 years later, Russell founded the International Paper Company, and created in Bellows Falls one of the largest paper-making centers in the world by the early 1920s. The company's consolidated holdings included pulp and paper mills in Hartford, Vt., and Lebanon, N.H., and sawmills in Hinsdale and Lancaster, Stratford, and Lisbon, N.H. Independent paper mills were later were established in Gilman, Vt., and Groveton, N.H.

Natural Resources and Economic Diversity

The Connecticut River Valley's industrial base grew in symbiotic relationship with the agricultural economy, stimulating the evolution from subsistence farming to the production of cash crops in butter, cheese, wool, maple sugar, and grain. Companies like the Vermont Farm Machinery Company, in Bellows Falls, made farming tools such as scythes and hand-cranked devices such as butter churns and cream separators. Farms and cooperative dairies in the region shipped butter and cheese and, later, milk, by overnight trains to Boston, New York, and Montreal.

Two decades after William Jarvis introduced Merino sheep to the Connecticut River Valley in 1808, the Monadnock Mills was established on the Sugar River in Claremont, N.H. (see Chapter 22, Early Agriculture). It was the first, and soon the largest, textile manufacturer

Shoe manufacturing employed people in many valley towns well into the twentieth century. This nineteenth-century photo is from the Ascutney Shoe Factory in Windsor, Vt.

A machine tool operator at the Jones and Lamson company in Springfield, Vt., early twentieth century.

in the upper Connecticut River Valley. As with the paper industry in Bellows Falls and the platform scale business in St. Johnsbury, the textile industry in Claremont transformed a rural village into an urban industrial town. Other towns, such as Littleton, N.H., and Windsor, Vt., saw similar growth follow investment in shoemaking. These growing companies attracted watershed residents off their farms and immigrants to the region who came seeking work. A new middleclass was created as incomes generally rose.

In other parts of the watershed, unique local industries influenced their surroundings and fed the new consumer economy. The Estey Organ complex in Brattleboro, Vt., was the largest organ manufacturer in the world in 1880, employing 500 men and women. It turned out more than 250,000 reed organs before pianos eclipsed their popularity. The Littleton, N.H., factory building still stands in which, from 1867 to 1909, the Kilburn brothers produced and distributed thousands of stereoscopic views. Their collection, largest in the world and collectors' items today, provided popular parlor entertainment for generations.

Rural electrification, made possible in part through the construction of major hydropower dams on the Connecticut River in the first half of the twentieth century, liberated manufacturers from riverside locations and dispersed manufacturing throughout the region. Electricity also dramatically increased the production capacity of industries formerly tied to streamflow volumes, and stimulated the consolidation of smaller companies into larger ones, notably in the paper and machine tool industries.

Springfield's first machine shop was built about 1810 near four other mills in what was then the village of Lockwood's Mills, through which the Black River tumbles on its way to the Connecticut. For the next 80 years, many businesses evolved to make machines for manufacturing textiles and wood and iron products, establishing an innovative machine-shop culture in town. Then, in the 1880s through the early 1900s, three companies were founded that drew on the creative and influential leadership of James Hartness, an inventor with 120 patents who later would become governor of Vermont. These were the Jones and Lamson Machine Company, the Fellows Gear Shaper Company, and Bryant Grinder Corporation. These businesses employed over 20,000 people during World War II. Indeed, Springfield lore has it that the city was so integral to the war effort that it was seventh on Hitler's list of U.S. bombing targets. All three businesses were purchased by larger corporations, and only Bryant remains in Springfield.

The Economy Turns Again

The same trends that led to the boom also led to a downturn in the region's manufacturing economy after about 1950. With consolidation came absentee ownership, severing long-standing direct relationships between mill owners and workers. Decisions in boardrooms outside the Connecticut River Valley sent local jobs to where labor was cheaper, in Southern states and overseas. Except for the logging and forest-products industries, whatever manufacturing industries remained in the region were no longer so closely tied to natural resources as they had been for the previous century.

Nonetheless, the physical imprint of this period remains. Many of our present rural villages and our largest commercial centers coalesced around the sites where early industries found their hydropower opportunities. Brick mills from the period survive to house new businesses or to serve residential and commercial uses. Many downtowns and village centers are remarkably intact, reflecting architectural styles from the 1870s to the 1920s, the era when the classic American "Main Street" was created. Libraries, schools, cultural centers, parks, and bridges—donated by the owners of long-gone industries—still serve their communities. Today, we may travel through the watershed, and like William Russell, stand on the banks of the Connecticut River and its tributaries, and stand in relation to the history that shaped the environment we see.

Richard Ewald served as the community development director for the town of Rockingham, Vt. He is the principal author of the story of the Connecticut River Valley, Proud to Live Here *(CRJC, 2002).*

For Further Reading

Albers, J. 2000. *Hands on the Land: A Story of the Vermont Landscape.* Cambridge, Mass: MIT Press.

Delaney, E. 1983. *The Connecticut River: New England's Historic Waterway.* Guilford, Conn: Globe Pequot Press.

Meeks, H. 1986. *Time and Change in Vermont.* Guilford, Conn: Globe Pequot Press.

Rolando, V. 1992. *200 Years of Soot, Sweat and Toil: The History and Archeology of Vermont's Iron, Charcoal, and Lime Industries.* Burlington: Vermont Archeological Society.

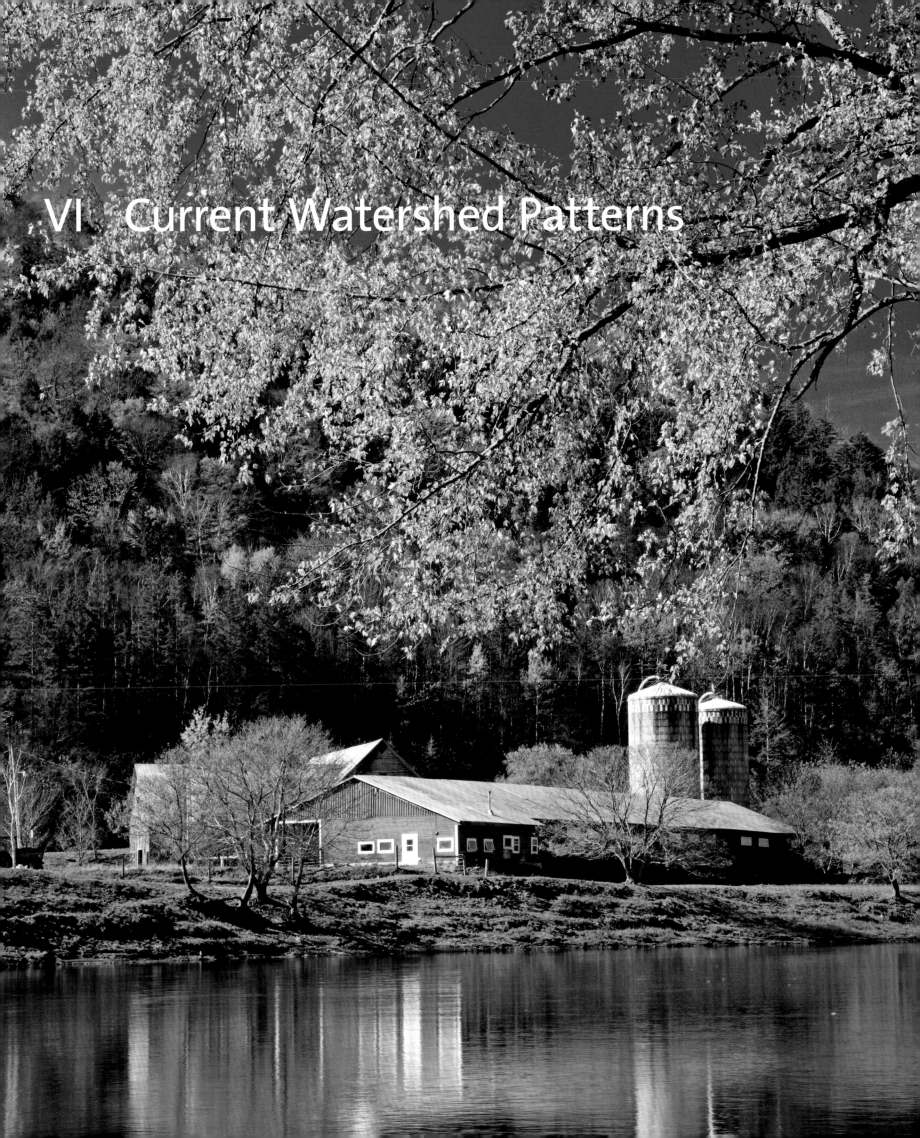

VI   Current Watershed Patterns

Introduction

Just as its landscape ranges from riverside meadows to rugged mountains, the human experience of the Connecticut River Valley takes very different forms. Town centers may hum with commerce based on new technologies, and just a few miles away farms still look like they have for generations. Some workers earn the salaries that make New Hampshire one of the richest states in the nation, and others struggle to make ends meet while holding multiple jobs.

Some communities, by design, good fortune, or both, have seen their economies move energetically into the postindustrial era, and are thriving with new opportunities in the arts, knowledge- and technology-based businesses, and in hospitality and heritage tourism. Other communities are still seeking effective ways to attract new businesses and residents. While residents in the Upper Valley region of the watershed have access to some of the finest medical care in the nation, those who live in the watershed's more remote areas find access to health care much more difficult because of lack of public transportation and a shortage of dentists and physicians.

New Hampshire as a whole is the fastest-growing state in the Northeast. Yet both New Hampshire and Vermont are losing young adult residents, as housing prices are outstripping salaries offered many workers in the early stages of their careers who are also trying to start families. In the watershed, the less-populated northern sections have more affordable housing prices, but lack the jobs and cultural opportunities that many young people seek. In these areas, the average age of the population is increasing more rapidly than in other parts of the states. Public schools are losing students, driving their per capita education costs higher.

The second-home market drives growth in many rural areas. Land use patterns show the influence as second homes grow in former farm fields, or perch atop steep ridges that many locals had considered not buildable. Outdoor recreation is affected as more land becomes "posted" or off-limits to public use. At the same time, in some parts of the watershed, concerted public and private efforts have resulted in an increasing amount of land being conserved for continued use as farms, timberland, recreational, or natural areas.

In many ways, economic and cultural change has come rapidly to the most rural parts of the watershed. In the north, it was scarcely over a decade ago that Internet service of any kind was either not available or a novelty. National newspapers were delivered a day late. One was hard-pressed to find a microbrewery, farmers' market, locally baked bread, organic produce, an alternative school, or a holistic health provider. Now, all of these are common. Today, many downtowns are experiencing new vibrancy as communities realize they can be a destination for people seeking "authentic" small-town experiences.

Steve Taylor continues his story of agriculture in the watershed by describing current trends, including the change in dairy farming to fewer but larger farms and the growth of "boutique farms" specializing in diverse products and enticing customers—both locals and tourists—with the farm "experience."

Kevin Geiger and Barry Lawson describe the trends in land use, and how some watershed communities are trying to encourage economic growth while maintaining their rural character. In Chapter 26, The Postindustrial Economy, Preston Gilbert and Rebecca Brown bring the story of the valley's economy to the present day, with the post-industrial mix of traditional businesses and emerging sectors. Joanna Whitcomb's sidebar to that chapter details changes in workforce composition and business sectors as the region evolves. In the final chapter, Demographics, Barry Lawson and Will Sawyer complement the economic development story by teasing out population trends in the watershed. The patterns of population growth, income, age, education, and other variables take shape when compared by county.

These chapters provide a snapshot of the current conditions of the watershed, and point toward a range of issues that the region will face going forward.

Dairy farms and cows remain an important part of the watershed's agricultural base, despite changes in the industry.

24 Contemporary Agriculture

Agriculture in the Connecticut River watershed is following two distinctly different tracks. Both continue trends that began in the 1970s and that seem likely to keep up in the next decade or two as population in the region grows.

The first track is traditional *bulk commodity agriculture*, which in the watershed has long meant dairy farming, and to a lesser extent, apple orchards. Some call the second track "niche" agriculture, others "new" agriculture. It is characterized by close ties between the producer and the consumer, exemplified by farmstands, pick-your-own produce operations, subscription/cooperative or "community supported" farms, enterprises growing for local farmers' markets, horticultural production for nearby markets, and an array of other market-led activities.

Dairy: Fewer but Larger Farms

Following similar trends in the rest of the Northeast as well as in the Midwest, dairy farms in the watershed are decreasing in number but increasing in size, as the remaining operations have expanded herd sizes and taken over cropland of neighboring discontinued dairies. The dairy industry is one of the most aggressive in adopting new technology, and the methods of crop production, animal feeding, and herd management have advanced so rapidly that average production per cow has nearly doubled since 1975. Efficiencies and economies of scale have compensated for relatively static milk prices over that time, and have kept dairying profitable for those operators willing to adopt new technologies and methods and who are capable of managing quite complex business enterprises. Figures 17 and 18 illustrate the trend to fewer farms with more dairy cows, and Figure 19 depicts the relative presence of dairy farming in the watershed's nine counties.

Dairy producers in the watershed face many challenges. They look ahead to price competition posed by lower-cost producers in a global market, the rising value of land due to development and speculative pressures, labor shortages, and the increasing regulation of the use of land. Dairy farms will become even more specialized, with many of the traditional tasks of tillage and harvesting turned over to custom operators with ever-larger and more efficient equipment. Farm owners will provide less labor themselves, and become managers of labor, capital, and physical assets. And milk will continue to be a commodity sold to a small number of processors who will convert it to any of hundreds of products sought by the consuming public.

The landscape of the watershed can be likened to a three-legged

Four Corners Farm in Bradford, Vt., is an example of a dairy farm that has grown through offering diversified products to the local retail market.

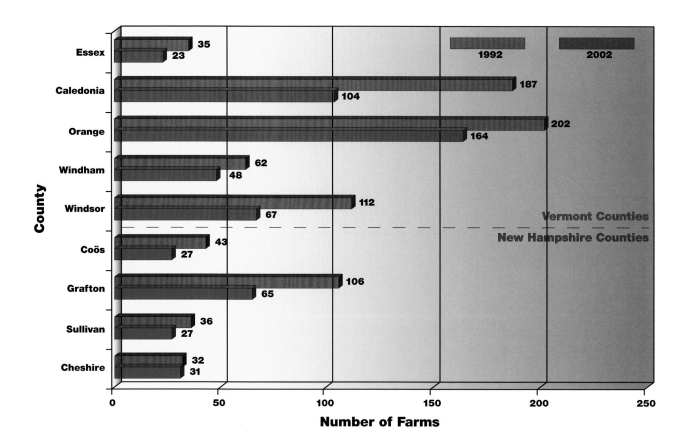

Figure 17. Number of Farms by County, 1992 and 2002.

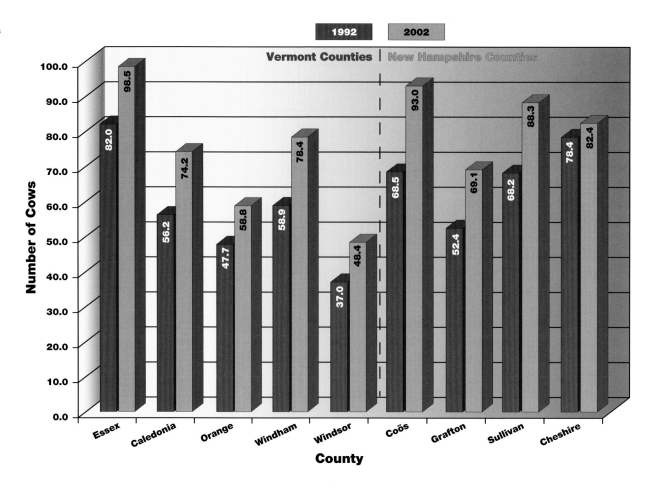

Figure 18. Average Number of Cows Per Farm, 1992 and 2002.

stool, with the legs being the forest, the built environment, and the fields, meadows, and pastures. Because much of the open land is kept open by agricultural activity, the vast majority of which is dairy farming, it is thus the most vulnerable of the three "legs" to change and loss. The close relationship among these elements is what gives the Connecticut River Valley and much of central New England its unique ambiance. The realization that this uniqueness can be lost to development has led to extensive efforts to preserve the best agricultural land. Some farmers have transferred development rights or placed conservation easements on their land, and some communities have adopted land-protection regulations. These efforts surely will continue in the years ahead.

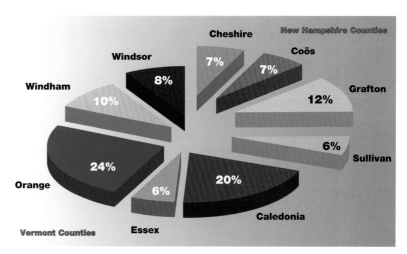

Figure 19. Percent of Vermont and New Hampshire Cows by County, 2002.

"New" Farms Are Growing

Though the Connecticut River Valley has witnessed a gradual decline in numbers of dairy farms in recent decades, the emergence of the second, or alternative, track of agriculture has helped to stabilize overall farm numbers and to foster modest increases in gross farm income. This new paradigm emphasizes careful development and expansion of markets rather than simply commodity output. While there is no crop grown in the region that can't be produced more cheaply or extensively elsewhere, local growers can appeal to the public with the idea that a product raised close by will be fresher, taste better, and represent a superior value.

Consumer interest in locally grown produce has prompted new farm stands, pick-your-own enterprises, and a proliferation of farmers' markets that provide attractive selling venues for smaller producers. Conventional food retailers also have been grasping the appeal of local products, as have food service and restaurant managers who have begun incorporating ingredients from nearby farms in their menus.

Some farms successfully take the raw commodities they produce and add value in the form of further processing and packaging. Farmstead cheeses, condiments, maple specialties, and milk packaged in returnable glass bottles are among the products that watershed farms are bringing to receptive nearby markets.

Diversity and New Opportunities

Meanwhile, the region continues to nurture other diverse types of agriculture. Consumer demand for floral and landscape materials has attracted numerous greenhouse, nursery, and field-grown horticultural operations, many of which are highly specialized and have far-flung customers. The equine sector includes various types of operations providing breeding, training, boarding, and other services to horse owners and recreational users.

Agri-tourism and "experiential agriculture" harness a farm's physical facilities, its ongoing activities, and the hospitality of the operators to generate entertainment and diversion for visitors. An orchard with a petting zoo, or a dairy farm that provides guests with lodging and meals for extended stays, are both examples of agriculture tapping the leisure market.

Traditional bulk commodity farms are adding other activities that market directly to nearby consumers. Some dairy farms have begun

Sheep's milk cheese from the Vermont Shepherd Farm.

Some sheep farms, like the Vermont Shepherd Farm in Westminster West, have found a niche market making cheese.

In Weathersfield Bow, Vt., center of the early nineteenth-century Merino sheep craze, a farm now raises goats of South African origin.

growing sweet corn and vegetables for a farmstand while others are converting manure into compost for sale to local landscapers and gardeners. In fact, a majority of farms in the watershed today likely will have multiple income streams from the use of their resources of land, labor, and equipment.

Looking ahead, agriculture in the Connecticut River watershed is sure to remain a dynamic and diverse part of the region's economy. A growing population will provide expanding market opportunities for farmers, while also presenting them challenges in the form of competition for land and regulation of agricultural operations.

A good infrastructure of suppliers and services, including veterinarians, feed stores, technical education, and reliable financing will need to be preserved, and local and state regulatory policies must remain attuned to the inevitable changes in technology and market opportunities that lie ahead. Consumer desire for locally produced commodities will be agriculture's greatest advantage in the watershed.

Steve Taylor is a farmer, a former newspaperman, and served as the New Hampshire Commissioner of Agriculture for 25 years. He lives and farms in Plainfield, N.H.

For Further Reading

Fritz, Sonja-Sarai. 2006. *New Hampshire's Changing Agricultural Land Use.* Keene, N.H.: Keene State College, Department of Geography.

Jager, Ronald. 2004. *The Fate of Family Farming: Variations on an American Idea.* Hanover, N.H.: University Press of New England.

Ruhf, Kathryn Z., ed. 1999. *Farmland Transfer and Protection in New England: A Guide for Entering and Exiting Farmers.* Belchertown, Mass.: New England Small Farm Institute.

Reidel, Carl. 1982. *New England Prospects: Critical Choices in a Time of Change.* Hanover, N.H.: University Press of New England.

25 Land Use

Early Settlement Patterns

The uses of land in the Connecticut River watershed derive from the inheritance of geography and the heritage of past generations, as well as from the needs and impulses of today's inhabitants. Before human settlement, the watershed was almost entirely forested, except for marshlands and moist meadows along the river bottoms, or land opened through natural disturbance like fire or hurricanes. Settlers who followed the river northward out of Massachusetts found the river bottom soils ripe for agriculture, and they systematically cleared land along the Connecticut to establish villages and family farms.

Settlers also followed the fan of rivers flowing into the Connecticut to reach the interior countryside, and towns blossomed around the waterpower furnished by the tributaries. This early settlement set the pattern of clustered village centers, extensive open farmland along the rivers and carved out of the surrounding hills, and steeper back land covered with trees, useful as woodlots.

The mix of land cover and land uses in Maidstone, Vt., and Stratford, N.H., in the northern river valley.

Old farms give way to new residential development up and down the valley. This conversion is in Orford, N.H.

The Valley Opens

Traditional patterns began changing in the mid-nineteenth century as individuals and families abandoned hill farms for more fertile soils in the West. Later, electrical transmission freed manufacturers from needing rivers to power their machinery. Dirt and gravel roadways were graded and paved, and residential and commercial development proceeded across more of the landscape. By the latter decades of the twentieth century, interstate highways made it easier for people to discover the valley and decide to move here.

Many small towns and villages in the uplands that had lost population have seen a residential rebound, driven by the second-home market, or by becoming bedroom communities to larger commercial centers such as Hanover/Lebanon and Littleton, N.H. The watershed's resurgence of population has followed some preexisting patterns in and around town centers, but is increasingly scattered among farmland, forests, and ridgetops. Many new settlers are drawn to large acreages with views and a sense of space. This new housing and the

road and utility infrastructure supporting it have fragmented formerly undeveloped areas. Chapter 27, Demographics, details the population trends in the watershed.

Loss of Agricultural Land

The post–World War II development boom dispersed new residences away from village cores, provided a plethora of new destinations called shopping centers, and created thousands of acres of new pavement for motor vehicle parking lots. Much of this development was at the expense of agricultural land. Farmland tends to be flat and free of trees and other obstacles, percolates well, and is inexpensive to develop. Sale to developers usually is more lucrative for the farmer than growing corn or milking cows. Although agricultural land in the basin is being converted to developed land at nearly 20 square miles per year, the fertile river terraces are still the largest and most cohesive expanse of agricultural land in New Hampshire, and represent a sizable portion of Vermont's total farmland as well.

Estimates by the U.S. Department of Agriculture from sample data collected every five years from 1982 to 1997 provide some insight into the broad changes in land use. During this 15-year period, developed land and agricultural land areas changed dramatically. The data suggest that the portion of developed land in the nine counties increased from 623,000 acres to 906,000 in the 15-year period, a gain of 283,000 acres. Land became developed during that period at a rate of nearly 19,000 acres per year, or 52 acres per day! Agricultural land decreased from 1,371,000 acres to 1,173,000, a loss of 198,000 acres at a rate of 13,200 acres per year or 36 acres per day. The remaining new developed land (16 acres per day) came at the expense of forestland. The effects on the towns, working landscapes, and local economies from these changes can be dramatic. The trend of converting agricultural lands to development is continuing sharply upward, especially in New Hampshire, the most rapidly developing state east of the Mississippi River after Florida. Figure 20 illustrates the difference in these changes in land use among the major categories between the two states, in thousands of acres, using the most recent data available at the time of writing.

Landscape change is illustrated in views from Sugar Hill, N.H. A farm, with the Franconia Range above cleared fields in the background, is depicted in an early twentieth-century drawing, above. Right, the similar view today. The background hills are completely forested, and the remains of the farmhouse and barn foundations are in the woods at right. The farm was abandoned by the 1930s.

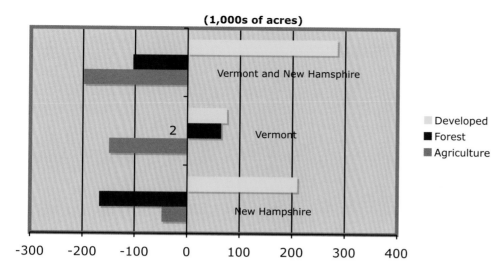

(1,000s of acres)

Vermont and New Hamsphire

2   Vermont

New Hampshire

-300   -200   -100   0   100   200   300   400

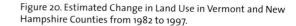
Figure 20. Estimated Change in Land Use in Vermont and New Hampshire Counties from 1982 to 1997.

As described in Chapter 13, Forests, the region's forests have grown back considerably after being cleared for farming in the 1800s. The region now is roughly three-quarters forest, although this percentage has peaked and forestland is now feeling the bite of development (see Map 41 and Figure 21).

Land Use Plans and Controls

In response to the quickening pace of growth, some watershed communities have revised their land-use ordinances or have created them for the first time. Town plans reflect the desires of local residents and provide guidance to local developers and the administrators of zoning ordinances and subdivision regulations. Municipal planning grants and other state and federal programs are available to support recreational, housing, historic, infrastructure, and other types of local projects.

The passage of Act 250 in Vermont in 1970, spurred by the new interstate highways that made the state considerably more accessible, mandates review by district environmental commissions of large-scale development using a set of criteria to protect the environment, community life, and the aesthetic character of Vermont. This program often consults local plans as guides for the compatibility of proposed commercial, housing, industrial, and supporting infrastructure. While the effectiveness of Act 250 has been debated, no comparable planning review process exists in New Hampshire.

Regional planning agencies analyze future trends and provide guidance and support to local communities trying to manage growth. For example, the Two Rivers–Ottauquechee Regional Commission in Vermont has identified several types of problems accompanying what it calls positive economic growth, including "indiscriminate commercial strips, residential sprawl characteristic of an urban setting, and the loss of open space . . . in some areas of the region, particularly those closest to interstate highways and heavily traveled roads." The commission also observes that "all municipalities in the region have planning programs, yet many are ill-equipped to deal with the complex challenges brought about by rising real estate and property taxes, and strained community services."

Similar issues have been identified by the Southwest (N.H.) Regional Planning Commission, which states, "strip development is a growing concern throughout the region. Its . . . visual effects and the traffic generated conflict with many residents' visions for their communities . . . This low density roadside development pattern also challenges Main Street commercial property."

In response to these types of concerns, and with the help of their regional planning commissions, some towns have adopted so-called smart growth initiatives focused on protecting ridge lines, farmland, scenic views, and critical environmental areas. Some towns direct that large subdivisions must set aside some permanent open space, and also may prescribe development densities. Zoning for minimum lot sizes of 5 or 10 acres no longer is seen as the way to keep a town rural, as had

Figure 21. Land Cover and Land Use in the Watershed.

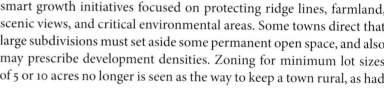

Forested wetland 2%

Open wetland 1%

Water 4%

Developed 3%

Transportation /utilities 3%

Other open 3%

Row crop 3%

Pasture 3%

Mixed forest 21%

Deciduous forest 37%

Coniferous forest 20%

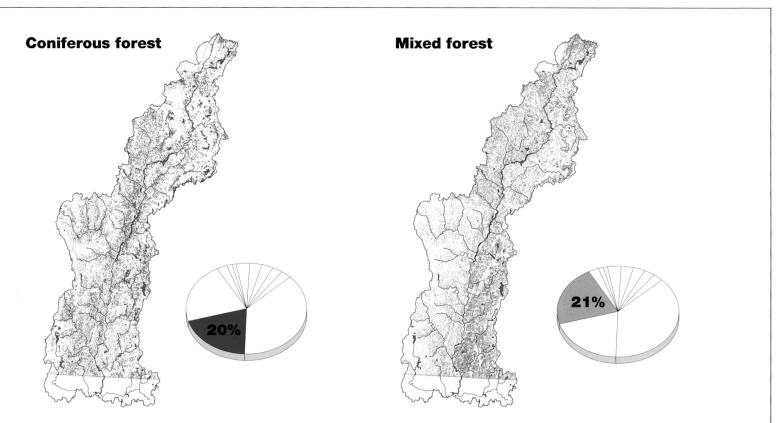

Coniferous forest

20%

Mixed forest

21%

While it is impossible at this size and scale to show a great amount of detail, the series of maps on this page provide a generalized view of the major categories of land cover and use in the watershed. These maps show how some of the more important components are distributed within the watershed.

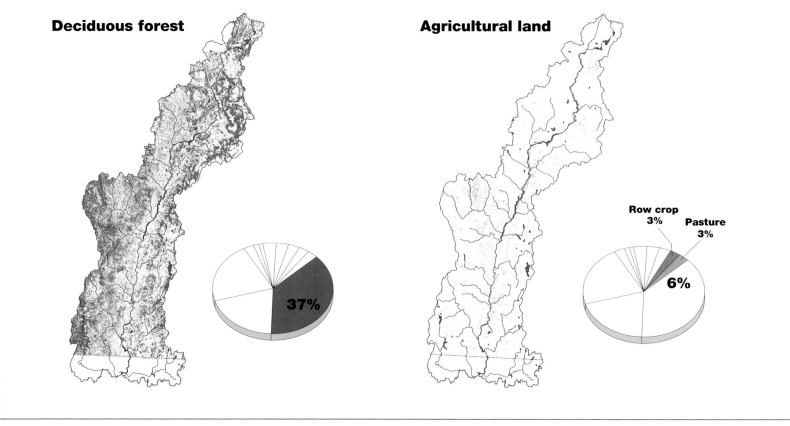

Deciduous forest

37%

Agricultural land

Row crop
3%

Pasture
3%

6%

Map 41. Land Cover and Land Use by Categories.

TABLE 4. Plans and Selected Ordinances in Towns Bordering the
Connecticut River, 2006

PLAN OR ORDINANCE	NEW HAMPSHIRE TOWNS	VERMONT TOWNS	TOTAL TOWNS, TWO STATES	% OF TOTAL TOWNS
	26	27	53	100.0
Town Master Plans	23	21	44	83.0
Zoning Ordinance	21	22	43	81.1
Subdivision Regulations	25	15	40	75.5
Shoreland Protection	8	19	27	50.9

once been the case. Rather, many towns when revising their regulations are keeping the 5 or 10 acres as a density level in rural areas, but lowering minimum lot sizes to one or two acres, and encouraging even smaller, clustered residential lots in planned subdivisions. Efforts such as Vermont's Designated Downtown and Village Center programs are promoting new commercial development within town centers, especially in existing buildings, instead of relegating new businesses to industrial parks or building on farmland.

Along the Connecticut River, some towns have enacted shoreland ordinances. Table 4 indicates the extent of these and other ordinances in towns that border the Connecticut River in both states. Ordinances and regulations are continually being enacted, or revised, and sometimes expire, so this chart provides only a snapshot of the status of these measures in 2006.

Land Conservation
Land conservation has blossomed over the past 30 years as nonprofit land trusts, state and federal agencies, and municipalities have conserved thousands of acres in cooperation with willing landowners. Large tracts of timberland have been conserved as working forest, helping maintain the forest products industry, and providing raw material for new fuel technologies based on cellulose. Farmland conservation is also a priority in the two states, and some premier agricultural areas along the Connecticut are now permanently protected by private landowners through conservation easements.

Tools for the Future
Aerial and satellite imagery, computer mapping by Geographic Information Systems (GIS), and other kinds of technology are being used by planners at the local regional and state levels. The use of GIS has totally revolutionized the field, and is now part of nearly every planning effort. Towns can now look at "development constraint maps" that identify steep slopes, poor soils, and wetlands. Computer-generated "build-out" analyses can assist a planning board to examine the ultimate effect of differing zoning regulations.

Not all communities are prepared for using these tools. Some towns resist interfering with what they consider private property rights. Nevertheless, many communities are moving forward to understand devel-

opment pressures, recognize the impact of future development on the local landscape and municipal budgets, and take measures to guide development in directions consistent with their residents' desires. More than ever, the towns and citizens of the Connecticut River Valley have the tools to understand their communities and the ability to keep them vibrant and special.

Kevin Geiger has worked for two regional planning commissions in Vermont over the last 17 years, serving over 80 towns. He believes that communities can, and should, decide their future. He is senior planner at the Two Rivers–Ottauquechee Regional Commission. He lives in Pomfret, Vt.

Barry Lawson, of Peacham, Vt., has a career-long interest in planning. He is the project coordinator for the Atlas.

Thanks to Ray Godfrey of the USDA Natural Resources and Conservation Service, who found and packaged land use estimates for the watershed.

FOR FURTHER READING

Harvard University. Landscape History of Central New England. Seven dioramas at the Fisher Museum, Harvard Forest. On-line at http://harvardforest.fas.harvard.edu/museum/landscape.html.

Foster, David R., and John F. O'Keefe. 2000. *New England Forests through Time: Insights from the Harvard Forest Dioramas*. Cambridge, Mass.: Harvard University Press.

Southwest Regional Planning Commission. 2002. *Guiding Change: The Southwest Region at the Beginning of the 21st Century*. Keene, N.H.: Southwest Regional Planning Commission.

Two Rivers-Ottauquechee Regional Commission. 2007. *2007 Regional Plan*. Woodstock, Vt.: Two Rivers-Ottauquechee Regional Commission.

Vermont State Environmental Board. 2000. *Act 250: A Guide to Vermont's Land Use Law*. Montpelier, Vt.: State Environmental Board, November.

26 The Postindustrial Economy

White River Junction evolves through the industrial era in three views of its Main Street, from 1919 (*top*), the 1940s (*below*), and today (*facing page, top*). A turn-of-the-twentieth-century postcard offers a glimpse of the future (*facing page, middle*).

New Markets

From the mid-twentieth century, a postindustrial economy has been growing and evolving in the Connecticut River Valley. There is an unmistakable pattern of modernization, a gradual shift from manufacturing to services, and increasing specialization within the two-state watershed. Some traditional industries remain, able to stay competitive by incorporating new technologies, while new businesses have emerged as global markets and competition reshape the economy.

For many businesses, the postindustrial economy has meant finding new markets or specializing within existing markets. Examples within agriculture include higher-value commodities such as farm-raised deer, artisan cheeses, and other specialty and organic foods. Some of these products are sold to local restaurants and hotels, themselves evolving to meet new market demands and opportunities (see Chapter 25, Contemporary Agriculture). The hospitality industry is seeking new markets by reinforcing the valley's sense of place and branding it to appeal to national and international travelers. The 2005 designation of the Connecticut River Byway as a National Scenic Byway is a significant example of this new kind of marketing initiative.

Reemergence of Downtowns and the Creative Economy

In the second half of the twentieth century, the development of the interstate highway system, suburban sprawl, and big box retailing all combined to reduce the vitality of many communities' historic downtowns and village centers. Since the early 1990s, communities on both sides of the Connecticut River have been working to reverse this trend through revitalizing their downtowns, often with the assistance of the New Hampshire Main Street Center and the Vermont Downtown Program.

Much of this focus on downtowns dovetails with regional efforts to quantify and promote what is known as the "creative economy." The creative economy encompasses writers, musicians, artists, craftspeople, and related galleries, retail shops, advertising and marketing businesses, performance spaces, restaurants, graphic design consultants, and related businesses and support services. Some communities, including Rockingham and Windsor, Vt., have made encouraging the creative sector part of their strategies for economic growth. Similarly, St. Johnsbury, Vt., has branded itself as a creative, heritage-minded community in its marketing to attract new businesses and residents.

Traditional Industries Evolve

The postindustrial economy is not without traditional and historic industries. Throughout the valley, traditional industries that remain have adapted to new global economic realities, sometimes by finding lucrative specialized markets. For instance, New England Wire Technologies, headquartered in Lisbon, N.H., has manufactured cables and wires for industrial use since 1898. It now supplies cable to a variety of modern sectors including medical products, telecommunications, robotics, and high-energy physics, to customers in China, Africa, and the Pacific Rim.

Fairbanks Scales, founded in 1824 and by the mid-nineteenth century a world leader in manufacturing weighing devices, put St. Johnsbury, Vt., on the map as a center of industrial manufacturing. Today, the company has incorporated sophisticated digital technology and focuses on specialty markets. Springfield, Vt., home of the machine tool industry, suffered devastating layoffs in the mid- and late 1980s, but has rebounded with a diversified manufacturing base, including operations aimed at modernizing traditional machine tools.

Health and Education Sectors Thrive

A significant growth area in the postindustrial economy is health care, as the population ages throughout the two states generally, and northern portions of the watershed in particular (see Chapter 27, Demographics). Dartmouth-Hitchcock Medical Center, based in Lebanon, N.H., has emerged as a leading health-care educator, research facility, and provider, and is a facilitator of health-related business development. By creating alliances with smaller hospitals up and down the valley, Dartmouth's medical centers also may provide some stimulus for smaller communities attracting new health-care industries.

The growth of Dartmouth-Hitchcock and of Dartmouth College, located next door in Hanover, N.H., is having a dramatic effect on surrounding communities. Upper Valley real estate prices are among the highest in the region, and Lebanon, once a sleepy crossroads, has a crowded commercial strip. Fast growth and rising wealth have sparked a thriving local arts scene, investment in historic preservation and conserving open space, and a growing movement to support local agriculture. As much as anywhere in the two states, the Upper Valley illustrates the movement of the postindustrial economy toward knowledge-based industries and the creative economy.

The watershed also has seen the start up and growth of many new businesses in the computer, health-care, financial, and information services sectors. Many of these are found in the Upper Valley, and some in Keene, N.H., home of Keene State College and a branch of Dartmouth-Hitchcock. The region boasts success stories of entrepreneurs, many connected with Dartmouth College, who founded small technology-based businesses that are now multinational operations.

White River Junction, Vt. in the future.

A designated Main Street community, Littleton, N.H., has emphasized revitalizing its downtown as part of its economic development strategy. Taking advantage of its location on the Ammonoosuc River, the town built a covered bridge in a traditional style. Private investors have renovated historic mill buildings into retail, restaurant, and office space.

Springfield, Vt., like many other towns in the watershed, is now promoting its creative economy along with manufacturing and other industries.

Amenities Attract New Businesses

Many communities in the watershed tout a range of business and lifestyle amenities or assets to attract new businesses. These assets may include skilled or highly educated workforces, lower construction and land costs (particularly compared to the New Hampshire seacoast and Massachusetts), access to interstate highways, a strong work ethic, and a rural lifestyle in a beautiful environment where people know their neighbors, have a sense of community, suffer relatively little traffic, and in the case of New Hampshire, pay no personal income tax and no sales tax.

The valley draws professionals seeking its quality of life, many of whom may have first experienced the area as vacationers or as students. In small towns many miles from Hanover and Lebanon, one- and two-person consulting firms work in technology, organizational consulting, product development, software writing, and so on.

Challenges Remain

While there are many success stories, the valley's transition to a postindustrial economy has not been seamless or easy. Service-sector jobs are not considered as well-paying as the manufacturing jobs they have replaced, and many workers lack health and insurance benefits. Communities in the northern part of the watershed in particular still face many economic challenges and uncertainties. Vermont's Northeast Kingdom and New Hampshire's North Country are rugged, lightly populated regions that traditionally relied on manufacturing and the forest products industry for employment and growth. That picture has changed rapidly in the last several years, as key industrial employers have shut down, likely never to return.

Generally, growth in northern communities is in tourism, recreation, and outdoor-oriented businesses and services, and the second-home market and attendant services like construction, landscaping, and maintenance. In New Hampshire, there is keen interest in developing biomass (wood) energy production as an alternative to the dying pulp and paper industry.

The evolution away from traditional industries is not necessarily steady and unidirectional, but the larger trends are clear. The postindustrial economy in much of the central and southern watershed is showing a strength and diversity that should serve its residents well for decades to come. The north faces some challenges, but the valley's overall creative and entrepreneurial spirit should support every region's postindustrial transformation in time.

The next chapter, Demographics, recounts other factors that are influencing the region's economic future.

Preston Gilbert is former director of the North Country Council, the regional planning commission based in Bethlehem, N.H. Presently, he is the operations director of the State University of New York Center for Brownfield Studies.

As a journalist, Rebecca A. Brown covered many traditional and emerging businesses. She is communications director for the Connecticut River Joint Commissions.

FOR FURTHER READING

Florida, Richard. 2002. *The Rise of the Creative Class.* New York: Basic Books.

Grogan, Paul S., and Tony Proscio. 2000. *Comeback Cities.* Boulder, Colo.: Westview Press.

New Hampshire Department of Employment Security. 2006. *Looking Forward: Preparing for the Future New Hampshire Economy.* Concord, N.H.: New Hampshire Department of Employment Security.

———. Published annually. *Vital Signs: New Hampshire Economic and Social Indicators.* Concord, N.H.: New Hampshire Department of Employment Security.

Vermont Department of Economic Development. 2002. *Research Innovations and Vermont's Economy.* Montpelier, Vt.: Vermont Department of Economic Development.

The Dartmouth-Hitchcock Medical Center is at the center of the region's growing health care services sector.

———. 2005. *Strategic Vision and Business Plan for Job Creation and Economic Development*. Montpelier, Vt.: Vermont Department of Economic Development.

Weiss, Michael J. 1988. *The Clustering of America*. New York: Tilden Press.

POSTINDUSTRIAL EMPLOYMENT TRENDS, 1960 TO 2000

JOANNA WHITCOMB

The traditional foundation of the region's economy is its natural resources and attendant high quality of life. Over the past century, jobs have shifted from utilization of these natural resources (i.e., forestry, farming, and resource extraction) to manufacturing to services. In the past 40 years, this shift has resulted in net losses in the primary sector (agriculture, forestry, and mining) and in manufacturing, and significant absolute and relative gains in the services. In 2000, employment in trade, health, education, and other services has gone from one-half to three-quarters of the labor force.

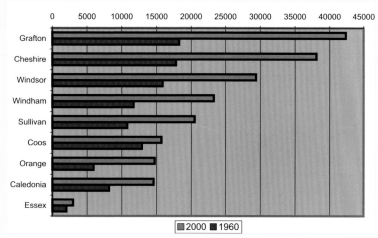

Chart A. Labor Force, by County, 1960 and 2000. U.S. Census Bureau, 1960 and 2000.

The overriding change in the watershed's economy is reflected in employment figures from 1960 to 2000 as shown in Chart A. Grafton County, N.H., influenced by the Hanover-Lebanon area, shows the most dramatic growth. Filling these jobs, many of which are in the Hanover-Lebanon area, and also in the retail complex that has grown in Littleton, are people commuting from other New Hampshire counties and from Vermont. Over 11,000 people travel into Grafton County daily for work. The only other county with net in-migration of workers is Windham County in southern Vermont.

The distribution of employment varies from north to south and across state boundaries. Manufacturing employment makes up a more significant portion of the labor market in the northern areas of the watershed (the Northern Forest region). In the labor markets in the central and southern regions, the professional service sector accounts for a significantly higher portion of employment. The map on page 173 illustrates the watershed's primary employment sectors, based on the 2000 U.S. Census. At the time of this writing, Coös County in northern New Hampshire is losing basic industries as pulp and paper mills continue to close. It may well be that by 2010, the primary markets in Coös County are forestry and agriculture, or recreation, rather than manufacturing.

Chart B makes clear the significant growth in the health and educa-

tion sectors, the decline of manufacturing, and the domination of the growing service sector between 1960 and 2000.

As the watershed's economy continues to mature, the patterns of that growth will change. Among the challenges facing the two-state region is the need to encourage balanced growth among sectors and subregions and to foster opportunities to share in that growth to all residents and communities. Simultaneously, residents would wish to be assured of access to productive employment and the essential services that, along with the outstanding environment, are necessary elements of a high quality of life and standard of living.

Joanna Whitcomb is a planner at Dartmouth College, where she is responsible for campus planning that integrates land use and buildings with natural resources, transportation, parking, and other infrastructure. She also works with local planners on regional issues. She lives in Hanover, N.H.

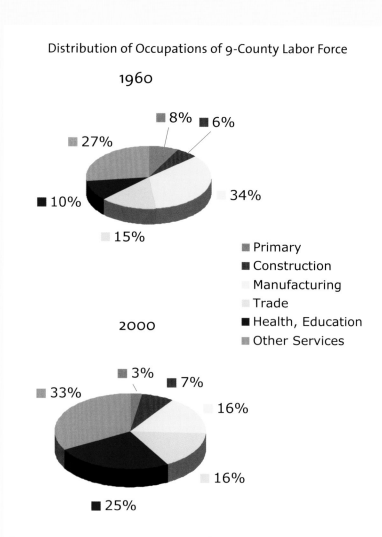

Chart B. Comparison of Industrial and Postindustrial Labor Force Patterns in Nine Counties, 1960 and 2000. U.S. Census Bureau, 1960 and 2000.

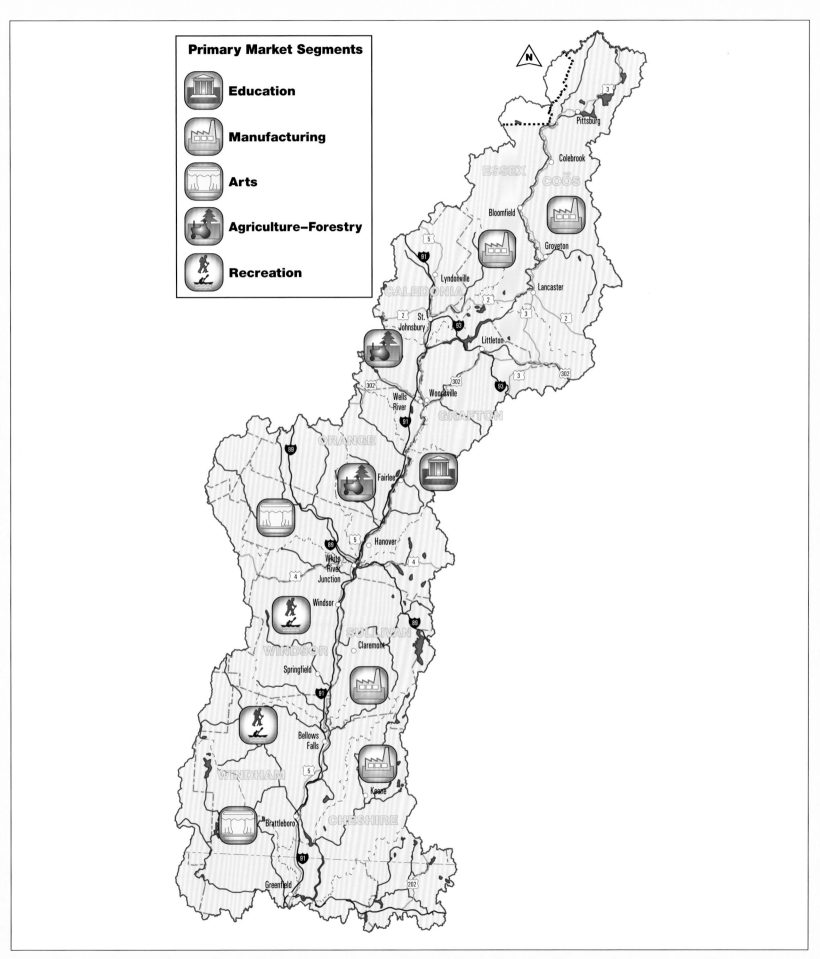

Primary Market Segments in the Nine Counties of the Watershed. Base map: VCGI and GRANIT data sets, modified by Northern Cartographic. Primary sectors graphics developed by Northern Cartographic from author's information derived from U.S. Census Bureau data.

27 Demographics

This chapter starts by considering historic population patterns in the watershed, and then explores demographic trends given current factors. These factors include long-term economic adjustments, improvements in transportation infrastructure, and the aging of the population. Demographic factors both influence and are influenced by changes in the economy region's economy, which is itself influenced by regional, national, and international forces. While this chapter is the most quantitative in the Atlas, it shares the underlying theme of interconnectivity throughout the watershed.

Population Change and Its Components
If someone living in the Connecticut River Valley in 1790 could reappear today, he or she would likely be very surprised at how settlement patterns have changed over two centuries. In 1790, the five most-populated towns on the Vermont side of the watershed were Guilford, Putney, Hartland, Westminster, and Woodstock, all in the southern counties of Windsor and Windham (see Table 5). Today, the five most-populated towns are Brattleboro, Hartford, Springfield, St. Johnsbury, and Lyndon, the latter two in Caledonia County in the north. Only three watershed towns were present in *both* of Vermont's top-20 lists of town population for 1790 and 2000: Brattleboro, Rockingham, and Woodstock.*

In New Hampshire, the pattern is similar, as seen in Table 6, but the largest aggregations of population remain in the southern half of

---

*The authors have included in their analysis of population significant towns and cities that lie only partly within the watershed, including Berlin and Keene, N.H., and Richmond, Vt.

TABLE 5. Top Five Towns by Population in Vermont Portion of Watershed, 1790 and 2000

	1790			2000	
TOWN	COUNTY	POPULATION	TOWN	COUNTY	POPULATION
Guilford	Windham	2,422	Brattleboro	Windham	12,005
Putney	Windham	1,848	Hartford	Windsor	10,385
Hartland	Windsor	1,652	Springfield	Windsor	9,078
Westminster	Windham	1,599	St. Johnsbury	Caledonia	7,571
Woodstock	Windsor	1,597	Lyndon	Caledonia	5,448

TABLE 6. Top Five Towns by Population in New Hampshire Portion of Watershed, 1790 and 2000

	1790			2000	
TOWN	COUNTY	POPULATION	TOWN	COUNTY	POPULATION
Westmoreland	Cheshire	2,018	Keene	Cheshire	22,563
Chesterfield	Cheshire	1,905	Claremont	Sullivan	13,151
Claremont	Sullivan	1,435	Lebanon	Grafton	12,568
Hanover	Grafton	1,380	Hanover	Grafton	10,850
Richmond	Cheshire	1,380	Berlin	Coös	10,331

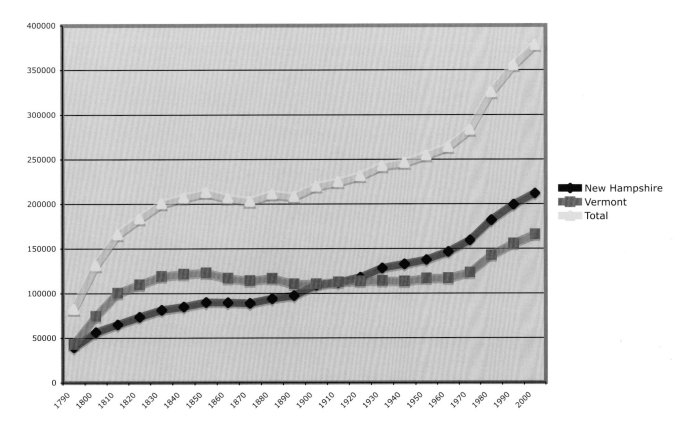

Figure 22. Total Population of the Upper Connecticut River Watershed, by State and Decade, 1790 to 2000.

the watershed. Hanover and Claremont appear in the top-five list for population in both 1790 and 2000. Indeed, Hanover has continued to grow and the Hanover-Lebanon, New Hampshire–Hartford, Vermont, area has become the leading area for population growth in the watershed.

Watershed Population

The estimated population of the upper Connecticut River watershed in 2000 was 378,000. In 1790, it was an estimated 82,600. The pattern of growth over the past 200 years has featured a rapid period of growth in the early 1800s, relatively slow growth between 1840 and 1970, including a marked loss during and after the Civil War, and a surge in the watershed's population from 1970 to 2000. Only once (1890–1900) in the period between 1830 and 1960 did the 10-year growth rate exceed 5 percent; since 1960, however, the rate has consistently been over 6 percent and even exceeded 14 percent in the decade between 1970 and 1980. Figure 22 shows the growth in population, by state during the past two centuries.

Distribution of Population with the Watershed

Table 7 illustrates the distribution and the ebb and flow of population growth and decline over the past two centuries by county. It reveals that the Vermont population in the Connecticut River watershed was larger than that of New Hampshire in the nineteenth century, but that

this pattern reversed in the twentieth century. Large areas of both states witnessed first growth, then decline, and then growth again over this period.

TABLE 7. Watershed Population Distribution as a Percentage, by County, for Selected Years (1790–2000)

COUNTIES	1790	1800	1850	1900	1950	2000
Cheshire, N.H.	23.9	18.6	14.2	14.3	15.2	19.7
Coös, N.H.	0.8	1.3	4.8	13.1	14.0	8.7
Grafton, N.H.	10.3	10.7	12.9	13.5	14.0	15.2
Hillsborough, N.H.	1.5	1.0	0.9	0.4	0.5	1.1
Sullivan, N.H.	11.1	11.1	9.1	8.2	10.4	10.8
Caledonia, Vt.	2.4	5.4	11.1	11.1	9.4	7.9
Essex, Vt.	0.7	1.1	2.2	3.7	2.5	1.7
Orange, Vt.	8.9	12.5	12.9	8.8	6.7	7.5
Windham, Vt.	21.3	18.0	13.7	12.2	11.3	11.8
Windsor, Vt.	19.1	20.3	18.2	14.7	16.1	15.4
N.H.—Conn. River watershed	47.6	42.7	42.0	49.5	54.0	55.6
Vt.—Conn. River watershed	52.4	57.3	58.0	50.5	46.0	44.4

Note: For purposes of this table, the small part of Hillsborough County, N.H., that lies in the watershed is included.

Population Growth, by Town, 1790 to 2000

Over the past 200 years, settlement generally flowed from south to north, from a starting point of over 75 percent of the 1790 population in what are now the four southern counties. But growth into the northern counties took different paths in the two states. The population in the northern three counties in Vermont (Essex, Caledonia, and Orange), for example, grew from roughly 12 percent of the watershed in 1790 to nearly 25 percent by 1810, and remained over 25 percent from 1840 to 1890. This subregion then started losing population relatively and steadily through 2000 (down to 17.1 percent). Changes in agriculture and industry, particularly in the natural resource–based economies, help explain the slowdown of population growth in the northern regions of both states. The northern New Hampshire counties of Grafton and Coös started at about the same population level as the northern Vermont counties in 1790, but grew more slowly and steadily throughout the nineteenth and twentieth centuries. Coös County has been losing population — the only New Hampshire county to do so in the 2000 census — while Grafton County has been the principal economic engine and growth center.

In 1970, for the first time since 1830, the southern counties of both states were each the two most populous of these regions within the watershed, and this pattern has remained relatively constant during the past three decades. The ebbs and flows of the northern and southern subregions of the two-state watershed over the past 200 years plus are shown in Figure 23.

Another watershed population dynamic is notable. As mentioned above, the period between 1830 and 1970 was characterized by slow growth, underscored by a growth in total watershed population of less than 7,000 in the 50 years between 1850 and 1900! Several pockets of

towns in both states experienced early rapid growth followed by sustained decline, due largely to economic opportunities elsewhere, both in the watershed and to regions west. In Peacham, Vt., for example, population peaked in 1840 at about 1,300 and fell gradually over the next 130 years to a low of about 400 in 1970. By 2000, its population had recovered to over 600. In the 1800s, Peacham was a sheep-raising area with nearly 10,000 sheep supporting the local economy; now it is a typical residential community with many retirees and small computer-based businesses. Another example is Bath, N.H., which contained 1,600 residents in 1830, but only 600 in 1960. It had grown to nearly 900 by 2000. These patterns are reflected in other watershed towns.

Population Changes in the Watershed

Maps 42 through 44 portray the towns in the watershed that gained or lost population in three major time periods between 1760 and 2000. The first, 1760 to 1840, is characterized by general settlement growth up the valley with only a couple towns experiencing net losses in that period (Map 42). The second period, 1840 to 1970, reflects the economic realities of the mid- and late-nineteenth and early twentieth centuries (Map 43).

The reasons for the loss of population in so many towns after 1840 are complex but two reasons stand out. First, some towns suffered losses as new transportation systems, primarily rail, provided people with a means for leaving areas with relatively poor farmland and moving out of the valley. Second, industrialization attracted workers from rural communities to some larger towns and cities. This is seen in the population increases in the growing commercial and transportation

Figure 23. Percentage of Watershed Population in Selected Subregions, 1790 to 2000.

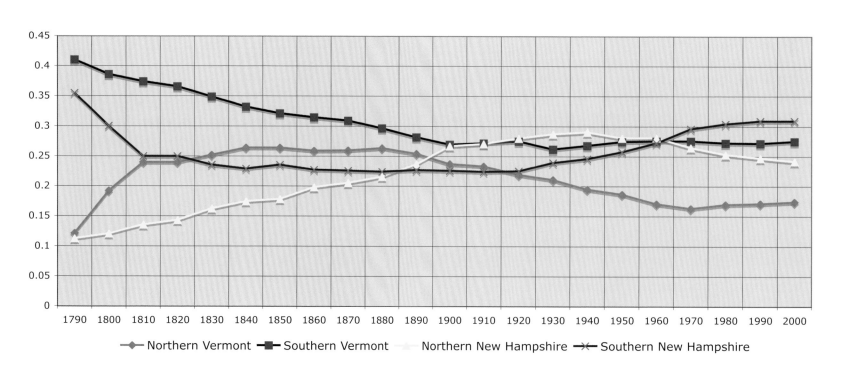

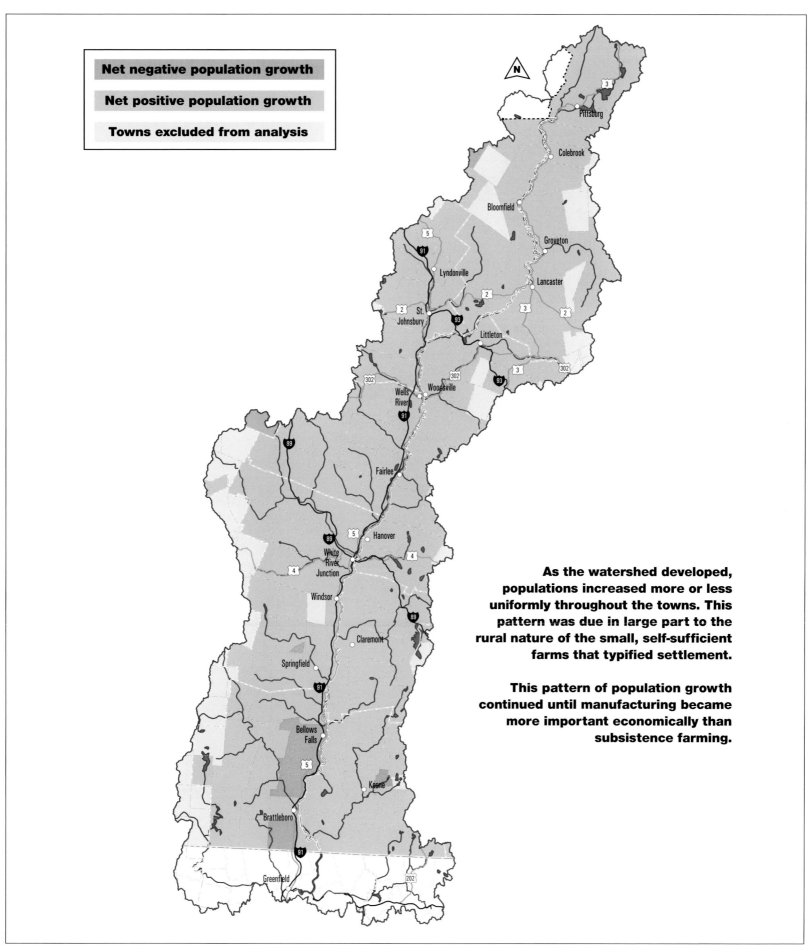

Net negative population growth

Net positive population growth

Towns excluded from analysis

N

Pittsburg

Colebrook

Bloomfield

Groveton

Lyndonville

Lancaster

St. Johnsbury

Littleton

Wells River

Woodsville

Fairlee

Hanover

White River Junction

Windsor

Claremont

Springfield

Bellows Falls

Keene

Brattleboro

Greenfield

As the watershed developed, populations increased more or less uniformly throughout the towns. This pattern was due in large part to the rural nature of the small, self-sufficient farms that typified settlement.

This pattern of population growth continued until manufacturing became more important economically than subsistence farming.

Map 42. Population Change, 1760–1840.

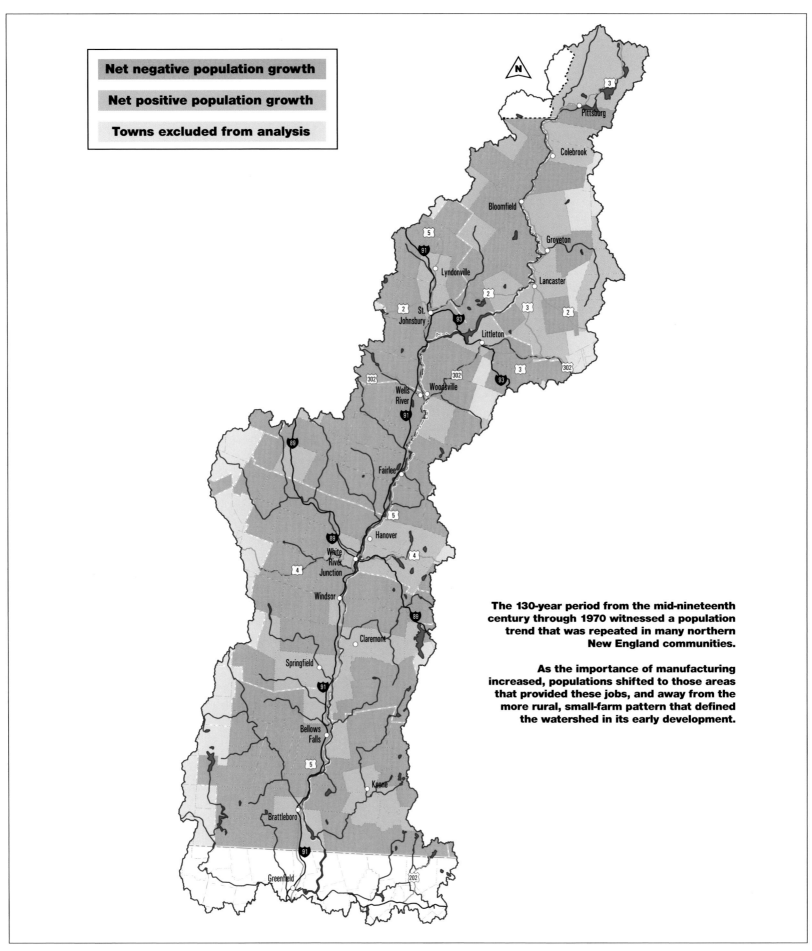

Net negative population growth

Net positive population growth

Towns excluded from analysis

Pittsburg

Colebrook

Bloomfield

Groveton

Lyndonville

Lancaster

St. Johnsbury

Littleton

Wells River

Woodsville

Fairlee

Hanover

White River Junction

Windsor

Claremont

Springfield

Bellows Falls

Keene

Brattleboro

Greenfield

The 130-year period from the mid-nineteenth century through 1970 witnessed a population trend that was repeated in many northern New England communities.

As the importance of manufacturing increased, populations shifted to those areas that provided these jobs, and away from the more rural, small-farm pattern that defined the watershed in its early development.

Map 43. Population Change, 1840–1970.

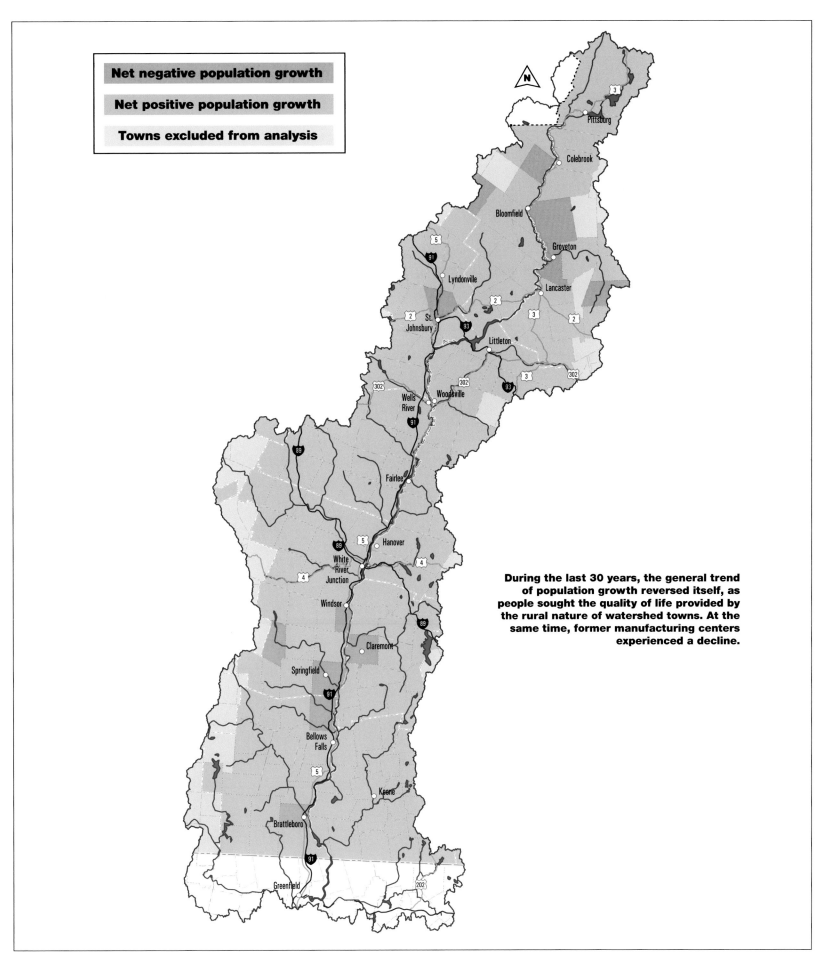

Net negative population growth

Net positive population growth

Towns excluded from analysis

N

During the last 30 years, the general trend of population growth reversed itself, as people sought the quality of life provided by the rural nature of watershed towns. At the same time, former manufacturing centers experienced a decline.

Map 44. Population Change, 1970–2000.

centers of Hanover–Lebanon–White River Junction, and in towns with burgeoning industrial manufacturing, including Brattleboro and Springfield, Vt., and Claremont and Keene, N.H.

Interestingly, as Map 44 (1970 to 2000) shows, some of regions that grew during the period 1840 to 1970 lost population after the middle of the twnetieth century. Manufacturing gradually gave ground to service industries and employees gained greater mobility with automobiles and new highways. Combined with new in-migrants, these changes led to a revived settlement of the surrounding rural areas.

Despite these ebbs and flows, we can also see that some towns have experienced continual growth during these two centuries. Other sections of the Atlas (notably Chapter 23, The Industrial Era, and Chapter 26, The Postindustrial Era) describe in some detail the reasons for this continual growth. Some towns that have shown growth in every decade since 1900 include Jaffrey, Keene, Hanover, Lebanon, Littleton, and Charlestown, N.H., and Fairlee and Hartford, Vt.

Social Characteristics of the Watershed Population

On average, the population of the Connecticut River watershed in the two states is older, slightly less well educated, and poorer than the population in other parts of the respective states. This population is not static, however, as shown by recent patterns of residential relocation and where people commute to work. These social characteristics are next considered one by one.

Age of the Population. As Table 8 portrays, the median age of the population of the watershed increased dramatically between 1980 and 2000, and is higher than the median age of the rest of either state. Four factors help explain this phenomenon. First, there are fewer young adults and parents as a proportion of the population. Fewer children are being born to this older population, exacerbating the trend. Declining enrollments in many schools are one manifestation.

Second, a growing number of retirees live in the watershed. Third, the postindustrial economy features an increasing number of high-tech and service businesses, especially those represented by home occupations or small firms that are linked electronically to markets or clients throughout the world. Many individuals in these businesses, while not of retirement age, are empty nesters whose children live elsewhere. A fourth factor in the increasing average age is that people are living longer.

Table 9 shows that almost all counties in the watershed have lower percentages of children under age 5 and under age 18 than their respective states as a whole, and a higher percentages of older people as well. Without in-migration of younger families with children, the aging of the watershed population will continue to have a dampening effect on population growth in the future.

Educational Attainment. In 2000, slightly over 50 percent of the watershed's population age 18 and over had received post–high school education, as shown in Table 10. Many current employment opportunities require some undergraduate, if not graduate, experience. Overall, residents of the watershed counties are comparable to their respective state averages in educational attainment. However, the northern counties in both states show a significantly lower percentage of the population with college degrees.

Household Income. The median household income in the watershed counties has increased dramatically from 1979 to 1999, as shown in Table 11. The percentage growth rate from 1989 to 1999 generally has been higher in these counties than it has been in the two states as a whole. Nevertheless, average median income in the watershed counties lags behind that of the two states. One aspect partially hidden in median household income figures is poverty levels. Table 12 shows the poverty rates in both states as well as in each county, with the northern counties showing the highest levels.

Conclusion

For the past two centuries, the upper Connecticut River watershed has been a dynamic place, with people and goods traveling through it and within it, first by birch bark canoes, now by 18-wheelers and other conveyances. Just as our imagined nineteenth-century resident likely would be surprised by changes in the locations of the population centers, we may surmise that a resident in the year 2100 will be equally surprised by population and demographic shifts compared to today. Pointing at potential effects of global climate change, some prognosticators see resettlement away from the nation's coastal and southern regions. It this prediction proves correct, the Connecticut River Valley may become a destination for people moving away from rising sea and temperature levels. Only time will tell.

Will Sawyer is an outreach professional and community data specialist with the Center for Rural Studies at the University of Vermont, where he specializes in outreach and technical assistance for local decisionmakers and entrepreneurs. He lives in St. Albans, Vt.

TABLE 8. Watershed Median Age, by County, for 1980 and 2000

COUNTY	1980	2000	ABSOLUTE CHANGE, 1980–2000	% INCREASE, 1980–2000
New Hampshire	30.1	37.1	7.0	23.3
Cheshire, N.H.	30.5	37.6	7.1	23.3
Coös, N.H.	32.5	41.5	9.0	27.7
Grafton, N.H.	29.3	37.0	7.7	26.3
Sullivan, N.H.	31.6	40.0	8.4	26.6
Vermont	29.4	37.7	8.3	28.2
Caledonia, Vt.	30.1	38.5	8.4	27.9
Essex, Vt.	30.7	39.0	8.3	27.0
Orange, Vt.	29.5	38.6	9.1	30.8
Windham, Vt.	31.3	40.0	8.7	27.8
Windsor, Vt.	32.2	41.3	9.1	28.3

TABLE 9. Watershed Age of Population, by County, 2000

STATE OR COUNTY	POPULATION ESTIMATE, 2006	POPULATION, 2000	% OF POPULATION UNDER AGE 5	% OF POPULATION UNDER AGE 18	% OF POPULATION AGE 65 AND OLDER	PERSONS PER SQUARE MILE
New Hampshire	1,314,895	1,235,786	5.6	23.1	12.5	137.8
Cheshire	77,393	73,825	4.8	20.7	14.1	104.4
Coös	33,019	33,111	4.5	20.2	18.2	18.4
Grafton	85,336	81,743	4.7	19.5	14.4	47.7
Sullivan	42,979	40,458	5.7	22.2	15.8	75.3
Vermont	623,908	608,827	5.1	21.3	13.2	65.8
Caledonia	30,842	29,702	5.2	21.6	14.0	45.6
Essex	6,567	6,459	4.1	21.1	15.1	9.7
Orange	29,440	28,226	4.7	21.5	13.2	41.0
Windham	43,898	44,216	5.0	20.8	14.2	56.0
Windsor	57,653	57,418	4.7	20.1	16.3	59.1
United States	299,398,484	281,421,906	6.8	24.8	12.4	—

TABLE 10. Watershed Educational Attainment of Population, by County, 2000

STATE OR COUNTY	% OF POPULATION AGE 18–24 ENROLLED IN COLLEGE OR GRADUATE SCHOOL	% OF POPULATION AGE 25 OR OLDER WITH LESS THAN 9TH GRADE EDUCATION	% OF POPULATION AGE 25 OR OLDER, HIGH SCHOOL GRADUATE OR HIGHER	% OF POPULATION AGE 25 OR OLDER WITH BACHELOR DEGREE	% OF POPULATION AGE 25–34 WITH BACHELOR DEGREE OR HIGHER
New Hampshire	38.6	3.9	87.4	28.7	30.2
Cheshire	56.0	4.0	86.2	26.6	24.0
Coös	16.4	8.6	76.9	11.9	10.1
Grafton	62.5	3.7	87.7	32.7	34.2
Sullivan	12.8	5.5	83.0	19.7	17.5
Vermont	43.1	5.1	86.4	29.4	31.2
Caledonia	35.4	7.1	82.6	22.5	18.6
Essex	10.0	10.5	75.0	10.8	11.5
Orange	32.4	5.5	84.1	23.9	21.1
Windham	30.5	3.9	87.3	30.5	28.6
Windsor	20.5	4.0	88.1	30.2	31.2

Barry Lawson is a consultant and researcher and has served as project coordinator for the Atlas project. The authors thank Tom Duffy of New Hampshire's Office of State Planning, who responded countless times to requests for state population data.

FOR FURTHER READING

Center for Rural Studies, University of Vermont, Vermont Community Data Bank. http://crs.uvm.edu/databank/.

U.S. Census Bureau, Census of Population and Housing, via American FactFinder, http://factfinder.census.gov/.

TABLE 11. Watershed Median Household Income, by County,
1979, 1989, and 1999

COUNTY, RANKED BY 1999 MEDIAN INCOME	1979	1989	1999	1989–1999 % GROWTH
N.H. — State	$17,013	$36,329	$46,467	27.9
Cheshire, N.H.	$16,037	$31,648	$42,382	33.9
Grafton, N.H.	$14,523	$30,065	$41,962	39.6
Sullivan, N.H.	$15,304	$29,053	$40,938	40.9
Vt. — State	$14,790	$29,792	$40,856	37.1
Windsor, Vt.	$15,360	$29,258	$40,688	39.1
Orange, Vt.	$12,867	$28,004	$39,855	42.3
Windham, Vt.	$13,696	$27,767	$38,204	37.6
Caledonia, Vt.	$13,131	$25,356	$34,800	37.2
Coös, N.H.	$13,699	$25,897	$33,593	29.7
Essex, Vt.	$12,369	$22,358	$30,490	36.4

TABLE 12. Percentage of Watershed Families
Classified at Below Poverty Level,
by County, for 1979, 1989, and 1999

COUNTY, RANKED BY 1999 FIGURES	1979	1989	1999
Essex, Vt.	17.2	13.9	13.7
Caledonia, Vt.	15.3	12.1	12.3
Coös, N.H.	11.7	10.1	10.0
Windham, Vt.	12.8	9.5	9.4
Vt. — State	12.1	9.9	9.4
Orange, Vt.	13.7	9.4	9.1
Grafton, N.H.	11.1	9.6	8.6
Sullivan, N.H.	10.5	9.8	8.5
Cheshire, N.H.	10.0	7.0	8.0
Windsor, Vt.	10.6	9.4	7.7
N.H. — State	8.5	6.4	6.5

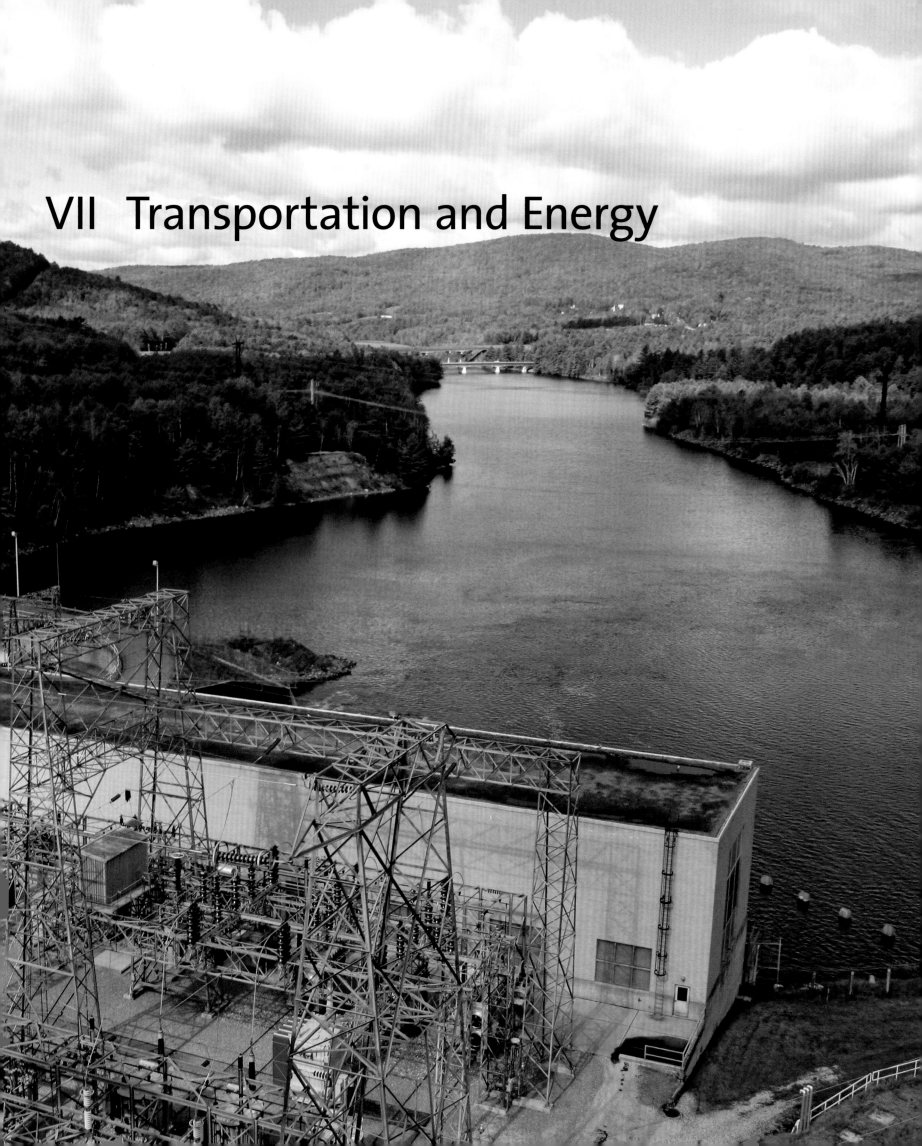

VII Transportation and Energy

Introduction

The Connecticut River and its major tributaries provided early transportation routes for Native people, white explorers, traders and trappers, loggers, and merchants. Later, innovative forms of waterborne transportation were tried here, with the steamboat enjoying a special place in local history, as Sharon Penney relates in the first chapter of this section.

The river valleys also invited overland travel, in some places offering the easiest way through the mountains. The first turnpikes and other official roads often followed the network of Native paths through the watershed. Paths worn smooth by Native foot travel gave way to dirt tracks furrowed by oxen and horse carts. "Corduroy" roads laid with lengths of timber evolved to gravel, stone, and eventually, pavement. Some of today's roads still follow the original routes. Sharon Penney and Barry Lawson provide an overview of the history of the watershed's roads in Chapter 29.

While the ascendance of the private automobile forever altered the development of the watershed by the mid-twentieth century, the railroad first revolutionized transportation. In Chapter 30, Nat Tripp and Sharon Penney track the story of the railroads, starting with their entry into the valley in 1847. Today, many miles of rail that once carried dozens of trains a day have been torn up, and people on foot, on bikes, or riding ATVs or snowmobiles enjoy the rail beds along the river and some tributaries. However, one may still catch a train to New York City and beyond, and specialty excursion lines offer a taste of what it would have been like to travel in style by rail car a century ago.

The valley's aviation history is surprisingly rich, filled with both bold characters and practical business decisionmakers, and continues today with a range of airfields. Many are still grass fields, while others offer modern services and connections to cities including New York. Roger Damon traces the history of aviation in the watershed and highlights a few of the many personalities who helped shape it.

For well over two centuries, the Connecticut River's flow has been used as a source of power, first for gristmills, and later for New England's largest hydroelectric project. In Chapter 32, John Marshall and Barbara Ripley tell the story of the river as a power source, as well as describing other energy resources in the watershed, from trees to "cow power."

An artist's depiction of an early barge of the type that was used on the broader, quieter reaches of the Connecticut River.

28 Water Travel

To Market by River

Sailing vessels, later known as "river" boats, were built in huge numbers in the population centers of the lower Connecticut River in Massachusetts and Connecticut during the 200-year span between the first European settlements and the coming of the railroads in the mid-nineteenth century. Trade flourished up and downriver with the advent of these vessels. But moving north, the large boats were impractical until the swift water, rapids, and waterfalls were tamed by a system of canals. The building of canals along the river from the 1790s to late 1830s hastened passage of goods in both directions and contributed to the growth and commercial importance of river towns in Vermont and New Hampshire.

The Vermont Legislature inaugurated the era of canal building in the upper river valley in 1791, when it chartered a canal so boat traffic could get around the ferocious Great Falls in Rockingham (now often referred to by the village name, Bellows Falls). Opened for riverboat traffic in 1802, this was the first navigation canal and lock system in the United States. The legislature later authorized canals to be built around Sumner Falls and Olcott, or White River Falls, near Wilder. These were opened in 1810. Eventually, flooding destroyed these northernmost canals and locks Carter 1945; Wikoff 1985).

Farther north, the river's varied widths, along with its many shallow oxbows, sandbars, spiny rock beds, and series of precipitous falls, prevented the use of the ships common along the lower Connecticut. Merchants and river men relied instead upon oversized canoes and later, the large "box" river rafts. These rafts were often 60 feet in length and 12 feet wide and were propelled by two sturdy men with huge oars. Often several of the box rafts were yoked loosely together by placing planked boxes over the solid hardwood pins that served as oarlocks. Linked together two boxes wide and three long, these so-called "divisions" carried great loads of lumber and other North Country goods downriver to the larger towns and cities. The fact that the rafts could be broken apart and made smaller to pass through narrow or rough water, then reconnected, made all the difference in the quantity of goods that could be transported in one trip.

Steam-Powered Watercraft Begets an Era

Robert Fulton, the American engineer and builder, usually is identified as the inventor of the steamboat. Fulton and Robert Livingston, the United States minister to France, successfully launched a steamboat on the Hudson River in New York State in 1807 and began regular

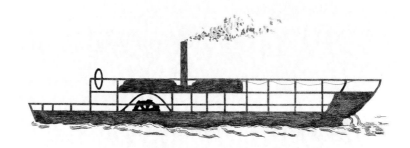

An artist's interpretation of Samuel Morey's *Aunt Sally*, the first steamboat on the Connecticut.

The *Barnet* chugs up the Connecticut toward her namesake village in a show of steamboat power.

Timber companies used the river as a highway for logs, men, horses, and supplies, as shown in this late-nineteenth-century photo from Hartford, Vt.

Falls. The steamboat's owner was the Connecticut River Company, a promoter of river travel and competitor with the canal advocates — all of whom were trying to win political and financial support for their projects.

The *Barnet* left Hartford, Conn., on her northern venture on November 17, 1826, but was unable to churn through the rapids upriver at Enfield. Fortified with "strengthened" machinery and 30 men armed with poles, the steamboat tackled the rapids a few days later and proceeded on her way. On through Massachusetts she traveled without incident. But arriving at the Great Falls in Rockingham, the crew found the *Barnet* too wide to pass through the locks. Nevertheless, the voyage of 125 miles, with an elevation gain of 200 feet, was deemed a tremendous achievement. It was apparent that for river travel to succeed, the locks would have to be enlarged, and the river dredged to allow the big boats' passage — expensive propositions both (Jacobus 1956). Another solution was to build smaller steamboats. One of these, the *John Ledyard*, journeyed north from Hartford, Conn., in June 1831 and made it as far as Wells River, Vt., before it became stranded on a sandbar. When it was finally freed, it floated back down to Springfield, Mass., and never ventured as far north again (Wikoff 1985; Blaisdell 1979).

The era of canals and locks as a way of surmounting the river's challenges proved fairly short lived. Ambitious proposals such as building canals all the way from Wells River to Montpelier and on to Lake Champlain, or linking Concord, N.H., with Plymouth and then on to the Connecticut River at Orford or Haverhill, were discussed but never attempted. Even Captain Morey avowed that should the huge sums of money and time needed for such a Herculean task of canal building become available, he would not sanction public projects that were "not needed and would never pay." According to his biographer Carter, Morey secretly foresaw a time when "steam would be applied to a carriage on a railroad" and the days of the canals would be through. Morey was right. By mid-century, steel rail was being laid along the riverbanks, and steamboats became an anachronism. The story of railroads in the Connecticut River Valley is told in Chapter 30.

service on that river the next year. At least 14 years before, however, Captain Samuel Morey, an enterprising inventor and engineer in Orford, N.H., took out a patent and successfully launched a steam-mechanized boat, propelled by a paddle-wheel in the prow. His little boat, said to be large enough for him, the steam boiler, the wheel, and a stack of wood for fuel, chugged along the Connecticut at about four miles per hour. Morey partisans claimed that Fulton incorporated the Orford inventor's work into his own designs and received unjust credit for the steamboat (Farrell 1915).

The steamboat proved a boon to river commerce, especially in the wide, slow expanses of the lower river. Even with canals, however, steamboating on the upper river remained challenging because of rapids, sandbars, and rocks. In *The Connecticut River Steamboat Story*, Melanothon W. Jacobus relates the fanciful story of the steamer *Barnet*, which was supposed to reach its namesake Vermont village and prove, during its voyage, that steamboats were the wave of the future. The village of Barnet was considered the head of navigation on the Connecticut, for just north tumbled the intimidating Fifteen Mile

The River Becomes a Sluiceway

The new nation grew steadily in the early nineteenth century, and so did the need for utilizing the vast resources of native timber growing along the upper reaches of the Connecticut. Wood for homes, wagons, and ships, and later, the advent of the new process of making paper from ground wood "pulp" instead of cotton rags, fueled one of the most dramatic uses of river as a means of transportation.

The great log drives on the Connecticut are part of the region's lore. They are described in Chapter 23, The Industrial Era. In his classic book *Spiked Boots*, Waterford, Vt., author Robert E. Pike tells with great elegance stories of the rugged men and brutal work of transporting logs down the length of the great river to sawmills and paper mills.

The spring of 1915 saw the largest and the last of the long-log drives on the Connecticut. Over 65 million feet of lumber floated down the waterway after ice-out that year. But business was changing, as the stands of huge timber had been cut and papermaking from wood pulp was growing. The river continued to be used, though on an ever-smaller

DONNA ROBERTS MOODY, JOHN MOODY, AND LISA BROOKS

No one is certain how old canoe travel is on the Kwanitekw (Connecticut River), or in the Americas for that matter. In some of the oldest Penobscot stories from the coast, the ocean-going canoe figures prominently. The Abenaki, Penobscot, and Passamaquoddy are known to have fished in Sobakw (the Atlantic Ocean) for cod and even swordfish over many thousands of years. From Tierra del Fuego to the Arctic, various forms of canoe and kayak travel are thoroughly documented from the fifteenth century to the present, with coastal and inland travel routes connecting indigenous communities throughout the hemisphere. Columbus's first hearing of the word *canoa* came from the Arawak (Taino) peoples he met at Hispanola in 1492, who promptly saved his crew and gear when one of their caravels got hung up on a reef!

The Diversity of Abenaki Water Travel

The usual chronology ascribed to river and lake canoes begins with the animal skin boat that the Wôbanakiak (Alnôbak or Abenaki) still make (*mozalagw*—"moose hide canoe"). By 7,000 to 3,000 years ago, the stone adzes and gouges (*wôleskahigan*—"hollow-out tool") associated with dugout canoe making (*wôleskaolagw*—"hollowed-out canoe") are found widely on the eastern seaboard. Dugouts in eastern North America have been carbon dated from 5,000 years ago down to the last 500 years. Spruce, birch, and elm bark canoes were also certainly possible here in those ancient times and they are well known to the present day. The proliferation and diversity of the dugout and bark canoes in this region suggests an ancient origin. The Abenaki call an elm or spruce bark canoe a *pkwaholagw*, a "peeled canoe," which is especially useful in a pinch, when one requires temporary transport.

The birch bark canoe or *wigwaol* was a singular innovation in this waterborne way of life. *Wigwaol* came in many sizes, from 8 to 30 or more feet, adapted to the diverse needs of communities and the ever-changing flow of free rivers. Abenakis called their bigger family or freight canoes *odôolagw*, and the equally grand war canoes *madôbadolagw* ("bigger water canoe or boat"). Each Native nation and each *wigwaol* maker had particular styles and methods. An Abenaki canoe made by a twentieth-century *nodtolid*, or canoe maker, can be seen at Fort No. 4 in Charlestown, N.H. (see Chapter 35, Tourism and Historic Sites).

Stripped or planked canoes (*kôkskolagw*—"cedar-sided canoe") are probably an older indigenous innovation from the north woods of Canada, but the nineteenth century saw this art form dramatically expand to a more varied and popular place in non-Native society much as the Inuit kayak has proliferated in recent years.

Canoeing History on the Kwanitekw

Accounts of Kwanitekw dugout and bark canoe travel abound in oral histories and the historical record. Perhaps the best-known tale comes from John Ledyard, who is said to have felled a pine tree "with some Indian friends" in the spring of 1773 in Hanover, N.H., after spending the winter with the Abenakis in northern Vermont. He then miraculously survived the dugout trip down the Kwanitekw to Long Island Sound, a journey replicated by Dartmouth College students to this day, though not, to our knowledge, with a green dugout weighing 200 pounds!

We know the Abenaki still canoed the Kwanitekw in the nineteenth century from remarkable accounts of Abenaki families using the river for long-range family travel. There are also stories that the Abenakis' eastern relations, the Penobscot of Maine, were still coming to the Northeast Kingdom of Vermont as late as the mid-nineteenth century to find surviving canoe birch with the *wigwasal* ("one canoe sheet of birch bark") to make their *wigwaol* the old, one-piece way.

The *wigwaol* tradition has survived to the present day as a tribute to the ingenuity of this indigenous mode of transport, a continuation of an ancient art, and as a symbol and model for a return to a quieter life on the waterways. The ethic that considers the Kwanitekw and other great rivers of the Americas to be vibrant, living beings is not an antiquated tradition of America's past. There is hope that these living waters will once again run clear, to sustain all life, including we human beings, for generations to come.

For additional information on the Native history of the watershed, see Chapter 20, Native Space.

Sources

Adney, Edwin Tappan, and Howard Chapelle. 1964. *The Bark Canoes and Skin Boats of North America*. U.S. National Museum Bulletin no. 230. Washington D.C.: U.S. Government Printing Office.

Mansfield, Howard, ed. 2006. *Where the Mountain Stands Alone*. Hanover, N.H.: University Press of New England. See pages 25–27 for a brief account of an Abenaki family traveling the length of the Connecticut River by canoe in 1882 to 1883 before settling in Keene, New Hampshire.

Parker, Trudy Ann. 1994. *Aunt Sarah: Woman of the Dawnland*. Lancaster, N.H.: Dawnland Publications. See pages x–xii for an account of the 1824 canoe trip from Odanak (St. Francis) to Lunenberg, Vermont.

Roberts, Kenneth G., and Philip Shackleton. 1983. *The Canoe: A History of the Craft from Panama to the Arctic*. Camden, Maine: International Marine Publishing Company.

scale, as transportation for the comparatively matchstick-sized pulp-wood. As steam, and later, diesel-powered railroad transport evolved, the use of water current as a major transportation medium for lumber was consigned to the past.

While no longer a commercial transportation route, the Connecticut is a destination for recreational paddlers, many of whom take to the water for several hours, some for multi-day journeys, and a few who travel its entire length from source to sea.

Sharon A. Penney worked as a transportation planner with North Country Council, the regional planning commission in Bethlehem, N.H. She lives in Franconia, N.H.

FOR FURTHER READING

Blaisdell, Katharine. 1979. *Over the River and Through the Years*. Littleton, N.H.: Courier Printing Co.

Carter, George Calvin. 1945. *Samuel Morey*. Concord, N.H.: privately printed. In *This American River*, ed. W. E. Wetherell. Hanover, N.H.: University Press of New England, 2002.

Farrell, Gabriel, Jr. 1915. *Capt. Samuel Morey Who Built a Steamboat Fourteen Years Before Fulton*. Manchester, N.H.: Standard Book Co.

Jacobus, Melanothon W. 1956. *The Connecticut River Steamboat Story*. Hartford, Conn.: Connecticut Historical Society, 1956). Reprinted in Wetherell, *This American River*.

Pike, Robert E. 1999. *Spiked Boots: Sketches of the North Country*. Woodstock, Vt.: Countryman Press.

Wikoff, Jerold. 1985. *The Upper Valley: An Illustrated Tour along the Connecticut River before the Twentieth Century*. Chelsea, Vt.: Chelsea Green.

29 Roads

The Connecticut River and its tributaries provided native tribes and early settlers major transportation routes in the eighteenth century and before. Military, trade, and political interests provided the impetus to carve roads through the wilderness. Native trails were followed by soldiers, traders, and settlers, and some evolved into designated routes as the colonial population grew.

Military Road Building

Military objectives inspired some of the earliest official roads. In Vermont, the Crown Point Military Road was built in 1759 and '60, during the French and Indian War. General Jefferey Amherst, commander of all British troops in North America, ordered its construction after his forces captured French installations at Ticonderoga and Crown Point, New York. Revolutionary War hero John Stark (who famously declared he would "Live free or die") was among the road builders. The road ran from Chimney Point, on the eastern shore of Lake Champlain, just across from Fort Crown Point, 77 miles southeast to the Fort at No. 4, the northernmost outpost on the Connecticut River in Charlestown, N.H. The road served as a route for resupply of materials, food, and men, both during the French and Indian War and later for the colonial effort during the Revolutionary War. In peacetime, it provided a major new route for settlers into the rugged territory of central Vermont. Today, the road is mostly gone, although a few lengths are still used as road, and some still exist as footpaths. Historic markers trace its route from Charlestown to Lake Champlain.

With the cessation of wars between settlers of the nascent United States and the English and Native tribes, colonial settlements flourished. A system of land-based transportation was needed to support these settlements and to connect them, for both mercantile and political purposes, with the population centers of coastal New Hampshire and with Boston and Portland. New Hampshire's political elite in the Portsmouth region saw establishing overland mail and travel routes as a way to link remote regions, first in the colony, and later in the newly independent state in a newly founded country. They also sought to capture the surplus of agricultural goods that began being produced in the upper Connecticut River Valley—trade that was going downriver to the benefit of Connecticut and Massachusetts, not New Hampshire. Clearly the solution was to construct a series of east-west highways to link together the two great river valleys of the Connecticut and the Merrimack with the coastal regions. Many of the earliest land-based routes followed old Native paths along waterways, sometimes

Early "corduroy" roads constructed with logs were considered an improvement over simple footpaths. They must have made for an exciting ride.

189

crossing the wide and flat floodplains, other places climbing into the rugged hills.

As early as 1763, leaders of the New Hampshire colony sought to build a road connecting the seacoast and the fertile and productive farm lands along the Connecticut River in the Piermont-Haverhill vicinity, ending where the village of Woodsville is situated today. The way was difficult—road-building techniques were still primitive, and the Revolutionary War disrupted maintenance, so after a few years only remnants of what was called the Old Province Road remained.

Across the Connecticut River in the village of Wells River, which is part of Newbury, another important early route took shape about a decade later. The Bayley-Hazen Military Road was proposed by Jacob Bayley, a colonel in the Continental Army and Newbury resident, as a way to speed supplies and reinforcements north to assist Benedict Arnold's attempt to seize Quebec. According to the Walden, Vermont, town history, Bayley employed 100 men "who were to be paid $10 a month plus board and a pint of rum per day" as road builders. But when the road reached Peacham in the summer of 1776, General George Washington had second thoughts about its ultimate destination. He wrote Bayley:

> Sir: I this Morning received yours of the 28th Ulto., and approve the measures you had adopted for opening the Road to St. John's, which may be still proper to pursue, but as our Army in Canada, since their retreat from Quebec has met with further Misfortunes, and thereby the strongest Reason to believe they will be obliged to abandon the possession of that Country, if they have not already done it; I would advise you, to consider well the Advantages and Disadvantages that will result from compleating the Work. If the Enemy will be thereby afforded an easy Pass to make Incursions into our Colonies and to commit Depredations, and the other Advantages we shall derive from it, will not greatly over balance these Inconveniences, it will be improper to carry it on. The Change which has taken Place in our Affairs in that Quarter may render now what was extremely right to be done some Thing very inexpedient and unadvisable. As you are well acquainted with the Country thro' which the Communication was designed to be made, and I am not, I shall submit the Propriety of compleating it to you, under the circumstances I have mentioned, not meaning to direct you to one thing or another.
>
> I am, etc. G. Washington

Continental Army General Moses Hazen received orders three years later to resume construction. Low supplies and British opposition forced his regiment to stop the effort at mile 50, in the town of Westfield, at a mountain pass now known as Hazen's Notch.

Building Roads, Building Economies

In 1791, New Hampshire began chartering "post" roads designated for the conveyance of mail, goods, and travelers. A few years later, both New Hampshire and Vermont authorized entrepreneurial construction of toll roads by private companies whose recompense rested upon charging toll fees from travelers. Fed up with twisting local arms to get

roads built, the legislatures hoped that by allowing private corporations to build and run roads for profit, people could ride from here to there without losing a wheel or having to bushwhack.

Among the significant turnpikes into and within the Connecticut River watershed of this era were the Second, Third, and Fourth New Hampshire Turnpikes (1799–1800) that connected respectively Amherst with Claremont; from Walpole through Keene and on toward Boston; and Lebanon to the Merrimack River in Boscawen. A branch of the last of these ran from Lebanon up toward Hanover. The Coös Turnpike Corporation was formed in 1805, and built a road from Haverhill Corner to the Baker River in Warren. For a thorough discussion of the early turnpikes, see Wood 1919.

In Vermont in 1795, a road was commissioned from the Massachusetts line to Newbury, along and as close to the Connecticut River as practicable; and two years later the Connecticut River Turnpike was authorized over the same route from Brattleboro (then on the Massachusetts line) to Norwich. Today, Route 5 follows much of the same ground. Other Vermont turnpikes in the river valley included the Green Mountain Turnpike connecting Clarendon with Rockingham; a road connecting Windsor with Woodstock; the White River Turnpike from White River Junction toward Royalton; and the Northern Turnpike linking Waterford to Lake Champlain. While travelers readily paid tolls at the numerous covered bridges crossing the Connecticut, extracting fees from them for road passage proved difficult. Apparently many enjoyed going through the tollgates for free whenever the toll keepers were not on duty. Tolls gradually were eliminated, especially when competing railroad lines were opened on nearby routes. The dissolution of the bankrupt toll companies "freed" the roads to become the unanticipated responsibilities of towns. Map 45 shows early turnpike routes.

For over a century, these "freed" roadways were maintained by local municipalities and their appointed road surveyors. Unable to meet the cost of regular maintenance, towns appealed to their state legislatures for help with road construction and maintenance, and the state road systems evolved. Many state roadways incorporate pieces of these freed roads to this day.

New England Interstate Highways

As more and more roadways began crisscrossing the states, state and federal governments recognized the need for some order. The first system for marking state highways used colored bands on telephone poles. These were assigned by direction (red for east-west, blue for north-south, and yellow for intermediate or diagonal routes). In 1922, the six New England states adopted a numbering system for their interstate highway systems, a precursor to the federal highway numbering system unveiled four years later. The federal system used odd numbers for north-south routes and even numbers for east-west— opposite of the New England system. The New England routes that did not become U.S. highways retain their old numbers.

A system of federal appropriations to support and expand state highway systems had begun in the early 1900s. This eventually led to the federal interstate system, championed by President Dwight Eisenhower in 1956. Interstate highways I-93, I-89, and I-91, constructed

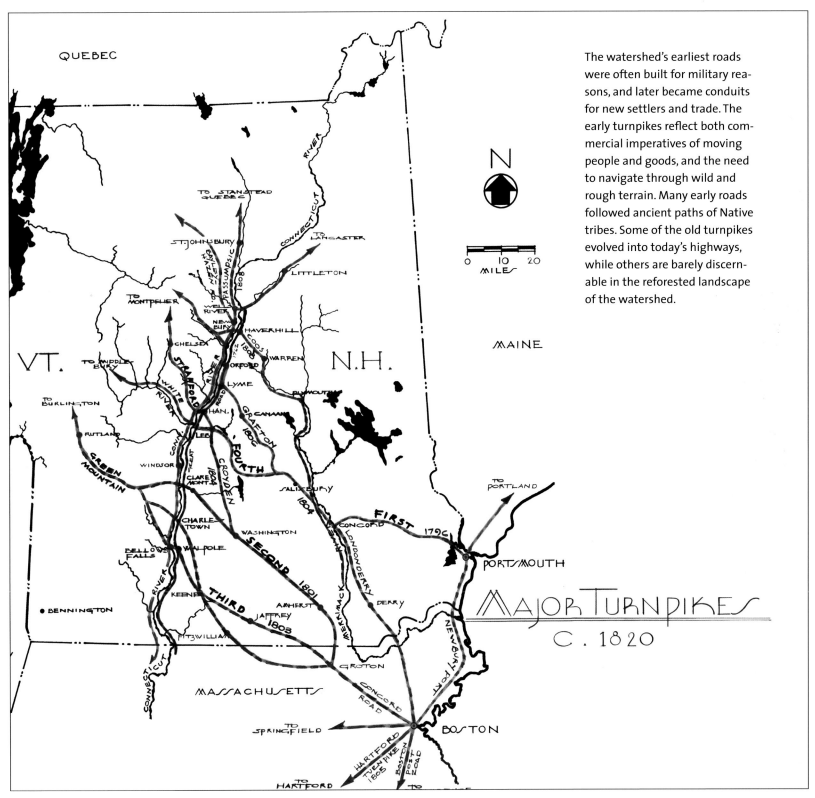

The watershed's earliest roads were often built for military reasons, and later became conduits for new settlers and trade. The early turnpikes reflect both commercial imperatives of moving people and goods, and the need to navigate through wild and rough terrain. Many early roads followed ancient paths of Native tribes. Some of the old turnpikes evolved into today's highways, while others are barely discernable in the reforested landscape of the watershed.

Map 45. Early Turnpikes.

From earliest times, the area of the confluence of the White and Connecticut rivers has been an important crossroads for overland and river travel. White River Junction became a major rail hub in the second half of the nineteenth century, and today is where Interstates 89 and 91 meet.

The first bridge across the Connecticut River, built by Col. Enoch Hale, is depicted in a c. 1792 painting by Frederick J. Blake, reproduced in an early postcard.

starting in the 1960s in New Hampshire and Vermont, echo the ancient paths of early travelers in the Connecticut River watershed. According to the U.S. Department of Transportation, New Hampshire and Vermont residents save on average over 40 hours of travel time per year by using these roads, with annual savings of close to $2,000 in safety, time, fuel, and other consumer costs. Anyone traveling I-91 north and south can attest to the truck traffic, much of it from or destined to Canada or to points south. It is estimated that perhaps as much as 70 percent of the goods shipped to and from the two states travels by truck on the interstates. Map 46 depicts today's major roads.

Bridges between the States

The first bridge ever built across the Connecticut was between Bellow Falls, Vt., and Walpole, N.H., constructed in 1785 by Colonel Enoch Hale, a Revolutionary War hero. On the rest of the river, ferry and scow boats continued crossing back and forth across the river. By 1796, two other bridges had been built across the river in the upper watershed: one at Cornish and one at Hanover, N.H. The Ledyard Bridge at Hanover has been rebuilt four times. Its 1859 iteration was the first bridge across the Connecticut where travelers could cross for free. Today's bridge was built in 1999.

Most early bridges were wooden and open — that is, uncovered — and rotting timbers plagued them. By the early 1820s, bridge builders adopted innovative designs that featured roofs and some enclosed walls. Covering the bridges made it pleasant for travelers, and most important, protected the integral wooden trusses from the weather. The bridges lasted much longer — many of them to this day. At one time, 35 covered road and railroad bridges spanned the Connecticut from New Hampshire to Vermont, but over the years many succumbed to floods and ice jams. Currently, three remain. At 460 feet, the Cornish-Windsor Covered Bridge is the second-longest covered bridge in the United States. The other covered bridges are found connecting Columbia, N.H., and Lemington, Vt., built in 1912; and the Mount Orne Bridge, built in 1911 between Lancaster, N.H., and Lunenburg, Vt. The first bridge at this site was built around the time of the Civil War and was destroyed by a log jam in 1908. The northernmost remaining covered bridge crossing the Connecticut was built in 1876 to connect the villages of Pittsburg and Clarksville.

Many covered bridges cross tributary streams in the watershed. The 1829 Bath-Haverhill Covered Bridge, which crosses the Ammonoosuc River just upstream of its confluence with the Connecticut, is reputed to be the oldest bridge remaining in the United States using the design of early-eighteenth-century designer Ithiel Town. The lure of covered bridges has grown as the years have gone by, and now many towns regard them with pride and visitors treat them as special destinations. Littleton, N.H., built a new covered bridge across the Ammonoosuc River in 2004, based on the design of local nineteenth-century bridge builder Peter Paddleford (see Chapter 26, The Postindustrial Era).

Travelers today still may use some of the oldest roads and bridges in the region. The guidebook *Northern Journeys* highlights five sce-

The Cornish-Windsor Covered Bridge is the fourth built at this location, with the first in 1796. Flooding swept away the bridges in 1824, 1848, and 1866. The bridge is designated a National Historical Civil Engineering Landmark.

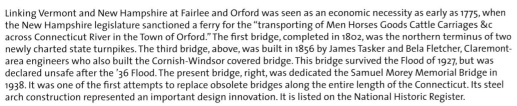

Linking Vermont and New Hampshire at Fairlee and Orford was seen as an economic necessity as early as 1775, when the New Hampshire legislature sanctioned a ferry for the "transporting of Men Horses Goods Cattle Carriages &c across Connecticut River in the Town of Orford." The first bridge, completed in 1802, was the northern terminus of two newly charted state turnpikes. The third bridge, above, was built in 1856 by James Tasker and Bela Fletcher, Claremont-area engineers who also built the Cornish-Windsor covered bridge. This bridge survived the Flood of 1927, but was declared unsafe after the '36 Flood. The present bridge, right, was dedicated the Samuel Morey Memorial Bridge in 1938. It was one of the first attempts to replace obsolete bridges along the entire length of the Connecticut. Its steel arch construction represented an important design innovation. It is listed on the National Historic Register.

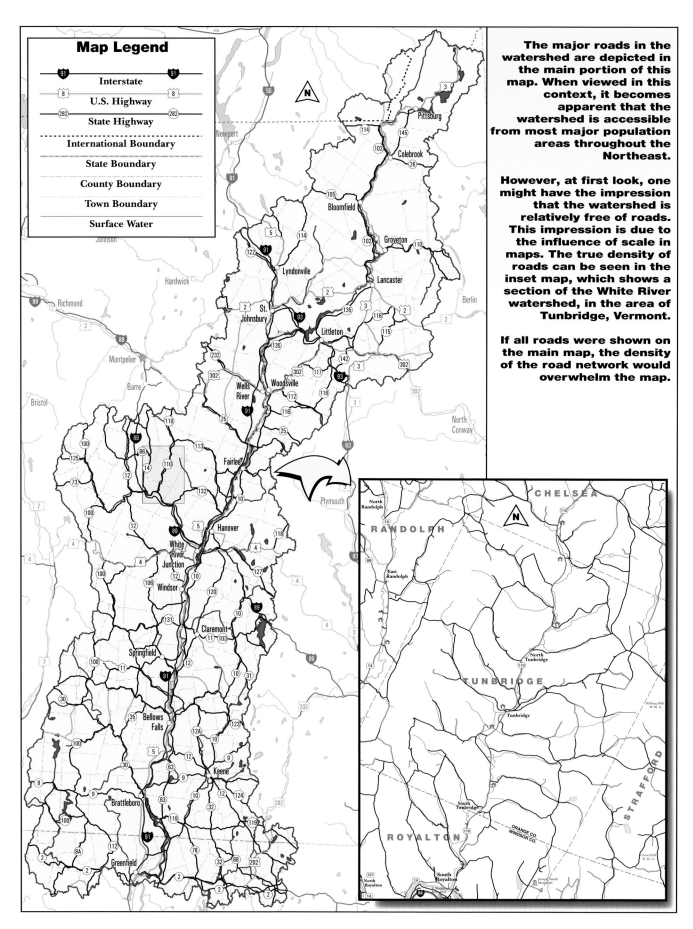

The major roads in the watershed are depicted in the main portion of this map. When viewed in this context, it becomes apparent that the watershed is accessible from most major population areas throughout the Northeast.

However, at first look, one might have the impression that the watershed is relatively free of roads. This impression is due to the influence of scale in maps. The true density of roads can be seen in the inset map, which shows a section of the White River watershed, in the area of Tunbridge, Vermont.

If all roads were shown on the main map, the density of the road network would overwhelm the map.

Map 46. Major Roads in the Connecticut River Watershed.

In Fairlee, Vt., Interstate 91, the rail line first laid down by the Connecticut and Passumpsic Railroad, and Route 5 (which follows the route of one of the valley's earliest roads), all squeeze into the space between the cliffs of the Palisades and the Connecticut River, which is a few hundred feet to the right of this photo.

nic and historic auto tours through northern New Hampshire (Jordan and McIntosh 2004). The Connecticut River Byway, a National Scenic Byway, traces some of the original roads constructed by early settlers, and highlights the historic bridges built over a century ago to aid travel and commerce along New England's greatest river.

Sharon A. Penney is a North Country native who resides in Franconia, N.H. Her professional planning background encompasses transportation, conservation, and regional community issues with over a decade spent at North Country Council in Bethlehem, N.H.

Barry Lawson is the project leader for the Atlas. Thanks to Frank J. Barrett Jr. and Ron Crisman, who made helpful suggestions for this section.

FOR FURTHER READING

Allen, Richard Saunders. 2004. *Covered Bridges of the Northeast*. Mineola, N.Y.: Dover.

Connecticut River Byway, www.ctrivertravel.net.

Garvin, Donna-Belle, and James L. Garvin. 1988. *On the Road North of Boston: New Hampshire Taverns and Turnpikes, 1700–1900*. Hanover, N.H.: University Press of New England.

Jordan, Charles, and James McIntosh. *Northern Journeys*. Littleton, N.H.: North Country Council, et al.

McCullough, Robert. 2005. *Crossings: A History of Vermont Bridges*. Barre, Vt.: Vermont Historical Society.

Northeast Vermont Development Association. 1997. *The Bayley Hazen Military Road Field Guide* (pamphlet). St. Johnsbury, Vt.: Northeast Vermont Development Association.

Wood, Frederic J. 1919. *The Turnpikes of New England*. Boston: Marshall Jones Company. Abridged edition, with an introduction by Ronald Dale Karr. Pepperell, Mass.: Branch Line Press, 1997.

30 Railroads

Picturesque New England has no more alluring gateway than that which tourists, bound from New York and the South for the glorious summer playground of the White Mountain region or Northern Vermont, are ushered through when they reach the far-famed Connecticut River Valley.

—Valley of the Connecticut and Northern Vermont
(Passenger Department, Boston & Maine Railroad, 1901)

From Steamship to Iron Horse

By the middle of the nineteenth century, great steam engines moved from powering boats on the Connecticut River to pulling cars on steel rail lines following the river's shores. Locomotives, or "Iron Horses," as they were sometimes affectionately called, supplanted horse-drawn vehicles and steamboats and helped usher in the great age of American industrial expansion. New railroads connected towns along the Connecticut River with each other and with other cities in North America, transporting products like milk and paper from the valley, and bringing in the tourists who would themselves become an engine of the local economy.

The development of railroads in the watershed was part of the new era of industrialism that spread from the commercial centers of the Atlantic seaboard, driven by the promise of the vast continent's natural resources. After the Erie Canal opened in 1825, Boston financiers and traders realized that New York had seized the trade advantage with access to the upper Midwest and the Great Lakes. These Bosto-

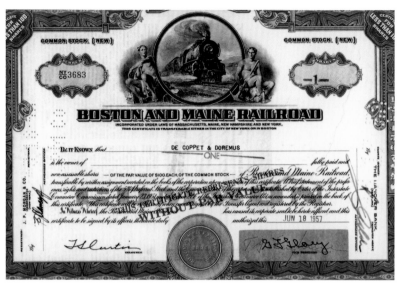

Boston and Maine Railroad stock certificate, 1957.

Boston and Maine Railroad Magazine, 1952.

WHICH SIDE ARE YOU ON?

BARRY LAWSON

The promise of the railroad led to some jostling between Vermont and New Hampshire communities over which side would attract the new technology first. For instance, when St. Johnsbury, Vt., business leader Erastus Fairbanks proposed a new rail line in the mid-1830s, Granite Staters objected. According to newspaper accounts, "This [plan] met with violent opposition from the New Hampshire folks who had pledged $100,000 to have the line run on their side of the river in Haverhill. Dartmouth College now has the broadside that was sent Mr. Fairbanks protesting that the Connecticut River was in New Hampshire anyway; that no bridges could be built across it safely because of the spring freshet, and that Vermont did not have as much stone as New Hampshire to build abutments and culverts."

Vermont prevailed, however, and in 1850 one passenger and one freight train ran daily between St. Johnsbury and Boston, a journey 10 hours in length.

SOURCE
Caledonian Record, April 16, 1938.

nians were aware of attempts ongoing in Great Britain at harnessing the power of steam to move materials and goods by rail—a novel and intriguing idea. As a result, by the late 1820s the idea took hold that, if Boston could not be connected to the interior regions of the country by canals as New York was, it could be connected by iron rail. In addition, canals (as well as the mighty St. Lawrence River) tended to freeze in the winter, and it seemed that the new-fangled railroad would not! The idea of railroads financed with Boston money and radiating out across New England toward the West took hold.

Many of the small regional lines built to link towns within the watershed and through the two states eventually came under the auspices of the great Boston and Maine Railway, whose web of rail lines through

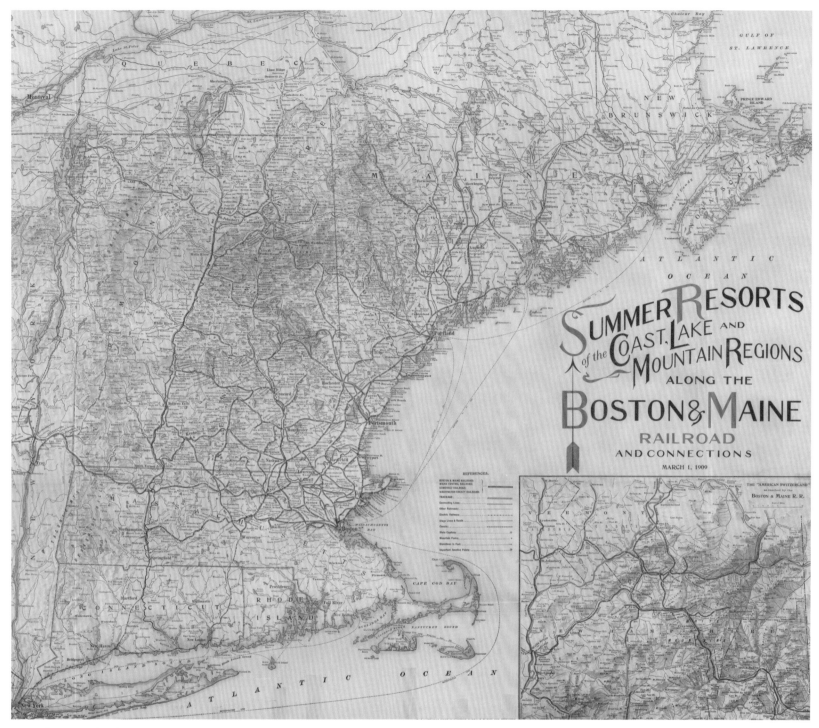

Boston & Maine Railroad map, 1909.

New England fanned out from Boston. The Boston and Maine reached into the valley with east-west connections to St. Johnsbury, Littleton, Wells River/Woodsville, White River Junction/Lebanon, Claremont Junction, Bellows Falls/North Walpole, and Brattleboro/Hinsdale.

The Central Vermont (CV) won the best rail route in the valley, running alongside the Connecticut River from its Atlantic coast connections to White River Junction, reached in 1848, and then following the White River over the height of land to Montpelier, Lake Champlain, and Canada. The Connecticut and Passumpsic Railroad followed its namesake rivers up the valley from White River Junction to St. Johns-

bury in 1850, and then eventually continued to Canada as well. The Rutland Railroad, always in competition with the CV, reached down the watershed of the Williams River to Bellows Falls in 1849, connecting that town to the west.

Many smaller branch lines followed, trumpeted by promoters as the next great transcontinental link. The West River Railroad was one such example, running out of Brattleboro and never getting beyond Londonderry, while the express passenger trains brought travelers up and down the Connecticut from Beechers Falls to Brattleboro, with connections to Portland, Montreal, Boston, and New York. While

The roundhouse at St. Johnsbury, c. 1870. Two men working together would position the "gallows" turntable to the locomotives.

A Network of Rails

always of dubious financial health, the smaller branch lines broke the isolation of small towns, revitalized textile mills on remote tributaries, and carried fancy merchandise to Main Street shops. Alas, for many young men and women, the lonely call of the whistle also spoke of more opportunity elsewhere, and just as the railroad brought, so did it take away.

A Network of Rails
White River Junction became the largest rail hub in the valley, where five railroads eventually converged, followed by St. Johnsbury, Wells River/Woodsville, and Bellows Falls with three railroads each. For the most part, the railroads followed the major waterways, with most traffic flowing beside the banks of the Connecticut, followed closely by the major tributaries such as the White River and the Passumpsic,

just as the precolonial Native American footpaths had. There were, however, some notable exceptions. The Canadian transcontinental between Montreal and Portland, Maine, crossed the uppermost valley at North Stratford in 1853, and in 1875, the Maine Central's Mountain Division crossed the valley at Lunenberg on its way from Portland to St. Johnsbury, having navigated some spectacular engineering feats in Crawford Notch.

Considerable freight traffic was generated from within the watershed for shipment to markets and ports in southern New England. The region also witnessed so-called "bridge" traffic that originated in Canada or other parts of New England and passed through the watershed on the way to distant markets. Milk and paper were two commodities that could be seen daily making their way to market. The railroads also opened up the watershed to more people. Stages met the northbound trains at various stations along the Connecticut River, providing con-

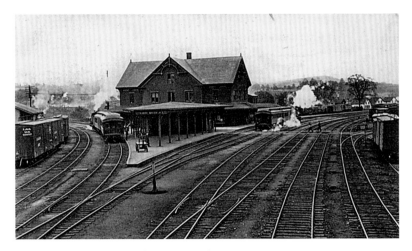

White River Junction, c. 1908, from a postcard.

White River Junction today hosts Amtrak service, remains a freight hub, and houses historic trains.

necting transportation to interior towns in both states. After the Civil War, tourists started visiting northern New England using the new and growing rail networks. The White Mountains, in particular, became a tourism destination. The Boston & Maine Railroad published a series of illustrated travel brochures, including a 64-page pocket guide to the beauty and attractions of the Connecticut River Valley and northern Vermont.

The Cog Railway has carried sightseers to the summit of Mount Washington since 1869. It is the world's only railroad running completely on a trestle, and is the world's second-steepest rail line.

As fluid milk shipments by rail grew, agriculture in the valley went through a renaissance after decades of decline and the daily "milk train" became an icon of rural life. A network of small, often privately owned logging and quarry railroads reached far into the hills, while trolley lines or "street railroads" served the residents of Brattleboro, Bellows Falls, and Springfield. Passenger service elsewhere, too, continued to grow. By 1900, St. Johnsbury, Vt., alone was served by 24 passenger trains every day headed north, south, east, and west. Industries there and throughout the valley were able to expand their markets and obtain raw materials at a greatly reduced rate.

Trestle B. & M. R. R., Woodsville, N. H.

Until the last passenger train left in 1954, Woodsville was a major stop for railroads in the river valley. Here, the train crosses the Connecticut into Wells River, Vt. Note the lower level of the bridge for automobiles.

Quechee Gulf Bridge, height 165 ft. On Woodstock Railroad, near Dewey's Mills, Vt.

Railroads Decline

It did not take long for the big railroads in Canada to realize the importance of the Connecticut River Valley as a connection to the East Coast, and the Canadian National, the Canadian Pacific, and the Grand Trunk all took over the biggest routes connecting Montreal with Portland, Boston, and New York. By the 1920s, however, local railroads in the upper Connecticut River Valley already were beginning to decline. The timber resources that had fed many of the smaller branch lines were gone; industry as well as agriculture continued to move west; and improvements in highway transportation siphoned off passengers and freight. Just as the railroads in the valley had begun by following the natural transportation corridor of the river itself, then its major tributaries, and lastly the smaller streams, the decline reversed the process, starting in the hills.

When the Rutland Railroad, part of which connected Bellows Falls to the west, failed in 1962, the state of Vermont set a precedent by purchasing the line and leasing operations to what later became the Vermont Rail System. It became a successful strategy, and was repeated most recently with the purchase of the former Boston & Maine and Canadian Pacific lines from White River Junction to Newport. New Hampshire, however, was not so willing to intervene at first, and as a result the valley lost all its eastern connections at Woodsville, Lebanon, Claremont, and Brattleboro.

Passenger service to valley residents, which had declined through the 1950s, halted for a while in 1966, but resumed again in the early 1970s when Amtrak re-introduced the overnight *Montrealer*. Today, the daily *Vermonter* stops at Randolph, White River Junction, Windsor, Claremont, Bellows Falls, and Brattleboro, with continuing service to New York and Washington.

Freight business is recapturing its share of the market as well with both "bridge" traffic and local service due to escalating trucking costs. The St. Lawrence & Atlantic crosses the head of the valley on the old Grand Trunk route. The New England Central follows the old Central Vermont route, while Vermont Rail Systems runs on both the old Rutland route out of Bellows Falls and the former Boston & Maine and Canadian Pacific line up the Connecticut and the Passumpsic rivers to Canada. All three lines run at least one train daily each way, and Vermont Rail Systems offers summertime passenger excursions and occasional passenger "specials" out of Bellows Falls and White River Junction. In addition, short lines New Hampshire Central and Claremont & Concord offer service when needed.

After many years of neglect, the active lines gradually are being upgraded. A recent example is the Bellows Falls Tunnel, which passes under some important structures and has long been a "bottleneck" with its low overhead clearance. The floor of the tunnel was excavated and lowered in 2007 in order to accommodate larger loads. Legislatures in both New Hampshire and Vermont have also recently been considering re-opening abandoned lines and increasing both freight and passenger service. Current and inactive railroads in the valley are shown in Map 47.

The Quechee Gorge Bridge, depicted here in an early postcard, is the oldest standing steel arch bridge in Vermont. Built in 1911, it replaced an earlier wooden truss bridge.

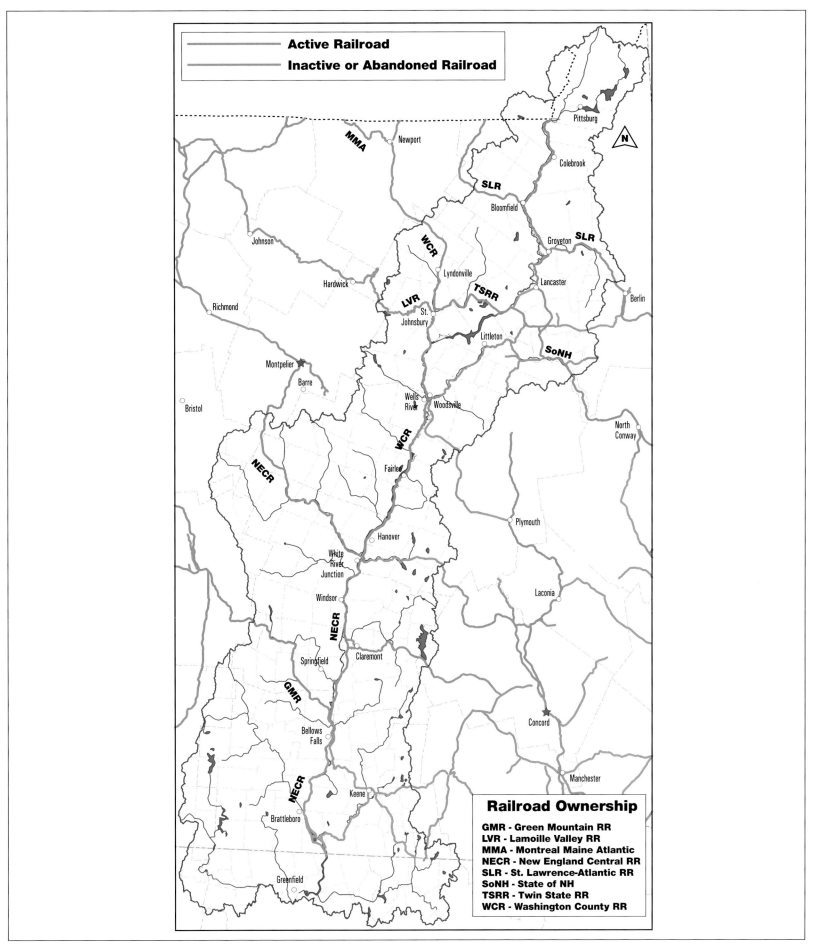

N

Pittsburg

Newport

MMA

Colebrook

SLR

Bloomfield

WCR

Groveton

SLR

Johnson

Lyndonville

Lancaster

Hardwick

TSRR

Berlin

Richmond

LVR

St.
Johnsbury

SoNH

Littleton

Montpelier

Barre

Wells
River

Woodsville

Bristol

WCR

North
Conway

Fairlee

NECR

Plymouth

Hanover

White
River
Junction

Laconia

Windsor

NECR

Springfield

Claremont

Concord

GMR

Bellows
Falls

Manchester

NECR

Keene

Brattleboro

Railroad Ownership

GMR - Green Mountain RR
LVR - Lamoille Valley RR
MMA - Montreal Maine Atlantic
NECR - New England Central RR
SLR - St. Lawrence-Atlantic RR
SoNH - State of NH
TSRR - Twin State RR
WCR - Washington County RR

Greenfield

Map 47. Active and Inactive Railroads in the Connecticut River Watershed.

Today, some residents long for a modern version of rail travel to alleviate the overwhelming dependence on autos and trucks. To others, rail stations and rail line rights-of-way present opportunities for new uses as tourism centers and as snowmobile and bicycle paths. The stations at White River Junction, Bellows Falls, and St. Johnsbury serve as waypoint centers for the Connecticut River Byway, and glimpses of the gilded past of the valley's railroad past also may be found at a number of other restored historic stations. Whatever their future, the railroads will continue to remind us of their role in the watershed's industrial growth and evoke fond memories of a time past.

Nat Tripp, of Barnet, Vt., has a lifelong love of trains and railroads.

Sharon A. Penney's professional planning background encompasses transportation, conservation, and regional community issues with over a decade spent at North Country Council in Bethlehem, N.H. She lives in Franconia, N.H. Thanks to Frank J. Barrett Jr. for his suggestions.

FOR FURTHER READING

Cheasley, Dennis. 1974. A quick run through New Hampshire history. *The New Hampshire Times Magazine*, April 4.

Jones, Robert C. 1993. *Railroads of Vermont*. Shelburne, Vt.: New England Press.

Lindsell, Robert M. 2000. *The Rail Lines of Northern New England*. Pepperell, Mass.: Branch Line Press.

31 Aviation

History

Aviation as a means of transportation and recreation came relatively slowly to the Connecticut River Valley. For one thing, the topography of mountains and steep-sided tributary valleys was not conducive to building many airports, and the major commercial activity in both states was focused elsewhere.

The first flight anywhere in New Hampshire was in 1910, at the Rochester Fair. The Wright Brothers had made their historic flight seven years earlier. New Hampshire's first airport opened in Concord in 1920. In 1923, the Balsams Resort in Dixville Notch, N.H., on the eastern edge of the Connecticut River watershed, started a company fleet of three planes. Each was a Curtis Oriole, and they made daily deliveries of newspapers, cut flowers, and fresh fish from Boston, New York, and Philadelphia in time for guests' breakfast.

By 1928, other valley operations had started, including the New Hampshire Aviation and Marine Co. in Keene, and flights started in and out of Twin Mountain, not far from the Bretton Woods Hotel. The Lebanon Airport, the valley's largest, opened in 1942 on 750 acres bought by the town. The Dillant-Hopkins Airport opened in Keene in 1943. Also in 1943, Richard Putnam of Hanover started Dartmouth Airways and started offering charter flights from Lebanon (New Hampshire Aviation Historical Society 2006).

James Hartness, an early proponent of a national air transportation system, built Vermont's first airport in Springfield in 1919. Hartness was a leader in the region's machine tools industry, and was elected governor in 1921. Several early airfields in Vermont remain active, but others have been abandoned or otherwise utilized. For example, the former St. Johnsbury Municipal Airport, replaced by a new state airport three miles away, is now an industrial park. Miller Airport, on the west bank of the Connecticut River a few miles north of Ascutney, was a busy 2,000-foot paved runway from 1947 to about 1986, when it no longer appeared in the Federal Aviation Administration Airport Directory. Built by the Miller Construction Company, it allowed its personnel quick access to works in process throughout New England. Similarly, Waterford, Vt., saw a very short paved runway constructed in the early 1970s by a concrete construction company. Its powerful single-engine Cessna routinely landed on highway construction projects throughout Vermont and New Hampshire.

Physical Environment: Terrain and Weather

The upper Connecticut River basin's topography demonstrates glacial sculpturing occurring over 10,000 years ago, leaving ridges, hills, and mountains whose axis runs generally north-northeast. Forested hills and narrow valleys leave little room for airports. Accordingly, most airports are in — or close to — larger river valleys.

Connecticut River Valley aviation is weather-dependent, perhaps to a larger extent than elsewhere in the United States (see Chapter 4, Weather and Climate). On calm nights, cooling air sinks into the valleys, generating ground fog that often lingers until mid-morning. On a larger scale, many major storms pass through the region. Moderate to strong winds interact with the rough terrain, creating low-level turbulence that affects the safety and comfort of flight. Summertime brings humidity and sometimes pollution-caused haze, often restricting flight visibility. Unstable moist air produces embedded thunderstorms that are difficult to detect and avoid by pilots flying smaller airplanes at lower altitudes. Year-round, a cold-front passage usually produces a few sparkling days with unlimited visibility. On the plus side, long spells of dreary weather are rare.

Weather creates two categories of aircraft operations: either Visual Flight Rules or Instrument Flight Rules. Due to mountainous terrain surrounding the northern Connecticut River, special handling is available from Flight Service Stations. Also, "flight following" is available from Air Traffic Control (ATC), workload permitting. However, in the northern reaches of the Connecticut River Valley, mountains intervene. Radio contact and radar coverage is not assured unless an aircraft is above 4,000 feet.

General Aviation Airports

Fifteen public-use facilities serve to move people and commodities in and out of the watershed (see Map 48 and Table 13). Of these, airports in Springfield, Vt., and Lebanon, Claremont, Whitefield, and Keene, N.H., are included in the FAA's National Plan of Integrated Airport Systems (NPIAS). These airports are considered significant in the national air transportation system. An airport must be included in the NPIAS in order to obtain federal funding from the FAA. Tower-controlled Lebanon Airport is the only airport in the watershed with scheduled air carrier connections. It offers daily commercial service to New York's LaGuardia Airport.

Airports with paved runways are adequate for single-engine aircraft and "light twins," the workhorses of charter operators. In winter, paved runways are usually plowed, while turf airstrips may be restricted to ski-equipped airplanes. Most airports provide fuel; several offer aircraft rental and maintenance, charter service, and flight instruction. Despite proximity to Canada, none of the Connecticut River Valley

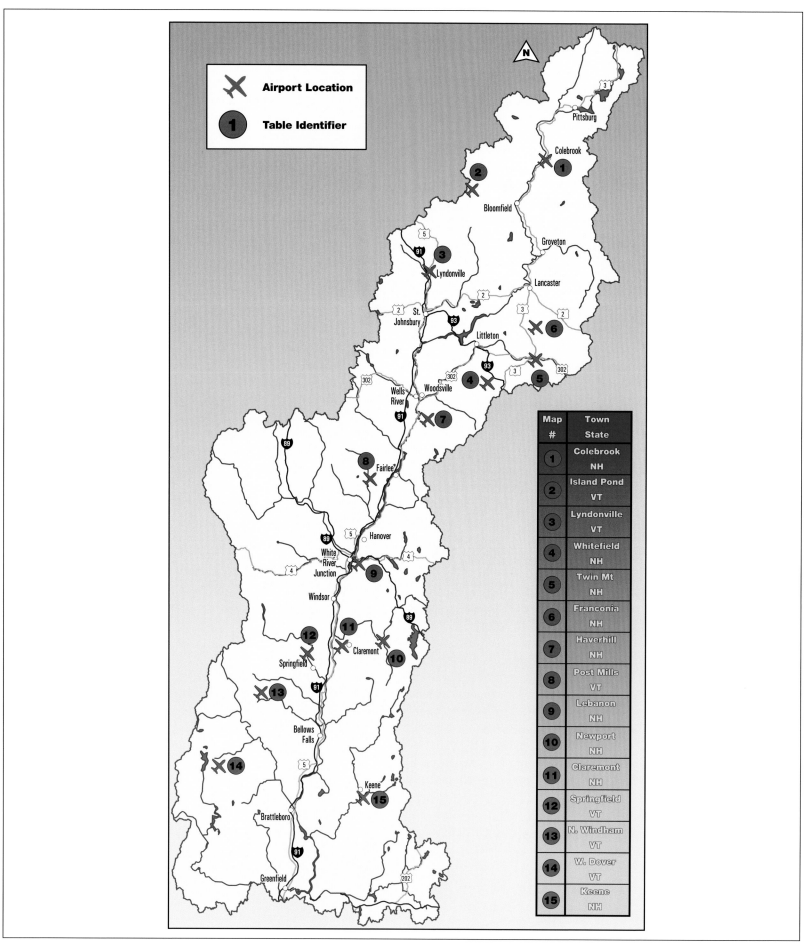

Map #	Town State
1	Colebrook NH
2	Island Pond VT
3	Lyndonville VT
4	Whitefield NH
5	Twin Mt NH
6	Franconia NH
7	Haverhill NH
8	Post Mills VT
9	Lebanon NH
10	Newport NH
11	Claremont NH
12	Springfield VT
13	N. Windham VT
14	W. Dover VT
15	Keene NH

Map 48. Public-Use Airports in the Upper Connecticut River Watershed.

TABLE 13. Airports of the Connecticut River Valley

MAP #	TOWN, STATE	NAME	IDENTIFIER	ELEVATION (FEET) MSL	RUNWAY LENGTH (FEET)	SURFACE (P)AVED/(T)URF
1	Colebrook, N.H.	Gifford	4C4	1010	2400	T
2	Island Pond, Vt.	Boylan State[1]	5B1	1194	2600	T
3	Lyndonville, Vt.	Caledonia Cty[1]	6B8**	1188	3300[2]	P
4	Whitefield, N.H.	Mt. Washington	HIE**	1074	4001[2]	P
5	Twin Mt., N.H.	Twin Mountain	8B2	1459	2600[2]	P
6	Franconia, N.H.	Franconia	1B5	970	2300	T
7	Haverhill, N.H.	Dean Memorial	5B9	580	2500[2]	P
8	Post Mills, Vt.	Post Mills	2B9	693	2900	T
9	Lebanon, N.H.	Lebanon Municipal	LEB*	603	5500[2]	P
10	Newport, N.H.	Parlin	2B3	784	3400[2]	P
11	Claremont, N.H.	Claremont	CNH**	545	3100[2]	P
12	Springfield, Vt.	Hartness State[1]	VSF*	577	5500[2]	P
13	N. Windham, Vt.	Robin's Nest	3N3 PPO	1750	2270	T
14	W. Dover, Vt.	Mount Snow	4V8**	1953	2600[2]	P
15	Keene, N.H.	Dillant-Hopkins	EEN*	488	6200[2]	P

*Precision Instrument approach(es) available (ILS).
**Non-precision instrument approach(es) available (GPS, VOR, NDB, etc.).
[1]State-operated airport.
[2]Runway lights activated on CTAF if not by tower.
PPO = Closed, prior permission only.

airports offer customs or immigration services. (These services are provided round the clock at Burlington and by prior arrangement at Newport, Vt.) Pilots should note runway lengths, remembering that a minimum of 5,000 feet is required for small business jets to operate safely. Airports having published Instrument Approach Procedures are noted in Table 13.

A number of these private, turf-surfaced airstrips are also located in the watershed. They may be found on sectional aeronautical charts but usually require prior permissions for use.

Helicopter Operations

Because helicopters don't need airports, their operations are more flexible than fixed-wing aircraft. They can utilize instrument flight. Their principal limitation is during icing conditions, as ice accreting on the rotor blades is dangerous.

Most helicopter operations in the Connecticut River basin are for urgent medical transportation. The principal operator is DHART, the Dartmouth-Hitchcock Air Rescue Team, based at the medical center in Lebanon. They will take emergency medical cases from wherever they can land to any hospital within their range—or farther with refueling.

Helicopters also perform routine low-level inspections of transmission lines and pipelines. Also, in the northernmost areas, helicopters from federal customs, border patrol, or immigration enforcement may appear anywhere as they conduct border surveillance. There is also increasing, though still proportionately small, use of helicopters by some commuters, particularly in the Upper Valley area.

DHART helicopters transport patients from throughout the valley to Dartmouth-Hitchcock Medical Center in Lebanon, N.H.

The Lebanon Airport is situated near other transportation crossroads—Interstate 89 meets I-91 in Vermont just west of this view, and the White River meets the Connecticut just north of here (to the left in the photo).

Military Operations

Three military areas exist over the northern portion of the basin. While civilian flight is not prohibited in these areas, extreme vigilance is mandatory, as an unwary pilot will be surprised to have an F-16 filling the windshield, executing violent high-speed maneuvers. Should you participate in a scenic flight over the White Mountains, ask your pilot if "either Yankee is hot." Military aircraft utilize an in-flight refueling track normally flown at 24,000 feet or above. Identified as IR800, it passes over the upper Connecticut watershed near Colebrook, N.H.

Other Aircraft

The Connecticut River Valley sees a variety of less common other types of aircraft, from ultralights, which are gaining in popularity, to gliders and balloons. The hills and mountains lining the Connecticut River Valley create orographic lifting of prevailing winds. Franconia, N.H., and Post Mills and Springfield, Vt., airports are centers for gliders, as rising air currents proliferate at these locations. Achieving altitudes exceeding 20,000 feet becomes possible when "mountain

An instructor and student from Morningside Flight Park in Charlestown, N.H., float over the Connecticut River with Mount Ascutney in the background.

Several little airports in the valley were once bustling enterprises, driven by local commercial needs and used by pilots who helped create the aviation history of the region. But conditions changed, and some of these airports came to be seen as more attractive for other uses even as their neighbors were growing. The stories of Lancaster and Whitefield illustrate the life cycle of some small rural airports and shed more light on the valley's aviation past.

Lancaster, N.H., is the home of Timberland Machines, a wholesale distributor of logging equipment. In the early 1960s, seeing the benefit of using an airplane to improve service to their customers, Timberland procured a single-engine airplane and arranged to use adjacent land. After smoothing and grass planting, Lancaster had a 1,500-foot airport.

About 1968, Timberland purchased a larger, twin–engined Aztec plane that needed a paved runway. The plane was based at the nearby Whitefield, N.H., airport, where Shirley Mahn became the pilot. For many years, Mahn had been Whitefield's flight instructor and charter operator.

Pilot and flight instructor Shirley Mahn.

Meanwhile, the town of Whitefield recognized a commercial opportunity, and built a longer, fully lighted runway to support area businesses and attract visitors to the White Mountains. The airport obtained an instrument approach at about the same time. More recently, the instrument approach to the Whitefield airport was upgraded to a more precise system, and the runway was again lengthened with improved runway identifier lighting.

Sadly, in 1974, Mahn took off into a low ceiling from Burlington, Vt., with a student in Timberland's Aztec. Take-off was normal, but moments after entering the overcast, the aircraft reappeared in a high-speed dive and crashed, killing Mahn and her student. The cause was never determined. Timberland did not replace the airplane.

With little use by planes, Lancaster's airport was recognized as

prime land for development. The approach end of the runway is now a McDonald's; further along is Lancaster's elementary school. Still there, although usually hidden in the grass, are halves of a yellow 55-gallon drum used as runway markers. A Quonset-type structure, used as a hangar for the original aircraft, collapsed under heavy snow in 2007.

Whitefield Airport, nestled in the shadow of the White Mountains, draws light commercial and private aircraft.

A hot air balloon drifts over Quechee Gorge during the balloon festival held each June.

slow stretches of the Connecticut, is the floatplane. Where powerboats are permitted to operate on a body of water, it is legal to land and take off in a floatplane. As long as an aircraft is waterborne, it is a boat in the eyes of the FAA. Occasionally a floatplane is observed either on the river or on one of the many lakes in the drainage, but there are no recognized floatplane facilities in the area. Similarly, you will occasionally find a ski-equipped airplane in the winter on the frozen northern lakes.

Col. Roger Damon Jr. (U.S. Army, retired) is an FAA-rated commercial pilot and flight instructor. He is a member of the Vermont Agency of Transportation Aviation Advisory Council. He lives in St. Johnsbury, Vt.

FOR FURTHER READING

New Hampshire Aviation Historical Society. www.nhahs.org.
New Hampshire Bureau of Aeronautics. www.nh.gov/dot/bureaus/
    aeronautics/index.htm.
Vermont Agency of Transportation. www.vermontairports.com.

waves" are being generated. Many a summer visitor has watched these quiet, elegantly long-winged soaring planes floating gently over the mountains and wished for a ride. Check the local airports for public soaring opportunities. The Morningside Flight Park in Charlestown, N.H., is a popular hang gliding and paragliding center, and hang gliders also launch from nearby Mount Ascutney. On pleasant days, colorful, dainty gliders may be seen floating above the Connecticut River.

The Quechee (Vermont) Balloon Festival held each Father's Day weekend draws balloonists from around the country and thousands of visitors who enjoy balloon rides, a crafts festival, and other games, sports, and entertainment. Balloonists also embark from other spots in the valley through the warmer months. The Post Mills Airport in Thetford, Vt., is a popular launching site. There are occasional opportunities to be a crew member in a "chase car"—staying in radio and visual contact with a free balloon, and assisting in landing site evaluation and retrieval. It may earn you a free balloon ride!

One surprisingly underutilized type of craft, given the wide and

32 Energy

For over 200 years, the flow of the Connecticut River and its tributaries has been harnessed for generating power. The energy and economic impacts have been significant. Power generation also has had environmental, recreational, and social impacts. This chapter traces the history of hydropower in the watershed, and then focuses on recent efforts to find a fair balance between energy needs and the environment.

Water as a Power Source

Hydropower, and the public laws which regulate it, both date back to Roman times. Small water-powered mills on the Connecticut River's tributaries were among the very earliest structures accompanying settlement. Nearly all the major towns of the valley grew beside tributaries that provided hydropower for industry. Claremont, N.H., on the Sugar River is perhaps the most spectacular example. Mills sawed lumber and ground flour, often using water built up behind rudimentary dams that were expected to wash away during freshets, only to be rebuilt again. Many dams only operated in the spring, when the water was high. As industry crept up the valley, larger dams were built to power new machines for carding and spinning wool, turning furniture and wagon parts, forging iron, or pressing apples. Today vestiges of that era can be seen at a restored circa 1798 gristmill in Littleton, N.H., on the Ammonoosuc River, and a circa 1870s sawmill on Garland Brook in Lancaster, N.H.

The first dam across the Connecticut River mainstem was built about 1792 at Turner's Falls, Mass. At around the same time, a dam was built between Guildhall, Vt., and Northumberland, N.H., and remained until the 1950s. By the twentieth century, the watershed's rivers were seen as resources for electric-power production, and the use of running water for mechanical power dropped off as electricity became available.

Hydropower

Hydroelectric facilities use water to move turbines. Water may flow through the turbines directly—called run-of-the-river—or may be impounded behind a dam, where it is stored and released through the turbines when power is needed. The earliest hydro dams were constructed in 1900 on the Ottauquechee, a tributary that joins the Connecticut in Hartland, Vt. Lights showed in windows of Bloomfield, Vt., and Stratford, N.H., for the first time in 1903, when a small hydro dam was built on the Connecticut at Lyman Falls.

A water wheel built in the style of the late eighteenth century powers a restored grist mill on the Ammonosuc River in Littleton, N.H.

Water power was the engine of early industrial development. Paper mills were common, such as this one in Bradford, Vt., on the Waits River, shown in an early-twentieth-century postcard.

A 1909 postcard depicts a still-novel source of electric power.

Operation of the major hydroelectric system on the upper Connecticut River began in 1909 with the opening of the Vernon Dam. New England Power Company used one of the earliest high-voltage lines in the United States to send power generated at Vernon to growing cities downstream in Massachusetts. Over the next 50 years, New England Power built five more hydroelectric generating facilities and two water storage dams on the upper river, as shown in Map 49. Fifteen Mile Falls, the fierce run of rapids and falls between Littleton and Monroe, N.H., and Barnet and Waterford, Vt., was flooded with three dams. Today, McIndoe Falls, Comerford, and Moore stations, collectively called the Fifteen Mile Falls project, comprise the largest hydroelectric generating complex in New England. The current owner is Trans-Canada Hydro Northeast. It renewed its federal operating license in 2002 (see sidebar, "The Fifteen Miles Falls Settlement Agreement," in Chapter 11, Water Management). TransCanada's power facilities have 476 megawatts of capacity. Chapter 11, Water Management, describes operations of the hydroelectric system. New England Power eventually sold its Connecticut River dams.

Three smaller hydroelectric facilities operate on the mainstem. Private businesses operate dams at Gilman and Dodge Falls, and Public Service of New Hampshire owns the dam at Canaan, Vt. Tributary hydro project owners include Central Vermont Public Service and several other private corporations. Some of these projects hold FERC licenses with environmental mitigation and enhancement conditions regarding aquatic habitat, temperature and dissolved oxygen, flow quantity, reservoir elevations, and other associated issues. Because of their small size, some hydroelectric projects are exempt from licensure.

In 1985, an electric cooperative, Vermont Electric Generation & Transmission Cooperative, developed an existing Army Corps of Engineers flood control dam at North Hartland, Vt., for peak hydroelectric generation. Operations ceased in 1996 after the cooperative filed for bankruptcy but resumed in 2006 after a private company acquired the facility.

Federal legislation passed in 1978 encouraged the development of small hydroelectric and cogeneration facilities. States were required to establish programs under which utilities purchased energy from these new, small suppliers and also paid them based on costs the utilities avoided by not having to build their own generation. As a result, developers built small hydropower facilities at 14 locations in the watershed, often at old dam sites that had been decommissioned or fallen into disuse. These projects added approximately 13.5 megawatts of capacity to the region's power supply.

In the early twenty-first century, hydroelectric facilities in the Connecticut River watershed represent approximately 10 percent of the power-generating capacity installed in New Hampshire and Vermont, and about 1.5 percent of New England's installed capacity.

Other Energy Resources in the Watershed

The Connecticut River serves as a resource for the generation of power in ways other than hydropower. The 620-megawatt Vermont Yankee Nuclear Power Station at Vernon, which supplies about one-third of Vermont's electricity, uses the river to cool water that the plant boils to generate electricity. It is called "non-contact" cooling water because

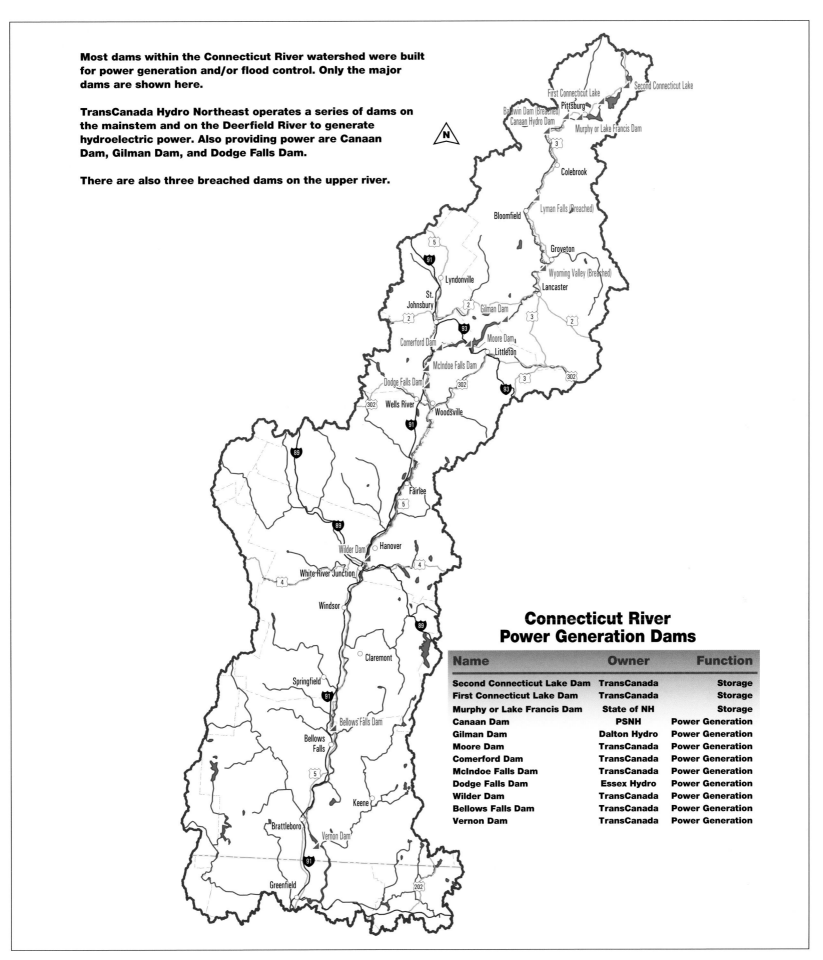

Most dams within the Connecticut River watershed were built for power generation and/or flood control. Only the major dams are shown here.

TransCanada Hydro Northeast operates a series of dams on the mainstem and on the Deerfield River to generate hydroelectric power. Also providing power are Canaan Dam, Gilman Dam, and Dodge Falls Dam.

There are also three breached dams on the upper river.

Connecticut River Power Generation Dams

Name	Owner	Function
Second Connecticut Lake Dam	TransCanada	Storage
First Connecticut Lake Dam	TransCanada	Storage
Murphy or Lake Francis Dam	State of NH	Storage
Canaan Dam	PSNH	Power Generation
Gilman Dam	Dalton Hydro	Power Generation
Moore Dam	TransCanada	Power Generation
Comerford Dam	TransCanada	Power Generation
McIndoe Falls Dam	TransCanada	Power Generation
Dodge Falls Dam	Essex Hydro	Power Generation
Wilder Dam	TransCanada	Power Generation
Bellows Falls Dam	TransCanada	Power Generation
Vernon Dam	TransCanada	Power Generation

Map 49. Major Hydroelectric Dams.

The New England Power hydro dam at Wilder, Vt., under construction, 1948 to 1950.

the water never touches radioactive material, including the closed-cycle water boiled to generate steam. The non-contact water absorbs heat and then is discharged back into the river, causing an increase in the background river temperature. Under a permit granted by the state of Vermont, for over 30 years this thermal discharge activity has been monitored closely for its effects on the river's insects, fish and other life.

A 20-megawatt generation facility located in Ryegate, Vt., also uses river water for cooling and as process water. The plant uses sawmill residue and tree chips as fuel. Paper mills at the Vermont river towns of Putney and Gilman have relied on river water for the production of paper since 1818 and 1901, respectively.

With its hydroelectric capacity largely tapped, new generation in the Connecticut River watershed is supplied increasingly by non-hydro resources, such as the woodchip (biomass) facilities at Ryegate, and at Bethlehem, Springfield, and Whitefield, N.H. These facilities are regarded as needed sources of power and contributors to the regional economy in New Hampshire's Ten-Year State Energy Plan adopted in 2002. At the time of this writing, interest is growing in building new biomass plants in northern New Hampshire, both for the renewable energy they supply, and as part of an economic development strategy to replace pulp and paper mills that have shut down.

Wind power is also drawing increased interest, pro and con. Wind energy proposals have sparked both intense local opposition based on aesthetic and environmental concerns, as well as fervid support by renewable energy advocates. Vermont's first commercial wind farm opened in 1997 in Searsburg. Owned by Green Mountain Power, 11 turbines generate 6 megawatts, enough to power about 2,000 households. Wind generation may be feasible on some of the watershed's other higher-elevation ridges. Wind farms are proposed in Sheffield and East Haven in the Northeast Kingdom, and are being discussed for high-elevation ridges in northern New Hampshire.

A "trash-to-steam" incinerator opened in 1987 in Claremont, N.H., as a repository for municipal waste from nearby Vermont and New Hampshire communities. The steam is used to produce electricity. Today, two-thirds of Vermont's waste is buried at a landfill in Coventry, the methane gas from which is used by the Washington Electric Cooperative to generate electricity.

Central Vermont Public Service offers another use of methane gas. Marketed as "cow power," the utility collects methane, or "biogas" from manure on dairy farms and uses it to generate electricity.

In 1997, the Portland Natural Gas Transmission System commissioned a pipeline, part of a network connecting the Canadian pipeline system near Montreal with the U.S. system near Boston. The pipeline, which enters the United States near Canaan, Vt., and passes through New Hampshire's Coös County and under the Connecticut River, is a potential source of fuel for cogeneration projects.

Emergence of Environmental Constraints

The biggest environmental issue caused by the presence of dams on rivers is the obstacle they create to fish moving up and downstream.

The Vermont Yankee nuclear power plant.

A plant in Whitefield, N.H., produces energy using wood chips, or "biomass."

Fish passage requirements are now routine in hydropower licenses, and for the Connecticut River a primary goal is to restore a naturally reproducing fishery for Atlantic salmon.

Water management is also an important issue in re-licensing. Historically, FERC and state agencies allowed generators to fluctuate the impoundment levels greatly to maximize energy generation. As these projects went through re-licensing, FERC imposed restrictions on the fluctuations and impoundment draw-downs along with constant, minimum-flow requirements through the dams to protect the fishery, restrictions that have reduced hydro facilities' output. While these restrictions have affected hydropower revenue, they reflect the importance of environmental and recreational quality of the river, both of which increased substantially following the federal Clean Water Act of the 1970s.

Other generation sources raise environmental concerns. The Vermont Yankee station's nuclear fuel, once used, must be stored and cooled in a pool located next to the reactor. Today, no off-site repository exists for the storage of spent nuclear fuel, and in 2005 the Vermont Public Service Board licensed a facility that will allow Vermont Yankee to store spent nuclear fuel next to the reactor building in air-cooled casks, which, like the pool, are close to the river.

Burning trash raises concerns about emissions such as mercury, lead, and dioxins. The Claremont operator had to retrofit its incinerator to meet state and federal regulations requiring significant reductions in mercury and other emissions by 2006.

What Does the Future Hold?

With looming concerns about global warning and the soaring prices of fossil fuels, policymakers and consumers alike are looking for sources of renewable energy. It is thus unlikely that the watershed's existing hydroelectric dams will be removed, despite actions in New England and elsewhere to restore the free flow of rivers. At the same time, however, concerns about the environmental effects makes the construction of new dams improbable. New Hampshire's Ten-Year Electric Energy Plan of 2002 cautions that it is doubtful that "many (if any) new [hydroelectric] sites" will be developed in the state in the foreseeable future.

While biomass and wind energy are attracting considerable attention, public approvals and the public and/or private investment needed to build new plants and transmission lines is by no means certain, and environmental impact is sure to be hotly debated.

The energy conundrum no doubt will continue, as public policymakers and entrepreneurs seek cleaner, renewable sources of energy that meet the needs of both the economy and the environment. The growing recognition of the challenges posed by global warming has given impetus to state policymakers to identify and innovate clean and green energy sources, while also accelerating energy conservation. Whether the need for clean renewable energy shifts investment back to water, or to wind, wood, or other sources, will be a major question in years to come.

John Marshall of Peacham, Vt., is the managing partner and CEO of Downs Rachlin Martin PLLC and chairs the firm's Public Utilities Group. He represents electric utilities that have built hydroelectric and other energy projects in Vermont.

Barbara Ripley of Montpelier, Vt., is also a member of the firm, also represents electric utilities on environmental matters, and was secretary of the Vermont Agency of Natural Resources from 1994 to 1998.

For Further Reading

New Hampshire Office of Energy and Community Services. 2002. *New Hampshire Energy Plan*. Concord, N.H.: Governor's Office of Energy and Community Services. November.

———. 2006. Energy Advisory Board annual report. Concord, N.H.: Governor's Office of Energy and Community Services.

Vermont Department of Public Service. 2005. *Vermont Electric Plan 2005*. Montpelier, Vt.: Vermont Department of Public Service. January 19.

VIII Culture, Education, and Recreation

Introduction

Just before daybreak on a midsummer morning, a delicate curtain of fog descends where moments ago everything was vividly clear. A kayak floats on a barely discernable current at the upper end of the Moore Reservoir, the paddler and red hull perfectly reflected in the glassy water. A loon takes shape in the near fog, moving closer for a look at the boat. Somewhere in the mist, another loon yodels.

The kayaker drifts near a stonewall that runs from the forested shore and, incongruously, dips beneath the water. Strange, until one learns that this placid stretch of river was once the beginning of the ferocious Fifteen Mile Falls, that beneath these calm waters lies the remains of a village. Both falls and village were swallowed over a half-century ago when New England Power built Moore Dam. Thoughts of rising waters take the kayaker's imagination back to when this valley echoed with the roar of the waterfalls and the shouts of river drivers working their logs. And even further back, to the White explorers and settlers who followed the river north into unknown wilderness, and back to the Native people who first made the wilderness their home.

The kayaker finally dips a blade and breaks the perfect symmetry of water and sky. The loon, satisfied of curiosity, cruises away. The Sun, now rising into a cloudless sky, shimmers through the fog. The river continues on its way to the sea.

This is the magic of the Connecticut River Valley. While it's a magnet for people who love to paddle, hike, ski, swim, hunt, cycle, fish, or ride a snow-machine, its heritage and culture are never far from the surface. The river itself guides the traveler through chapters of its history, flowing from the vast forests where lumbermen still work, through verdant farm fields cleared by early settlers, past grand homes expressing nineteenth-century prosperity, by the factories where workers of many nations once toiled.

This part of the Atlas starts with an overview by Rebecca Brown of the wide range of cultural life and heritage in the valley. In Chapter 34, James Wright tells the story of Dartmouth College, whose history is so integral to that of the region. Judy Hayward and Rebecca A. Brown sample the watershed's many public historic sites, as well as architectural styles that give the region its flavor. In Chapter 36, Adair Mulligan presents the vast opportunities for recreation through all the seasons.

Like the changeable New England weather, patrons may discover an astonishing range of cultural experiences in a single day in this valley. One may visit a museum of science or fine art, historical sites from the nation's founding, and homes of renowned artists and United States presidents. One could take in a play in a community opera house, attend a performance in a modern concert hall, or enjoy a reading by a local writer in a public library. If people are first drawn here for recreation, they soon discover a whole community of art and culture and the rich heritage and traditions of the valley.

The Cornish Colony Museum houses an outstanding collection of paintings, illustrations, and sculptures by colony artists, including this oil painting by Maxfield Parrish (1870–1966), *The Canyon*, 1923. Quechee Gorge was an inspiration for the work.

33 Cultural Institutions

Arts, culture, and education have a long and rich history in the Connecticut River Valley, and are a significant part of life today. From the earliest days, the region has drawn artists from afar and developed its own. Storytellers carry on the tradition of the spoken word, craftspeople have converted old factory space to studios, and audiences fill public spaces built over a century ago to enjoy professional and community performances of all kinds. Public education is the focus of community support and pride, and private schools flourish. Museums and local historical societies interpret the history and heritage of the region, and public libraries are centers of cultural programs in many communities. Following is an overview of the mosaic of cultural life in the watershed.

Visual Arts: The Romantic and the Heroic
The watershed's intricate landscape has inspired generations of artists, attracted to the variety of forms from verdant meadows to rugged cliffs, and mesmerized by changes in light, mood, and season. The region's artistic heritage is rooted in the Romantic aesthetic of the nineteenth century, when painters and poets sought in nature and wilderness a sense of purity and the prospect of renewal, an antidote to increasingly crowded, industrialized urban areas. In Europe, artists flocked to the Alps, and in America they traveled to the West, to the Adirondacks, and to northern New England. The Connecticut River Valley was a favorite landscape subject for what became known as White Mountain art. New Hampshire native Benjamin Champney (1817–1907), who first visited the mountains in 1838, is credited with starting the movement.

The arrival of the Irish-born and New York–raised sculptor Augustus Saint-Gaudens (1848–1907) in Cornish, N.H., in 1885 marked the beginning of the one of the early art colonies in the United States. The Saint-Gaudens National Historic Site in Cornish conserves the artist's home, studio, and gardens, and displays some of his best-known sculptures, including the heroic Robert Shaw Memorial. Saint-Gaudens is the only unit of the National Park Service in New Hampshire, and the first unit devoted to a visual artist. The Cornish Colony Museum, across the river in Windsor, Vt., interprets the fascinating history of the artists' community and has an outstanding collection of art.

Today, painters, photographers, craftspeople, and other artists draw inspiration from many of the vistas portrayed by their predecessors over a century ago. Some celebrated landscapes have been conserved by the White Mountain National Forest and through other conservation efforts. Other views exist only in the historic landscape paintings or in memory.

In towns throughout the watershed, numerous galleries offer fine arts and crafts in a variety of media. Local arts councils play an important role in promoting arts education, and several provide gallery space. Some towns are making the "creative economy" a central focus of their business development strategies, and are promoting the reuse of mill and other factory buildings as studio space for painters, woodworkers, potters, weavers, and other craftspeople. Music, dance, and theater are also part of the creative economy effort (see Chapter 26, The Postindustrial Economy).

Performing Arts through the Valley
In the late nineteenth century, many valley towns joined a national trend of building community opera houses to host local and traveling theater companies and musical groups. Over the years, some of these spaces fell into disrepair or were absorbed into municipal offices. Today, many communities have restored or upgraded public performance places as part of fostering new cultural energy and a regional creative economy.

The 1890 Briggs Opera House in White River Junction is the intimate home of Northern Stage, which presents professional theater productions and theater education for children and adults. In Randolph,

Jennifer Powers of Twin Mountain is one of many artists who capture the valley's landscape. Here she is at work at the Pondicherry National Fish and Wildlife Refuge in Jefferson, N.H.

Jeanette Fournier, *One Last Look*, 2004, watercolor, 5½" × 6½", Bethlehem, N.H.

Vt., the 1907 Chandler Music Hall is a thriving cultural arts center. The Lebanon Opera House, built in 1924, is home to Opera North, which produces professional operas each summer and brings in nationally known musicians and other performers. In Keene, N.H., the Colonial Theatre has been an important regional arts center since 1924. Bethlehem, N.H., also hosts a historic Colonial Theatre — renovated and reopened as a film and performance space by a new community nonprofit arts organization. In nearby Littleton, efforts are ongoing to restore the historic town building and opera house. Alumni Hall in North Haverhill, N.H. (once the Grafton County Courthouse), has

found new life as a performing arts space and as a Waypoint Center on the Connecticut River Byway.

Up and down the valley, amateur and professional productions perform in town halls and community playhouses. The Weston Playhouse features Vermont's oldest professional theater company, and the Springfield Community Players are the state's oldest continuously running amateur theater group. The small town of Monroe, N.H., on the banks of the Connecticut, annually hosts a "Madrigal Dinner," performed by the North Country Chorus. Across the river, St. Johnsbury is home to the Athenaeum and the Fairbanks Museum (see sidebar), as well as Catamount Arts, which presents films and live performances and has gallery shows. A regional arts center is taking shape in Colebrook, N.H., at the northern end of the valley, while at the valley's southern entrance, Brattleboro, Vt., is a nexus of community artistic activity.

Many institutions, including Saint-Gaudens, hold summer concert series. Marlboro College has for years hosted the world-renowned Marlboro Festival, founded by Rudolph Serkin and Pablo Casals. Members of the North Country Chamber Players spend their summers in and around Sugar Hill, N.H., and present a series of concerts in the valley. Classicopia sponsors musical performances in public spaces, as well as in private homes around the Upper Valley. The Hopkins Center for the Creative and Performing Arts at Dartmouth College draws nationally known performers, and is a center of community as well as student creative life.

It would be impossible to mention let alone do justice to all of the arts organizations in the region. Many may be found through the state councils on the arts and other Web sites listed at the end of the chapter.

The Literary Tradition

The four-time Pulitzer Prize–winning poet Robert Frost (1874–1963) lived at various times in Vermont and New Hampshire. His influence

In Bellows Falls, Vt., the renovated train station houses the Connecticut River Byway Waypoint Center with an interpretive display of area history, and hosts events including musical festivals like Roots on the River.

Summer stock theater is popular throughout the region. The Weathervane Theatre in Whitefield, N.H., presents a variety of performances in repertory, including *Guys and Dolls*, shown here.

Two notable Connecticut River Valley museums are the Montshire Museum in Norwich, Vt., devoted to science education, and the Fairbanks Museum and Planetarium in St. Johnsbury, Vt., a monument to its nineteenth-century founder's interest in natural history.

St. Johnsbury industrialist Franklin Fairbanks opened his namesake museum in 1891 to house examples of nature's artistry and diversity that he collected throughout the world. Its main floor displays pieces from Fairbanks' remarkable collection, from mounted birds and mammals to Native American and Near East artifacts. Gallery space is also devoted to contemporary displays. The museum is home to the state's only public planetarium, and a weather center from which daily "Eye on the Sky" forecasts are broadcast.

The main gallery of the Fairbanks Museum.

The Montshire Museum, situated on the Connecticut River in Norwich, is a private nonprofit museum dedicated to hands-on experience and education in the natural and physical sciences, ecology, and technology. It also serves as an education center for the Silvio O. Conte National Fish and Wildlife Refuge.

continues at the Frost Place in Franconia, N.H., a nonprofit arts center based at a farm he bought in 1915. The Frost Place has in residence each summer an emerging American poet, holds an annual poetry conference and festival, and offers workshops for poets and teachers. Vermont Poet Laureate, novelist, and social activist Grace Paley (1922–2007) made her home in Thetford.

Rudyard Kipling (1865–1936) worked on *The Jungle Book* and other stories while living in Dummerston, Vt., from 1892 to 1896. He came to Vermont to marry, and designed and built the home he called Naulakha, now a National Historic Landmark.

An icon of children's literature, the ever-upbeat Pollyanna, stands in bronze in Littleton, N.H., on the lawn of the public library. Eleanor H. Porter (1868–1920), author of *Pollyanna*, was born in Littleton.

The literary novelist Ernest Hebert (*The Dogs of March*) and poet Cleopatra Mathis are on the English faculty at Dartmouth. Cornish is

the home of J. D. Salinger (*The Catcher in the Rye*). Noel Perrin (1927–2004), also a Dartmouth English and environmental studies professor, captured the flavor of rural life in his many essays. Storyteller Willem Lange, formerly of Etna, is a well-known voice on public radio and in print. Walter Wetherell of Lyme is nationally recognized for his many books about the river, ranging from flyfishing to history.

Howard Frank Mosher is a Vermont novelist and essayist well known for his evocative portraits of the Northeast Kingdom in works including *A Stranger in the Kingdom*. Vermont poet and literary novelist Jeffery Lent of Tunbridge has won acclaim for *In the Fall* and *Lost Nation*, both set in the watershed's northern regions. Reeve Lindbergh, of Barnet, Vt., is the author of numerous children's books, as well as *No More Words: A Journal of My Mother, Anne Morrow Lindbergh*. Her spouse, Nathaniel Tripp, is the author of a *Confluence*, which treats the Connecticut River as a metaphor in exploring a host of ecological, political, and historical issues.

Several other contributors to the storytelling tradition in the watershed bear mention. The Center for Cartoon Studies in White River Junction draws teachers and students from all over the world. It was founded by cartoonist Inky Solomon, creator of the strip "Freightcar Fritzy," who visited White River Junction (arriving by train), in 1936. The well-known documentary filmmaker Ken Burns lives in Walpole, N.H., and feature filmmaker Jay Craven operates his studio in Barnet, Vt.

Public Libraries

The valley is home to a network of public libraries that are thriving centers of town activity. Some present fine examples of American architectural styles. The St. Johnsbury Athenaeum was built by Horace Fairbanks as a public library and given to the town in 1871. The Fairbanks family, whose patriarch invented the platform scale and founded the Fairbanks Scales Company early in the century, were generous community philanthropists and civic leaders (see Chapter 23, The Industrial Era). The adjacent art gallery opened in 1873, shortly

Public libraries are a cultural center in many valley communities.

after the announcement of the purchase of the monumental painting, *The Domes of Yosemite*, by Albert Bierstadt. This work—Bierstadt's largest—remains the centerpiece of the gallery. The building itself is an elegant French Second Empire style.

Littleton, Claremont, and Whitefield, N.H., and Rockingham, Vt., feature Carnegie libraries built in the Classical Revival style. Steel magnate Andrew Carnegie funded the construction of over 2,500 free public libraries throughout the world. The 1906 Littleton Public Library is notable for its display of White Mountain art, and its extensive collection of stereoptic views manufactured by the Littleton-based Kilburn company, the nation's leading stereoptic card maker after the Civil War.

Public and Private Schools

Public schools are a focal point of community life up and down the watershed. The Dresden School District, linking the river towns of Hanover and Norwich, is the country's first interstate school district. A second cross-river school venture, the Rivendell District, was formed by the towns of Orford, N.H., and Fairlee, West Fairlee, and Vershire, Vt.

The valley's private schools attract students from surrounding towns and around the world. Among them in New Hampshire are the White Mountain School in Bethlehem; the Crossroads Academy in Lyme; Kimball Union Academy in Meriden; and the Cardigan Mountain School in Canaan, a small boys' school founded by former Dartmouth president E. M. Hopkins in 1945. Among many private schools on the Vermont side of the river are the St. Johnsbury Academy, Thetford Academy, Vermont Academy in Saxton's River, the Putney School, the Compass School in Westminster, and the Austine School for the Deaf in Brattleboro. Burke Mountain Academy in East Burke was one of the first schools to integrate academics with serious training in Nordic and Alpine skiing. The Lyndon Institute in Lyndonville was founded in 1867. One of its major patrons was Theodore N. Vail, first president of American Telephone and Telegraph Company (AT&T).

Postsecondary Education

While Dartmouth commands attention as the valley's leading college (see the next chapter, Dartmouth College), other public and private colleges and university affiliates offer a variety of programs and degrees. Marlboro College, just west of Brattleboro, is one of the country's most innovative liberal arts institutions. Lyndon State College in Lyndonville enjoys a national reputation in meteorology. Community College of Vermont offers classes in Springfield, St. Johnsbury, Brattleboro, and White River Junction, and St. Johnsbury hosts a branch of Springfield College. The School for International Training in Brattleboro is widely known for its study abroad program. The Vermont Technical College in Randolph Center offers programs ranging from computer-assisted design to biotechnology.

In New Hampshire, Keene State College is known for its degrees in safety studies, education, and health science. Also in Keene, Antioch New England Graduate School is highly regarded for its programs in environment studies and management. Lebanon College has served

Upper Valley residents for over 50 years. Granite State College offers adult courses in Claremont and Littleton, and White Mountains Community College, based in Berlin, has academic centers in Littleton and Woodsville.

Rebecca A. Brown is communications director for the Connecticut River Joint Commissions and editor of the Atlas. Thanks to Marion Bratesman for her contributions to this chapter and to Frumie Selchen for her thoughtful review.

FOR FURTHER READING

The Arts Alliance of Northern New Hampshire, www.aannh.org, maintains a comprehensive listing of cultural listings and events, and links to regional arts organizations.

Ewald, Richard J., with Adair D. Mulligan. 2003. *Proud to Live Here.* Charlestown, N.H.: Connecticut River Joint Commissions.

New Hampshire galleries, listed by region: www.nhliving.com/galleries/index.shtml.

New Hampshire State Council on the Arts: www.nh.gov/nharts

New Hampshire theaters: www.directorynh.com/NHArt/NHTheatre.html.

Vermont galleries: www.vtliving.com/galleries/index.shtml.

Vermont Arts Council: www.vermontartscouncil.org

Vermont theaters: www.vtliving.com/theatres/rutl.shtml

34 Dartmouth College

Dartmouth's setting on the Hanover Plain, bordered by the Connecticut River and the nearby mountains, has deeply affected the college's development and its character. For centuries, Dartmouth has distinguished itself as a leader in education, offering an exceptional liberal arts education enhanced by excellent graduate programs in the arts and sciences, business, engineering, and medicine. Yet the Dartmouth experience involves more than the college's academic offerings. Life and learning are influenced by a sense of place, a deep appreciation for the beauty of the landscape, and a shared responsibility for the environmental legacy and the college's setting within the Upper Valley community. Although the center of campus has always been defined by the Green, Dartmouth was never bounded by the outer edges of its own buildings. Students, faculty, and staff historically have expanded the learning environment to include the river, the mountains surrounding the campus, and the world beyond.

Eleazar Wheelock, a congregational minister, and his Mohegan student Samson Occom provided the vision and the resources for the founding of the college to educate Native Americans and others for the ministry. With a charter from King George III, donations from the Earl of Dartmouth and others, a gift of 500 acres of land from the Royal Governor of New Hampshire, and additional land granted by the towns of Hanover and Lebanon, Wheelock moved up the Connecticut River to settle in what is now called the Upper Valley. He served as president of Dartmouth College from 1769 to 1779. The college graduated its first students in 1772. That same year, an energetic young man named John Ledyard joined Wheelock's small band of students and later would come to epitomize the Dartmouth spirit of adventure.

While at Dartmouth, Ledyard's love of literature grew, as did his passion for outdoor endeavors. He led classmates on winter backpacking expeditions; trudging through feet of snow, Ledyard and his compatriots followed a portion of what is now the Appalachian Trail. Awed by the pristine, natural splendor of the Connecticut River Valley and emboldened by his Dartmouth experience, Ledyard set out to behold the world's beauty. He paddled downstream in a self-crafted dugout canoe, carrying only his provisions and a bearskin, a Bible, and a copy of Ovid—making the first recorded journey down the Connecticut River. That trip was the beginning of his life's adventures, but he never forgot Dartmouth. After leaving Hanover, he wrote, "the Acquaintance I have gained there is dearer than I can possibly express! . . . that you may flourish in immortal green . . . ye, thro' Time & Eternity farewell!" (Zug 2005)

Dartmouth has indeed continued to flourish. Recreational and

Baker Library and the Green.

The Hanover Plain.

John Ledyard navigates the Connecticut River in his hollowed-out canoe.

Eleazar Wheelock, founder and first president of Dartmouth College, in a portrait by Joseph Steward, 1793–1796.

athletic opportunities are central to Dartmouth's learning experience. Each year, an annual student-led canoe trip — the "Trip to the Sea" — revives Ledyard's spirit and replicates his journey down the Connecticut. Other students enjoy the river on shorter outings, borrowing canoes and kayaks from the Ledyard Canoe Club, a 10-minute walk from the campus green, to spend time on the water.

The Dartmouth Outing Club (DOC), founded in 1909 by Fred Harris from the Class of 1911, plays a critical role in Dartmouth's student experience. Up to 90 percent of each entering class participates in the group's student-led trips to remote tracts of New Hampshire and Vermont. The DOC's offerings include hunting and fishing, cycling, rock climbing, canoeing, and hiking; members of the Cabin and Trail Club show their appreciation for the natural environment, maintaining 75 miles of the Appalachian Trail. Closer to home, runners enjoy the unspoiled trails of "Pine Park" and a frozen polar bear swim in Occom Pond is an annual highlight of Winter Carnival.

The College's intimacy with its natural setting has profoundly affected its curriculum and research. Dartmouth's interdisciplinary Environmental Studies Program, one of the oldest in the country, focuses attention on international and local issues. Dartmouth's organic farm, located just north of the campus, serves as a critical resource for the program and is used by faculty teaching classes in biology, education, engineering, geography, and religion.

The Dartmouth faculty, passionate and committed teachers all, are at the forefront of their fields and pride themselves on sharing their

Morning practice on the Connecticut River.

knowledge with students. Undergraduate students work together with graduate students, postdoctoral fellows, and research faculty in the Arts and Sciences, the Dartmouth Medical School, the Tuck School of Business, and in Thayer School of Engineering, in an environment that encourages active learning. An unusually collaborative culture encourages imaginative and creative disciplinary and interdisciplinary work across the institution. Undergraduates outnumber graduate students by a significant margin and benefit from the full range of opportunities and programs.

The sense of adventure embodied by the first president, Wheelock, has continued in the College's relentless drive to innovate. Dartmouth was an early leader in the development of professional programs in medicine, engineering, and business, creative approaches to the teaching of languages, the introduction of selective admissions, and the use of technology in the learning process. Dartmouth also embraces its historic commitment to educating students from different backgrounds, circumstances, and experiences. Wheelock opened the college to Native Americans from the very beginning, and Dartmouth was among the first institutions to admit an African-American student when Edward Mitchell arrived in 1824. President John Kemeny (1970–1981) recommitted the college to this original goal. The College

Winter Carnival, c. 2003.

Rauner Special Collections Library houses the college's rare books and manuscripts and the college archives.

President James Wright awards diplomas.

aspires to create a community of students, faculty, and staff where the perspective is global and learning about different cultures and viewpoints is an integral part of the education with the understanding that diversity is critical to the educational experience of all students.

Dartmouth's ninth president, William Jewett Tucker (1893–1909), recognized the school's obligation to build students' characters through service and consideration for others. He urged, "Do not expect to make a lasting impression on the world through intellectual power without the use of an equal amount of conscience and heart." At home in Hanover and beyond the Upper Valley, Dartmouth people strive to make a difference. Under the leadership of President John Sloan Dickey (1945–1970), the college became more mindful of international issues and encouraged students to be accountable to the global community, for, as Dickey told students, "the world's troubles are your troubles . . . and there is nothing wrong with the world that better human beings cannot fix." Faculty and students through their teaching, scholarship, and service look for ways to affirm these broader responsibilities.

Dartmouth continues to help young people build character; in 2005, the consulting firm Booz Allen Hamilton named the college to its list of the "world's most enduring institutions." Dartmouth's consistent spirit of intensity and innovation is exemplified as community members take mindful action in countless realms. In 2005, while Dartmouth alumni scaled Mount Everest, researchers back in Hanover invented the world's smallest robot. Dartmouth graduates are characterized by their passion for involving themselves in the world and their deep affection for the school and its idyllic setting. John Ledyard lives on through generations of students.

James Wright is the sixteenth president of Dartmouth College. He received a bachelor's degree from Wisconsin State University–Platteville, and master's and doctoral degrees in history from the University of Wisconsin at Madison. Wright specializes in American political history.

FOR FURTHER READING

Zug, James. 2005. *American Traveler: The Life and Adventures of John Ledyard, The Man Who Dreamed of Walking the World*. New York: Basic Books.

35 Tourism and Historic Sites

The rich natural and human heritage of the Connecticut River Valley draws visitors from all over the world, and is a source of pride to residents. The river was named an American Heritage River in 1999. The designation of the Connecticut River Byway as a National Scenic Byway in 2005 recognized the natural, artistic, cultural, and historic attractions of the region. This chapter presents a sampling of the many public historic sites in the valley, as well as the architectural styles reflecting the evolving aesthetic of the valley and the growing nation. It also shows how changing transportation technology, from the introduction of the railroads to the ascendancy of the private automobile, influenced aspects of the valley's culture and development.

Ancient Cultures

The story starts with a culture that is difficult to witness now: the earliest inhabitants, Paleo-Indians, who lived in the valley more than 10,000 years ago. Archeological digs in Vermont and New Hampshire have unearthed evidence of these hunter-gatherers, who coexisted with mastodons, mammoths, caribou, and other mammals inhabiting the subarctic tundra after the retreat of the last glaciers. Connecticut River Valley archeological sites dating from this period include Colebrook, Jefferson, Hinsdale, and Swanzey, N.H. Skitchewaug, a site on the floodplain in Springfield, Vt., is considered to hold the earliest evidence of agriculture in the valley. These sites are not open to the public, but research findings and other information are available through the State Archeological and Rescue Program within the N.H. Division of Historical Resources. Information about Vermont's archeological work may be found through the state Division of Historic Preservation and the Vermont Archeological Society.

Colonial Era

Vestiges of early European settlement and American colonial history are much easier to find and observe. A visit to the Fort at No. 4, a reconstructed fortification in Charlestown, N.H., is a great way to begin understanding the region's early settlement (see Chapter 21). Built in 1743, the fort was an important military center during the French and Indian War, and again in the Revolutionary War. The Fort at No. 4 was reconstructed in the 1960s, not far from its original site, and is now open as a living history museum.

The Old Constitution House in Windsor, Vt., interprets the contentious nature of settlement, politics, and geographic boundaries during

The Fort at No. 4 in Charlestown, N.H., gives visitors a glimpse of early American life. In 1735, the Massachusetts General Court established 26 land grants, or "plantations" along the upper river valley. Northernmost was No. 4, on the banks of the Connecticut across from its confluence with the Black River, a strategic crossroads of Native American water and overland travel. The first settlers made the arduous journey to No. 4 five years later, only to find themselves in the midst of King George's War, a European conflict that had spread to the English and French forces in North America. In 1743, the settlers began constructing a fort to provide protection.

the last quarter of the eighteenth century. On July 8, 1777, representatives of the new Republic of Vermont ratified their constitution at the building, then Elijah West's tavern. Today, several blocks from its original location, the restored tavern is operated as a state historic site (see Chapter 21, Settlement).

The oldest remaining one-room schoolhouse in Vermont stands in Springfield. The Eureka Schoolhouse was built between 1785 and 1790 along the route of the Crown Point Military Road running from Fort No. 4 to Lake Champlain (see Chapter 29, Roads). The school closed in 1900, and the building eventually was disassembled and rebuilt on a spot more available to visitors. Today it is owned by the state and operated as an attraction by the Springfield Area Chamber of Commerce.

The Old South Church in Windsor, Vt., built in 1798, exemplifies the grand style of Federal architecture.

American Heritage, Growing Wealth, and Architectural Styles

From 1780 to 1810, the valley experienced a building boom as the population increased sevenfold on both sides of the river (see Chapter 27, Demographics). The region retains an abundance of American Federal architecture reflecting the prosperity of the time. A leading builder of the era was Asher Benjamin, a Connecticut native who spent some time living and working in Windsor, Vt., where he designed the Old South Church. Benjamin wrote two popular architectural plan books, *Country Builder's Assistant* (1797) and *American Builder's Companion* (1827). His influence may be seen in Federal homes throughout the two states (Tolles 1979). Seven homes on "The Ridge" facing the main street in Orford, N.H., exemplify the style. Another outstanding example is "Aspet," a brick tavern built about 1800 in Cornish, N.H. The tavern later became the home of sculptor Augustus Saint-Gaudens and is now part of the Saint-Gaudens National Historic Site (see Chapter 33, Cultural Institutions).

The wealth and rise of the middle class brought on by the Industrial Revolution left a legacy of several architectural styles. Greek Revival, popularized from the 1820s until the Civil War, celebrated temple-like design elements of ancient Greece in homage to the forbearers of American democracy. Examples of this style may be found in many towns along the river. The Romantic revival styles followed. They are collectively called "Victorian," and include Gothic Revival, Italianate, French Second Empire, Romanesque, and Queen Anne.

A fine Gothic Revival home is the centerpiece of the Justin Smith Morrill Homestead in Strafford, Vt. As a U.S. congressman and senator, Morrill was a leading proponent of public education. The 1862 Morrill Act enabled land grant colleges. The Morrill historic site includes the gardens he designed in the Romantic landscape style.

Industry, Railroads, and Tourism

While agriculture drove commerce in the eighteenth and early nineteenth-century valley, the engine of the Industrial Era was manufacturing. Fueled by waterpower from the Connecticut and its larger tributaries, mills and factories started producing textiles, paper, shoes, machine tools, firearms, drilling equipment, and more. The region around Claremont, N.H., and Springfield and Windsor, Vt., became known as the "Precision Valley" for the dominance of the machine tool and related industries (see Chapter 23, The Industrial Era). The American Precision Museum in Windsor, housed in the former Robbins, Lawrence and Kendall Armory, tells the story of how handcraftsmanship evolved into precision manufacturing.

Driven by the needs of growing industries to move goods and receive raw materials, the railroad came to the valley in 1847 (see Chapter 30, Rail). It is possible today to take train excursions with local rail tour operators. The Green Mountain Flyer offers tours in restored 1930s coaches along the Connecticut and Williams rivers between Bellows Falls and Chester Depot. The White River Flyer travels from White River Junction up the Connecticut to the Montshire Museum in Norwich. Glimpses of the valley's railroad history also may be seen at restored rail stations in several valley communities, including

A former tavern, Aspet is preserved on the grounds of the Saint-Gaudens National Historic Site in Cornish, N.H.

The American Precision Museum in Windsor, Vt., housed in the former Robbins & Lawrence Armory. Note the firearm weathervane.

St. Johnsbury, Vt., where the station is also a Waypoint Center on the Connecticut River Byway.

The railroads made it possible for the very wealthy from Boston, New York, and beyond to build summer retreats in Vermont and New Hampshire. Today, the region features a number of important historic sites that interpret the artistry and lifestyle of America's Gilded Age. These include Saint-Gaudens; The Rocks, summer retreat of Chicago industrialist John Jacob Glessner, in Bethlehem, N.H.; and The Fells, the summer estate of John Hay, the international statesman and private secretary to President Lincoln, on Lake Sunapee in Newbury, N.H.

The changing economic life of the Industrial Era allowed leisure time and vacations for the growing segment of well-to-do. The new "leisure class" sought to leave the crowded, dirty cities and enjoy respite and rejuvenation in the mountains of northern New England and the Adirondacks. The quickly expanding network of railroads granted their wish, and ushered in the era of the grand resort hotels. Towns throughout the eastern slopes of the watershed bustled with summer tourists deposited by the trainload. Grand hotels drew families who stayed the entire summer, and employed rafts of workers from all over the East Coast. Most of these of huge hotels were gone by the mid-twentieth century. They were victims, ironically, of the next

revolution in transportation — the automobile — that allowed middle-class families more mobility and shorter vacations. A few of the grand resorts still welcome guests. Relaxing in a rocker under the portico of the Mountain View Grand in Whitefield, perambulating the massive porch at the Mount Washington Hotel in Bretton Woods, or playing croquet on the lawn at The Balsams in Dixville Notch — all transport guests back to an earlier, Gatsbyesque time.

Conservation and Agricultural Heritage

Automobiles and improved road building encouraged John Wingate Weeks, a Lancaster, N.H., native and foremost conservationist who made his fortune as a Boston financier before being elected to Congress, to build his country retreat back home in 1913. The Weeks Historic Site features his grand home, perched atop Prospect Mountain and accessible by auto road, and 420 acres of forest. The home commands splendid views of the White Mountain National Forest, created after the 1911 Weeks Act establishing national forests in the East.

Railroad wealth played a part in the creation of a historic site devoted to conservation and agricultural history. The Marsh-Billings-Rockefeller National Historical Park in Woodstock, Vt., honors George

The Balsams Grand Resort in Dixville Notch, N.H., is one of the watershed's destinations where guests step back to an earlier time.

Perkins Marsh, who created the estate. Marsh was one of the nation's first environmental thinkers, publishing the influential book *Man and Nature* in 1864. One of those inspired by his ideas was Royalton, Vt., native Frederick Billings. Billings, who joined the California Gold Rush and went on to head the Northern Pacific Railroad, purchased the Marsh estate in 1869 and established a progressive dairy farm and professionally managed forest. The historical park was created in 1992.

Not far from the Billings Farm at the watershed's western edge is the small community of Plymouth Notch, birthplace and boyhood home of President Calvin Coolidge. The Coolidge Homestead is a state historic site, and the village retains the look and feel of the early 1900s. Coolidge and seven generations of his family are buried in the town cemetery.

Agricultural heritage at an intimate scale is at found at the 100-acre Poore Family Farm in the northern New Hampshire town of Stewartstown. J. C. Kenneth Poore (1885–1983) lived on the farm his entire life and wanted to see it preserved as a museum after his death. He created the Poore Family Foundation for North Country Conservancy, and today a passionate group of volunteers and staff works diligently bringing the farm's history to life.

On the other side of the river, a new heritage initiative focuses on "geotourism" in Vermont's rural Northeast Kingdom. Residents, community organizations, and businesses teamed with the National Geographic Society to produce a mapguide of favorite cultural, historic, and natural sites and events. Information on obtaining the mapguide is listed below.

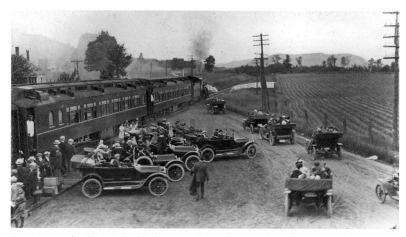

Tourists came by the trainload to the mountains of Vermont and New Hampshire. In this c. 1920 photo, they disembark at Fairlee, Vt., for Camp Quinibeck.

The main house at the Marsh-Billings-Rockefeller National Historic Park, Woodstock, Vt. The park was created as a gift to the nation from Billings' granddaughter, Mary French Rockefeller, and her husband Laurance. The Rockefellers also founded the Woodstock Foundation, which operates the Billings Farm and Museum as a working dairy farm and agricultural history museum.

The Poore farm in Stewartstown, N.H., is conserved as a museum of early agricultural life. Starting in 1832, generations of the Poore family roughed out fields from the rugged and rocky forest on the eastern slopes of the Connecticut River Valley.

Historic sites in the Connecticut River Valley are rich and varied, offering a window on the region's and the nation's evolution of commerce, leisure, industry, and agriculture. Details on the many historic sites and nationally designated historic districts may be found on the Web sites for state historic preservation listed below. In addition, town historical societies are rich with local information, and some maintain intriguing small museums. The Connecticut River Byway and N.H. State Welcome Center in Colebrook houses the Great North Woods Interpretive Center, and Byway waypoint centers in Lancaster, St. Johnsbury, Wells River, Haverhill, White River Junction, Windsor, Claremont, and Bellows Falls include interpretive displays of local and regional history.

Rebecca A. Brown works as communications director for the Connecticut River Joint Commissions from her circa 1790 home and office in Sugar Hill, N.H.

Judy Hayward is executive director of the Preservation Education Institute and Historic Windsor, Inc. She is a specialist in preservation building skills education and conference director for the Traditional Building Exhibition and Conference, the largest tradeshow in North America dedicated to historic preservation and traditionally inspired new construction.

FOR FURTHER READING

Many brochures, mapguides, and booklets are devoted to exploring the valley. They are available at the Connecticut River Byway waypoint centers, listed at www.ctrivertravel.net, or contact the listed organization. Among them are: *Bellows Falls Neighborhood Historic Self-Guided Walking Tour*, a brochure; *From Mills to Main Streets*, a brochure featuring industrial heritage from Brattleboro to St. Johnsbury; *Historic Northern New Hampshire*, a mapguide published by the Arts Alliance of Northern New Hampshire, www.aannh.org/heritage/index.php; *Heritage Guide of the Vermont Northeast Kingdom*, a 68-page pamphlet, and *Mapguide of*

Vermont's Northeast Kingdom, both available from the Northeast Kingdom Travel and Tourism Association, www.travelthekingdom.com.

Connecticut River Byway, www.ctrivertravel.net.

Ewald, Richard J., with Adair D. Mulligan. 2003. *Proud to Live Here*. Charlestown, N.H.: Connecticut River Joint Commissions.

New Hampshire Division of Historical Resources, www.nh.gov/nhdhr. Historical markers: www.nh.gov/markers/index.html.

State Archeological and Rescue Program, N.H. Division of Historical Resources, http://mysite.verizon.net/ddboisvert/index.html.

Tolles, Bryant F., and Carolyn K. Tolles. 1979. *New Hampshire Architecture: An Illustrated Guide*. Hanover, N.H.: University Press of New England.

Vermont Division for Historic Preservation, www.historicvermont.org.

Wikoff, Jerold. 1985. *The Upper Valley: An Illustrated Tour Along the Connecticut River*. Chelsea, Vt.: Chelsea Green Publishing Co.

36 Recreation

The Connecticut River Valley has long attracted visitors seeking adventure and respite from the nation's growing urban centers. In the early 1800s, Yale University's famously itinerant president, Timothy Dwight wrote, "The Connecticut valley is a prominent part of this landscape. In its extent it is magnificent; in its form it is beautiful" (Dwight 1823).

Many others followed Dwight to sample the forested footpaths, mountain views, and tumbling waterfalls for themselves. Henry David Thoreau took such a trip with friends on a sunny day in 1856, hiking up Mount Wantastiquet to enjoy its prospect over Brattleboro, Vt. Rustic hunting and fishing camps appeared in the nineteenth century near headwaters streams and ponds, lit by kerosene lanterns and the glow of fellowship over a fine day's catch. Mountain hospitality evolved from farmhouse rooms offered to travelers to a later nineteenth century burgeoning of grand hotels that hosted families for entire summers.

Today, the Connecticut River Valley's appeal for recreation and tourism is rooted in its authenticity, in historic white-steepled villages, mountain views, working farms, home-grown crops and crafts, and outdoor pastimes such as hiking, fishing, paddling, and watching wildlife. The Connecticut River Byway explores over 500 miles of roads bordering the river in Vermont and New Hampshire. In recognition of the tremendous cultural, historic, and recreational assets of the valley, the Byway was designated a National Scenic Byway in 2005.

A Tradition of Water-Based Recreation

Canoe paddles have flashed in the sun on these waters for centuries. In 1773, John Ledyard, the adventurous Dartmouth student, made what is believed to be the first trip downriver all the way to the Atlantic Ocean—by dugout canoe. Construction of hydro dams on the Connecticut River 150 years later created pools deep enough for motorboat propellers, beginning with elegant little steam-powered craft. Today, the Connecticut River offers a broader range of boating opportunities than any other water body in the region, from whitewater kayaking to a quiet paddle to power boating on impoundments. Of the river's 271 miles in New Hampshire and Vermont, about half is free flowing and half is impounded behind dams.

Canoeing has always been a fine way to enjoy the river up close, and kayaking has now become just as popular, particularly at Sumner Falls at Hartland, Vt., and on many of the tributaries. The natural beauty of the river corridor, the rising numbers of paddlers seeking an extended river experience, and the willingness of landowners to share their conserved riverfront property with the public has prompted creation of a string of primitive canoe campsites. Map 50 shows boat launches on the Connecticut.

The Northern Forest Canoe Trail, an east-west water route traversing the Northern Forest region of New York, Vermont, New Hampshire, and Maine, follows the Nulhegan, Connecticut, and Upper Ammonoosuc Rivers in the Connecticut River watershed. With its challenging portages and stiff rapids as well as lovely quiet stretches, the canoe trail offers paddlers the experience of Northern Forest heritage and a great outdoor adventure.

Rowing and sculling draw people of all ages who enjoy the exercise and exhilaration of slipping quickly across the wide flat water of the impoundments. Organized adult, college, and high school crew teams practice and compete on the river near Hanover, N.H., and Putney, Vt., hosts the Green Mountain Head race.

Fishing is a nearly year-round sport on the Connecticut River. Tournament anglers seek trophy pike, trout, and other species in the impoundments, and fly fishers try matching the hatches of spring and summer. In winter, hardy fishermen tend rigs set over holes drilled through the thick ice on the impoundments and setbacks where tribu-

Stretches of the Connecticut River above and below McIndoe Falls are popular with paddlers.

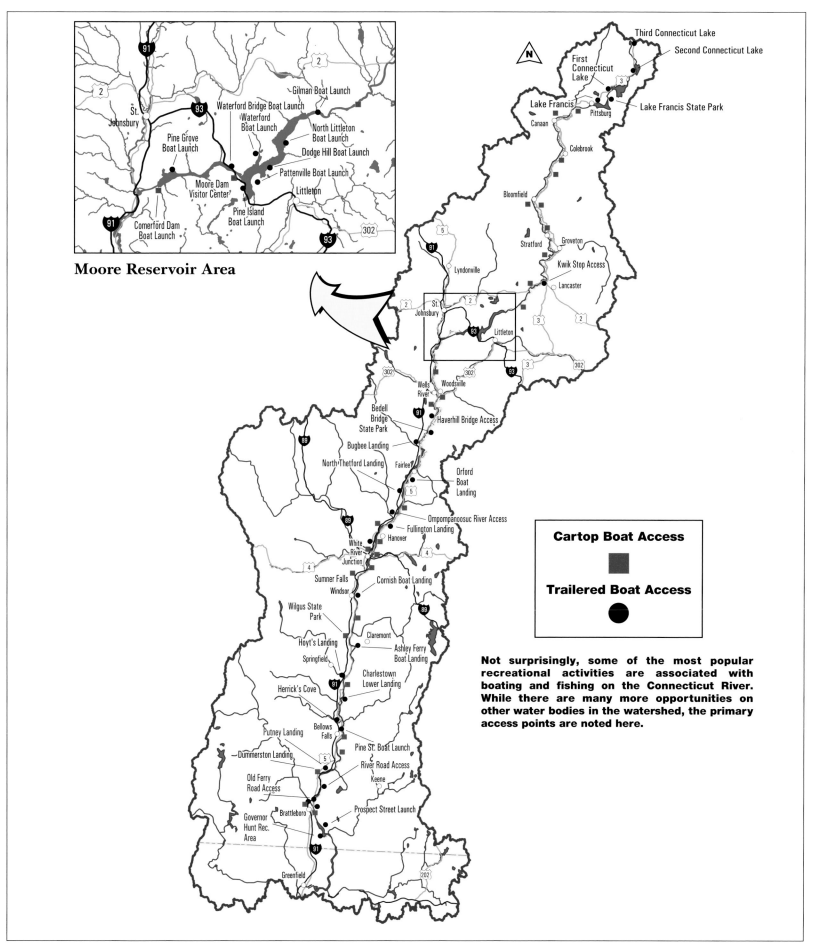

Moore Reservoir Area

Inset labels:
91
2
2
91
93
St. Johnsbury
Gilman Boat Launch
Waterford Bridge Boat Launch
Waterford Boat Launch
North Littleton Boat Launch
Pine Grove Boat Launch
Dodge Hill Boat Launch
Pattenville Boat Launch
Moore Dam Visitor Center
Littleton
91
93
Pine Island Boat Launch
Comerford Dam Boat Launch
302

Main map labels:
N
Third Connecticut Lake
Second Connecticut Lake
First Connecticut Lake
Lake Francis
Lake Francis State Park
Canaan
Pittsburg
3
Colebrook
Bloomfield
Groveton
Stratford
Kwik Stop Access
Lancaster
5
91
Lyndonville
2
St. Johnsbury
302
93
Littleton
3
302
302
Wells River
Woodsville
91
Bedell Bridge State Park
Haverhill Bridge Access
89
Bugbee Landing
North Thetford Landing
Fairlee
5
Orford Boat Landing
Ompompanoosuc River Access
89
Fullington Landing
White River Junction
Hanover
4
4
Sumner Falls
Cornish Boat Landing
Windsor
Wilgus State Park
89
Claremont
Hoyt's Landing
Ashley Ferry Boat Landing
Springfield
Charlestown Lower Landing
91
Herrick's Cove
Putney Landing
Bellows Falls
Pine St. Boat Launch
Dummerston Landing
5
River Road Access
Keene
Old Ferry Road Access
Brattleboro
Prospect Street Launch
Governor Hunt Rec. Area
91
Greenfield
202

Cartop Boat Access

Trailered Boat Access

Not surprisingly, some of the most popular recreational activities are associated with boating and fishing on the Connecticut River. While there are many more opportunities on other water bodies in the watershed, the primary access points are noted here.

Map 50. Public Access Boat Launches on the Connecticut River.

The Hanover
High School crew
practices early in
the morning on the
Connecticut River.

The Hanover High School crew practices early in the morning on the Connecticut River.

Ice fishing is popular on shallow river setbacks and on area lakes and ponds. Here, two men check their tip-up on Post Pond in Lyme, N.H.

taries meet the river. Many tributaries and the northern river offer fine angling for cold-water fish including rainbow, brown, and the native brook trout, and the mainstem impoundments shelter warm water species such as perch, pickerel, bass, and walleye.

By Foot and By Wheel

Hiking trails and footpaths have long followed the valley, starting with paths used by Native Americans, then white soldiers and settlers, and more recently, hiking trails built for recreation. The Appalachian Trail, which runs from Maine to Georgia, travels through the heart of the upper Connecticut River Valley, crossing from Norwich, Vt., to Hanover, N.H., on a bridge named for John Ledyard. Other trail systems, large and small, meander the watershed, including the recently established 162-mile Cohos Trail, which runs from the southern Presidential Range to the Canadian border above the Connecticut Lakes. An example of a community trail system is Cross-Rivendell Trail, conceived by the interstate Rivendell School District, linking the towns of Vershire, West Fairlee, and Fairlee, Vt., with Orford, N.H. Schoolchildren have helped build this community trail, beginning at the summit of Mount Cube in Orford. Strong interest in this region's abundant trails prompted formation of the Upper Valley Trails Alliance, creating a network among trail users and maintainers.

A century ago, the Connecticut River and its tributary valleys echoed with the sounds of locomotives following the waterways as they moved timber, freight, tourists, and other passengers. Today, many miles of converted rail trails host walkers, joggers, bicyclists, and horses in summer, and snowmobiles in winter. Bicycle touring, mountain biking, and even bicycle commuting have become popular in the region in the last few years.

Winter Recreation

In a region that an artful New Englander once said "offers six months of winter and six months of poor sledding," there are many forms of cold-weather recreation. Old-fashioned pond skating and coasting on farm hills are joined these days by cross-country skiing on frozen golf courses and snowmobile trails, and backcountry skiers tackling the highest mountains. Snowshoes, once a necessity for getting around a farm and the woods in deep snow, are now choice gear for exploring winter trails. Relatively new to the region are dog sledding and ski-joring (where harnessed dogs pull people on skis), often on a competitive basis. Some communities have revived their traditions of winter carnivals, and several chambers of commerce in the Littleton, N.H., area hold an annual Frostbite Follies celebration in February. The Hulbert Outdoor Center in Fairlee hosts an annual winter festival on Lake Morey, and the Dartmouth Winter Carnival is a long-standing tradition. Lancaster hosts an annual Snodeo and Ride-In for snowmobilers.

American skiing got off the ground in 1934 in the Connecticut River Valley, when a Ford Model T engine powered the first ski lift, a rope tow up a sloping farm pasture in Woodstock, Vt. European instructors at the nation's first ski school in Sugar Hill, N.H., added to the sport's novelty. Soon ski areas—and Nordic jumping hills—opened throughout the valley. Over the years, this region has sent many athletes to compete in the winter Olympics in both alpine and Nordic skiing.

Snowmobiling has become popular throughout the region, after making its debut in Lancaster in 1959. A vast network of snowmobile trails, especially in northern Vermont and New Hampshire, has become a destination for riders from throughout the Northeast. The first good snow cover brings a cavalry of snow machines onto hundreds of miles of well-coordinated snowmobile trails linking most towns. Volunteers from local clubs such as the Pittsburg Ridge Runners and the Colebrook Ski Bees care for these trails and organize derbies and other events.

Wildlife Watching and Hunting

Wildlife-related recreation has become the most popular form of recreation in Vermont and New Hampshire, with 86 percent of residents in each state spending time watching, feeding, and/or photographing wildlife. Moose viewing at Pittsburg's "Moose Alley" in New Hampshire's Headwaters region is legendary. The growing popularity of

Moose watching is a huge draw in the northern watershed. This cow moose seems intent on crossing busy Route 2 in Lunenburg, Vt.

Hunting is a traditional and popular pastime in the valley.

bird watching led to creation of the Connecticut River Birding Trail, a series of 126 different wildlife-viewing sites stretching from the warbler paradise at Fourth Connecticut Lake, the river's source, to the waterfowl-rich waters of Retreat Meadows in Brattleboro. While the birding is especially rewarding in spring and summer, wildlife tracking captures the imagination of many in winter. Hunting remains a strong tradition in both states. Hunters and their dogs jump grouse and woodcock in the golden days of October, look for waterfowl in marshes and river setbacks, and generations of families head to deer camp in November.

Fairs and Quests

Back in town, Connecticut River communities have a long tradition of festivals, parades, Old Home Day celebrations, and county fairs for family fun. Among the many events are the annual Moose Festival in Colebrook, the Keene Pumpkin Festival, the Strolling of the Heifers through downtown Brattleboro, and the Quechee Balloon Festival. Each fall, the Tunbridge World's Fair draws thousands to a tiny hill village in Vermont, a tradition going back over 135 years.

Many of the watershed's special places and unique features are the subject of another family recreational activity of growing popularity, "questing." Valley Quest, a program of Vital Communities based in White River Junction, Vt., offers treasure hunts that illuminate local history, leading explorers on their quests to ancient hidden cemeteries or the secrets of a downtown square.

Dams and Reservoirs

U.S. Army Corps of Engineers reservoirs offer diverse opportunities for high quality, year-round outdoor recreation in the watershed.

All are open for hunting, fishing, hiking, picnicking, and swimming. Developed recreation areas and beaches are available at all the reservoirs. For additional information on the recreation currently available at these reservoirs see the Army Corps New England website, www.nae.usace.army.mil.

TransCanada's six hydroelectric dams and two water storage dams are known for their public recreation opportunities, as is Murphy Dam at Lake Francis, which TransCanada manages. Hunting is permitted on TransCanada land. ATVs are not allowed, but snowmachine corridor trails run through some of the areas. Areas are open year round, but remote parking lots are not plowed. They are open for day use only. Paddlers will find a portage trail or steps up from the river at each dam.

The annual Moose Festival in Colebrook, N.H., draws visitors and residents.

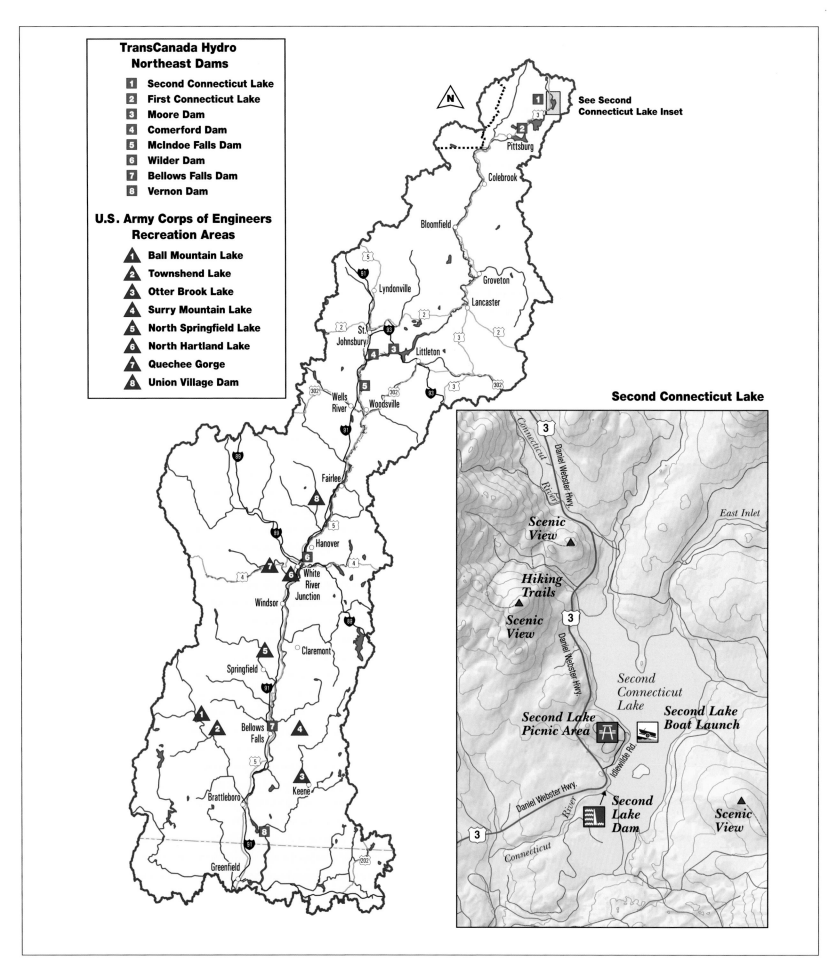

TransCanada Hydro Northeast Dams

1. Second Connecticut Lake
2. First Connecticut Lake
3. Moore Dam
4. Comerford Dam
5. McIndoe Falls Dam
6. Wilder Dam
7. Bellows Falls Dam
8. Vernon Dam

U.S. Army Corps of Engineers Recreation Areas

1. Ball Mountain Lake
2. Townshend Lake
3. Otter Brook Lake
4. Surry Mountain Lake
5. North Springfield Lake
6. North Hartland Lake
7. Quechee Gorge
8. Union Village Dam

See Second Connecticut Lake Inset

Second Connecticut Lake

Map 51. Dam-related Recreational Opportunities.

TransCanada's dams are working facilities, and may be called on to generate power at any time. With power generation may come significant changes in water levels below the dams. Anglers, swimmers, and boaters should be aware of the upriver boundaries (marked with buoys) and obey warning signs. Loudspeakers and a lighting system at the dams announce gate openings. Schedules for power making and predicted flow levels may be found on the Web at www.h2oline .com. Army Corps and TransCanada dam recreation areas are shown on Map 51.

Public Users, Private Land

Public recreation in today's valley benefits from the previous century's investments in public land. The Appalachian Trail traverses large areas of the federally protected Green and White Mountain National Forests. Dozens of state-owned parks offer residents and visitors opportunities for camping, hiking, and personal encounters with nature.

Northern New England also has a long and honored tradition of public use of private land for recreation. Concern for the loss of access for the public led both Vermont and New Hampshire to protect this tradition when major tracts of private timberland came up for sale in the late 1990s. In 1997, the state of Vermont and the Silvio O. Conte National Fish and Wildlife Refuge conserved 132,000 acres in the Nulhegan River and Paul Stream basins and at West Mountain in the Northeast Kingdom. A few years later, the state of New Hampshire invested in the largest land protection project in its history, protecting 171,500 acres at the headwaters of the Connecticut River.

These landmark conservation successes have protected the public's right to use those wild and beautiful lands for recreation. The challenge of maintaining the quality of life enjoyed here will continue to be tested as the region's visitor and resident population grows. Greater numbers of people are leaving behind urban and suburban sprawl, some for a week and others permanently, as the beauty of New England's greatest river will continue to draw people, just as it did 200 years ago.

Adair D. Mulligan is the conservation director for the Connecticut River Joint Commissions, and co-author of Proud to Live Here *(Ewald with Mulligan 2003), a description of the history and life in the Connecticut River Valley. She hikes, skis, and snowshoes in Lyme, N.H. Thanks to Mike Curran of the U.S. Army Corps of Engineers for his contribution to this chapter.*

For Further Reading

Connecticut River Watershed Council. 2007. *The Connecticut River Boating Guide: Source to Sea*. Guilford, Conn.: Globe Pequot.

Dwight, Timothy. 1823. *Travels in New England and New York*. London: W. Baynes and Son, and Ogle, Duncan & Co.

Kibling, Mary L. 1989. *Walks and Rambles in the Upper Connecticut River Valley*. Woodstock, Vt.: Countryman Press.

MacKay, Dick. 2003. *Adventures in Paradise: Exploring the Upper Connecticut Valley of Vermont and New Hampshire on a Bicycle*. Hanover, N.H.: Faculty Ridge Books.

Silverberg, Judith K. 1997. *New Hampshire Wildlife Viewing Guide*. Helena, Mont.: Falcon Press.

Vital Communities. 2001. *Valley Quest: 89 Treasure Hunts in the Upper Valley*. White River Junction, Vt.: Vital Communities.

Vital Communities. 2004. *Valley Quest II: 75 More Treasure Hunts in the Upper Valley*. White River Junction, Vt.: Vital Communities.

Epilogue

Opportunities and Challenges

Readers of this volume have explored the movement of continents in deep, deep time. They have absorbed the advance and retreat of glaciers, and the forest primeval. They have glimpsed Native Americans in the Connecticut River Valley thousands of years ago, and the European settlers who much later cleared land for farms, and built mills, churches, and houses. They have witnessed tides of change: the evolution of agriculture from subsistence, to sheep, to cows, and more recently to specialized crops. They have encountered waterfalls that first powered grain mills, then machine tools, and now—amplified by hydroelectric dams—export power into the national power grid.

Over time, people and place have intertwined. Fine alluvial soils along the river helped turn subsistence settlers into successful farmers. Tumbling waterfalls turned the wheels of mills, and innovative mill workers evolved with the times to become machine tool makers. The Connecticut River watershed is studded with villages, most of them small, nestled among the hills. Generation after generation, people here have evolved a culture based on church suppers, school basketball games, local theaters and crafts, upon looking out for each other, and upon grass roots democracy expressed at annual town meetings.

The proportion of settlement to nature favors nature, and the natural world of forests and the open fields of farms are only a few minutes away for most valley residents. The watershed's geography has fostered practical lives that for the most part use, but don't exhaust, sustaining waters, soils, and forests. The landscape also affords inspiration. All who live here have experienced those "Maxfield Parrish" moments of awe when rosy cumulus clouds pile up in a vivid blue sky, even if the rest of us can't quite paint the picture as he did.

Natural history and human history are stories of the forces of change, and how people adapt to some changes and are driven to create others. As years go on, the interplay will continue. It will take place between old timers and newcomers, and between people and the river and hills, soils and wild creatures that shape this remarkable valley. To an important extent, changes in the valley may come from forces elsewhere, such as population growth, rising costs of transportation and of food, nonnative species, airborne emissions, globalization, and a changing climate.

People who believe the upper Connecticut River watershed to be a pretty fine place can look ahead into the twenty-first century and identify a number of questions, the answers to which will shape the next chapters in the valley's identity and integrity. Some of these questions follow. We will have done our job if this Atlas gives valley residents and visitors a condensed human and natural history that will illuminate the choices ahead.

Will the defining features of the landscape and history of the valley be cherished and preserved as a part of its culture and quality of life and livelihood? Connecticut River Valley communities, with their preponderance of historic structures, enjoy a wealth of visible history, rare in the United States, and impressive compared to the rest of New England. This resource is beginning to be recognized as the basis for economic revitalization through heritage tourism and the Connecticut River Byway. Preservation of historic town halls, academy buildings, white steepled churches, old brick mills, and large main street houses is not assured, however, and no government program channels support into historic preservation the way public support is provided for parks, forests, or water quality.

Communities, landowners, and legislatures increasingly are recognizing that lands valued for their natural qualities—scenic vistas, productive farms or forests, wildlife habitats, river and stream buffers—should have legal protection, either as a park, forest, or wildlife refuge in public ownership, or through the certainties of conservation easements, administered by a land trust.

Will the valley continue to progress in safeguarding and improving water quality? While federal and state agencies have long taken the lead in requiring, financing, and enforcing pollution prevention or treatment, their resources to do so face increasing competition from other public purposes such as the war on terror, homeland security, and health care. Aging wastewater treatment plants, village sewers that overflow untreated into rivers when it rains, unvegetated riverbanks that erode sediment, failing septic systems, overfertilized lawns, and increased impermeable surfaces all play a role in diminished water quality. Public support for water quality is as high as ever, but this support needs to translate into continued commitments to progress on the part of agencies, communities, landowners, and those responsible for discharges. As technical knowledge advances about how pollutants affect natural habitats and people, public education will need to keep abreast of the science.

Will the watershed have as rich a diversity of fish, wildlife, and birds fifty or a hundred years from now as it enjoys today? We are diminished as a people when we lose any of our fellow voyagers on Planet Earth. The federal Endangered Species Act was passed by Congress in

1973 in recognition of this principle. Yeoman restoration efforts by the U.S. Fish and Wildlife Service and many partners have returned the bald eagle to the Connecticut River Valley for our awe and enjoyment. Restoration of a fading species is much more difficult and expensive than protection of adequate habitat for dynamic populations and biodiversity to continue to thrive. As human activity expands, protection of habitat becomes ever more important. In the Connecticut River watershed, no habitat is more valuable for fish, wildlife, and birds than the riparian areas along the Connecticut River, its tributaries, and feeder streams. Natural vegetation along river and stream banks provides cooling shade for fish, filters pollutants and nutrients, and provides travel corridors for wildlife and feeding and nesting places for birds.

People who may love to fish, see a moose, or hear the thrush's song, still may not recognize the need for commitments to preserve the habitats that ensure long-term species survival. Partnerships will be needed between landowners and organizations like Audubon societies, fish and wildlife associations, and land trusts, as well as with the state agencies established to protect habitat and educate the public. Congress created the Silvio O. Conte Fish and Wildlife Refuge in 1991 to catalyze habitat conservation in the Connecticut River watershed. Both state and federal agencies have meager funding compared to their missions. When these wheels of government finally turn, however, hundreds of thousands of nonverbal residents and migratory campers in the valley will gain security.

Will sufficient open space be preserved to sustain the natural biodiversity that characterizes New England? Biodiversity embraces the natural interactions among soil, plants, wild creatures, sunlight, precipitation, and climate that foster biological productivity. Healthy forests and agriculture are based in healthy soils and plant diversity. Invasive species and monocultures often undermine biological health. Landowners at all scales are going to need ready access to good science that can help them manage lands for long-term as well as short-term productivity and biodiversity.

Will agriculture and forestry again be major contributors in the valley's economy, and can these resource-based industries reshape their economic prospects to succeed in the local and regional marketplace and compete globally? The globalization of food and timber production and distribution has significantly undercut the markets for Connecticut River Valley timber, milk, cheese, and other farm products. The loss of a sustaining economic role for farm land and forests too often can leave the landowner with little option except to sell, with scattered development the result. The trend has started to turn through the growth of farmers' markets, community supported agriculture, chefs who use local foods, and the creation of value-added local wood products. The preponderance of food and wood sales in the valley, however, still comes from the global marketplace, to the detriment of the farms and forests that give the valley its enduring character.

How can the region create a sustainable economy, fueled by innovation and offering a viable future for those who grow up here? The consolidation of agriculture and decline of local manufacturing jobs has made it difficult for many young people to stay near their families and look forward to a secure economic future. The loss of a youthful population is happening in rural communities all across America, so the question is a societal one. That does not mean, however, that communities, entrepreneurs, and educational institutions in the Connecticut River Valley should not make an effort to shape our own destiny and to create communities that will be sustainable for this generation and the next.

How will climate change affect the Connecticut River watershed? People all over the world are asking a similar question about their river valley, seacoast, or forests. Our Atlas is published at a time when widespread awareness of climate change is growing, though still in an early phase. Science, technology, public policy, and private choices are starting to come to grips with the fact that the climate is warming, and that the warming is due primarily to carbon emissions from burning fossil fuels. Unchecked, climate change is destabilizing ecosystems, and may force the relocation of human populations and other species. Ecosystems are dynamic and can change rapidly.

Earlier forces of change in the valley — the advent of interstate highways, or the shift of machine tool manufacture to Asia — happened as a result of federal investments or global market decisions, and the Connecticut River Valley lived with the consequences. This time, people in the valley have a larger role. Climate change is happening in a new information age when computers can model differing scenarios and when every classroom can have access to a wide range of knowledge about the effects of a changing climate on biota, ecosystems, water supplies, agriculture, and more. A citizenry informed is also a citizenry empowered, and thus individuals, organizations, corporations, communities, state and federal governments all have an array of options before them for addressing climate change and minimizing its adverse effects. Dartmouth College and other educational institutions in the valley are providing leadership in developing solutions, through science, technology, and in public policy. Creative innovation is addressing renewable energy, energy conservation, and appropriate technologies.

In this great challenge, everyone has a stake: teachers, students, parents, home owners, commuters, employers, employees, nonprofit organizations, towns, cities, counties, state agencies, the Congress, and federal agencies. It would be a mistake if people simply pointed fingers and said it's somebody else's problem to solve. Another mistake would be if people and institutions think that taking one step will be sufficient. Offsetting climate change will necessitate a quantum leap in technical and behavioral adjustments. From now on, climate protection will need to become part of the math of everyday business and life.

Will people in valley communities continue to draw strength, and resolve issues through local community participation? Outsiders are astonished at the amount of time spent at town meeting debating the merits of whether to purchase a new fire truck or enact a new zoning proposal. In many towns, however, attendance at town meetings is down. Some people have too many other demands on their time. Some may not want to give up a Saturday or a Tuesday, or may not like driving at night, preferring to stay home. Those who do participate not only engage in gutsy debate, but also make decisions that will affect their neighborhoods and pocketbooks for a long time to come. People in other parts of the country—indeed the world—regard New England's town meeting form of government as the purest form of democracy anywhere. No aspect of local government is more important to the topics addressed in this Atlas than the role of local planning boards (in New Hampshire) and planning commissions (in Vermont). Town by town, these are the people who do the homework, educate their townspeople, develop the ordinances that protect water quality, and determine whether development is concentrated in village centers or sprawls across fields and hills. Both states have encouraged and supported regional planning commissions to do the important mapping and analysis in support of volunteer town planners. "Local control" has been a way of life in Connecticut River Valley towns for 200 years, yet is challenged today by a culture that emphasizes fictional entertainment over the dramas of real life conflict and cooperation.

How can people in the Connecticut River Valley respond to challenges facing the watershed? A look at the topographic map and a review of geology show the Connecticut River watershed to be a unit, with the river running through it and all waters descending to that river. Up close, we realize that the river has been determined to be a boundary between two states rather than the unifier of a watershed. "Political ecology" has its own rationale, just as much as environmental ecology, and the two overlay each other's maps. But they are very different. Moose, bear, and beaver may wander from one side of the river to the other oblivious of whether they are in Vermont or New Hampshire. People who live in valley towns may play soccer, date and chose mates, or go to concerts and shop in stores in one state or the other. It's one place: this watershed—yet part of two distinct states.

A voice for the watershed was born in the late 1980s when the New Hampshire and Vermont legislatures had the foresight to establish commissions to work with each other and ensure a united bi-state approach to watershed issues. The Connecticut River Joint Commissions develop the river management plan that guides both states, watershed communities, and landowners. The commissions crossfertilize, advocating in Vermont shoreland protection provisions such as those of New Hampshire, and advocating in New Hampshire phosphorus controls similar to Vermont's. Bi-state cooperation is voluntary, and depends upon good will, a self-renewing source of social energy. The Connecticut River Joint Commissions teamed up with Dartmouth College and Northern Cartographic to create *Where the Great River Rises* as a tool for holistic, watershed-framed understanding. Through the Atlas, all of us gain a wider perspective of the Connecticut River, the strong thread that binds us all.

Sharon F. Francis is the first executive director of the Connecticut River Joint Commissions, a position she has held since 1990. A graduate of Mount Holyoke College in political science, she has worked in the environmental field for over 40 years, including senior level appointments in the U.S. Department of the Interior, the White House, and at the Environmental Protection Agency. She received the EPA's lifetime achievement award in 2005. She is a resident of Charlestown, N.H.

Bibliography

Part I. The Physical Landscape

1. Physiography and Bedrock Geology (pages 5–11)

Cheney, J. T., eds. 2003. *Guidebook for Field Trips in the Five College Region*, 95th Annual Meeting of the New England Intercollegiate Geological Conference, B1-1–B1-31.

Denny, C. S. 1982. *Geomorphology of New England.* U.S. Geological Survey Professional Paper 1208.

Doll, C. G., W. M. Cady, J. B. Thompson, and M. P. Billings Jr. 1961. *Centennial Geologic Map of Vermont.* Vermont Geological Survey, scale 1:250,000.

Eby, G. Nelson. 1995. *Third Hutton Symposium on Granites and Related Rocks, Pre-Conference Field Trip Guide*, Part I: White Mountain Magma Series, 1–23.

Geological Society of America. 1999. Geologic Time Scale, product code CTS004, Compilers: A. R. Palmer and J. Geissman.

Hibbard, J. P., C. R. van Staal, D. W. Rankin, and H. Williams. 2006. Lithotectonic Map of the Appalachian Orogen, Canada–United States of America. Geological Survey of Canada, Map 2096A, scale 1:1,500,000.

Johnson, C. 1998. *The Nature of Vermont.* Hanover, N.H.: University Press of New England.

Karabinos, P., S. D. Samson, J. C. Hepburn, and H. M. Stoll. 1998. Taconian Orogeny in the New England Appalachians; collision between Laurentia and the Shelburne Falls Arc. *Geology* 26: 215–18.

Kim, J., R. Coish, M. Evans, and G. Dick. 2003. "Supra-subduction zone extensional magmatism in Vermont and adjacent Quebec: Implications for early Paleozoic Appalachian tectonics." *Geological Society of America Bulletin* 115, no. 12: 1552–69.

Lougee, R. J.1939. Geology of the Connecticut River watershed. In *Biological Survey of the Connecticut Watershed*, Survey Report No. 4. Concord, N.H.: New Hampshire Fish and Game Department.

Lyons, J. B., W. A. Bothner, R. H. Moench, and J. B. Thompson. 1997. *Bedrock Geologic Map of New Hampshire.* Concord, N.H.: New Hampshire Deparment of Environmental Services and United States Geological Survey.

Moench, R. H., and J. N. Aleinikoff. 2002. Stratigraphy, geochronology, and accretionary terrane settings of two Bronson Hill arc sequences, northern New England. *Physics and Chemistry of the Earth* 27: 47–95.

Press, F. and R. Siever. 1986. *Earth.* New York: W. H. Freeman and Co.

Ratcliffe, N. M., T. R. Armstrong, and J. N. Aleinikoff. 1997. Stratigraphy, geochronology, and tectonic evolution of the basement and cover rocks of the Chester and Athens Dome. In *Guidebook to Field Trips in Vermont and Adjacent New Hampshire and New York*, ed. T. W. Grover et al., B6 1–55. New England Intercollegiate Geological Conference, vol. 89.

Ratcliffe, N. M., W. E. Hames, and R. S. Stanley. 1998. Interpretation of ages of arc magmatism, metamorphism, and collisional tectonics in the Taconian Orogeny of western New England. *American Journal of Science* 298: 791–97.

Raymo, C., and M. E. Raymo. 1989. *Written in Stone: A Geological and Natural History of the Northeastern United States.* Chester, CT: Globe Pequot Press.

Schneiderman, J. 1989. The Ascutney Mountain breccia: Field and petrologic evidence for an overlapping relationship between Vermont sequence and New Hampshire sequence rocks. *American Journal of Science* 289 (June): 771–811.

Spear, F. S., M. J. Kohn, J. T. Cheney, and F. Florence. 2002. Metamorphic, thermal, and tectonic evolution of central New England. *Journal of Petrology* 43, no. 11: 2097–2120.

Sprear, F. S., J. T. Cheney, and J. M. Pyle. 2003. "Monazite geochronology and the Alleghenian Assembly of central New England." In *Guidebook for Field Trips in the Five College Region*, eds. J. B. Brady and J. T. Cheney, 95th annual meeting of the New England Intercollegiate Geological Conference, Amherst and Northampton, Mass.

Stanley, R. S., and N. M. Ratcliffe. 1985. Tectonic synthesis of the Taconic orogeny in western New England. *Geological Society of America* 96: 1227–50.

Thompson, P. J., and T. B. Thompson. 2003. Prospect Rock thrust: Western limit of the Taconian accretionary prism in the northern Green Mountain Anticlinorium, Vermont. *Canadian Journal of Earth Sciences* 40: 269–84.

Tucker, R. D., and P. Robinson. 1990. Age and setting of the Bronson Hill magmatic arc: A re-evaluation based on U-Pb zircon ages in southern New England. *Geological Society of America Bulletin* 102: 1404–19.

Van Diver, B. 1987. *Roadside Geology of Vermont and New Hampshire.* Missoula, Mont.: Mountain Press.

van Staal, C. R. 2006. "Pre-Carboniferous Metallogeny of the Canadian Applachians." http://gsc.nrcan.gc.ca/mindep/synth_prov/appalachian/index_e.php.

van Staal, C. R., J. F. Dewey, C. Mac Niocaill, and W. S. McKerrow. 1998. The Cambrian-Silurian tectonic evolution of the northern Appalachians and British Caledonides: History of a complex, west and southwest Pacific-type segment of Iapetus. In *Lyell: The Past is the Key to the Present*, ed. D. J. Blundell et al., 199–242. Geological Society Special Publication 143.

Williams, H., and P. St-Julien. 1982. The Baie Verte-Brompton Line: Early Paleozoic continent ocean interface in the Canadian Appalachians. In *Major Structural Zones and Faults of the Northern Appalachians*, ed. P. St-Julien et al., 177–208. Geological Association of Canada Special Paper 24.

Wilson, M. 1989. *Igneous Petrogenesis: A Global Tectonic Approach.* London: Unwin Hyman.

2. Glacial Geology (pages 12–15)

Bierman, P. R., P. T. Davis, and M. W. Caffee. 2000. *Old Surfaces on New England Summits Imply Thin Laurentide Ice*. Reno, Nev.: Geological Society of America, Annual Meeting.

Boothroyd, J. C., J. H. Freedman, H. B. Brenner, and J. R. Stone. 1998. The glacial geology of southern Rhode Island. In *Guidebook to field trips in Rhode Island and adjacent regions of Connecticut and Massachusetts*, ed. D. P. Murray, C5-1-25. New England Intercollegiate Geologic Conference, 90th annual meeting.

Brigham-Grette, J. 2001. Drainage history of Glacial Lake Hitchcock and paleoclimatic implications of late Quaternary sediments and terraces in the central Connecticut Valley, New England (abstract). *Geological Society of America Abstracts with Programs, Northeastern Section*.

Davis, P. T. 1999. Cirques of the Presidential Range, New Hampshire, and surrounding alpine areas in the northeastern United States. *Géographie physique et Quaternaire* 53: 25–45.

Doll, C. G., W. M. Cady, J. B. Thompson, and M. P. Billings Jr. 1961. *Centennial Geologic Map of Vermont*. Vermont Geological Survey, scale 1:250,000.

Jacobs, E. J. 1950. *The Physical Features of Vermont*. Waterbury, Vt.: Vermont State Development Department, Vermont Geological Survey.

Larsen, F. D. 1985. The last great ice sheet and the origin of Quechee Gorge. *Window of Vermont Magazine* (Summer).

Lougee, R. J. 1939. Geology of the Connecticut River watershed. In *Biological Survey of the Connecticut Watershed*, Survey Report No. 4. Concord, N.H.: New Hampshire Fish and Game Department.

Raymo, C., and M. E. Raymo. 1989. *Written in Stone: A Geological and Natural History of the Northeastern United States*. Chester, Conn.: Globe Pequot Press.

Ridge, J. C. 2003. The last deglaciation of the northeastern United States: A combined varve, paleomagnetic, and calibrated 14c chronology. In *Geoarchaeology of Landscapes in the Glaciated Northeast*, ed. David L. Cremeens and John P. Hart. New York State Museum Bulletin 497.

Ridge, J. C., M. R. Besonen, M. Brochu, et al. 1999. Varve, paleomagnetic, and 14c chronologies for Late Pleistocene events in New Hampshire and Vermont, U.S.A. *Géographie physique et Quaternaire* 53: 79–107.

Springston, George S. 2000. *Surficial Geology of the Newbury 7.5 Minute Quadrangle*. Open File Report. Waterbury, Vt.: Vermont Geological Survey.

Stewart, D. P., and P. MacClintock. 1970. *Surficial Geologic Map of Vermont*. (Waterbury, Vt.: Vermont Geological Survey, Department of Water Resources. Scale 1:250,000.

Thompson, W. B., B. K. Fowler, and C. C. Dorion. 1999. Deglaciation of the northwestern White Mountains. *Géographie physique et Quaternaire* 53.

Van Diver, B. 1987. *Roadside Geology of Vermont and New Hampshire*. Missoula, Mont.: Mountain Press.

3. Soils (pages 16–22)

Brady, N. C., and R. R. Weil. 2002. *The Nature and Properties of Soils*. Englewood Cliffs, N.J.: Prentice Hall.

Kohnke, H., and D. P. Franzmeier. 1995. *Soil Science Simplified*. Long Grove, Ill.: Waveland Press.

U.S. Department of Agriculture-Natural Resources Conservation Service.

1999. *Soil Taxonomy, a Basic System of Soil Classification for Making and Interpreting Soil Surveys*. USDA-NRCS, Agricultural Handbook 436.

Part II. Climate and Weather

4. Weather and Climate (pages 25–28)

Ludlum, David. 1976. *The Country Journal: New England Weather Book*. Boston: Houghton Mifflin.

Zielinski, Gregory A., and Barry D. Keim. 2003. *New England Weather, New England Climate*. Hanover, N.H.: University Press of New England.

5. Extreme Weather Events (pages 29–32)

Bazilchuck, N. 1999. At nature's mercy: Vermonters prove their mettle through floods, flu and blizzards. *Burlington Free Press*, March 29.

Olson, S. A. 2006. Flood of October 8 and 9, 2005, on Cold River in Walpole, Langdon, and Alstead and on Warren Brook in Alstead, New Hampshire. *U.S. Geological Survey Open-File Report 2006-1221*.

PBS Online. 2002. American Experience: The hurricane of '38. http://www.pbs.org/wgbh/amex/hurricane38/index.html.

Scotti, R. A. 2003. *Sudden Sea: The Great Hurricane of 1938*. Boston: Little Brown and Co.

Zielinski, G. A., and B. D. Keim. 2003. *New England Weather, New England Climate*. Hanover, N.H.: University Press of New England.

6. Climate Change (pages 33–36)

Intergovernmental Panel on Climate Change. 2007. *Climate Change 2007: The Physical Science Basis*. IPCC Secretariat, World Meteorological Organization, Geneva, Switzerland, February 5.

Lines, G., C. P. Wake, et al. 2006. *Cross Border Indicators of Climate Change over the Past Century: Northeastern United States and Canadian Maritime Region*. Gulf of Maine Council on the Marine Environment.

Union of Concerned Scientists. 2006a. *Climate Change in the U.S. Northeast: A Report of the Northeast Climate Impacts Assessment*. Cambridge, Mass.: UCS Publications.

———. 2006b. *The Changing Northeast Climate: Our Choices, Our Legacy*. Cambridge, Mass.: UCS Publications.

Wake, C. P., and Cool Air–Clean Planet. 2005. *Indicators of Climate Change in the Northeast 2005*. Durham, N.H.: The Climate Change Research Center, University of New Hampshire.

Zielinski, G. A., and B. D. Keim. 2003. *New England Weather, New England Climate*. Hanover, N.H.: University Press of New England.

Part III. The River and Watershed

Introduction (page 38)

Grant, Ellsworth S. 1967. The mainstream of New England. *American Heritage* (April 1967). Reprinted in W. D. Wetherell, ed., *This American River:*

Five Centuries of Writing about the Connecticut. Hanover, N.H.: University Press of New England, 2002.

Hard, Walter. 1947. *The Connecticut.* New York: Rinehart & Company.

8. Groundwater *(pages 49–51)*

Flanagan, S. M. 1996. "Geohydrology and water quality of stratified-drift aquifers in the Middle Connecticut River Basin, West-central New Hampshire," *U.S. Geological Survey Water-Resources Investigations Report 94-4181.*

Hodges, A. L., Jr., and David Butterfield. 1967–1968. *Groundwater Favorability Maps of Eleven Major Basins in Vermont.* Vermont Department of Water Resources.

Medalie, Laura, and R. B. Moore. 1995. Ground-water resources of New Hampshire: Stratified-drift aquifers. *U.S. Geological Survey Water Resources Investigations Report 95-4100.*

Moore, R. B. 2004. Quality of water in the fractured-bedrock aquifer of New Hampshire. *U.S. Geological Survey Scientific Investigations Report 2004-5093.*

9. Streamflow *(pages 52–58)*

Cooke, M. G., Roy S. Socolow, and J. L. Zanca. 2004. A century of service—100 years of streamflow-data collection on the Connecticut River, Montague City, Massachusetts. *USGA Fact Sheet FS-2004-3049.* Montague City, Mass.

Keirstead, Chandlee, R. G. Kiah, S. L. Ward, and G. S. Hilgendorf. 2005. *Water Resources Data for New Hampshire and Vermont, Water Year 2004.* U.S. Geological Survey Water-Data Report NH-VT-04-1.

Kiah, R. G., Chandlee Keirstead, R. O. Brown, and G. S. Hilgendorf. 2006. *Water Resources Data for New Hampshire and Vermont, 2005.* U.S. Geological Survey Water-Data Report NH-VT-05-1.

Moore, R. B., C. M. Johnston, K. W. Robinson, and J. R. Deacon. 2004. *Estimation of Total Nitrogen and Phosphorus in New England Streams Using Spatially Referenced Regression Models.* U.S. Geological Survey Scientific Investigations Report 2004-5012.

Randall, A. D. 1996. *Mean Annual Runoff, Precipitation, and Evapotranspiration in the Glaciated Northeastern United States, 1951–80.* U.S. Geological Survey Open-File Report 96-395.

10. Water Quality *(pages 59–64)*

Evers, David C. 2005. *Mercury Connections: The Extent and Effects of Mercury Pollution in Northeastern North America.* Gorham, Maine: Biodiversity Research Institute.

Evers, David C. et al. 2007. Biological mercury hotspots in the northeastern United States and southeastern Canada. *Bioscience* 57, no. 1 (January).

Federal Security Agency. 1951. *Connecticut River Drainage Basin: A Cooperative State-Federal Report on Water Pollution.* Federal Security Agency, Public Health Service.

U.S. EPA. 2006. *Connecticut River Fish Tissue Contaminant Study: Ecological and Human Health Screening (2000).* Prepared for the Connecticut River Fish Tissue Working Group by Greg Hellyer, Ecosystem Assessment Unit.

North Chelmsford, Mass.: USEPA–New England Regional Laboratory, May.

11. Water Management *(pages 65–71)*

Field, John. 2006. *Fluvial Geomorphology Assessment of the Northern Connecticut River Tributaries.* Charlestown, N.H.: Connecticut River Joint Commissions.

———. *Fluvial Geomorphology Assessment of the Northern Connecticut River, Vermont and New Hampshire.* Charlestown, N.H.: Connecticut River Joint Commissions.

Lambert, Kathy Fallon. 1998. *Instream Flow Uses, Values and Policies in the Upper Connecticut River Watershed.* Charlestown, N.H.: Connecticut River Joint Commissions.

Nislow, Keith H., Francis J. Magilligan, Heidi Fassnacht, Doug Bechtel, and Ana Ruesinka. 2002. Effects of impoundment on the flood regime of natural floodplain communities in the upper Connecticut River. *Journal of the American Water Resources Association* (December).

Part IV. The Natural Environment

12. Habitats and Natural Communities *(pages 75–81)*

DeGraaf, Richard M., and Mariko Yamasaki. 2001. *New England Wildlife: Habitat, Natural History, and Distribution.* Hanover, N.H.: University Press of New England.

DeGraaf, Richard M., Mariko Yamasaki, William B. Leak, and Anna M. Lester. 2006. *Technical Guide to Forest Wildlife Habitat Management in New England.* Burlington, Vt.: University of Vermont Press.

Sperduto, Daniel, and W. Nichols. 2004. *Natural Communities of New Hampshire.* Concord, N.H.: New Hampshire Natural Heritage Bureau and The Nature Conservancy.

Sperduto, Daniel D., et al. 2000. *Black Gum (*Nyssa sylvatica*) Marsh in New Hampshire.* Concord, N.H.: New Hampshire Natural Heritage Inventory.

Thompson, E., and E. Sorenson. 2005. *Wetland, Woodland, Wildland: A Guide to the Natural Communities of Vermont.* Waterbury, Vt.: Vermont Department of Fish and Wildlife and The Nature Conservancy.

13. Forests *(pages 82–89)*

Bormann, F. H., and M. F. Buell. 1964. Old-age stand of hemlock-northern hardwood forest in central Vermont. *Bulletin of the Torrey Botanical Club* 91: 451–65.

Bormann, F. H., and G. E. Likens. 1979. *Pattern and Process in a Forested Ecosystem.* New York: Springer-Verlag.

Braun, E. L. 1950. *Deciduous Forests of Eastern North America.* New York: Hafner Press.

Cline, A. C., and S. H. Spurr. 1942. The virgin upland forest of central New England: A study of old growth stands in the Pisgah Mountain section of southwestern New Hampshire. *Harvard Forest Bulletin* 21.

Cogbill, C. V., J. Burk, and G. Motzkin. 2002. The forests of presettlement New England, USA: Spatial and compositional patterns based on town proprietor surveys. *Journal of Biogeography* 29: 1279–1304.

Parker, Trudy Ann. 1994. *Aunt Sarah: Woman of the Dawnland*. Lancaster, N.H.: Dawnland Publications.

Stewart-Smith, David. 1998. *The Pennacook Indians and the New England Frontier, 1604–1733*. PhD dissertation, Union Institute.

Thomas, Peter. 1990. *In the Maelstrom of Change*. New York: Garland Publishing.

21. Early Settlement (pages 137–144)

Bacon, Edwin M. 1911. *The Connecticut River Valley and the Valley of the Connecticut*. New York: G. P. Putnam.

Daniell, Jere R. 1981. *Colonial New Hampshire: A History*. Millwood, N.Y.: KTO Press.

———. *Experiment in Republicanism: New Hampshire Politics and the American Revolution, 1741–1794*. Cambridge, Mass.: Harvard University Press.

Doan, Daniel. 1997. *Indian Stream Republic: Settling a New England Frontier, 1785–1842*. Hanover, N.H.: University Press of New England.

Williamson, Chilton. 1949. *Vermont in Quandary, 1763–1825*. Montpelier, Vt.: Vermont Historical Society.

22. Early Agriculture (pages 145–150)

Benes, Peter, ed. 1995. *Plants and People*. Dublin Seminar for New England Folklife. Boston: Boston University.

Goodwin, Harry Samuel. 1986. *The Clock Turned Back: Reminiscences of a Nineteenth Century Childhood*. Portsmouth, N.H.: Peter E. Randall.

Hudson, Robert F., ed. 1976. *The Yankee Farmer*. Topsfield, Mass.: Americana Archives.

Russell, Howard S. 1982. *A Long, Deep Furrow: Three Centuries of Farming in New England*. Hanover, N.H.: University Press of New England.

Walker, Joseph B. 1906. *Chronicles of an Old New England Farm: The House and Farm of the First Minister of Concord, NH, 1726–1906*. Concord, N.H.: n.p.

Wilson, Harold Fisher. 1936. *The Hill Country of Northern New England: Its Social and Economic History, 1790–1930*. New York: Columbia University Press.

23. The Industrial Era (pages 151–156)

Abbott, Collamer. 1973. *Green Mountain Copper: The Story of Vermont's Red Metal*. Randolph, Vt.: Herald Printery.

Albers, J. 2000. *Hands on the Land: A Story of the Vermont Landscape*. Cambridge, Mass: MIT Press.

Aldrich, Roger W. 1996. *The Iron Industry in Franconia and Sugar Hill, 1805–1860?* Sugar Hill, N.H.: self-published.

Delaney, E. 1983. *The Connecticut River: New England's Historic Waterway*. Guilford, Conn: Globe Pequot Press.

Gove, Bill. 2003. *Log Drives on the Connecticut River*. Littleton, N.H.: Bondcliff Books.

Hammarstrom, J. M., J. C. Jackson, R. Barden, and R. R. Seal. 1999. *Characterization of Mine Waste at the Abandoned Elizabeth Copper Mine, Vermont* [abstract]. Geological Society of America, Abstracts with Programs, New England, vol. 31, A-20.

Meeks, H. 1986. *Time and Change in Vermont*. Guilford, Conn: Globe Pequot Press.

Pike, Robert. 1975. *Drama on the Connecticut*. Eatontown, N.J.: The HH Press.

———. 1999. *Spiked Boots: Sketches of the North Country*. Woodstock, Vt.: Countryman Press.

———. 1999. *Tall Trees, Tough Men: A Vivid, Anecdotal History of Logging and Log-Driving in New England*. New York: Norton.

Rolando, V. 1992. *200 Years of Soot, Sweat and Toil: The History and Archeology of Vermont's Iron, Charcoal, and Lime Industries*. Burlington: Vermont Archeological Society.

WGBY. 2005. *Dynamite, Whiskey and Wood: Connecticut Log Drives 1870–1915*. Video. Springfield, Mass.: WGBY.

Part VI. Current Watershed Patterns

24. Contemporary Agriculture (pages 159–162)

Farming Magazine. St. Johnsbury, Vt.: Moose River Publishing Co.

Fritz, Sonja-Sarai. 2006. *New Hampshire's Changing Agricultural Land Use*. Keene, N.H.: Keene State College, Department of Geography.

Jager, Ronald. 2004. *The Fate of Family Farming: Variations on an American Idea*. Hanover, N.H.: University Press of New England.

New England Country Folks. Weekly newspaper. Palatine Bridge, N.Y.: Lee Publications.

New Hampshire Department of Agriculture, Markets and Food. *Weekly Market Bulletin*. Concord, N.H.: New Hampshire Department of Agriculture, Markets and Food.

Reidel, Carl. 1982. *New England Prospects: Critical Choices in a Time of Change*. Hanover, N.H.: University Press of New England.

Ruhf, Kathryn Z., ed. 1999. *Farmland Transfer and Protection in New England: A Guide for Entering and Exiting Farmers*. Belchertown, Mass.: New England Small Farm Institute.

———. *Northeast Farms to Food: Understanding our Region's Food System*. (Belchertown, Mass.: Northeast Sustainable Agriculture Working Group.

Vermont Agency of Agriculture, Food and Markets. *Agriview*. Montpelier, Vt.: Vermont Agency of Agriculture, Food and Markets.

U.S. Department of Agriculture. *Annual Bulletin, New England Agricultural Statistics*. Concord, N.H.: U.S. Department of Agriculture National Agricultural Statistics Service.

25. Land Use (pages 163–167)

Foster, David R., and John F. O'Keefe. 2000. *New England Forests through Time: Insights from the Harvard Forest Dioramas*. Cambridge, Mass.: Harvard University Press.

Harvard University. Landscape History of New Englad. Seven dioramas at the Fisher Museum, Harvard Forest. http://harvardforest.fas.harvard.edu/museum/landscape.html.

Peacham (Vt.) Planning Commission. *Peacham Zoning Bylaws*.

Southwest Regional Planning Commission. 2002. *Guiding Change: The Southwest Region at the Beginning of the 21st Century*. Keene, N.H.: Southwest Regional Planning Commission.

Two Rivers-Ottauquechee Regional Commission. 2007. *2007 Regional Plan*. Woodstock, Vt.: Two Rivers-Ottauquechee Regional Commission.

Vermont State Environmental Board. 2000. *Act 250: A Guide to Vermont's Land Use Law*. Montpelier, Vt.: State Environmental Board, November.

26. *The Postindustrial Economy (pages 168–173)*

Florida, Richard. 2002. *The Rise of the Creative Class*. New York: Basic Books.

Grogan, Paul S., and Proscio, Tony. 2000. *Comeback Cities*. Boulder, Colo.: Westview Press.

Mansfield, Howard. 1993. *In the Memory House*. Golden, Colo.: Fulcrum Press.

New Hampshire Department of Employment Security. 2006. *Looking Forward: Preparing for the Future New Hampshire Economy*. Concord, N.H.: New Hampshire Department of Employment Security.

New Hampshire Department of Employment Security. *Vital Signs: New Hampshire Economic and Social Indicators*. Concord, N.H.: New Hampshire Department of Employment Security, published annually.

Pindell, Terry. 1995. *A Good Place to Live*. Ontario: Henry Holt Publishers.

Ray, Paul, and Sherry Ruth Anderson. 2000. *The Cultural Creatives*. New York: Three Rivers Press.

Sears, John F. 1989. *Sacred Places*. Amherst: University of Massachusetts Press.

Vermont Department of Economic Development. 2002. *Research Innovations and Vermont's Economy*. Montpelier: Vermont Department of Economic Development.

Vermont Department of Economic Development. 2005. *Strategic Vision and Business Plan for Job Creation and Economic Development*. Montpelier: Vermont Department of Economic Development.

Weiss, Michael J. 1988. *The Clustering of America*. New York: Tilden Press.

27. *Demographics (pages 174–182)*

U.S. Census Bureau. American FactFinder. http://factfinder.census.gov/home/saff/main.html.

Vermont Community Data Bank. Center for Rural Studies, University of Vermont. http://crs.uvm.edu/databank/.

Part VII. Transportation and Energy

28. *Water Travel (pages 185–188)*

Adney, Edwin Tappan, and Howard Chapelle. 1964. *The Bark Canoes and Skin Boats of North America*. U.S. National Museum Bulletin no. 230. Washington, D.C.: U.S. Government Printing Office.

Blaisdell, Katharine. 1979. *Over the River and Through the Years*. Littleton, N.H.: Courier Printing Co.

Carter, George Calvin. 1945. *Samuel Morey*. Concord, N.H.: privately printed. In *This American River*, ed. W. E. Wetherell. Hanover, N.H.: University Press of New England, 2002.

Falcon, Thomas. 1967. *The Ledyard Canoe Club of Dartmouth*. Hanover, NH: 1967.

Farrell, Gabriel, Jr. 1915. *Capt. Samuel Morey Who Built a Steamboat Fourteen Years Before Fulton*. Manchester, N.H.: Standard Book Co.

Jacobus, Melanothon W. 1956. *The Connecticut River Steamboat Story*. Hartford, Conn.: Connecticut Historical Society, 1956. Reprinted in Wetherell, *This American River*.

Parker, Trudy Ann. 1994. *Aunt Sarah: Woman of the Dawnland*. Lancaster, N.H.: Dawnland Publications.

Pike, Robert E. 1999. *Spiked Boots: Sketches of the North Country*. Woodstock, Vt.: Countryman Press.

Roberts, Kenneth G., and Philip Shackleton. 1983. *The Canoe: A History of the Craft from Panama to the Arctic*. Camden, Maine: International Marine Publishing Company.

Weinraub, Ann Plane. 1990. *Logboats of New England: Amerindian Interaction with Euro-Americans over Three Centuries*. Unpublished masters thesis, Boston University.

Wikoff, Jerold. 1993. John Ledyard. *Dartmouth Alumni Magazine* 85, no. 9: 18–25.

———. 1985. *The Upper Valley: An Illustrated Tour along the Connecticut River before the Twentieth Century*. Chelsea, Vt.: Chelsea Green.

29. *Roads (pages 189–195)*

Allen, Richard Saunders. 2004. *Covered Bridges of the Northeast*. Mineola, N.Y.: Dover.

Garvin, Donna-Belle, and James L. Garvin. 1988. *On the Road North of Boston: New Hampshire Taverns and Turnpikes, 1700–1900*. Hanover, N.H.: University Press of New England.

Jordan, Charles, and James McIntosh. 2004. *Northern Journeys*. Littleton, N.H.: North Country Council, et al.

Northeast Vermont Development Association. 1997. *The Bayley Hazen Military Road Field Guide* (pamphlet). St. Johnsbury, Vt.: Northeast Vermont Development Association.

Walden Public Library. 1986. *The History of Walden, Vermont*. Sponsored by the Walden Public Library. Randolph Center, Vt.: Greenhill Books.

Wikoff, Jerold. 1981. Historically speaking. *Valley News* [Lebanon, N.H.], October 27, 13.

Wood, Frederic J. 1919. *The Turnpikes of New England*. Boston: Marshall Jones Company. New abridged edition, with an introduction by Ronald Dale Karr. Pepperell, Mass.: Branch Line Press, 1997.

30. *Railroads (pages 196–202)*

Cheasley, Dennis. 1974. A quick run through New Hampshire history. *The New Hampshire Times Magazine* [Concord, N.H.], April 4.

Jones, Robert C. 1993. *Railroads of Vermont*. Shelburne, Vt.: New England Press.

Lindsell, Robert M. 2000. *The Rail Lines of Northern New England*. Pepperell. Mass.: Branch Line Press.

31. *Aviation (pages 203–208)*

New Hampshire Department of Transportation. 1993. *New Hampshire State Airport System Plan, 1993 and Update*. Concord, N.H.: Division of Aeronautics, State Department of Transportation.

———. 2006. *Recommendations for the Ten Year Transportation Improve-*

ment Plan, 2007–2016. Concord, N.H.: New Hampshire Department of Transportation.

Vermont Agency of Transportation. 1998. *Vermont's Airport System Policy Plan*. Montpelier, Vt.: Vermont Agency of Transportation.

32. Energy (pages 209–213)

New Hampshire Office of Energy and Community Services. 2002. *New Hampshire Energy Plan*. Concord, N.H.: Governor's Office of Energy and Community Services, November.

———. 2006. Energy Advisory Board annual report. Concord, N.H.

Vermont Department of Public Service. 2005. *Vermont Electric Plan 2005*. Vermont Department of Public Service, January.

Part VIII. Culture, Education, and Recreation

33. Cultural Institutions (pages 217–220)

Ewald, Richard J., with Adair D. Mulligan. 2003. *Proud to Live Here*. Charlestown, N.H.: Connecticut River Joint Commissions.

34. Dartmouth College (pages 221–224)

Zug, James. 2005. *American Traveler: The Life and Adventures of John Ledyard, The Man Who Dreamed of Walking the World*. New York: Basic Books.

35. Tourism and Historic Sites (pages 225–229)

Ewald, Richard J., with Adair D. Mulligan. 2003. *Proud to Live Here*. Charlestown, N.H.: Connecticut River Joint Commissions.

Tolles, Bryant F., and Carolyn K. Tolles. 1979. *New Hampshire Architecture: An Illustrated Guide*. Hanover, N.H.: University Press of New England.

36. Recreation (pages 230–235)

Connecticut River Watershed Council. 2007. *The Connecticut River Boating Guide: Source to Sea*. Guilford, Conn.: Globe Pequot.

Dwight, Timothy. 1823. *Travels in New England and New York*. London: W. Baynes and Son, and Ogle, Duncan & Co.

Kibling, Mary L. 1989. *Walks and Rambles in the Upper Connecticut River Valley*. Woodstock, Vt.: Countryman Press.

MacKay, Dick. 2003. *Adventures in Paradise: Exploring the Upper Connecticut Valley of Vermont and New Hampshire on a Bicycle*. Hanover, N.H.: Faculty Ridge Books.

Silverberg, Judith K. 1997. *New Hampshire Wildlife Viewing Guide*. Helena, Mont.: Falcon Press.

Vital Communities. 2001. *Valley Quest: 89 Treasure Hunts in the Upper Valley*. White River Junction, Vt.: Vital Communities.

———. *Valley Quest II: 75 More Treasure Hunts in the Upper Valley*. White River Junction, Vt.: Vital Communities.

Wetherell, W. D. 1991. *Vermont River*. New York: Lyons Press.

———. 1991. *Upland Stream: Notes on the Fishing Passion*. Boston: Little, Brown.

———. 1998. *One River More*. New York: Lyons Press.

Connecticut River Joint Commissioners

This Atlas has benefited from the insights and contributions of all who have served as Connecticut River Joint Commissioners, 1990–2008.

New Hampshire Connecticut River Valley Resource Commission

Robert Christie, Lancaster
Bruce Clement, Westmoreland
Michael Dannehy, Woodsville
Joan DeBrine, Charlestown
Irene Domini, Charlestown
Glenn English, North Haverhill
Richard Fabrizo, North Haverhill
Nancy Franklin, Plainfield
Robert Harcke, Westmoreland
Erling Heistad, Lebanon
Cleveland Kapala, Canterbury
Robert Kline, Plainfield
Robert Love, Claremont
Denise Meadows, Keene
Robert Michenfelder, Piermont
Jeffrey Miller, Walpole
Kully Mindermann, Keene
George Moulton, Charlestown
Mary Sloat, Northumberland
Hugh Sullivan, Lebanon
Henry Swan, Lyme
Ann Sweet, Sullivan
John Tucker, New London
Lawrence Underhill, Piermont
George Watkins, Walpole
John Wolter, Pike

Vermont Connecticut River Watershed Advisory Commission

Annalei Babson, Island Pond
Kenneth Bishop, Springfield
Dennis Borchardt, Randolph
Leonard Buchanan, Brattleboro
Charles Carter, St. Johnsbury
Mary Daly, Ely
Peter Daniels, Weathersfield
Geoffrey Dates, Hartland
David Deen, Putney
Kevin Geiger, St. Johnsbury
Peter Gregory, Hartland
Richard Hodge, Ely
Thomas Kennedy, Ascutney
Scott Labun, Newbury
Thomas Lauritsen, Perkinsville
John Lawe, Norwich
Stephen Long, Corinth
Beverly Major, Westminster
James Matteau, Brattleboro
Timothy McKay, Peacham
Alison Meaders, St. Johnsbury
Gary Moore, Bradford
Gayle Ottmann, Quechee
Jeffrey Owen, St. Johnsbury
Peter Richardson, Norwich
Joseph Sampson, Bradford
Lew Sorenson, Brattleboro
Michaela Stickney, Waterbury
Stephan Syz, Montpelier
Nathaniel Tripp, Barnet
Stephen Walasewicz, Perkinsville
Brendan Whittaker, Brunswick
Norman Wright, Putney

Atlas Advisory Group

Richard Birnie
Rebecca Brown
Charlie Browne
Emily Bryant
Laura Conkey
Jere Daniell
George Demko
Sharon Francis
Andrew Friedland
Bob Gagliuso
Kevin Geiger
John Harrigan
John Lawe
Barry Lawson
Timothy McKay
Richard Moore
Adair Mulligan
William Murphy
Fred Pond
Sarah Rooker
Michaela Stickney
Ned Swanberg
Stephen Taylor
Nathaniel Tripp
Stephen Walasewicz
Walter Wetherell

Illustration and Table Credits

Page 151. Courtesy of American Precision Museum.

Page 152. Courtesy of Vermont Landscape Change Project, Collamer Abbott Collection, Bailey/Howe Library, University of Vermont.

Page 153. Frank J. Barrett Jr. collection.

Page 154. *Bottom:* Courtesy of Christopher Grotke. *Top:* Courtesy of Christopher Grotke.

Page 155. Bottom Courtesy of Windsor Historical Society.

Page 156. Courtesy of Springfield Historical Society.

Page 154. *Top:* Frank J. Barrett Jr. collection.

Page 157. Jerry and Marcy Monkman/EcoPhotography.com photo.

Page 158. Rebecca Brown photo.

Page 159. Rebecca Brown photo.

Page 161. Beverly Major photo/Connecticut River Joint Commissions.

Page 162. *Top:* Beverly Major photo. *Bottom:* Rebecca Brown photo.

Page 163. Jerry and Marcy Monkman/EcoPhotography.com photo.

Page 164. *Top:* Rebecca Brown photo. *Bottom left:* Rufus Perkins collection.

Page 164. *Bottom right:* Rebecca Brown photo.

Page 168. *Top:* Frank J. Barrett Jr. collection. *Bottom:* Frank J. Barrett Jr. collection.

Page 169. *Top:* Rebecca Brown photo. *Middle:* Frank J. Barrett Jr. collection. *Bottom:* Rebecca Brown photo.

Page 170. *Right:* Rebecca Brown photo. *Left:* Rebecca Brown photo.

Page 171. Courtesy of Dartmouth Hitchcock Medical Center/photographer Mark Washburn.

Page 183. Photo Courtesy of TransCanada.

Page 184. New England Transportation Museum collection, from Vermont History, October 1955.

Page 185. *Top:* New England Transportation Museum, Susan Berry Langsten illustration. *Bottom:* New England Transportation Museum collection.

Page 186. Courtesy Hartford Historical Society and Vermont Landscape Change Project.

Page 189. Frank J. Barrett Jr. collection.

Page 192. *Top:* NAIP 2003 orthophoto acquired from NH GRANIT: http://www.granit.sr.unh.edu; Originator: USDA FSA APFO Aerial Photography Field Office, NAIP Countywide MrSID Mosaic; map created by Emily Bryant in Dartmouth College Earth Sciences Department ASA Lab, courtesy of Richard Birnie. *Bottom:* Frank J. Barrett Jr. collection.

Page 193 *Top:* Connecticut River Joint Commissions photo. *Bottom left:* Frank J. Barrett Jr. collection. *Bottom right:* Rebecca Brown photo.

Page 195. Rebecca Brown photo.

Page 196. *Top:* Collection of New England Transportation Museum. *Bottom:* Collection of New England Transportation Museum.

Page 197. Courtesy of Dartmouth College Library.

Page 198. Collection of New England Transportation Museum.

Page 199. *Top left:* Frank J. Barrett Jr. collection. *Top right:* Rebecca Brown photo. *Bottom:* Collection of New England Transportation Museum.

Page 200. *Top:* Collection of the New England Transportation Museum. *Bottom:* Collection of the New England Transportation Museum.

Page 205. Courtesy of Dartmouth-Hitchcock Medical Center/photographer Mark Washburn.

Page 206. *Top:* Courtesy of Lebanon Airport, photo by Chapin Photography. *Bottom:* Photo courtesy of Morningside Flight Park.

Page 207. *Left:* New England Transportation Museum collection. *Right:* Rebecca Brown photo.

Page 208. Rick Russell photo/courtesy of the Hartford Area Chamber of Commerce.

Page 209. Rebecca Brown photo.

Page 210. *Top:* Frank J. Barrett Jr. collection. *Bottom:* Frank J. Barrett Jr. collection.

Page 212. *Top:* Frank J. Barrett Jr. collection. *Bottom left:* David L. Deen photo. *Bottom right:* Rebecca Brown photo.

Page 215. Eric Aho, *Connecticut River Looking South*, 2005, oil on linen, 22 x 40 inches. Private Collection. Image courtesy of Eric Aho.

Page 216. Parrish, Maxfield (1870–1966). *The Canyon.* Oil on board. 19.5 x 15 inches. Private collection. From the archives of Alma Gilbert. Used with permission.

Page 217. Dave Govatski photo.

Page 218. *Top:* Image courtesy of Jeanette Fournier. *Bottom left:* Tony Elliot photo/courtesy of the Rockingham Arts and Museum Project. *Bottom right:* Photo courtesy of the Weathervane Theatre.

Page 219. *Right:* Rebecca Brown photo. *Left:* Photo courtesy of the Fairbanks Museum.

Page 221. Joseph Mehling/Dartmouth College Photographer.

Page 222. *Top left:* Joseph Mehling/Dartmouth College Photographer. *Top right:* Dartmouth College, Hood Museum of Art. *Bottom:* Courtesy of Dartmouth College, Rauner Special Collections.

Page 223. *Top:* Joseph Mehling/Dartmouth College Photographer. *Bottom:* Natalie Koch photo.

Page 224. *Left:* Joseph Mehling/Dartmouth College Photographer. *Right:* Joseph Mehling/Dartmouth College Photographer.

Page 225. Photo courtesy of Fort at No. 4.

Page 226. *Top:* Rebecca Brown photo. *Bottom:* Rebecca Brown photo.

Page 227. Rebecca Brown photo.

Page 228. *Top:* Rebecca Brown photo. *Bottom:* Frank J. Barrett Jr. collection.

Page 229. *Right:* Rebecca Brown photo. *Left:* Photo courtesy of the National Park Service.

Page 230. Rebecca Brown photo.

Page 232. *Top:* Joey Kulkin/Connecticut River Joint Commissions photo. *Bottom:* Adair Mulligan photo.

Page 233. *Top left:* Adair Mulligan photo. *Top right:* Gary W. Moore photo. *Bottom:* Edith Tucker photo.

FIGURES

Figure 1. Modified from Wilson 1989.

Figure 2. Modified from Geological Society of America 1999.

Figure 3. Modified from Stanley and Ratcliffe 1985 and Kim et al. 2003.

Figure 4. Modified from Press and Siever 1986.

Figure 5. Graphic developed by Northern Cartographic from author's text.

Figure 6. Graphic developed by Northern Cartographic. Soil picture from NRCS.

Figure 7. Courtesy of Clean Air—Cool Planet, *Indicators of Climate Change in the Northeast*, 2005.

Figure 8. Courtesy of Clean Air—Cool Planet, *Indicators of Climate Change in the Northeast*, 2005.

Figure 9. Courtesy of Clean Air—Cool Planet, *Indicators of Climate Change in the Northeast*, 2005.

Figure 10. Graphic developed by Northern Cartographic, modified from data provided by the U.S. Army Cold Regions Research and Engineering Laboratory, Hanover, N.H.

Figure 11. Provided by USGS.

Figure 12. Provided by USGS.

Figure 13. Graphic developed by Northern Cartographic, derived from USGS streamflow data.

Figure 14. Graphic developed by Northern Cartographic, based on author's text.

Figure 15. Graphic developed by Northern Cartographic, modified from author's image.

Figure 16. Graphic developed by Northern Cartographic, derived from author's data.

Figure 17. Graphic developed by Northern Cartographic, derived from author's data.

Figure 18. Graphic developed by Northern Cartographic, derived from author's data.

Figure 19. Graphic developed by Northern Cartographic, derived from author's data.

Figure 20. Ray Godfrey, U.S. Department of Agriculture.

Figure 21. VCGI and GRANIT data sets, modified by Northern Cartographic. Land cover/use data from VCGI and GRANIT data sets, derived from Thematic Mappers satellite data, extracted and categorized by Northern Cartographic.

Figure 22. U.S. Census Bureau, Census of Population and Housing, various years; the Center for Rural Studies, University of Vermont; and Office of Energy and Planning, State of New Hampshire.

Figure 23. U.S. Census Bureau, Census of Population and Housing, various years; the Center for Rural Studies, University of Vermont; and Office of Energy and Planning, State of New Hampshire.

MAPS

Map 1. Modified from Hibbard et al. 2006.

Map 2. Base map: VCGI and GRANIT data sets, modified by Northern Cartographic.

Ecological units: Modified from J. Keys, Jr., et al. 1995. *Ecological Units of the Eastern United States—First Approximation*. Atlanta, Ga.: U.S. Department of Agriculture, Forest Service.

Map 3. Modified from Ridge 2003.

Map 4. Modified from Stewart and MacClintock 1970.

Map 5. Modified from Department of Geosciences, University of Massachusetts, Amherst (personal communication with J. Brigham-Grette, 2007).

Map 6. Base map: VCGI and GRANIT data sets, modified by Northern Cartographic. Lithological data from USGS surficial geology datasets.

Map 7. Base map: VCGI and GRANIT data sets, modified by Northern Cartographic. Soils: NRCS digital soils data.

Map 8. Map created by Emily Bryant with data from NH GRANIT and VCGI, using the Dartmouth College Earth Sciences Department ASA Lab, courtesy of Richard Birnie.

Map 9. Base map: Derived from Northern Cartographic data sets. Storm tracks: Derived from E. Van Cleef 1908. Is there a type of storm path? *Monthly Weather Review* 36: 56–58.

Map 10. Base map: National Elevational Dataset, VCGI, and GRANIT data sets, modified by Northern Cartographic.

Map 11. NRCS and USGS National Watershed Boundary Dataset. Some watershed names modified by CRJC staff.

Map 12. NRCS and USGS National Watershed Boundary Dataset. Some watershed names modified by CRJC staff.

Map 13. Base map: National Elevational Dataset, VCGI, and GRANIT data sets, modified by Northern Cartographic.

Map 14. Base map: National Elevational Dataset, VCGI, and GRANIT data sets, modified by Northern Cartographic.

Map 15. Base map: National Elevational Dataset, VCGI, and GRANIT data sets, modified by Northern Cartographic.

Map 16. Base map: National Elevational Dataset, VCGI, and GRANIT data sets, modified by Northern Cartographic.

Map 17. Base map: National Elevational Dataset, VCGI, and GRANIT data sets, modified by Northern Cartographic.

Map 18. Base map: National Elevational Dataset, VCGI, and GRANIT data sets, modified by Northern Cartographic.

Map 19. Base map: National Elevational Dataset, VCGI, and GRANIT data sets, modified by Northern Cartographic.

Map 20. Base map: National Elevational Dataset, VCGI, and GRANIT data sets, modified by Northern Cartographic.

Map 21. Base map: National Elevational Dataset, VCGI, and GRANIT data sets, modified by Northern Cartographic.

Map 22. Base map: National Elevational Dataset, VCGI, and GRANIT data sets, modified by Northern Cartographic.

Map 23. Provided by USGS.

Map 24. Provided by USGS.

Map 25. Provided by USGS.

Map 26. Base map: VCGI and GRANIT data sets, modified by Northern Cartographic. Dam names and locations: VCGI and NH DEP dam datasets.

Map 27. Base map: National Elevational Dataset modified by Northern Cartographic. Slope/aspect data developed by Northern Cartographic.

Map 28. Base map: VCGI and GRANIT data sets, modified by Northern Cartographic. Forest legacies data from author.

Map 29. Base map: VCGI and GRANIT data sets, modified by Northern Cartographic. Forest legacies data from author. Source: U.S. Forest Service, Forest Inventory and Analysis.

Map 30. Base map: VCGI and GRANIT data sets, modified by Northern Cartographic. Forest legacies data from author. Source: U.S. Forest Service, Forest Inventory and Analysis.

Map 31. Base map: VCGI and GRANIT data sets, modified by Northern Cartographic. Wetlands data derived from National Wetlands Inventory datasets.

Map 32. Base map: VCGI and GRANIT data sets, modified by Northern Cartographic. Wetlands data derived from National Wetlands Inventory database.

Map 33. National Wetlands Inventory data, NAIP 2003 orthophoto, and other GIS data acquired from NH GRANIT: http://www.granit.sr.unh.edu; Originator of NAIP orthophoto: USDA FSA APFO Aerial Photography Field Office, NAIP

Countywide MrSID Mosaic; map created by Emily Bryant in Dartmouth College Earth Sciences Department ASA Lab, courtesy of Richard Birnie.

Map 34. Base map: VCGI and GRANIT data sets, modified by Northern Cartographic. Plant extents provided by author.

Map 35. Base maps: Northern Cartographic datasets. Atlantic Flyway and bobolink information developed by Northern Cartographic from U.S. Fish and Wildlife data sources.

Map 36. Base map: VCGI and GRANIT data sets, modified by Northern Cartographic. Fish ranges developed by Northern Cartographic from U.S. Fish and Wildlife data sources.

Map 37. Base maps: Northern Cartographic datasets. Data developed by Northern Cartographic, derived from N.H. Wildlife Action Plan, 2005; and Andrews, Atlas of the Reptiles and Amphibians of Vermont, 2005.

Map 38. Base map: VCGI and GRANIT data sets, modified by Northern Cartographic. Native names provided by the authors.

Map 39. Base map: VCGI and GRANIT data sets, modified by Northern Cartographic. Town information developed from author-supplied information.

Map 40. Base map: VCGI and GRANIT data sets, modified by Northern Cartographic. Sheep population by town derived from author-provided data.

Map 41. Base map: VCGI and GRANIT data sets, modified by Northern Cartographic. Land cover/use data from VCGI and GRANIT data sets, derived from Thematic Mapper satellite data, extracted and categorized by Northern Cartographic.

Map 42. Base map: VCGI and GRANIT data sets, modified by Northern Cartographic. Population change data developed by Northern Cartographic, derived from U.S. Census Bureau data, 1760–2000.

Map 43. Base map: VCGI and GRANIT data sets, modified by Northern Cartographic. Population change data developed by Northern Cartographic, derived from U.S. Census Bureau data, 1760–2000.

Map 44. Base map: VCGI and GRANIT data sets, modified by Northern Cartographic. Population change data developed by Northern Cartographic, derived from U.S. Census Bureau data, 1760–2000.

Map 45. Courtesy of Frank J. Barrett, Jr.

Map 46. Base map: VCGI and GRANIT data sets, modified by Northern Cartographic. Roads information derived from VCGI and GRANIT data sets.

Map 47. Base map: VCGI and GRANIT data sets, modified by Northern Cartographic. Railroads information derived from VCGI and GRANIT data sets.

Map 48. Base map: VCGI and GRANIT data sets, modified by Northern Cartographic. Airport locations derived from VCGI and GRANIT data sets and from author-supplied data.

Map 49. Base Map: VCGI and GRANIT data sets, modified by Northern Cartographic. Dam Names and Locations: VCGI and NH DEP dam datasets.

Map 50. Base Map: VCGI and GRANIT data sets, modified by Northern Cartographic. Boat launches derived from CRJC, *Boating Guide to the Connecticut River*.

Map 51. Base map: VCGI and GRANIT data sets, modified by Northern Cartographic. Inset map from Northern Cartographic, produced for former PG&E recreational booklet.

TABLES

Table 1. Source: U.S. Department of Agriculture, Natural Resources Conservation Service.

Table 2. Source: National Watershed Boundary Dataset.

Table 3. Source: Federal Security Agency, Public Health Service, *Connecticut River Drainage Basin: A Cooperative State-Fedearl Report on Water Pollution*, 1951.

Table 4. Source: Connecticut River Joint Commissions and various regional planning commissions.

Table 5. Source: U.S. Census Bureau, Census of Population and Housing, various years; the Center for Rural Studies, University of Vermont; and Office of Energy and Planning, State of New Hampshire.

Table 6. Source: U.S. Census Bureau, Census of Population and Housing, various years; the Center for Rural Studies, University of Vermont; and Office of Energy and Planning, State of New Hampshire.

Table 7. Source: U.S. Census Bureau, Census of Population and Housing, various years; the Center for Rural Studies, University of Vermont; and Office of Energy and Planning, State of New Hampshire.

Table 8. Source: U.S. Census Bureau, Census of Population and Housing, various years; the Center for Rural Studies, University of Vermont; and Office of Energy and Planning, State of New Hampshire.

Table 9. Source: U.S. Census Bureau; State and County QuickFacts; the Center for Rural Studies, University of Vermont; and Office of Energy and Planning, State of New Hampshire.

Table 10. Source: U.S. Bureau of Census, Census of Population and Housing, 2000.

Table 11. Source: U.S. Census Bureau, Census of Population and Housing, various years.

Table 12. Source: U.S. Census Bureau, Census of Population and Housing, various years.

Table 13. Source: Federal Aviation Administration, www.airnav.com.

Index

mountain-building events (orogenies), 5, 7–9
mountain lions, 78, 123, 124
Mountain View Grand (Whitefield, N.H.), 227
Mount Orne Bridge, 192
Mount Washington Hotel (Bretton Woods, N.H.), 227
Mount Washington Observatory, 27
mudpuppy, 118
Murphy Dam, 65
museums, 217, *219*, 219, 226
music festivals, 218, *218*
muskrat, 126
mutton, 146

Nash Stream, 38
National Audubon Society, 107
National Historical Civil Engineering Landmark, *193*
National Historic Register, *193*
National Plan of Integrated Airport Systems (NPIAS), 203
National Watershed Boundary Dataset (WBD), 39, 39 table 2
National Weather Service, 53
National Wetlands Inventory (NWI), 90, 91–93 (maps 31–33)
Native Americans, 65, 123. *See also* Abenaki people
natural communities, 75–81; biodiversity threatened in, 79, 236–37; defined, 75; five resource elements of, 75–79, 77 map 27; floodplain forest, 94; forest stand types and, 80–81; mapping of, 80–81; visit recommendations, 76; wetland, *76*, 90. *See also* habitat
Nature Conservancy, 71, 78, 94, *104*
Naulakha (Dummerston, Vt.), 219
Nelson farm (Ryegate, Vt.), *146*
Newbury (N.H.), 227
Newbury (Vt.), 14, 21 map 8, 22, 69, 190
New Connecticut, 142
New England Central Railroad, 200
New England Interstate Water Pollution Control Commission, 51
New England Power Company, 68, 210, *212*, 216
New England region: town incorporation in, 139–42; weather in, 25
New England Wildflower Society, 94
New England Wire Technologies, 169
New Hampshire: alternative energy facilities in, *212*, 212; archaeological sites in, 225; auto tours in, 195; bedrock geology in, 4, 11; biomass energy development in, 170; birding resources in, 108–10; boundaries of, 142–44; development rate in, 121, 164; drought management plan in, 31; early migration from, 138; first airport in, 203; fish consumption advisories in, 62; floods in, 30, *31*, 56; forest communities in, 85; gold mining in, 152; growth of, 158; Hills and Plains region, 19; hurricane damage in, 30; land conservation in, 235; land-use

regulation insufficient in, 165; natural communities in, 76; population patterns in, 174, 174 tables 5–6, 176; railroad decline in, 200; road-building in, 189–90; species reintroduction in, 124, *125*; state tree of, 85; taxes in, 170; Ten-Year State Energy Plan, 212, 213; tornadoes in, 32; town governments in, 142; trout fishing in, 115; turnpikes in, 190; USGS gaging stations in, 54 map 23; Vermont interconnected with, 1–2, 4; Vermont secession from, 142, 143 map 39; water management in, *70*; water pollution in (ca. 1950), 59. *See also specific place*
New Hampshire Audubon Society, 108, *127*
New Hampshire Aviation and Marine Co. (Keene, N.H.), 203
New Hampshire Division of Historical Resources, 225
New Hampshire Fish and Game Department, 115
New Hampshire Reptile and Amphibian Reporting Program (RAARP), 122
New Hampshire Series, 7, 11
New Hampshire State Soil, 19
New Hampshire Turnpikes, 190
New Hampshire Water Supply and Engineering Bureau, 51
New Hampshire Water Well Board, 51
New Haven (Conn.), 151–54
New London (N.H.), 76, 93
New London Conservation Commission, 93
Newport (R.I.), 200
Newport (Vt.), 205
newspapers, early, *140*
New York City, railroad connections to, 197, 200, 227
New York State, early boundaries of, 138–39
"niche" agriculture, 159, 161, *162*, 168
nitrogen, 60, 76
nor'easters, 25–26, 31
North Country Chorus, 218
Northern Cartographic, 238
Northern Forest, *84*
Northern Forest Canoe Trail, 230
Northern Stage, 217
Northern Turnpike, 190
North Hartland (Vt.), 210
North Haverhill (N.H.), 218
Northumberland (N.H.), 209
North Walpole (N.H.), 197
Norwich (Vt.), 105, 142, 219, 220, 226
nuclear power, 210–12, 213
Nulhegan Basin, 94, 105, 235
Nulhegan River, *96*, 230

oak, *82*; harvesting of, 146; northern hardwoods replaced by, *86*; red, 98; re-establishment of, after glacial retreat, 82
Occom Pond, 222
Occom, Samson, 137n, 221
Ockett, Molly, 137

Odzihozo (Abenaki deity), 133, 133n
Olcott Falls, 185
Old Constitution House (Windsor, Vt.), *144*, 225
Old Man of the Mountains, 14
Old Province Road, 190
Old South Church (Windsor, Vt.), 226, *226*
Ompompanoosuc River, 44 map 16, 152
One Last Look (painting; Fournier), *218*
opera houses, 217–18
Opera North, 218
opossum, 123
Orange County (Vt.), 84, 176
orchids, 94, *95*
Orford (N.H.): as birdwatching site, 105; Federal architecture in, 226; ferries in, *193*; flow data collection at, 52; glacial formations near, 14; interstate school district of, 220; NWI survey map for, 93 map 33; public library in, *219*; recreation in, 232; residential development in, *164*
organic foods, 168, 222
organ manufacturing, 156
oriole, Baltimore, 107
Orleans County (Vt.), 98
osprey, 108
Ottauquechee—Black—Williams/Mascoma—Sugar watershed, 45 map 18
Ottauquechee River, 74; glacial geology and, 14, *15*; gold mining near, 152; hydro dams on, 209; watershed of, 45 map 18
otter, river, 126–28, *129*
outwash deposits, 12, 15, 50
owl: barred, 107; boreal, 105; great gray, 105; habitat of, 105–7, 126; migration of, 105; northern hawk, 105; saw-whet, 105–7, 126; snowy, 105
oxbow ponds, *100*, 100–102, 101 fig. 14
oxbows, 185
oxygen availability, 75–76

Paddleford, Peter, 192
Paleo-Indians, 225
Paley, Grace, 219
Palisades, 108, 195
Pangea (ancient land mass), 7–9
paper industry: communities transformed by, 155, 156; decline of, 170; hydropower used in, *210*, 212; log drives for, 186; railroads and, 198; wood pulp as raw material for, 151, 153, *154*, 155
parades, 233
paragliding, 208
Paris, Treaty of (1763), 138
parking lots, 164
Parrish, Maxfield, *216*
Partridge Brook, 46 map 19
Passamaquoddy people, 187
Passumpsic River, 59, 60, 197, 198, 200
Passumpsic watershed, 43 map 14
Pattenville (N.H.), 65
Paul Stream Basin, 235
paving, 56
PCBs, 59, 62

Pearl Lake Brook, *70*
peat lands, 97
Penobscot people, 187
perch, 112
performing arts, 217–18, *218*
Perkins, George H., 152
Perrin, Noel, 219
pesticides, 51, 59, 62, 107, 108
Philbrick-Cricenti Bog, 76, 93
phosphorus, 76
physiographic regions, 10 map 2, 11, 19
pickerel, 111–12; chain, *111*
pickerelweed, 100
pick-your-own produce businesses, 159, 161
picnicking, 233
Pierce, Mount, *125*
Piermont (N.H.), 14, 69
pigeon, rock, 107
pike, 111, 114, 230
Pike Hill Mine (Corinth, Vt.), 152
Pike, Robert E., 186
Pilgrims, 115
pine-oak forest, 82
pine, 82, 84, 146
pitcher plant, 93
Pittsburg (N.H.), 56, 65, 94, 142, 192, 232
planetarium, 219
plate tectonics, 5, 5 fig. 1
platform scale manufacturing, 156
Plath, Sylvia, 1
Pleistocene epoch, 12
Pliny Range, 9
Plymouth Notch (Vt.), 228
polar jet stream, 25
polar vortex, 25
political ecology, 238
Pollyanna (Porter), 219
Pondicherry National Wildlife Refuge, 93, *94*, 107, *217*
ponds, oxbow, *100*, 100–102, 101 fig. 14
pondweeds, 100, *100*
Poore Family Farm (Stewartstown, N.H.), 228, *229*
Poore Family Foundation for North Country Conservancy, 228
Poore, J. C. Kenneth, 228
poplar, 82
population: aging of, 180, 180 table 8, 181 table 9, 237; distribution of, 175, 175 table 7; educational attainment levels, 180, 181 table 10; growth patterns, by town, 176, 176 fig. 23; historic pattern changes, 174–75, 174 tables 5–6, 176–80, 177–79 (maps 42–44); impact of climate change on, 180; median household income, 180, 182 table 11; poverty-level, 182 table 12; of watershed, 175, 175 fig. 22
Porter, Eleanor H., 219
Portland (Me.), railroad connections to, 197, 198, 200
Portland Natural Gas Transmission System, 212
postindustrial economy, 158, 168–73; challenges of, 170, 237; "creative economy" in, 168, 169, *170*, 217; downtown

spruce, *84*; as bird habitat, 105–7; black, 84, 105–7, 123; canoes made from bark of, 187; as natural community, 83–84; red, 82, 83; re-establishment of, after glacial retreat, 82; as witness trees, 85
stagecoaches, 198–99
Standing Pond Formation, *7*
Stark, John, 189
starling, European, 107
steamboats, 184, *185*, 185–86, 196
steam power, 196
steel-arch bridges, *193*, *200*
stereoptic cards, 220
Stewartstown (N.H.), 69, 228, 229
St. Johnsbury (Vt.): average summer temperatures in, *33*; "creative economy" in, 168; education in, 220; historic sites in, 229; ice jams in, *28*; industrialization in, 151, 156; performing arts in, 218; population patterns in, 174; precipitation patterns in, *35*; public library in, 219–20; railroad connections in, 196, 197, *198*, 198, 199; snowfall extremes in, *31*; tourism in, 226–27; weather data for, *27*. *See also* Fairbanks Museum and Planetarium
St. Johnsbury Academy, 220
St. Johnsbury Athenaeum, 218, 219–20
St. Johnsbury Municipal Airport, 203
St. John's-wort, *98*, 98
St. Lawrence & Atlantic Railroad, 200
Stone, Livingston, 111
stonewalls, 147
storms: aviation and, 203; blizzards, 31; floods caused by, *29*, 29–30, *31*, 52, *58*, 69; forest regrowth after, *85*; hurricanes, 30, 86; ice storms, 31–32, 86; impact of climate change on, 86; nor'easters, 25–26, 31; streamflow impact of, 52, 56, 56 fig. 13; tornadoes, 32; tracks of, in U.S., 26 map 9; water quality impact of, 60
storytelling, 219
Strafford (Vt.), 151, 226
Stratford (N.H.), 102 fig. 15, 103, 155, *163*, 209
stratified drift, 50
Stratton Mountain, 53
streamflow, 52–58; alteration of, 70; annual flow, 52; data collection, 52–53; defined, 52; gauging stations, 52, 54 map 23; impact of climate change on, 34–35; impact of storms on, 52, 56, 56 fig. 13; low flow and water demand, 58; management of, 69–70; mean annual flow, 52, 53, 55 map 24; as power source, 184; runoff, 53–56, 57 map 25; seasonal patterns, 53
St. Regis Paper Company, 153
strip development, 165
Strolling of the Heifers (Brattleboro, Vt.), 233
subdivisions, regulation of, 165, 167 table 4
subduction, 7
suburbanization, 108, 168, 235
succession, 90–93
Sugar Hill (N.H.), *97*, 152, *164*, 232

sugar maple-silver maple white ash floodplain forests, 76
Sugar River, 45 map 18, 209
Sumner, David, 153
Sumner Falls, *62*, 185, 230
Sumner Falls Dam, 112
Sunapee, Lake, 227
Sunderland (Mass.), 52
sundew, 93
sunlight, 76, 77 map 27
swallow: barn, 107; tree, 105
swamps: alder, *76*, 90–93, *94*, *96*; black spruce, *96*; northern white cedar, *97*; red maple-black gum, *76*, 76, 93; spruce-fir-tamarack, *76*, 90, *94*, *96*; as wetland ecosystem, 90–93
Swanzey (N.H.), 225
Swift, Esther, 135
swimming, 216, 233, 235
sycamore, 98, 100

Taconian Orogeny, 7
tamaracks, *84*
tanager, scarlet, 107
Tarleton, Lake, 107
Tasker, James, *193*
taxation, 139–42, 165, 170
technology, 158, 167
temperate lichen talus barrens, 76
temperature patterns, 24, 26–28, 33, 33 fig. 7
terranes, 7–9
textile industry, 155–56
theater, 217–18, *218*
Thetford (Vt.), 139, 208, 219
Thetford Academy, 220
Third Connecticut Lake, 38, 53
Thoreau, Henry David, 230
thrush: Bicknell's, 62, 105, 107, 108; hermit, 107, *107*
thunderstorms, 86
till deposits, 12, 15, 19–20, 50
timber. *See* logging
Timberland Machines (Lancaster, N.H.), 207
titmouse, tufted, 108
toads: American, 119, *121*; Fowler's, 118, 119
toll roads, 190
tornadoes, 32
tourism, 225–29; Abenaki and, 137; auto, 195; geotourism, 228; heritage, 158, 225–29; hospitality, 158, 168; impact of climate change on, 35; postindustrial economy and, 158, 168, 170; railroads and, 199, *199*, 226–27, 228; winter, 35. *See also* recreation
town centers, 156, 158, 163, 164
town historical societies, 229
town meetings, 142, 237–38
towns, incorporation of, 139–42
trade, 146–47, 185–86, 189–90, 198
TransCanada Hydro Northeast, 65–67, 68, 210, 211 map 49, 233–35, 234 map 51
"transformer" stories, 133n
transportation, 184, 225. *See also* aviation; railroads; roads; water travel

trapping, 123, 128
"trash-to-steam" incinerators, 212, 213
treaties: Paris (1763), 138; Webster Ashburton (1842), 142
trilobites, 4
Tripp, Nathaniel, 219
trout: brook, 111, 114, 115, *115*, 126; brown, 111; fisheries, 114; fishing for, 230; lake, *111*, 111; rainbow, 111, *111*; Sunapee, 111
Trout Unlimited, 115
trucking, 200, 202
Tucker, William Jewett, 224
Tunbridge World's Fair, 233
turkey, 78, 108
Turner's Falls (Mass.), 209
turnpikes, 184, 190, 191 map 45
turtle: painted, 121; snapping, 118; spotted, 118, *119*, 120 map 37; wood, 118
Twin Mountain (N.H.), 203
Two Rivers—Ottauquechee Regional Commission, 165

United States Agriculture Department, 164
United States Army Corps of Engineers, 67–68, 69, 210, 233, 234 map 51
United States Environmental Protection Agency (EPA), 51, 62, *62*, 121
United States Fish and Wildlife Service, 81, 90, 237
United States Geological Survey, 39, 49, 52, 54 map 23
United States Natural Resources Conservation Service, 39
United States Surgeon General, 50–51
United States Transportation Department, 192
Uplands physiographic region, 11, 19
Upper Ammonoosuc River, 230
Upper Connecticut River Mitigation and Enhancement Fund, 68
Upper Valley Land Trust, xv
Upper Valley Trails Alliance, 232
uranium, 50

Vail, Theodore N., 220
Valley Quest (White River Junction, Vt.), 233
Van Cleef, Eugene, 26 map 9
Van Dyke, George, 153
Van Dyke, Henry, 38
varves, 14
Vermont: alternative energy facilities in, 212; archaeological sites in, 225; bedrock geology in, *4*, 4, 11; birding resources in, 108–10; boundaries of, 142–44; copper mining in, 151, *152*, 152; development rate in, 121; establishment of, 142, 225; first airport in, 203; fish consumption advisories in, 62; floods in, 29, *29*; gold mining in, 152; hurricane damage in, 30; land conservation in, 235; land-use regulation in, 165, 167; natural communities in, 76, 81; N.H. interconnected with, 1–2, 4; N.H. towns admitted to, 143 map 39; Northeastern Highlands, 19; oldest

schoolhouse in, 225; poet laureate of, 219; population patterns in, 174–75, 174 tables 5–6, 176; railroads purchased by, 200; species reintroduction in, 124, *125*; state soil of, 19, *19*; temperature extremes in, 27; tornadoes in, 32; turnpikes in, 190; USGS gaging stations in, 54 map 23; water management in, *70*; water pollution in (ca. 1950), 59, *61*. *See also specific place*
Vermont Academy (Saxton's River, Vt.), 220
Vermont Archaeological Society, 225
Vermont Breeding Bird Atlas, 108
Vermont Designated Downtown Program, 167, 168
Vermont Division of Historic Preservation, 225
Vermont Ecostudies Center, 108
Vermont Electric Generation & Transmission Cooperative, 210
Vermonter (magazine), 119
Vermonter (train), 200
Vermont Piedmont, 19–20
Vermont Public Service Board, 213
Vermont Rail System, 200
Vermont Reptile and Amphibian Atlas, 122
Vermont Shepherd Farm (Westminster West), *162*
Vermont State Bird, *107*
Vermont Storm Events Database, 32
Vermont Village Center Program, 167
Vermont Water Supply Division, 51
Vermont Yankee Nuclear Power Station (Vernon, Vt.), 210–12, 213
vernal pools, 94
Vernon (Vt.): ancient trees in, 93; floods in, 30; natural communities in, *76*, 76; nuclear power station at, 210–12, 213; temperature extremes in, 27; wetlands near, 93
Vernon Dam, 67, 114, 210
Vershire (Vt.), 151, *152*, 152, 220
veterinarians, 162
vireo, red-eyed, 107
Visual Flight Rules, 203
vulture, turkey, 108

Waits—Ompompanoosuc—Eastman—Mink watershed, 44 map 16
Waits River, *210*
Waits River Formation, *7*
Walden (Vt.), 190
walleye, 111, 112, *112*
Walpole (N.H.), 56 fig. 13, 190, 219
Wantastiquet, Mount, 76, 230
warbler: blackpoll, 107; chestnut-sided, 108; habitat of, 105–7; migration of, 105; population trends, 108
Warner (N.H.), 123
Warren (N.H.), 190
Washington (D.C.), railroad connections to, 200
Washington Electric Cooperative, 212
Washington, George, 142, 190
Washington, Mount: average precipita-